Fast Talk, Full Volume

Fast Talk, Full Volume

Edited by Alan Spears

GUT PUNCH PRESS
Cabin John, Maryland

COPYRIGHT NOTICES AND ACKNOWLEDGEMENTS

First edition

Copyright © 1993 by Alan Spears

Library of Congress
Cataloging in Publication No.: 92-72284

ISBN: 0-945144-04-0

Cover photograph by Charles Steck

Gut Punch Press
PO Box 105
Cabin John, MD 20818

Foreword

Consider the experiences of a people, a nation. How would one get to the core of that existence? Define it or rationalize it? Past efforts have tried to exact grandiose generalizations and themes about African-Americans and other ethnic minorities, from a handful of poems. Dubious suppositions based upon our pathology, rhythm, anger, backsliding, progress, color, hysteria, victimization, spirituality, or lack thereof. But in truth, there is only one place from which to begin piecing together our collective history. Our "schizophrenia," tragic and triumphant, in being both Africans and Americans. We must hear from the individual.

Fast Talk, Full Volume has no grandiose purpose. There is no desire here to thrust aside the barriers of contemporary poetry with innovation and design. Rather, the need is to pull and tug the collective consciousness of all peoples in a winding series of opposite directions. To point out the flaws in what has become the contemporary orthodoxy of African-American thought, mainstream and radical. To document the thoughts and ideas of the "trees" when all others are preoccupied with the forest.

Sometimes humorous, sometimes violent or provocative, the poetry of individuals and free thinkers is represented within these pages. Good riddance to the African-American hegemony. Death to the "Black monolith". Hail the rise of the black woman and black man, and the independence of the souls of black folks.

Collected within the pages of this anthology are some of the best and most promising African-American poets of our time. Most are unpublished or under-published (as of this date). Therefore, a primary objective of *Fast Talk, Full Volume* is pure and simple exposure.

Many of us are newcomers. So be prepared to experience a breadth of style, technique, execution, and even a few imperfections, as we strive towards establishing our voices. Allow us to beg your indulgence. To be heard, seen.

More seasoned veterans, such as Wanda Coleman, Reuben Jackson, Kenneth Carroll, Michelle Parkerson, and Meri Danquah, will slake the thirst of the ardent poetry enthusiasts for consistently powerful and proven work. Following in the footsteps of their foremothers and forefathers, these poets have achieved national (and sometimes international) acclaim. All the while maintaining their place as cornerstones of local literary communities.

There are several features that make *Fast Talk, Full Volume* different, notable, and unique. First and foremost would be the strong and independent voices of the women writers selected for this anthology. Gone are the days when black women wrote support poetry for the "black male revolution" and then shut up to make more coffee! Contemporary women, Jennifer Vest, Kweli Smith, and Toni Blackman for example, candidly address the onerous plagues of rape, sexism, and male violence, which pervade our neighborhoods and bedrooms. And, in the new "tradition" of black feminists such as Pearl Cleage, they demand a better showing from their black male counterparts.

Will we listen?

Check out Kenneth Carroll's "White Woman Blues" and note with pride the awareness of certain black men!

Second, an increasing number of black poets are examining the subject of black on black violence. In this the same period that writer Essex Hemphill editorialized that he feared young black men more than he feared the Ku Klux Klan, *Fast Talk, Full Volume* contains several poems which take up and expand the discussion of black pathology. Brian Gilmore's "Black on Black Homicide #2" and Akilah Oliver's "Encounter with a Young Brother" both leap to mind.

Adding to the patchwork are the poems of two native American women, Kim Nault and White Deer Woman. This inclusion is more than a token political gesture. In fact, a greater sampling of poetry by Native peoples was intended for this edition, but here time itself was the enemy. Pressed by the decision to choose between some and none, I chose some. However awkward, I stand by these selections, and promise a more solid effort in the future.

Any questions so far?

I would like to apologize to all of the poets we missed this time around. Allow me to boldly assert that all of the missing pieces to the picture might be included in a future *Fast Talk, Full Volume*. So please continue to write and express yourselves.

I wish to thank Dr. Elias Blake, Jr., whose generous assistantship helped make this book possible. Derrick Hsu of Gut Punch Press, who expressed interest in this project from its inception. Jennifer Lisa Vest, who helped with the first stages of editing and collecting poetry. Katya Frischer and Mia Anderson. Emily and Wallace Spears & Pooh. Wanda Coleman for the West Coast connection. Richard Peabody for the red pen and editorial assistance. Sunil Freeman and The Writer's Center for typesetting. And the always affable E. Ethelbert Miller, who sent so many aspiring poets my way. I thank you all.

And to Kristine Miller: What I do for the ages has taken great inspiration from your beauty. Prosper!

> Alan Spears
> January 8, 1992
> Washington, D.C.

Introduction

*If it's possible for us to stay alive,
then it's possible for the whole world
to stay alive.*
— Paula Gunn Allen

Fast Talk, Full Volume

When Alan Spears asked if I would be interested in writing the introduction for *Fast Talk, Full Volume*, I immediately said yes. There were several reasons for accepting, the major one being curiosity. As a literary activist, I wanted to know what was happening in our literary communities. What our new writers were saying at this moment in history.

There are two traditions operating within African American culture, one oral, the other literary. At times they intersect and influence each other. Some writers borrow readily from the oral tradition and attempt to "stretch" their text into being more responsive to sound, music, and mobility. How you sound is still important within the African American community.

A quick observation and survey would probably lead to the conclusion that Rap is the manner in which most of the new African American poets are expressing themselves today. However, the work included in *Fast Talk, Full Volume* shows that this assumption is false, and that is one more reason why this anthology is an important publication.

There are several performance poets in *Fast Talk, Full Volume*, although how comfortable they are with this label I don't know. I have seen excellent performances by Kweli Smith, Michelle Parkerson, Kenneth Carroll, and Darrell Stover. I vaguely remember Reuben Jackson on stage with a guitar one evening at d.c. space, but I still don't know what he was doing. Perhaps, there are a few contributors to this anthology who would like to be called rappers. I wonder about Rabia Rayford . . .

I believe this new collection of poems extends and broadens our rich literary tradition. The decision by Alan Spears to include the works of two Native American poets (Kim Nault and White Deer Woman) is an important one. It emphasizes the similarities between people instead of the differences. This book moves beyond the rhetoric of the 1980s, a period which introduced us to such concepts as the rainbow coalition and multiculturalism. As we move forward into the next century there will be conflict and resolutions between people of color. We already see it occurring between Asian Americans and African Americans. While the changing political landscape will hopefully bring us together to establish a new American agenda, it must be the work and responsibility of writers and artists to establish the essential cultural links and bridges.

In their own literary books such as *Fast Talk, Full Volume* are shaped by such things as geography. This anthology is a west coast/east coast production. Almost all the contributors reside in the Los Angeles and Washington, D.C. area. Is this a poetry conspiracy?

The inclusion of Wanda Coleman in the book should be a clue to readers and critics that *Fast Talk, Full Volume* is not a collection of newcomers. Several poets in this book have significant reputations; others only lack a book of their own in order to obtain wider recognition. Jennifer Vest told me last year that a new generation of literary voices was emerging. What makes this generation of African American writers different from the last?

In *Fast Talk, Full Volume* I find the "changing same." African American music is still present in the work of these writers. One can hear the blues and jazz. Many poets can be found extending their hands and hearts to Africa. However, the treatment of African Americans in America is still the overriding concern. Several writers are concerned with black on black crime and the increasing homicide rate for African males. The seriousness of the situation is best expressed by Darrell Stover when he writes about the death of Jay Bias and says "the news is no different with the TV off or on."

Yet somehow we survive, the South African poet Dennis Brutus once wrote. We survive through memory. Although there has been a considerable erosion of activism and commitment during the last decade in which a new conservatism coincided with an increase in homelessness, drugs and crime across America. Even love poems take on a new meaning in this age of AIDS.

Contemporary poets must compete for listeners and readers. Where Baldwin once spoke of the writer as witness, there is now a need for all of us to become more involved. New technology is shaping our language and our values. The impact of film and television has made us more visual. "Fast Talk" is what it takes to be heard. With so many changes occurring in Africa, and throughout the world, it is critical that we keep writing and dreaming. This is the responsibility of all new writers working on the cultural front. The "changing same." The struggle to define and secure freedom for the individual and the group. The poets included in this anthology extend traditions, they push our borders forward almost to the beginning of a new era. We will hear about the future before we see it.

Fast Talk, Full Volume will mark the first major publication for several of its contributors. Hopefully, it will help launch a few more careers. I tell folks to stand back and give space to Reuben Jackson and Kenneth Carroll, and emerging poets such as Natasha Tarpley. *Fast Talk, Full Volume* is a testimony to the abundance and talent in our communities. Here are voices that heal . . .

E. Ethelbert Miller

*   *   *   *   *

Additional information on the poets who contributed to this project can be obtained by writing to *Fast Talk, Full Volume*, care of:

Gut Punch Press
P.O. Box 105
Cabin John, MD 20818

Table of Contents

Fast Talk, Full Volume

Meri Nana-Ama Danquah

Right on Time

It was a freedom thing

the lawyer called it
temporary insanity
folks 'round the neighborhood
gossiped maybe the pet was rabid
maybe it had gotten loose
sank some of its evil into him

nobody understood

used to be a time
when him and his buddies
hung tight on the courts
scratchin' each other's asses
talkin' shit
then they'd get a brew
catch prime time
maybe smoke a joint
talk some more shit
'til sleep set into the room

life was easy then

pop and smacky
joined the service
bobby got shot
over some petty he say/she say
died a couple of days later
cisco went off to college
came back dashikid
with big words, africa
and revolution on his tongue

1

her love came right on time

for a while
there was travel, dancing
making love 'til dry mouth
and play-doh muscles begged "no more"
then marriage and the kid
when she said jump
he'd leap right out of his shoes
love's high was that good
he never wanted to come down
it was then that the dream began

he repeatedly feared
he rhythmically dreamed
first month by month
then week after week
until soon whenever eyes closed
he saw it
flesh in flames of confinement
dripping
freedom which would not rest
in the palm of his hands

that night
when he blew his kiss
through the skulls
of their picket fence future
he drowned
in his own pool of dry tears

he had loved them
but not more than life

sometimes if you stay too long
in an escape
it can turn into your prison

nobody understood

it was a freedom thing

Akbar the Mad Poet

otherwise known as someone else, take luther
alphonse rivers or david ravon smith

half black half white, a brown eye on his left
his right eye blue

he regurgitates anguish as brutality
what is in his gut goes to his head

on one occasion Akbar is spotted in downtown
Manhattan slamming the head of his true love thru
a plate glass window. this earns his straightjacket
time and diagnosis as schizophrenic

(ain't dat de natch'l order o Niggah Universe?
all Blacks are schizo. African vs American
we jes can't get along with ourselves)

after that episode
he abandons the apple for the orange

one sunny afternoon Akbar is found wandering nude
along the stretch of Venice Beach his face bloody
his blue eye freshly plucked out of its socket
the offender crushed
in his own avenging hand

Heritage

the Dakota man came to the party
among strangers — mainly whites
at our table my husband told him that i, his wife
was part Sioux (a breed indian)
embarrassed that he would tell this story to
an *authentic* of tribal origin
i was nevertheless polite and did not deny my history
otherwise there wasn't much we had in common
for in me the afro-american dominated the aboriginal
to state my case until, reaching for a butter knife
my hand next to his. except for color
they were the same

Chuck Man

that loosiana swamp dog put some funny stuff
on me. tells me I quiver his liver

he got the fish head eyes, smells like whiskey
pig feet and old smokes

he brings me okra and black-eyed peas
steady comes round to get his ham bone boiled

he do the belly rub
he do the jelly roll
he a back door man with front door ambition
he piss sweet water

we honky tonk we gut bucket

he feed me catfish
he feed me divorce lies

he scared to leave his wife she a two-headed
woman. the fix go deep

he ain't strong enuff to leave her
i ain't strong enuff to make him stay

on odd mornings he come round early
tryin' to catch another niggah in my bed

to work his mojo he lick my pearl to
feel it glow. makes my hair grow

Casting Call (2)

schemin' and dreamin'

something about Amos. he wore his hat like
an aviator and drove that cab like a dive bomber
scoping in on enemy installations, sported that
jacket with pride debonaire, not to mention
he always made good sense

more than lightning who, I would discover years
later, was merely caught in the act of being himself

more than tall Mr. Andrew H. Brown, foil and
thick-lipped good-natured sidekick whose
dome-lidded bowler was an extension of his head
and there wasn't much in either. his expression of
shock was manifest ugly, an ill-fitting cigar
popping out as his mouth froze into an O

even in black and white i imagined his gums a
pinker blush than Veronica Lake's thighs when she
did a peek-a-boo

the only thing i dug 'bout Amos 'n Andy
were the grand opening credits which rolled
across a mock urban skyline to a choir singing
as if in nigger heaven. i'd imagine myself grown-up
sitting in a bar, sipping the beer that made
Milwaukee famous, looking fine and dressed to the nines

i never guessed time would
peg me in the role of King Fish

Daddyboy

1

with papa walking toward sunset
along the old railroad tracks in watts off 103rd
i am five in braids and bangs
and the blue cornflower print jumper mama made
the sun, a big copper smile
peeks over thunderheads
papa holds my tiny brown hand in his huge
boxer's fist. we wave at the switchman as we
walk past. i skip to keep in his giant's step
kicking granite pebbles as i go
watching them skitter in our path
home to mama

2

me & brother george have been up to mischief
we think we can outrun daddyboy
and break for the front door. he runs us round
the house twice then passes us, laughing
we uh-oh surprise, stop in our tracks
and run back the other way
he spins round, catches us, hold me
in the vise of his calves as he
plucks george high into the air
and takes the tar out of us

3

daddyboy surprises mommygirl
with fats domino's latest hit, *honey chile*
they go into a clinch/kiss and we start to sniggle
they put it on the victrola and
show us how to boogie woogie and lindy hop
we ooh ahh as he flips her over his back
and swing her between his legs
then they put on something slow
and send us off to bed

4

"daddyboy daddyboy daddyboy's home!"
we run to greet him
"don't call me that no more!" his bass
is sharp and harsh. we run crying to mommygirl
"your father's black. white people
disrespect black men by calling them boy
call him anything but"

5

we've been fighting. mom's gonna tell pop
our rear ends ache in anticipation
another whipping. mom uses a peach tree limb
all pop needs is those powerful black hands
home, he lectures us. brother and sister
should love and respect. at 10 & 12
we're too big for such nonsense

george gets his first
i figure a way to save my butt. i stuff my britches
with a book wrapped in a towel like i saw on tv
george is hot tears and snot. it's my turn
WHOP WHOP WHOP. i fake a boo hoo
"what's this?" surprise he reaches in, pulls out
he laughs and laughs so hard
he's almost crying and spanks me at the same time
and i'm laughing and crying and we're
laughing together
and shit does it hurt

6

one terrible morning pop came home in a sweat
he'd gone to the shop as usual
everything was gone. the printing presses
the desks. the files. the ledgers. every damn thing
his partner ripped him off

"what we gonna do?" mom wailed
"i don't know" he said real quiet
i went hot and cold
he paced the room, slammed open the door
and went back to the streets

it is the only time i've ever seen him cry
and they was killin' tears

7

the phone screams. i jump up from my sleep
it's mama. can i come? papa's fallen
against the bathroom door. she can't get it open
she doesn't know if he's hurt

it's the seizures again brought on by scar tissue
from where they removed the tumor. yes
i'm on my way. and as i'm about to leave
the phone rings again. no
i don't have to come. the boys are coming
she says

but i go anyway

8

i take my father to the hills of zion
for wednesday night prayer meet
i'm long since a woman
he's long since grayed and grandfather
he goes into his wallet for the card and gives
it to me, his hands swollen/cushioned with
illness. perhaps i'd like to come some time?
when i'm not too busy? they have a good choir.
i take the card, say okay say maybe
and wait patiently as he struggles
get out of the car with the aid of his cane
and makes his way toward the light
of the open door

Love the Letters

written in thin penned impermanent ink/a
young black woman's fever

pages in sealed envelopes
how soon forgot the "my love for you will never dies"
how buried dust deep the
"there will never be anothers"
"you are my lasts"
"i can't live without yous"
buried with time and the apt shovel of experience

such comedy first love
love always
the dizzy spin/hyperventilated ache
torture and sweat of it
give all to give of it

letters/pain pressed thin from
storage for review
tell me how stupid i was then
and how stupid i remain

Dream 522

young bloods got me riding in the car
yes i value my life yes like on tv or a bad movie
they say "empty your purse" and of course i cooperate
they are young, impatient
in do rags and earrings
the one in front pulls out the *beretta*
he doesn't like what i say
that i say anything
"please don't shoot me"
and the gun throbs the bullets bites thru
my stomach. i feel a second slug lodge in
my forehead
i keep thinking i don't want to die so young
i don't want to die this way black on black
black against black
i want to see my son grow to man
and my lover — how hurt he'll be
i slump into the back seat of the car
hear one of them say
"come on man — let's get out of here"
they don't know and they don't care
as I wake up monday morning
late for work

Walkin' Paper Blues

give me my walkin' papers
and wave yo hand goodbye
give me my walkin' papers
and wave your hand goodbye
the day i miss yo drudgin'
that's the day i die

if yo think i'm comin' back he-ah
hold yo breath and pee
if yo think i'm comin' back he-ah
hold yo breath and pee
my rear end in the wind
last black thing you'll evah see

Refrain:

if'n yo don't fire me soon
i'm leavin' he-ah today
if'n yo don't fire me soon
i'm leavin' he-ah today
mah soul nevah been je-ah
mah heart been gone fo days

got a fifth o mad dog
to celebrate this day
got me a fifth o mad dog
to celebrate this day
a year of unemployment
and two weeks severance pay

A Man Who Smacks Congos (A Go-Go Poem)

he put fire on the hide of
a million dead cows
when he play
          he make me feel
like
a raga muffin
boogaloo man
last disciple
of the music of the ancients

rawness of the breakdown
send some
into oneness
          they bounce between the streets
          and the walls of this sanctuary,
          the spinning rhythms
          bouncing walls, spirits, stretching
          to all parts of frames, holy spasm
          the music

rawness of the breakdown

get down get down
          get down get down

others sit in awe
jungle boogey
sock it to'em
so hard
stillness of their face

say

their soul is dancing
                    dancing
                    dancing
                    dancing . . .

As She Sleeps

A woman grinds herself
to ecstasy

while I lie there,

scanning the room for signs of daylight,

And paper
for a poem I will work on
As she sleeps.

Country Music

white men nurse beers,
guard the six foot gulf
separating
my table from the nearest blonde.

i am nervous
as a steel guitarist moments
from an audition with ferlin husky.

when a fight destroys a picture window
should i join the laughter?
would my silence be perceived as uppity?

a man the size of texas
buys me a bud,
then asks if those singers would make it in the soul arena;
he wants an answer.

three hours later,
he's stuffing the jukebox with quarters
as if it's collection time
at the church of merle haggard,

and plays nothing but love songs,
just like my dad.

Driving to Newport

(for J.C. Burns)

"Good fences make good neighbors"

— Robert Frost

john
burns
and i
spent an
autumn sunday hugging
the right lane of
interstate 14.

we marveled
at how frost's
mending wall
rolled across the hills
like music

followed us to canada
like a runaway slave

through
hardwick, craftsbury, east craftsbury,
craftsbury common, mill village, west
glover,

foliage rattled —
pom-poms
cheering us on.

Studio A

(for Jimi Hendrix)

down the
carpeted
stairs

into a
curved room
where

blues
and
double stops

spun
off
his
fender

a percussionist and

two
not so
background
vocalists

added
funk

a battleground
of beauty

silent

save for
our footsteps

the click
of an anxious
minolta

our host
dims the lights

leaving me

in the studio
where

the symphonies
of my
adolescence

were recorded

i recall
mrs. slezak's
dismissal of
those songs
as "inappropriate
for classroom discussion"

a current heartache

the artist's
fatal brush
with doubt

Old Music

writing poems
about old music
is beginning
to make me feel
funny,
like maybe
i've turned
into one of
those relatives
you consciously avoid
at gatherings.

the ones who
think today's
songs are
groovy enough,

but just let them
tell you
about some
ghost they
saw at
the fillmore,
the apollo,

wherever.

i don't think
my passion
for hendrix
puts me
in that
boat.

but this isn't
the same as
discovering
one's blackness
in the mirror,
baby.

it's more like a chive
on your tooth,

spaghetti
stains
on your
sweater.

everyone's
giggling.

you're the last
to know.

Autumn '59

doc weston
closed
his pharmacy
and
soda fountain
before i
could take
part in the
world i saw
on television

no more
densely
freckled
girls named
amy
sipping
cokes

looking
dreamily
at the
leaves
passing
by the
window

no more
playmates
staring
quizzically
at the negroes
on my fathers
album covers

my brothers
dancing

their every
jump shot
an homage
to bob cousy

sarah goldfarb
looked just like
the girl
in the
royal princess
tea set commercial
even though her
father said

it's not possible
sarah's jewish

there are no
jews on television

rocco quinzani
was a dead ringer
for ricky nelson

who and where
was i

Teddy

big ears
and clown face

played left flanker

the section of playground
where cobwebs grew

and
yardmarkers
ceased

this did not stop him
from awkward
stabs at perfection

size 13 keds
jostling one another

turning post patterns
into 15 yard
tragedies

starring himself

it was a conspiracy
he shouted

and he was right

offense and defense
laughed so loud

we did not
hear the pistol

rumor was
it pierced the
left temple

death by conspiracy
we asked
each other

the morticians
smoothed all clues away

Sixty-third & Broadway

my hotel room's small.
no space
for leaves
that swirl
above the idle
fountain of
lincoln center.

who's the statue
in the nearby
park?

(its benches
lined with
chronic shadows.)

a block away
is the church
where billie holiday's
funeral was held —

and further west,
the lowercase skyline
of new jersey

gazing across the hudson
i don't think
of landfills,
jimmy hoffa,
or bruce springsteen,

but thelonious monk's
last exile:

standing on nica's
balcony
in "catsville,"

resisting the piano's
advances
and the city
where i am happiest
alone.

For My Neighbors

they turn everything
up to ten:

arguments,
bath water,
gospel music,

did i mention
commodores
albums?

do you want to know what hell is?

being bedridden
with influenza,

hearing lionel richie
sing
"easy like a
sunday morning"

20 or 30 times.

F Street Elegy

in the window
of olsson's
books and records

beneath a sign
marked
new releases

a compact disc
with two smiling
guitarists/brothers
on the cover

one is the unsuspecting
stevie ray vaughan

Roundball Two

thank god
i'm not
the president of
a college
whose funding
rests upon
my genetically assumed
prowess
at the
foul line,
or any other
aspect of this game

Michelle T. Clinton

Why I Hate Music
(for & against the blues aesthetic)

I wanna talk bad about you
I wanna confiscate your comforter
strip off your party noise
& force the remains of a semi-conquered race
into the soft center of your ears

I wanna dissect your demi-gods
those media drunk heroes & she-rose
their pedicured fine-ness
their lame tame lyrics
that xerox & recycle
the tickle of romantic love
like all we got to do
(in this life) (in this world)
& fuck the fuckable
& endure the breaks

inside the music is a history we betray
inside the saxophone is a trace of holocaust wisdom
lesson burned into underclass
skin we go dumb to

pay attention: black
ass slaves distilled
the hurt of humiliation
into a musical code
the nouveau negro jesus
partied in christian tents

& hallucinated grace
that mutated into jazz
& transfigured the negritude
blues into white metal rock & rap
& here we are
in the wake of the neo-upper class
colored entertainers
who do benefits for african famines
who do charity for burnt out farmers
here we are w/ ex-ghetto brothers
rapping & lounging &
lusting their zillion dollar homes
once fame invades their body space
they swell up like a greedy penis
& hire mexicans to cut their weeds
they do interviews
they give intimacy to airbrushed photos
& admit/ they knew it/ they were special
from the start. you eat
their trance like a tranquilizer

I hate you because you're happy
because a cd & heavy duty speakers
erase your genetic grief
because a rhythm & wordless melody
pacifies you like a common beast
you are soothed
you are cooled
& your numbers
are enormous.

Bernard Harris, Jr.

Peaceful Evening

Last night the phone rang . . . I think.
Someone knocked on my door,
(two or three times).
Outside I heard a friendly horn blow,
right beneath my bedroom window,
right after the screaming sirens
had just died off into the distance.
I believe I heard about some bad news in and between
some meaningless commercials and the illest be-bop-hip-
hop-non-stop-rap record around,
on the radio.
Fortunately, the only one I let in . . . was you.

Wake Up People!

Wake up people, hear what I'm saying.
The hour is late, there's no time for playing.
Realize and open your eyes,
injustice will induce our ultimate demise.
Racism . . . makes life unliveable
makes me feel like a social criminal
sly real slick and subtly subliminal
done discreetly, neatly, completely,
a camouflaged conspiracy
designed to defeat me.

Wake up people, try to understand
what I'm talking about is the brotherhood of man,
hypocrisy and prejudice is not in God's plan.
But he won't help you until you take a stand,
grab a hand of the brother of color
then hug his dad, sister and mother, then maybe, ultimately,
we'll all act like the human family,
and then we won't act
it may come naturally.
Perhaps not tonight, but eventually.

Wake up people, we need to get busy now,
on the double.
Can't you see the very earth is in trouble.
No more jungles,
a big hole in the sky,
acid showers and planes that don't fly.
(no respect for nature if there's any wonder why)
All the movers and shakers and policy makers
suffering serious shut-eye.

Wake up people, hear what I'm saying,
by now we should be on our knees praying.
Instead our own kind we keep slaying,
perpetuating, discriminating,
raising generations to grow up hating,
the black man, the yellow, brown and red one,
believing the only good one is a dead one.

Wake up people, people wake up.
I only have time for a few more minutes
and I intend to stretch this to the very limits.
And if you can't get to that
then you're not even in it.

Wake up people! Wake up!
The time is now.

Paranoia

Of all the millions of women
in the universe, she is
certain that her personal
business is neon sign worthy.

New York Times front page
worthy like everybody
gives a damn about a black
woman's state of affairs.

Anyhow, paranoid or not it's
her business and it's important
for women not to put their
business in the street. So

She tucks hers away in poems
and stores them in cobwebbed
corners in boxes behind the
linen in the closet.

She has a "particular" friend
who has a key to go in and
remove the boxes in case she
has an automobile accident/dies.

Unlike radical feminists who
whine "the personal is political"
or the good poet who has mastered
the art of circumlocution, she

Thinks her business is to tell
the truth without telling a lie.
Not telling her business is lying
by omission but since it's

Important for women not to put
their business in the street,
I've tucked hers in the
spaces between these lines.

Zora

in boiling sun
i look among the weeds
of eatonville for you
who strutted hats
cocked and feathered
draped-down pants when
women knew their
places

most townspeople
never heard of you
i pronounce your name
more deliberately
z o r a n e a l e
h u r s t o n
hunted
jook joints
of mississippi
for the souls
of her people

a dusty finger
points out your
house among a dull
row of shanties
the one with the
sanctified screen door
drying on dried hinges

in boiling sun
i search the
splintered wood
the taller brush
for your stone
the one alice
had engraved
a genius of the south

i want to break bread
drink wine
with you who
spit back hell from
the niggerati
your brazen tongue
died cold in hand

a charge to keep i have
a god to glorify
who gave her sun
my soul to save
and fitted for the sky

by half moon
i turn graves
to find your
oyster knife
suspended between
my thighs

The Trial (Ramona)

are you a liar
    objection

why am I here and not you
    objection

        you must revere america
        you must wash your feet in
        water blazing law and order
        we have borders around difference

        foulmouth bullhorn mattedhair
        difference

objection

        justshutup
        be a revolutionary pit bull
        but shutup about it

are you a liar
    objection

here I stand the charred
remains of no mothersday
morningglories
for spacious skies
see my arms
see my back
see my lungs
my scars
smell the smoke
who am I

        theyateoutofgarbagecans

tenthousand rounds of ammunition
seventy armed hard hats

    createdaserioushealthhazard

helicopter grinding beating circles

    oralsexonthestreet

the bomb
vietnam hiroshima
dachau auschwitz

    violentradicalgroup
    stockpiledweapons

watercanons 2000 gallons a minute

remember
the flesh peeling screams
the kids are coming out
the kids are coming out
the showers poison smoke
fire fire fire

are you a liar
    objection

  whose eye is this
  whose eye is this
  whose teeth are these
  does this skull fit
  this spine whose foot
  whose shin bone femur
  nine-year-old

12
male or female
animal or human
    objection
     this is america
     this is america

these are babies
screaming bullets
blown back roast
flames leaping out lungs
man
you can tell the
future of a nation
by how it loves
its children
hear ye hear ye
this court was
never in session

see my arms
see my back
see my lungs
my scars
smell the soot
I am the autopsy
of a lethal eviction
the crust of
a white tornado

    objection

a red tornado
eviction
don't be such a
smart ass

why am I here and not you

    radicalbacktonaturegroup
    fedchildrendogmeat

11 people dead
blood in your eyes
on your shirt
dripping fingers
dripping strings
shoes dripping
a neighborhood
no charge
you free by the people
for the people

   africa a handyman withathirdgradeeducation

I charred and charged
conspiracy attempted assault
riot

you are a liar
      objection

are you a
murderer
      sustained

are you a
terrorist
      objection

are you a
holocaust
tornado
      sustained

I can feel you
whirl suck
slamkick
this wood
funnel your rage
shriek lock
the wood in the
stove 6221 osage

burn the dark devils
pitch black ashes
and all

    I think we did everything
    possible to negotiate and
    bring about a peaceful resolution

Sixties

The sixties
our era to rage
now
after the purge
we ignore
racism

The eighties
a poem about race
is not a poem
people say that's
sixties rhetoric
anger no longer
the correct response
to white supremacy

We put on grandboubas
not dashikis dread our hair
no longer bushes call ourselves
kwekuhodarikunjufu
tote incense peddle oils
and vegetarian sermons
write safe poems about
trees in nicaragua cover
eyes with blue contact lenses
watch our sister host
fosyth county georgia on
national television
go back
tom fetchit step
and be safe
the sixties was our
era to purge

Deny charred holes
in harlem watts
14th street dc

southeast
is a bantustan
glass chrome
granite marble
monuments to racism
rise from connecticut avenue

Forget
heads rolled off the tip
of hoover's tongue
forget
draft cards clogged sewers
so johnny could come marching home

peace be still
forget
james cleveland ordained
nikkigiovanni poet arsonist
forget
panthers parked rifles
between rightwing liberal eyes
police pigs broke many backs
broke no spirits
smash racism
jam the rubble down its
red white and blue throat
the sixties was our era
to rage

Remember
flames
shattering glass
tvs and stereos
running down the city streets
remember
no forty acres
not one mule only
screams and uniformed
militia national guard
blank faces blocked

clenched fists angry
teeth "black power burn
baby burn" and water the water
tripping over water and fat
firehoses and more water

My water broke right after
the King was murdered
my daughter pushed fragile
and tightfisted against
walls of resistance

Maybe she will remember

Billie's Birthday

(tough on black artists)

in papitos restaurant
no other black patrons
beside my daughter and me
hail and sleet clog the air
hard eyes rocks
against our faces
we have trespassed
something sacred
this is italy's antipasto
not ethiopian cabbage
a standoff between
hog and sheep

sixty years ago
gave Billie
the ice
burnt corked
her face
wrong color
in the band
too light black
in the toilet
she read comicbooks
too black to
sit at a
whitebar

It's April
Billie's Birthday
I got to think about Billie
what she did
what she said
how she did it
her body simmered
folktales like a
caldron

what Billie could do was feel
feel the humiliation
arrests convictions
addict junky headlines
dead momma sadie hardrot
in her gut in her bones and
bleed bleed
celebrate blood in the public
bleed style into that
cold metal penis

her tongue scorched
words into smoke rings
every period every question mark
comma dot sang

my man don't love me
treats me awful mean
my man don't love me
treats me awful mean

wasn't just you Billie
Sarah's gone now
Sassy left the other day
laid down her horn somewhere
between the florida avenue grill
and blues alley gone

no two people on earth
are alike its got to be
that way in music or it
ain't music   gone

cry Billie
cry and call

gardenia momma
no money off the table
cept in the palm a yo hand

What's it gonna be tonight Blackie
heroin hunger or rejection

redneck mothafucker
I will beat yo ass
if you don't git that
goddamn cigarette ouffa
my mink coat

Style Billie
sandpaper rubs the soul
sometimes Godnoise screaming
applause sometimes
a littlevadkagin sometimes
a tortured monkey gone wild
blow your horn girl

cry and call
bleed laugh
quiver and shake

the trenchcoat trenchmouth
mothafuckin shadows
lurkin street corners
bar corners

handcuffed

Sing anyway
Billie
sanctified blues
like it ain't never oughta been
like it still is
in these United Whitefolks of
America lowdown tricky men
laugh Billie shake

Explode

needletracks
prison
indeed

It's April
Billie's Birthday
this is a party for Billie
orchurch orsomething

antipasto friedchittlins
grapeleaves and greens

call the names
of our honored guests Billie Sarah
BessieSatchmo
PresDukeCount Mahalia
AlbertaNat JosephineMoms

witness
witness
Can I get
a witness

This is a party a service
A Worshipservice Birthday
Party

I got to talk to Billie
We got to talk about
how she is
how I am
how we be

It's tough on Black Artists

I need Billie
I need Billie's blood

A Round Peg Over a Square Hole

I walk backwards away
from myself into
stiff brown chairs
chalk dust over
my fingers over my art
a round peg over a square hole,

My teaching too black
for the system
I keep trying to bolt it back
teach the children a tomato dance
teach french pearcoring
teach appalachian humming.

I walk past myself out of
fear and habit into
prison walls
painted wardens
stabbing air with letter openers
sloshing bull ships guarding
me from myself,

Keep the niggers in line
trash independent thinking
reward conformity, teaching
black children to think is still
against the law punishable by
social isolation and a lowered
performance rating,
teach em to be
good gluttonous consumers
sing all praises due
i magnin, nieman marcus,
saks 5th avenue
limit that
black pride stuff to february.

Take the money girl! just keep movin
you been teachin long enough
do it by rote go on in there
an git that check they owe you that.
it's dirty money. hell! you crazy!

The length of the lights makes me dizzy
I suffocate, from sand and feet
pounding toward my room, sugar brown
faces, the adolescent crust layered
in baby fat, the chubby fingers kneading
tugging pulling come on please.

Most wardens
are light skinned
some darker tones have
risen the ranks light or dark
brainless wonders rule the roost.

You like to teach all that
thinking stuff. I want em quiet.
they're too noisy.

Fuck her! smile talking angry
to myself a mad woman no
a round peg over a square hole

The customs, the cross
the nomenclature/CBC
crush black children
designed to fail the grim
nasty links, the barbedwire

I like to teach the song
It's alright to cry
I never do I'm empty

For years
I crawled between
cracks for fresh lilacs
wild berries and freely gave from my catch

For years
I rode the schedule
the stinking train on the skinny track
the death track starched manners
peroxide, wooden corsets swimming
in pork fat earmarked self-destruction,

Now eight-thirty gets later and later
I remove the shackles,
unfasten the helmet, the yoke
the collar and inch off
this trained slave toward myself.

Dancer

(for Nina Montgomery)

How we fall between
the cracks of difference
depends on the distance
we need to keep from ourselves

your face
a benin mask
stretched and patched
by fire and plastic surgery

your head
thrown back
breasts arched forward
announce your arrival

I watch you
walk on water
your long taut
limbs embrace the sun

dance designs
on my senses
you are monk
you are mingus

you offer me your hand
I hesitate
my clay eyes trace
the contours of your scars

your hands are not whole
I was always told
it is impolite to stare
I want to understand your hands

I want to know
how you were burned
if you still feel pain

you laugh easy from your
ribs
I weigh my need
for understanding
on your scale
of self-acceptance

I am not steady
I squeeze your hand
kiss your cheek for
reassurance

Akili

Bird

as a bird i fly above the trees
i feel the breeze of the wind
wind my wings with warmth
flying free
my flight defies the force
of gravity
at this height my sight
sees with clarity
the unity
connectedness of all that exists
oceans valleys rivers mountains
merely fountains
of colors blending together in shapes
textures
sketching patterns
on terrestrial easels
celestial scenes above
reflect in constellations
the configurations on earth
slopes plains prairies
rolling greenery
as it is in heaven
pleasant scenery
stars planets galaxies
similarities abound
between sky and ground
as i fly around

Kenneth Carroll

Ill-logistics

"people running 'round in circles,
don't know what they heading for
everybody crying peace on earth
just as soon as we win this war."

i don't support drug dealing
but i support the drug dealers

     say what? you say
four red white & blue sheets in the breeze
grasp the logic in your hand like gusts of wind
     accessible like strawberry letter 22

     i don't support murders
     but i support the murderers

     you are smiling
catching the bait now instead of the hook
bend this logic in half like running water
     any fool can do it, why can't a nation

i don't support rape
but i support the rapists

     if a lumberjack chops down a tree & nobody hears it
     does the sky wear a yellow until he clears the forest
     does he get a purple heart for the splinter in his hand

i don't support child molesting
but i support the child molesters

only thing about the fire you stand is the heat
all this logic is messing with your reason
your reason for supporting a weird war

i don't support exploitation
but i support the exploiters

you don't have to listen to dan quayle
to hear things plain absurd
if a man stands in the rain & curses its wetness
is he crazy or patriotic

your mind is at war
senseless parroted ideas march across your conscience
armed with government propaganda & paper-thin rationality

on the home front
your common sense is bunkered down
reeling against thoughtless tirades
exploding like bombs piercing your brain

i don't support bullshit
i just like the smell

stop making sense
specious reasoning
let's stand for nothing
roguish logic passing for intelligence

i don't support the war
but i support the soldiers

h.g. wells is scratching his skull
this is deep like quagmire deep
like freud would lose his own mind deep
like discount family therapy deep
& if soldiers fight wars . . . & we're against the war . . .

"y'know if silence was golden you couldn't raise a dime
because your mind is on vacation
& your mouth is working overtime" *

suddenly superman can fly
white boxers named rocky can beat black heavyweights
tarzan did run africa before the boers came along
milli vanilli didn't lip sync
vanilla ice is better than chuck d
ronald reagan never dyes his hair
bush always knows what he's talking about
& bart simpson is not a cartoon

if all this ain't making sense
that's only because there ain't
no words to this poem
because i hate poetry
but i support dem poets

now get ta dat!

* excerpt from Mose Allison.

60

Never Piss Off a Poet

don't try to play me chump!
cause i'll meet you in a back alley
on a rainy moonless night
wit a loaded verse in my pocket
push a sawed-off simile 'gainst your nose
as a dog that looks like your sister
drains the last swig from a dead thunderbird bottle
& a black cat humming bessie smith blues
wit a haiku stainless steel stiletto
pulls a jack move on your brother
as a rat recites dolomite
while me & a signifying monkey
press a sharp analogy against your throat
'til it drips blood red rhymes

keep messin' 'round hear
you might find your gov'ment
looking down the bizness end
of an ugly metaphor
i'll slap a cold metal stanza against the temple
of every republican-democracker i see
to shinin' sea
i'll make george bush lick my italian sonnets
give ronald reagan a quarter to shine my meter
make nancy reagan shop at woolworth's
with a free verse credit card

i'll hold your family hostage
'till you decipher every ismael reed poem written
i'll put your mother's mother
father's father
ancestors in a bawdy ballad
tie an epic poem round yo neck
drop you in the river styx
let my man charlie tuna go through your pockets
full of poesy
shoot a blazing lyric through your covered wagon

sneak up behind you
in the middle of town
at high noon
& put a bullet in your back
'cause i'm an inkslinger with no code
i'll peel your cap with some tomahawk imagery
'til the sun sets in the west in one
long narrative poem describing your demise
& buzzards sail in a crooked sky
ashes ashes
you'll all get beat down sucka

i'll put you on a leaky canto back to england
drop a barakian bomb on yo shakespere club, make 'em say,

"to be, yeah dig that baby, like not to be, dig it"

make stagger lee the poet laureate
bust a satire cap in the ass of your humanities dept.
i'll let shine steal your girlfriend
while crooning a funky rhyming couplet
that sounds like cannonball adderly live in detroit
i'll push you in the middle of a fight at
the crazy-bard lounge
on friday night
have two muses from chicago take you for a drive
then maybe you'll finally learn
that pissing off a poet
is as dangerous as oppressing
black people!

bang! bang! ya dead!

Depocricy

voting for president
is
like
peeing
in the
ocean
while the
electoral college
points at your urine
& laughs

Small Difference

What's

the
difference
be
tween

Jeanne
Kirkpatrick's

face

and
her

soul?

Her

soul
is
uglier

and

whiter

White Woman Blues

14 dead
montreal moans
blood drips from the pages
why am i not surprised
only sick

this is the inheritance of europe's female children
it begins with eve-justification
proceeds through witch burnings-affirmation
& continues with friday 13th-confirmation

young & beautiful & white & woman & will not save you
in this culture
freddy krugerrand will hunt you down
as madison ave. grins and strokes its erection
sex becomes foreplay for murder
witness:
montreal is weeping
history is an open wound
why am i not surprised
only sick

my ancestors, whose bones swell the ocean, atlantic knew
massa thomas jefferson bedded his negro wenches then tried
to hide their mutilated bodies beneath a hypocrites constitution

the lakota & cheyenne knew
it. custer & his boys slaughtered squaws with their
colt .45 penises, the american public promoted him to general,
such popular support for a rapist

the women of latin america know
american trained men-turned animals assault according to
    instructions
in a cia manual, phallic bayonets are paid for by usa
    women-taxes

philippine women know
as american soldiers purchase them like cheap watches
and discard them like same

and maybe you thought it would be just the foreign females,
who lacking blonde hair & blue eyes were destined for brutality
but
14 are dead
montreal tolls its bells
my t.v. is bleeding
why am i not surprised
only sick

for a small fee you can enjoy this masascre of maidens
in the privacy of your own home
ted bundy was a handsome murderer, a real lady-killer, they said
a made for t.v. special starring you as prey
screams & cash register rings
hunting for vaginas is as profitable as mining for africans
and more fun

hollywood features you fucked and filleted in
stereo sound & technicolor
hollywood: an ugly reflection in the distorted mirror
of your history
where everything is reduced to bitches & niggers & gooks &
savages
& spics & white men with guns
white men whose masculinity is predicated on the debasement
of human beings

these white men who man your churches
who make your movies
who run your governments are not space monsters
they did not land in upstate n.y. on halloween
they are not the figment of h.g. wells or orson welles'
imagination

they are your fathers
& brothers &
lovers
women haters eat apple pie
drive chevrolets
and become president

this is your culture
jeanne kirkpatrick & phylis schlafly are your sisters
providing justification as your brothers provide horror
as is their historical legacy

you are raising another generation of
murdering masturbation misogynists
who cheer gleefully as jason hunts down women
killing the promiscuous ones first,
the dumb ones next,
and the beautiful ones last

what a horror to find that your knights, white
seek to slay fair maidens

your macho men are plotting your demise
as they stroke your flowing hair

a change must come
america must have a conscience, it has none now
you will not be able to e.r.a. yourselves to safety
the roots of this weed must be pulled, examined, then destroyed
you cannot remain "white" women if you are to survive
you must be human, allied only to that which is right
because
14 are dead
montreal must teach
these men cannot surprise me
only make me sick
you should be sick too.

Assassin

like BANG!
and he was dead.
I got him right 'tween his lying eyes
caught his moldy ass in mid-dis
information

it was a high tech take-out
an *infrared* removal
it was so sweet
like a laser shot
quick!

i put ah capper on da gipper (gypper)
and watched
as his white lies
were zapped into the
beautiful Black truth.

120 Degrees

(For Lance Cpl. Jason J. Rother)

Wilderness is deaf
African hearts break loudly, bake in the heat
blind is this desert
stolen children are discarded, uncared for
burning sun mocks the unseen
tears fry at 120 degrees
water heavy moon deceives
alienation drips through sweaty pores
stars mock, twinkle dispossession
dumb terrain will not speak
at a 120 degrees
it is dangerous to presume visibility
unforgiving, unrepentant is this ground
                  it is ugly here
dreams die, African hearts break
                  at a 120 degrees

only the vapors are visible.

Semper Fi
(For Lance Cpl. Jason J. Rother)

24 hours later, no one even noticed the absence
and the sun burns like america's ugly lies
40 hours later, it was almost as if you never existed
you wait for the sound of your marine brethren
running wildly into the desert, splitting the day with concern;
it is quiet, like mourners waiting for a funeral
the desert's eyes are beautiful like death
a vulture paints the searing sky
a presumptuous belief seasons your dreams

40 hours later, two pale faces converse:
"Hey jack, how many niggers went on patrol with us?"

Huh . . ."

4 months later they find your remains
a baked jawbone marks the last leg of your journey into eternity

"He almost made it," remarks the marine search party
the vulture with deceit on his breath knows,
you weren't even close.

Someday

Black people will be a people someday
Able to stand tall amongst people anywhere
With a homeland, a religion, a purpose, a name
Black people will be a people someday
Able to work out their own destinies
No longer enslaved, no longer afraid
Black people will be a people someday
With the strength that comes in unity
Ready to make their place, ready to take a stand
Yes, Black people will be a people someday
Black people *will* be a people someday
For they'll soon realize they're Kings & Queens dethroned
And move to gain their crowns once more
They'll see the chains which have them bound
And cast them off, for good, at last
Yes, Black people will be a people someday
My people will be a people someday

Jennifer Lisa Vest

Survivor's Poem #1

Who will receive
My anger?
In the form of a baseball bat
Blow
Across the brow?
Or better, the bloodletting
of broken teeth,
the crunch of splintered ribs,
The shattering of broken kicked shins?

Who will take my anger?
Package bomb parcel post
Express
Who will deliver me
of this hateful birth;
This suddenly remembered
Child's terror,
This misty recollection
Forming a cloud
Raining on my
Everything
That was sanity
Purity
Sanctity.

Who will take from
My weary arms
This burden too heavy
To hold?

Rambo-Woman

My friends tell me
I have no business
Being 'Rambo-Woman'
On the streets
of D.C.
(talking back to rudeass
boys at bus stops)
That in return
For my bravado
My John Wayne
Don't – mess – with – me attitude
I will only end up dead
Or worse; raped
In any case
Left in some condition
My parents won't
Recognize.
And that instead
of demanding
Respect
I need to swallow
My pride
Lose a little dignity
Cower in the presence
Of Brothers on street corners
Strung out on drugs
College boys in cars
Lecherous middle aged
Married men
And learn fear
Because (they insist)
The only way I can
Stay alive
Intact

Altogether
Is to lie
To hide
To acquiesce
And to surrender to my fate:
The fate of all my sisters.

But that's not me.
I don't agree
Because like any man
I deserve my peace;
Personal and private
Control of my own
Body
And its sanctity

From the Beginning – For Miri

If it ever
Wasn't obvious
If ever in my running
My flighty long-winded explanations
I didn't carefully explain
If ever it was unclear
And I never sat still long enough
To speak simply
To talk about love,
Forgive me.
My sentiment never felt
The restriction of my words
And I have been loving you
Wordless
From the beginning.

Return From Jail

He likes to look
In mirrors now
Flex his muscles
Joke about torture.

He's a big man
Precarious and too proud
To cower
So he walks tall
The scars they left are small.

Hard for a stranger to see.

I have no more
Any ego
Any need of an ego
He says
Hiding his wounds
From his mother
He must go home
Strut young
Talk fast
Use long smooth words
And live.

He's a big man
To cower
Precarious but proud
The scars they left are small
He walks tall
And tells us they
Left no scars at all.

Hair

Monica friend Sharon
Say she straighten her hair
Cause back when she was natural
She couldn't get none,
And hey she ask
How I'm spose to go
Without dat?

Monica say
When she went 'natural'
Just one day
Up and got nappy
Her boyfriend cried
Right there
Sittin on the bed
Big as he was
Big strong black man
But, she say
Smiling cool breeze like,
He got over it.

Kalika is angry
Her hair ain't
never been
Laid back
Pressed flat
Always been
Growin toward the sky
Like it spose to
And she wanta know
Why all these sistas
Is making it so hard
For her just to be
A straight-up (unstraightened)
Black woman?
And why they always
Wanna touch her hair

Like she got somethin
They don't.

Betina who
Dread her lock
Not too long back
Say we
Need ta have a
Conference on hair
For all these confused
Colored folk
Who she say
Like her locks cause they long
She was in the 'nappy stage'
Wiv them short locks
Be pointin every which
Way
Didn't nobody
Wanna touch it then.

Austin F. Wooten

The Nameless People

We are the nameless people with many names.
We have been called many names by many people,
such as Blacks, coloreds, and Negroes.
We have called ourselves people of color,
Afro-Americans, and Creoles.
Some of us have used X or triple X
for the name that we have never known.
Sometimes,
we make up names of our own.
Some of us refuse to use a name
and refer to "us" as "we."
Because we are the nameless people with many names.
Yet we have features among our many faces
to represent the whole human race.
We have many names,
and yet no one name.
Are we no one? Are we everyone?
We are the nameless people with many names.

Kim Taylor

Love's Kansas City Caper

Love made its presence known to me
On a Kansas City night
Love will not be ignored, it's true
Though I tried with all my might

It tapped me on the shoulder
It whispered in my ear
At first, I was so stubborn
Determined not to hear

But Love can be persistent
On a Kansas City night
Despite all my resistance
It set out to win the fight

It just kept right on nagging
It would not leave me be
I said "Go away," Love
Go away RIGHT NOW!

I have no time, you see

When suddenly Love raised its voice
Defying all convention
Leaving me no other choice
Demanding my attention

I had to think of something
And I had to do it quick!
'Cause I was getting caught up
In a Kansas City trick

So, I steeled myself with firm resolve
To bring Love to its knees
But when I glared into its eyes
Love winked and smiled at me

I said "Love, you surprise me!
So soon you admit defeat?"
Love said "Don't be a fool, my dear
My mission is complete."

"For you and one other
Have cast me one long look
So now I have the two of you
Forever on my hook."

With those words Love tipped his hat
Then kindly wished me well
And to this day, I am indeed
Held captive by its spell

So, when in Kansas City
Be careful of the night
And watch out for
The eyes of Love

They'll make your heart
Take flight!

Susan Anderson

Buffalo Soldiers

Once they rode together
Slave and Indian
Across the Nueces
And below the Rio Grande

1.

First there is nothing
But the spirit
Left behind like a scent

Then there are the voices
Howls

Then the blue
Of cavalry uniforms
The peaked caps

2.

Geronimo called them
Buffalo Soldiers
It was the warrior.
Naming his betrayer.
He saw their hair,
Like buffalo,
And sensed the doom.

3.

When they howled
It might have been
For all the years of dying.
What makes a killer ride,
Churning up
The white dust,

Chewing the corrosion,
Screaming an old song
Once meant for God?
What makes the fear
Billow around him
In his own voice?

4.

It has been nearly two years,
This pursuit.
Geronimo eludes.
The Sierra Madre hold him.
How powerful is memory?
Vittorio had prophesied,
"You must not trust them
The land is not in them."
Now the mountains groan.

5.

The patrol approaches
The border
Which stretches ahead
Gouged in the cheek
Of the skin called Texas

Cattle will soon follow
The Buffalo Soldiers
And bankers
And the other gods
Of History
Now the men follow
The scent of death
The frontier

6.

They ride at night.
When the sun goes down
They awaken with their shoulders
Aching against boulders.
Their legs are stretched
Along the ground
Taut as telegraph wires.
They reach for their rifles.
They talk and pick their teeth
With pocket knives.
They think of victory.

Texas Town

There is money in this place
It blares
Like a rodeo tune
Everywhere
Kennedy is in
And the black people
Are relieved
It is as though
Some promise has been kept

In the neighborhood
Old Man who owns the corner store
Thrusts his gargoyle head
At the candy hungry children
To keep them from stealing

Everybody is trying
The best they can
Ma Dear among the toilets
In office buildings downtown
Her daughter Willie Ruth
Works spells
In other people's kitchens
After school the little boy
Runs curly-headed
Through the Dallas wilderness

At night the boy
Sleeps like a hostage
Grateful for the darkness
Willie Ruth has left him
For the all night prayer meeting
At the Apostolic Mission
Her cologne still drifts
Across the living room where
Ma Dear sits
In the Waxy yellow window light

Lamenting that Dallas
Is such a rough town
She puts her trust in God
While she reads the Tarot cards

When Ma Dear's husband
Was a young man
They called him Hot Shot
And Dallas was too tame for him
The city could not match
The pure worship of morning
On the country roads of Marshall
The nighttime dangers in those woods
When the crackers strolled
Hot Shot said
Even the white men in Dallas
Were small time
Sneaking their pistols
Shaded by their stetsons
Stinking with money

They shipped Hot Shot
To the Philippines
When the white men
Made their war
He drove trucks
In the jungle
Hauling supplies
To beat the Japanese
He had a hell of a time
Among those Army Negroes
Bourbon heavy at night
They sang a soldier chorus
It was the same old labor
As in Dixie
But now Hot Shot swung
The truck's gearshift
For Democracy
He worked his soul thin
And willingly

It was his only aria
The war
Better than Dallas ever was
Or ever could be

Twenty years later
Hot Shot took off again
No amount of Ma Dear's scrubbing
Or Willie Ruth's praying
Or the little boy's running
Could make Hot Shot stay
Kennedy was in
And the man got restless
They should have seen it coming
Ma Dear, Willie Ruth, and the big-eyed boy
They should have known
When Hot Shot told them
That money haunted him
That money made Dallas weak
Content to just stand there
Like a barkeep
With his elbows on the counter
And the patience of greed
Waiting
For an old-fashioned shoot-em-up
To bring in business

Ruby Bates' Escape From Huntsville

*Ruby Bates and Victoria Price were the two white women who
testified against the Scottsboro Boys in the famous 1930s rape
trial. Ruby Bates later recanted her testimony and worked for
the defense of the black teenagers.*

Oh, honey
The movies they show!

Sitting in the fertile
Mad dark of the cinema
After all the royal passions
Have faded
And the credits roll
In the Jim Crow theater
Her lamenting chin
Is thrust into her breast
Eyes closed
Thinking
"What a place
Fucking Alabama
To be a queen of romance."

The cotton mill job ran out
And the vagrancy went to her head
She was ready to tell big lies
And see wild places on her own
She had a right
Seventeen years old and foreboding
Her back stooped with grime
Her chest whistling through her cigarette
Her nights spent loving in the arms of a millhand
Loving his coughing flesh
Sleeping in the dead wet night
Like a convict
Alert with longing
Waiting for the right freight train

This depression earth
Ain't giving up nothing, sister
And politics has passed you by
If a man can do it
Why not you?
Haul your treacherous flesh
Over the state line to Chattanooga
In a fire snorted by an engine
Going north or west or anywhere
Away from this prescription

She travels butch with Vicky Price
Who is older
With a body like the anxious clay
In drought time
Vicky is the hard one
Burning under her overalls
Dry from so many dollar bills
Stuffed up her crotch
Soaking up her tears

Ruby snares a whiskey-powered demon
In the hobo jungle
His mouth funnels fumes over her
Knowing she is an imposter
The idea of all that wiry cotton
Sprouting through the man's fly
Of her disguise
Is too much
She weathers the burst of his sour rain
The coins chime in her pocket
She snaps them inside
And swallows an appetite more aroused

Ruby finds Vicky at the hobo fire
And shares some boiling coffee
Their paltry words flicker
in the damp spring night

Down the track
They see the camp
Set up by the nigger bums
Waiting, too
For the speeding boxcars
Scottsboro bound

Notes On a Storefront Church

Preacher deaf from the steel mill scream
Strides through the urban shambles
Wafting the holy scents of whiskey and aftershave
The steel mill pays his money
But this is his real job:
Finding the pitch of his spirit
In the long wail of Wednesday nights

Louisiana man on crutches
Talks of a polio childhood
Women gather on the shabby concrete
Wearing the best suits welfare can buy
Children chase street cats and the shadows
Of trees

Light from the door sprawls across the sidewalk
Night brings a rumor of industry downwind
Slaughterhouses a few blocks away
Still alive in the christian dark

Organ tremolos reach outside
Worshippers pull up anchor
Hushed expectant as Christmas morning
They go indoors
Merge with the light
Leave the bloody air
To the meatpackers on swingshift

Illumination

Our traffic battered car
Rolls over the rough asphalt
Into the church parking lot
My father stills the machine
My mother sighs with the triumph
Of arrival

They rouse us
Their children in the back seat
We are heavy-eyed with nostalgia
For our beds

Inside
The sun slides itself
Back through the church windows
After having gone prodigal during the night
In the church pews
Even the old ladies
In fur coats shiver
The light
From the stained glass windows
Cuts like ice
We children rub our hands
To keep them warm
And watch our breath
make its jailbreak
From our mouths

The old sanctuary
Is experienced at winter
Built as it was against the cold
The wood creaks
The bodies settle into pews
The congregation whispers
The organ is pumped into life
The choir rustles like a flock of farm birds
Restless for feeding

The hymn finds its way
Out of the desolation of its beginning

From the altar
As the men's choir sings
My father's solo tenor rises
Above the old slave chorus
That rhythms on
Until its end
And the silence
Its tone
Is suspended still
Still
Still
In that air

This Morning

Somehow this morning speaks to us
And we feel what a shape we are
Of mammal and upright and, worse, sinner
We are welcomed to this rock of faith
In the city's hidden center
And foretold (trembling already)
Of the shouting good time that will be had
This morning

This morning, this morning the sun circles
Around our heads through
The patchwork glass of windows
In the rumble of old wood
This morning

Somehow this morning holds its breath
For the heart to be heard
Beating in these pews
And when the preacher's wife
Claims the piano
Its keys beat, too

It is the beat that sounds
Everywhere in this city
When the breath is held
For the heart to be heard
Out of the pavement chase
Out of the warehouse shoes
Out of the truck growl
And the car grimace
And the hammer hands
That reach for the truth
In a day, its hours
As far as the ocean edge
With its mouth calling

From the berths and piers
And the dock pounding
And the ship impatience
And the body rocking loose
Into the wind dash
Into the lung gulp
Into the rain drive
Out of the blue born
Out of the cetacean dark

And the voices of the choir
Don't relent this morning
This morning which has lifted
The entire world and spun it
On the long note of a gospel solo
And there is life
All the way from our sun-flamed heads
To our feet
And beneath our feet
Beneath even the floor
There is life pushing ahead through the deep
Which it knows
And which the voices of the choir
Take us back to

This morning, this morning we remember
What it is we hold in our throats silently
Until it leaps out full volume
From the dark below
And we clench our eyes shut
And shake our heads from side to side
Because it has surfaced
In the first scream
In the legends of blood and night
In the memory of sanctuary

When life dangled by its neck
From the pain of slavery everywhere
Even the sky rained it
And we built a small shelter of wood
Against the downpour
Against the horror that was human
And was made by humans
And we tried for one Sunday moment
To find a voice
And call it divine

This morning, this morning
We try again
(In the fugitive city
By the inescapable sea)
Igniting the fire of our hearts
In one somber song
One freedom

Bag Lady

Earth
That old woman
Has shoved her shopping cart
Under the freeway
And stained her fingers
With the ink of tears
She lives in a muttering shadow
Her knit cap over her ears
Her black skin branded
By fear

The refuse
Of the human heart
Is piled up in her cart
Gathered from those
Who have stopped waiting
For the Promised One
In the locked laboratories
In the arsenals
In the high places
They have prepared for her funeral
It will be a public burning
There will be no music
Not even the blues
And no one will be left to grieve

She Was a Painting (. . . And I Wished to be an Artist)

i could wildly kiss her
remove her lipstick
wipe off her clothes

or

wipe off her lipstick
remove her clothes
wildly kiss her

it doesn't matter
only her face on my canvas
"still lifed"
and water based

soon she shall
be hanging in my
bedroom
I can see
exotic colors
on strokes of my brush

    lightly recreating delicate
    details of
    brown
    skin

    lightly recreating
    african nudity with
    bold emotions

soft hands . . .

gentle feet . . .

passionate places . . .

i paint nudes slow and deliberate because heat
in my house works best when needed most

i paint nudes best because you only see chill
bumps when you are close to someone

i paint nudes life-like because i never was
good at faking orgasms

i painted this nude because

i could wildly kiss her
remove her lipstick
wipe off her clothes

or . . .

Horror Movie

stop counting spooks . . .

. . . this addition and subtraction
of   abnormality
                                 is
                                 insignificant
we have plenty of ghosts
                    in
the dc govt but the schools
tell you that
the   first slave
couldn't   count to 10.

in atlanta
the   govt is haunted
but nobody in   washington
                                           is afraid,

and philly
has some   real   scary   werewolf
                                types

who think
raw
meat
smoldering with a taste of
brick is   GOODddddddddd.
around inauguration time we

                                     count spooks

                                     "carefully"

                          and accuse wildly if
one
                          frankenstein monster
if one frankenstein creation with a brain that's
been dropped on concrete and juggled around
like jell-o

doesn't get a chance
to fight the wolfman or the mummy or the invisible
men.
but remember igor,   "mastah . . . mastah . . .
                                   it's time."

                    — sound familiar?

now the cowardly lion had something:

"i do believe in spooks, i do believe in
spooks, i do i do i do believe in spooks,"

damn that lion, he should have been a scarecrow

because
frankenstein
was
not a
man
and
i never have been afraid of the dark.

When Minds Meet

(for D.P. & the B.S.M.)

and u know
we have
been
thru
this
love
thang
many many times
baby
me luvin u
u luvin me
but never
us lovin
us

call
it wavelengths
baby

rhythm

like
maybe
i need
to learn
to dance
so i can
be in
step with
yo
sweetness
yo
gracefulness
so i can
see

you sparkle
on the floor
in front of my
eyes with yo
tenderness:

yo ankles.
yo knees.
yo hips
yo waist
face
eyes
ears
hair
nose
thighs
calves
fingers
toes.

i'm up
and down
on you
and smilin
seein
all of you
just like i love
it:

black

beautiful

and

ready to
kiss you

anywhere . . .

America and the Ant Message
(for Amiri Baraka)

maybe ants are too deliberate.
                  too conformist.
                  too obedient.
                  too organized.

and maybe ants are too much like the
military,
                  too much like
                  those guys in
                  orwell's *1984*
                  under the rule

of
the

thought
         police. (God forbid that.)

and maybe, just maybe
ants are too un-american,
because
         you can't eat steak everyday
         if you constantly think of
         all the others.

when i was younger,
i would marvel at their order,
how they collected crackers
calmly,
how they rebuilt their destroyed homes
after young "uncivilized" maniacs
stepped on their civilization
for cheap laughs.

but still,
ants just seem too refined for
america,
seem too unalarmed,
too civilized.

then again,
i haven't ever seen an ant
beg for money or sleep on
a heat grate.

Broken Pencils

james baldwin has always been dead.
held the funeral before jimmy
was even born.
held it on college campuses,
high schools,
broadway
press rooms,
publishing houses,
printing companies,

one huge burial for
10 million invisible fingers
dead from writer's cramp.

you see awhile ago
this guy shot jimmy b,
shot jimmy b & sonia s,
amiri b & maya a,
june j & haki m,
gwendolyn b & ethelbert m,

shot them all in the back while
their granddaddies wrote down
little verses down by the creek
for them to read when they grew up,
shot them all & tossed broken
pencils in the creek until
little black boys &
girls got lead poisoning in the brain
from drinking creek water.

after the funeral
they buried them all together
in a bunch,
all of our smoke kings and manchilds,
homegirls and sulas,
sonny's blues singers
and caged bird crooners.

all piled up in one big grave
with a million others
& a giant epitaph reading

"RICHARD AIN'T WRIGHT . . .
BIGGER KILLED MARY . . ."

Upon Becoming Black

cliff tried to warn us.
it was a camp director's duty,
our mommas would have slapped
him if he hadn't

we were young.

the beach air was fresh,
smelled like
perfumed feathers
of a rare bird,
banishing distant thoughts
of concrete jungles.

the beach was white:

sand.
clouds.
salt.

people.

cliff tried to warn us,
we were young.

he told us they would
look at us,
they would stare,
they would send messages
without uttering the slightest
word.
he told us about the water where
we could swim and play free,
where we wouldn't have to worry
as much about those frowns,
and those thousand eyes calling

us
                    monkey.

on the boardwalk the storekeepers set us
straight from the start,
felonious frowns from civil war cinema,
confederate tales tacked in time,
antebellum anger arranged and
arrogant.

we didn't want trouble,
didn't even want to buy anything,
just wanted to be like
everyone else,
we were dr king's kids,
we came to start trouble,
we were all the same
it was said.

we tried every store,
they were all the same,

1960 and selma is a beach,
1860 and maybe i would
have laughed,

so we went to swim like cliff said,
talked about the white beach
and white sand
about storekeepers with
broomsticks and telephones
ready,

and how everything would be different
from this day forth because we were
no longer innocent and no longer
young.

Black on Black Homicide #2

the bengal tigers
were
all
locked
in a zoo.

the bengal tigers
were told they were alley
rats.

the bengal tigers
were given
no food.

the walls were covered
with paintings
of bengal tigers
eating garbage.

the zookeeper
dropped in some garbage.

the killing began . . .

Stone Cold Hustler

he was cool
a
stone cold
hustler
laying still like ice
one day out of the meat freezer
bullet frozen in his brain.

Afrikan B-Ball

(for Kenny Anderson, and all the other Afrikan brothers shooting college hoop in 1990 and on . . .)

we be
havin
ropes
connected
to our hands
hips that
swivel
like barstools

chests and
backs that
got hands
too

the ball
out in
front
we with
bruises on our knees
from
smacklin the
rim

it is reggae
up in the
lights
jazz
on
the
scoreboard
nosebleeds
we
brothers
have
lookin

down at
the
hateful
world

have
you
got your
ticket
on
this jet plane
the one
goin
to
afrika

we
can
paint
pyramids
on the
backboard
sweat
water
from the
nile
dunk
racism
through
the hoop
and laugh
while
y'all
cheer
our blackness
and ask over
and over:

how'd
that niggah do that?

Bow to Allah

in america
people
treat
christmas
like
the hajj

only
mecca
is a
mall.

To Be Or Not To Be . . .

ACT I

polonious is still alive,
rosencrantz is still spying,
guildenstern is taking pictures of
all the niggahs thinking. thinking
and waiting until the ghost returns,

returns with news of our end,
in a place that reminds me of denmark
and looks like america,
or it is a place that reminds me of america
and looks
like
south africa?

ACT II

the king has banged our momma. the king has killed
our daddy. the king with
       the ship
       and the quest for
       gold.
       the king with guns and powder
       and daddy with the spear that's
       broken

we are reciting soliloquies and forever
loving our uncle.

ACT III

"there is something rotten in denmark . . ."
something old
rewritten
and performed
at too many theatres.

denmark is unsafe for spooks.

ACT IV

malcom was mad. dr. king was mad.
garvey
nat t
fred d
were all mad.
there is method to their madness,
says the king.
they did not think,
thinkers read soliloquies and slowly become
yorick.

ACT V

we are hamlet. we were warned by
our fathers.
there are too many poison cups
too many poison swords
too many niggahs
behind the curtain with polonious

the king is banging our momma
and killing our daddy
as we recite soliloquies
and defy the visit
of the ghost.

Thoughts of Africa

My thoughts of Africa
               were
of a dark and deep
               jungle,
populated by wild animals and
               wild people.

But then I saw your
               Dark face.
With your accent, thick and
               African.

Then Africa for me,
               Became you,
Dark, deep beautiful and wild.

Thank God I'm Africa's distant child!

Kim Nault

The Holy Land

The tree of peace
is growing stronger,
standing taller,
for those who wish to follow.

We have begun to uproot
the wisdom and knowledge of the Great Law.
These white roots of peace
reaching to all directions
on this Turtle Island.

Soon,
very soon,
we as a nation
will stand under the Great White Pine
of this Holy Land.

Bodies unfolding
in a brilliant hue.
Skies unravel the mysteries
of forgotten truths.
And changing times quickly melt away.
Time is now,
   time is forever.
The seasons begin to collide.
The magic moments are here to stay.

To stay.
  In this Holy Land.

Michelle Parkerson

lest we forget

These

black, brown, beige faces

of the least in life

took the streets

defied empires

woman to woman

man to man

It began ablaze

high tacky queens

blood-soaked crinolines

tear gas and mace

A few fearless

freaks: flip, flamboyant

fed up

on police brutality

the menace of the vice

Spontaneous riots bushfire

round Stonewall Bar

Meanwhile

the 6 o'clock news brings you

the blatant courage

of the fag frontline

America discovers sexual preference

still believes in Rock Hudson

It is 1969

Black & Puerto Rican sodomites

proud leather dykes

in a faceoff

with the world

for three nights

Greenwich Village is a minefield

Are you there?

Let us now praise

a few good women & men

ripe for insurrection

on a chafed June night

pushed to the wall

beaten into shadows

cutting back the night

These, the fringe

black, brown, beige faces

of the least in life

ignited a movement

to love in the light

Are you there?

notes from amistad II

This migration was always:

Jubilee

El Norte

Up South

A legacy of freed wanderers/ex-slaves.

In urban climates

we grew as strangers.

we barely remember our chains.

under the influence

those moments

you enter me

unannounced

i dial a few airlines

then come to my senses

perched on

a transatlantic leap

for love

if some brighton mornings

bring serenading

beneath your balcony

that tense

yearning sound

mistaken for moondust

is me

sons of the pioneers (a litany)

Bill of rights

Bud Lites

KKK

CIA

Tarzan

Ed McMahon

Layaway plan

Frank Perdue

Ollie North, too

IBM

ABM

Boesky

Borke/Baake

Rambo

Nixon

Ellie Mae

Rockefeller

Son of Sam

Billy Graham

All sons

True sons

All sons

True sons

All sons

True sons

of the pioneers

golden girls

Three from the charmed set

doyenne of avant-garde

eccentric

white women

well to do

with   conscience

eternal friends

clutching

beaded throats

experiencing revolution

from their opera box

encouraging the bright

young coloreds

to excel

meaning it

even if it means

destruction

of the gilded halls

which bred them

statistic

In 1944

the lives of black boys

were worth nothing

and you were

no stranger to bloodshed

or the drives of men

in a Southern sawmill town

That carolina dawn

came tender

and two white girls

raped and murderd

led to a black boy's door

You were 14

no stranger to bloodshed

or the drives of men

In newspaper photos

eyes caved with wisdom

lips without question

a child resigned

to a man's fate

In 1944

the lives of black boys

were worth nothing

and George Stinney, Jr.,

was given the chair

The youngest face

on Death Row

was dark

silent

Now the sons

he never fathered

learn his lesson well:

You are black and male

in america

You are never

too young to die

reasoning

We cling to old lovers

in spite of risk

cling to life

via condom

Simulate sex

on video

orgasm by proxy

three minute toll call fantasies

the interactive passion

of PC's

This is karma

in the age of AIDS

Never have so many

felt so little

Never have so many

never dared

for cece

chicago is

a strange place

to find you

with all this wind

i could have missed

your beauty

because you are white/working class

because america lies to us both

how you cut through history

i will never know

but you take me

girl

without notice

i follow

i want your breasts

your sorrow

just for a night

so

c'mon

men at work
(for essex and etheridge)

Show us

what sweet promise

lurks beyond puberty

Give and take it

like a man

In dark places

beat our hearts

with iridescent roses

Leave no dare undone

Push hard tears

with hard talk

Handle us

By night

invade these borders

You chase love

Force tenderness

on the wind

for the horror on the corner

Here fart the gargoyles

a bevy of hardcore

homeboys

dreamt of darkly

in flashbacks of rape

and other unnatural acts

forced in broad daylight

on pooltables/ in subways

boasted over beer

The victim is

always unidentified

a woman

sodomized repeatedly

body discarded

on turnpike curbsides

by some mother's son

You

smash what you cannot touch

mutilate what

you cannot master

Some other life

you could have been a brother

I might have been queen

Keith Antar Mason

A Boy's Poem

Describe yourself?

I am black coffee, please . . . manners
are important. I am a boy's poem.
I nursed older boys lumps and read
big brother's porno mags . . . he was
proving himself all the time too.

How'd you feel about that?

Quiet, like boiling water . . . my
fingers would twitch . . . we sound
like insect worlds. She was nothing to us . . .
they made us — me —
feel like shit.

How long were you out there?

The whole winter, skullin' is
the only thing that pleases me.
There are shackles in my bone marrow.
Spurs — kicking it up.
Rememberin' myself — when I can,
it's important.

Could you explain that?

Getting paid. Working crew. You
indited my culture. "The wild
Thang" is a rap song — a document
of blood — not the event. Getting

paid. Working crew. I'm teaching
you now. Listen — what you want
from me? How you gon' get it? Take
my life! What you want? This is a
boy's poem. "Don't send me no
doctor — fillin' me up . . . ."

What's going on now?

Inside Superman's mind, not Clark
Kent's, I am Lex Luther's shadow.
Fury — rap songs gone ancient —
field holler and uzi's wail coming
from the children in the bellies of
slaveships . . . caught in the under
current of today — drowning in the
sewage of Amerika. God!
Prometheus is inside me . . . tearing
himself apart like a rotted tooth
being torn from a gum . . . my mouth
is bloody . . . only I an't noble like
a vampire . . . just a monster . . . just a
nigga . . . help me.

What made you do it really?

I don't know . . . don't you get it?
We are born and then we learn
something's got to die, like me,
something black and scary gots to
die . . . something black and scary and

loud gots to die . . . don't you know that . . .
doctor, I know that . . . doctor . . .
don't send me no doctor . . .
filling me up . . .
ain't nobody come out and said it but
something like me has got to die,
and I hate you. I hate you for
hating me and I hate myself for
that too — hating you but something
black has got to die.

On Nigga Terms

On the proving ground
I come
the missing light
from dead eyes.
I see the same faces
everywhere
back east
at home
out here
in the popped joints
snapped in the rhythms
of sinewed marriages
of bastard children
starving on the streets
or in the rock houses
this bitches brew
makes coltrane go down easy.

In black august we scream out the conditions
con-ditions
the seditions of this
broken heart
and black male privilege
does not exist
who mistook my pain for power.
Is it in the way
i stand in alleyways
praying for a sign?
Who mistook my sufferings
for messiah like glory?
Dam you , Christians
Anti-Christ
black skin is still a cross
only no resurrection is coming
in the darkness
I scream
a million no's

my god
has abandoned me
and in between the sweet thighs
of the goddess
I fake myself out
for a while
till her screams overwhelm me
flash!
I am rapist/lover
unwanted boy taking up space
cruel hand
handsome nigga man
sung about in her womanhood blues

playing with her clit
I turn magical for myself.
I am skateboarding on the issues
of serious grey matter
black and male and intimate
kill me.
I must be screaming out to you
beyond male silence
in North Carolina
poems are being written
about my personal arrogance
how I smell afterwards
from cleaning toilets
but my soul rots
from smiling a chicken shit grin
knowing that my cousins
died on a poplar tree, nearby
blood riot on distant time
on nigga terms I wish to explain
my late night riding uzi's singing
my work songs now.
My field hollers.
Whispering in random gunfire
this is the wages of war.
Terror is in my bones
I am scared for myself
I fear me.

My sweat tastes like god's blood,
am I the communion wine of
this high mass?
Is this good friday gone bad
for me?
I weep for my father.
I weep for my childless brothers,
shot down.
What mistake did we make —
how am I to blame?
If I understand how I am guilty
then maybe
the cross' shadow wouldn't block
my children's ascension.
We split atoms in Egypt
ate pancakes first.
Now ain't yo momma
on the pancake box?
Shames me
on the proving ground
naked and branded
I enter into the labyrinth
to find me a lover.
Defined as the man
I dress me up
muscle hard
the scars make me complete
Remember how I got them
in Memphis
Soweto
Harlem
Paris . . .
Round midnight I'll be drinking
blood.
Wondering if I still got the shit
like a gunfighter
in a ghost town,
I come to be the missing light
in dead eyes.
I come to be the same faced

nigga boy
i will always be.

Prometheus

Wanting bus fare
waiting
in a Birmingham jail
praying in Mecca
crying
because somebody,
some fool,
mistook my pain for glory.

Rabia Rayford

Sisters

. . . and we are not one daughter of the same
mother's child breathing one breath
from a multitude of mouths?
— From the Sisterhood Songs of the Yenga Nation.

OK
So
She's on drugs.
And
I'm
not.

OK
So I say She
Sell it and
She
Say
I
give
it
away.

OK
So
She
Gang Bangs
And has been
Bang Ganged
And I
Run alone

Individual.
Virginal.
Madonnal.
OK.

OK
So she is
Homeless
And I
Paid
My rent
This Month.

OK
So she had a
Crack baby
And I
breast fed

OK

So she
wears colors
And I
Garb
Sometimes.
OK
So
She
Goes to the
Rock house
And I
Party
At the
Playhouse
Fast
We moving
Fast
Away
From
Each other.

Guess none of us
Feel any pain.

Guess none of us

Can
Help
Each
Other
Out . . .

OK
OK
OK

Name Change

She had an Afrikan name.

       Once.

But I guess it didn't jibe with huh new image

        Of

False eyelashes and red, rouged cheeks . . .

She was given an Afrikan name, once.

Her brother wrote her, long distance.
   It wuz beautiful
   — Soft, melodic,
       With meaning
          Even.

But

it didn't

          Jive

          With her new image
  of red/tight/red/hot
     Hot pants and
     Mask On!

     Painted faces . . .

She had an Afrikan name.

      Once

      But it didn't

Go go

With huh new

Yuppeh/Buppeh

Image . . .

Of Mer ke dees cars
And Soo She bars
            'n razor lines up
                    aquilines

She had an Afrikan name, once.

But she decided

It just didn't SUIT
            (As in three-piece)

Huh

kNew

I

                    mage

So she ain't gone

Use
It

            no 'mo.

Wouldn't it Be a Shame? (Where is Motown?)

Wouldn't it be a shame
    Black music died?
If all that survived was
    Rock?
Thousands of years
  And Tons of sand
the only jams left be
—the Average White Band?
(After years of excavations
    To discover our past
        They find no soul music
          —Only watered down jazz
        No rhythm and blues
          No reggae or soca
            Cause down Black musicians
            All had to crossover.)

Picture an archaeologist
    Not knowing what
      jazz or blues
        rhythm and blues
       reggae
       soca
         gospel
   or Calypso
  —was?
No congas, no steel drums,
    no shakers or cowbells
      Just wang wang wang
        And speaker feedback.
Wouldn't it be a shame?

      Wouldn't it be a shame
      if the only
        Dance

That survived was

Ballet?
No more funky chicken
No tapping, no
bebop, jazz, no jitterbug
no breaking and popping,
High Life,
Jump up,
skank, no

get on down, bump,
shake your booty
no dudumba
or funga
no get out on the floor

and sweat
no samba
rhumba
freak
watusi

just u
p?

on the toes?

on the tippy, tippy toes . . .

and leaping like a swan?
like a white, white
swan?

Wouldn't it really be a shame?

Wouldn't it be a shame
      if only
            Classical Music
            Survived?

Aaaaaa
   Aaaaaa
      Aaaaaarias and
      Italian lyrics
         Per la Gloria, but no
         R E S P E C T

What if wailin'
   And moaning
      Shouting
      and
            SCREEEEEEEAMIN'
               was forgotten
               as an ART FORM?
               No Pleeeeeeeeeaaaaase Babeh, Babeh
               No Ow! Wit You Bad Self
                  No Come on now HUH!

         No Woooooooooo!
No hmmmmmmmmmmmm yes mmmmm

         No BOOM laka laka laka
      BOOM laka laka Boom BOOM!

   No
puh a hu aha
   puhpuhpuhpuh
   puh a hu a hu

      puhpuhpuh

      No whee uh whee whee
No no'
Sockittomesockittomesockittome
   sockittomesockittomesockittome

sockittome
sockittomesockittomesockittome
sockittomesockittomesockittome
sockittomesockittomesockittome
sockittome
sockittome
sockittome oh yeah!

no runs

— Starting at Bass
And eruptin' in soprano . . .
— pumpin' up at a hum
and ending in a
Shout . . .

. . . Any y'all know what I'm talking about?

Wouldn't them archeologists
Really miss out?
If all that was left
was Lalala

and yeah, yeah, yeah?

Wouldn't that be

A REAL

shame?

Old Black Women

**(for my Mother, Caroline Joumiette Rayford & all
elder sisters)**

Old black women are special
  hey tell you about yourself in a minute/just by a glance . . .
    they smile at you
      and a warmth starts up in your chest
    i never see 'em cry
tho i know they got pains . . .
—and doo de wop
  be bop is not

        too distant a thunder
        'cause lots of 'em can still
        hear the A train
          . . . and feel it
          . . . and want it
          . . . and neeeeeeed it more than slumber

    in a
     single
     old
      ladies
      bed . . .

grandkids fill up lots of gaps
  but itching never cease, tho
  bleedings do.
    A hand held in old age
          is rare
          rare
          rare

    rare as a thousand-year-old wine
    'cause old black ladies are scarce
    tho not as scarce as old black men

they sigh
ride the bus
wish
—gray haired and giddy—
for saviours

they smile
and their lives open up for a moment
"Yes ma'am. You are Queen of the world. Your face
is the face
of your
God
Can
You
Stand it?"

Old ladies, old black women are special, don't you know.
they look at me
and frown questions
—ain't you a old lady yet?
No ma'am, but I'm on my way . . .

Nobody but us
Can frown that old black woman frown

or smile
that Holy mama smile.

Nobody can sing
That black woman scat

Who can dance that
Dahomy dance but she?

— and me?

our hair/lines
grey and silver/oak bark, like
      etched above an earth face, not sky . . .
    black and someday wiry/wigs
        dread/short
         long/pressed
           for centuries
              natty fo days
                we look and see,
                  'cause

        Nobody cries
        like an old black woman

      — 'cept me.

. . . Tell you 'bout yourself in a minute
        say
    "Honey, ain't you a old lady YET?"

No ma'am
Soul/goddess of the sphere
    No ma'am
        Mother/Mama/Nana Supreme
        No ma'am
            Sister/Auntie/Star
            No ma'am,
            but I AM
            on my
            way

      . . . No ma'am
    but I am on my way.

Apartheid Blackout

They close the country like a window closing on a dirty deed,
But we see. Botha behind the curtain
defiling the whole Black world.
Smiling for the cameras,
Copping a feel on the ig
No Rant
Be
Hinds
Of Certain
LeAduhs
Apartness
is a real
BLACKOUT
in South Afrika . . .

. . . They close the country
So we cannot see
But we seeeeeeeeeeeeee . . .

Decision to Have an Abortion

i'd love
to father this child with you
raise him on carrot juice
and watermelon
and grow her
into
a
revolutionary.

then i sweat
night
dreams
remembrances
of romance
broken.

and living through
the brokeness
of my previous fatherhoods
. . . it is too much grief.

so i will go with you to the clinic
and hope no one holds a sign
of a dead fetus
in
my
face.

i go with you to the clinic

release the dream of a sweet, dreadlocked child with you.

i release the dreams, all of them
and nightmare
about the suction tubes
snaking
inside
your
womb . . . .

Decision to Have an Abortion. Too. Two

i wish
that you would
scrub yourself with salt
        place a pot of herbs beneath my belly
and breathe me and our child straight into you . . .
            but I see the deadline
                and friends
                and me
                    str
                        ugg
                            ling
                                with children
                                    alone.
                                        i
                                    fear.
        this baby loves her father, though
        my nausea disappears
                    when you approach me.

            yet we are not the revolutionaries
            we thought we
                were

                and so i am sure
                my nightmares
                will continue
                    for a
                        thousand
                            years.

Wings

(for my children Saahir and Naeem Brewington)

(Written on the occasion of a sister saying to me, "Just wait'll
your wings get clipped, and you get put back in your place.")

my wings *have* been clipped.
they have been slit, sliced and severed
thrown back at me
as a souvenir of my own destruction . . .

but with the hands of my children

i replaced them, with blood,
bugars and spit

haaaaaaaaaaaamered them to my back,
and now I fly,
creaking
dripping
and proud

anyways,

oh, yes, honeh

don't you know somebody *stole* my wings?

and left two helpless infants
on my cloud
as anchors

but the male child became Shango
and lifted me with his fires

the earth daughter became
Oya
and her breath
is a mooooooooooooving breeze . . .

oh yes, my wings have been clipped/cripped

mistaken for lost,
hell, i gave 'em away once
to a dog who did a very good impression of a lion

but i got 'em back

by sitting, still as obsidian
in a cracked house

when i pounced
he thought it was a nightmare
my wings beating across his face . . .

    nah see sistuh
i ain't very attached to my wings
    too fragile.
  toooo delicate

my allegiance goes to these back muscles
        that pull and do and strain
with or without
        wings . . .

to these legs that walked us outta death
and kick a path for my
righteousway when i need it

to this mouth o' mine
that whispers the words of Jah
O Allah Oludumare and oh yes
screams these thoughts outta my head . . .

Wings?

Wings?

why, they are such angelic things
    and even with wings,   you need your arms
    to hold a child   like i have done.

wings ain't nuthin'

but my dreadlocked daughter
and my clear-eyed son.

Wings.

Christopher Nickelson

Untitled

i don't get
the hidden meaning,
the allegory or the
symbolic gestures
or the references to
the part to the whole
or the whole to the part
but it
sounds real pretty, it
sounds real nice

so
gimme your hand
i mean gimme
the part to
the whole

Toni D. Blackman

For My Brothers Who Chant the Pussy Song

obsessed with
vaginal chants of
regions of
acts of nonsense

not moving us forward
stagnant we remain
clutching
to those concepts
with which they have
brainwashed us
with which they have
controlled us

sex
can be/hypnotic if
u allow it to be

sex
can be/an escape if
u allow it to be

the only true
escape from reality is
death

and
we are allowing
it
to happen
one by one by one

u
are endangered
species

sex
is not for
our people
we cannot allow
it
to happen

we
must
make love!

No Sell-Outs!

Unity!

    Chants in unison

Echoing across
    a campus full of empty students
    with empty minds and empty ideas

No justice
No peace!

    Chants in unison

that echo across
    a city under siege
    leading scorer/average/a death a day

It's not the Man
It's not the issues!

    Chants in unison

that echo across
    a nation asleep and
    ignorant of reality.

Philip Henderson

A Reflection On My Youthful Vagabondage

I look over this trunk of experiences
that is me, and open myself up
and touch what is inside, and
whatever is there
from many years past
spent roaming the cities
and jungles and deserts of the world
is still raw and vivid.
A train ticket may hurt me,
or a restaurant bill fills me with happiness.
Still more some old Tunisian stamp
fills me with excitement —
but a Greek stamp angers me.

I have done much but I feel it is time to move on.

My youthful years have ended.

It is time to throw off the excess baggage.

Natasha Tarpley

North
To Ophelia

Just a note to say that I have found myself well in Chicago
and have secured an apartment with a man called Fred
who is also from the South, Arkansas
We have two rooms and a window
in a building with thirty floors
I have never been up so high
Even Papa's hayloft don't compare
Sometimes I feel like I'm looking down on the sky
But I still can't see the stars at night
I go to that window and it's like there ain't nothing out
there, nothing to let your eyes rest on or look towards
I miss Memphis, Ophelia the air there is so thick
My lungs must be covered
in the black of all these cars and factories I wish to God
I could say soon I'd be back for you and the baby,
but I have not found a place to work
Each morning Fred and me and the other men ride
the bus out to Gary where there's a big steel mill
We ask if they're hiring coloreds and every time
they say tomorrow
We hear that there may be work on the pier, but it's not for
certain
I must be going I hope you are well
It pains me that I won't be there when the baby comes
Please tell him about me I am

yours always
Albert

Pregnancy

In my dreams I am straight
and smooth, flat as a drum
But beneath my corset
I am spreading out from all places
I am fat with pickles and grits and Albert,
has gone to the factories, to the North
where the night swallows him like dust,
where he cannot find
the stars beneath his windowsill
Each day it's harder
to fasten the clasps on my dress,
I have already lost the rhythm
that kept me tight and regular
Soon I will lose my toes to this swelling,
to this devil, who eats me from the inside out
But I am trying Albert, to save all of this,
to hold myself in until your hands
let loose the roundness of my belly

Sometimes

(For Rosalyn)

Mornings are hard on brown girls
in the wake of sleep's yellow-skinned
yearnings, the awful trick of dreams,
she rises from blue-eyed wonders,
to ash collecting at her knees

Under this uncompromising sun
was not the blond caress
of thin-lipped lovers,
but the wide-legged glances
of crooked black men;

was dead ends and heated irons,
was rain scarves and greasy scalps,
was morning breaking on
sameoldplainfacedblackgirl
grown

Girl ashamed of your lips
(under what crown would you)
lay your cotton down

and raise your whole head

Keeper

For you
loudman daddyman thief
lover of bottles like wives

I swallow nights
of your alcoholic breath
dislodging me from sleep,
of mama's hip,
bruised when the cigarettes
were all gone

We forgave
those nights like scars
against our tongues

We forgave
broken kitchen glass,
the wet spot in your pants
as if age had lost you,
had sent you back
to where you couldn't quite remember
how letters came together,
and numbers were only fingers

We forgave
until forgiving was just wanting
and wanting was only waiting
for morning to come
like a cool breeze

To you
loser of houses,
of babies misborn

This is just to say
we are alive
daddy

we are alive
and the days keep coming
in the space where you took to the earth
your bloated heart,
where you left me
in the midst of twelve years

To you
lifegiver
I loved you like fire

But I like you best
when you are sleeping

To Aunt Jemima's Children
(For Marlene)

And it shall come to pass
and these two planets,
the one of darkness,
the other of supreme light and benevolence,
will converge to a greater entity
where goodness prevails all ways
and darkness will be a period of rest
commemorating those times when god put down
his hands

I must tell my children
that it was not as simple as bodies
or planets
or bibles

I kept my hair tied
because missus wanted
a new wig

I must tell you children
that it was not as simple
as the capturing of the stars

Twenty long-eyed Galileos
examined my firmaments
on the Carolina block.

I must tell you children
that they emptied heaven's secrets
like coins into their pocketbooks,
and made up the papers
for those who would pay
to put their name to a star

They say my name
comes from the stars of Gemini
Gemini
Jemima

I must tell you children
that no man can own a star
but the law is in the papers

and I been saving years
of hot greased nickels
because you belong to heaven
and I aim to give you back.

Feel Free

The year the white women came like the plague
was when me and my girls took to backwater
cornfields and the shimmy
"girl I love the way you shake"
Time lunch bell rang, we was out at Roderick's field
barefoot and loose headed
Marva pounded a beat on her thigh and Frieda
stepped
      stepped
like walking to Jesus
"do the snake girl"
and wound herself up to trembling
We would come in then, hard and fast,
shaking till sweat dripped from our fingers
Marva stopped her beat, but we would still be going on
the sound of our own feet, the screaming of crows and wind
slapping
cornstalks, even a heartbeat
Some say we was begging for the devil
But we was just dancing
And when we got through, that field vibrated,
like all of Memphis rolling beneath us
in the place where Frieda stood,
the ground was worn to the roots
Even the earth could not resist the power of that
step

We was bad bad girls

To Alabama
(For My Granddaddy And My Daddy)

i-95 is quicker,
but 50 is better for colored folks
Halfway between Chicago and Alabama
they stretch their bones and open their baskets
to fried chicken wings and strawberry pop;
where a man named Slim sits by
the only colored indoor toilet 'til Alabama,
counting out sheets of toilet paper
(a nickel for ten)
This was the stop where we didn't worry;
where daddy stretched along the front seat
and me and my brother ran until our legs burned,
until we couldn't do nothing but lie on the hood and wait
for the stars to come
When it got dark, Slim would get a fire going
and all of the families gathered around,
most of us from the North headed back South
to visit our people
The adults would talk about the problems
of the Black man, and how to spot the klan at night
while Slim gave all the kids peppermints
Me and my brother sucked ours real slow
and didn't even bite once
On the way out in the morning,
my daddy always gave Slim a dime and asked
"How far to Alabama?"
Slim would put his hand up to his eye
as he looked out toward the road and answered

"Still got a long way to go"

Yearning

(For Shawn)

When will I
hold music
in my hands;
greet the gospel
open mouthed;
learn to tremble
like she trembles
under the long notes
with arms raised,
making voices out of bodies,
movement into salvation
She pulls me back to the hot pews
of Arkansas, of Chicago
raises to my tongue the desire
to say "Yes Lord, yes"
I am yearning for that frenzy,
for gospel,
for Aretha and Mahalia,
for Chicago and Arkansas,
"Yes Lord, yes"
Give me the tambourine
and I will play
play
play

Tanya Seale

Embarrassing

I saw him again
followed him with my eyes
my stomach registered no twinge
I must remember that
though I did look
Now the warmth of sexuality returns
should I enjoy the pleasure
(simply)
or challenge myself to discover
where these feelings are coming from?

Melvin E. Lewis

Doors #4

I get excited
when your flowers open
and I feel your
nectar flowing

Doors #5

When I see you
I become a roll of wheat
reaching for the sun

When you move a little
I bend to get closer,
to sing to you and draw you back

I expand my kernels to catch your eye,
I fluff them up when you look
and make them blow in the
slow summer wind

Doors #6

I feel safe
when I hold you

It's one of the few
times the clouds open
and I see the sun

Doors #16

Your hands are my ink
you nod up and down
the sun moved west while I slept

Doors #17

The dark humus meets the orange waters near Manaus [*]
Orange waters of the Amazon River kiss
the decomposing soil del Rio Negro
we are somewhere floating in the black waters

[*] Manaus is a river, region in Brazil.

Doors #18

(For Ronald)

Sometimes things fall off the wall
fall out of our life

We wish them come down
not able to move
to hold them up,
catch life before it falls apart

Doors #19

When you opened your dreams
the path you spread was lined with
mountain tops, moist persimmons,
cherry blossom air from an April, Potomac breeze

I tried to put my dreams in yours

Our dreams are crystals we make in the
cup of our hands,
the space water can stand in the lines,
ridges of a closed palm.

Doors #20

The sandy, arid roads of Havana province,
half-open windows on school buses
with long hard choir seats
banners blowing from the walls of Jose Marti Airport:
Bienvenido a La Brigada Venceremos,
Amistad y Paz con los Pueblos del Mundo
Welcoming us to a little bit of the new world.

On the beach you can point your antenna north or west
hear Ray Charles, Cuban teenagers singing,
"Lonely Night In Georgia,"
we are asked to do the "Bump" in *las plazas*
we hear the stark actions in Alabama, D.C.
of Tricky Dick or George "stand in the doorway" Wallace,
we're close enough to smell the rotting of 20 Emmett Tills
in the slow waters of the Florida Everglades
the ripe fields, orchards of California, Michigan,
some of our fathers are lynchers,
some of our fathers are the lynched.

We pass open pastel doorways in the evenings on our way
a la casa de Julio Antonio Mella
in April evenings the road to, from this place
from this day are dry, flat.

We go around *el bloque*, the blockade
in disguises, sunglasses, beards, frog hats
we sat in the corners of Montreal, Mexico City
hiding behind novels,
wearing tourist clothes over blue hammer and sickle tee shirts
carrying poems on our chest with two wings of the same bird,
one free, one hostage, one that sings, one that is silent,
waiting all night in bunches
anywhere that will allow us to run the blockade

The nights are smoother, quieter in Havana and Oklahoma
both are open places where we can breathe
the hills are outlined by slow, easy stairs,
wooden bridges where we escape,
shed cold northern thoughts,
conga circles invite us in.

We shared the small brown ports,
piers where thin boats smuggled ideas
into the high roads, teeth of the Sierra Maestra
I saw you walking alone, in the fragments of Che's base camp.
We walked along the hand cut, machete trails of the second
        column.
The bullet holes in the weathered walls of *el Moncado*
stilled our accents.
Where are screams, thirty-year-old shouts,
blood in each street in central *Santiago de Cuba*

At night there is lemon, salt in the air
salt with rice in the shaker
pan fried *pescado, frijoles negroes con arroz, y cerveza fria.*
At dinner you invite us in,
your mother listens as we struggle for social words
for ways to describe our family, house
the sound of our mothers at Sunday dinner.

Your mother writes our mothers on a brown-flowered note card
wishing them a happy Mother's Day.
Telling them, that she is looking out for,
feeding their wandering children
who want to hold the wind
blow new seeds, seasons to southern, western sounds, souls

At the entrance of the gateless, free baseball stadium
where Cuban men with long lines,

edges etched in their faces and hands
chew cigars while watching their favorite teams
we sat free, watching the game

People walk the streets at night
stand outside popular restaurants, nightclubs
beneath blinking neon signs
praising the worker
It's short sleeves April warmth
the women have removed their pattern work, sun scarves
they move in cotton dresses, arched eyebrows
the wind holds you from walking fast
it's the first drag of a cool drank,
KOOL, strong cigarette,
the first pull on POPULARS, white and blue, white & red
when you haven't smoked in a long time,
the note in a song where you start tapping your feet

Where you want to sit on the edge of the wall
that holds *el Mar Caribe*
from slashing into Havana

Sit, watch white, gray seagulls dive into the bay
to capture drops of water on their long thin beaks
Watch skinny brown, black children in short pants,
bare chests play on rocks, boulders.
Water shines in their wet, curly hair
the sun glows on the laughter, shouts of their jumps,
hops from stone to stone, stone to sea
they rest wet, smiling
we rest standing on the edge of the wall
that holds the edge of the sea

The lights from the harbor
clear May stars, full Caribbean moon embrace over Santiago
they merge at
el Monumento de Hèroes.

You lower your eyes
soften your voice when you walk around
the marble figures of armed people in motion
of people holding light,
fighting for a new season, in a new world, wind
creating, connecting a new whirlwind

The low monument raises the sky
the stone out, cried over,
stands, talks to *los niños del Che*.
we read the placards, lower our heads,
become a little closer to the children of Che,
to the children of the whirlwind.

Fancy Dancer

Standing on the edge of time
eyes momentarily closed
gates of the next opened wide
wrapped in the protection
of dream designs
it begins
Chant swelling drumbeats
carry shawled wings
and cut glass beaded feet
spinning radiant light
into the heading warrior state
beyond illusionary gravity
traveling to the spirit world
out among the stars
gathering up peacemaker medicine
to share upon
last honor beat return

Sometimes it gets this strong

Shit Talk on the Venice Boulevard Bus Heading East One Summer's Night

Bus Stop I

i am on the bus
& the people around me
they talk crazy
some lady in a bruised eye
dribbles shit
ending every insult with
yo momma
the young brother
across the aisle from her
trades euphemisms
they weave an instant
friendship bonded by blood
they talking so scandalous
about this & that
nothing & oh yeah
fuck you too you
long-legged watutsi bitch
i'm from chicago
she spews at a tall slip
afroed woman passenger
who's clutching an overhead
bar for support
cause the bus operator
driving like a fool
lurching here & there
mad cause won't nobody lissen
when he tell them
to shut up

Bus Stop II

smelling of the little
half pint of gin
she carried on board
bruised eye gin she
kept ranting along
so loud & long
until some smart-assed
young T-shirted muscles
laughingly tell her
that all the cheap gin
she done drank
must be kicking off
& young muscles continues
to tell moms
to cool out
& bruised eye gin
had to ask him
is he missing
a motha' fucking mama
cause if he is
she ain't it
& don't be calling
her moms
wit' his narrow ass

Bus Stop III

sitting behind white
T-shirted muscles
this other brother
with a serape crisscrossed
his shoulders keeps
talking about he just
come back from
the beach & baby
what's your name
she got on at
hauser & venice

he said he'd always
remember this corner
as he bent over
to tear off a strip
of paper from a smudgy
newspaper trampled
in the aisle
so she could
write it down
her phone number
so she did

Bus Stop IV

ain't no radio playing
the bus driver reminds everyone
so a small dude with a tail
hanging down his neck
took a bite out of his
hamburger before he hollered back
ain't no eating either man
the chorus of passengers
cracks up laughter spilling
from reluctant lips
causing one woman
of shopping bags & a
bulge-eyed little girl
to shake her head
chuckle & ask why
niggas got to act
so ignorant
so the little girl admits
i don't know
then she hid a laugh
behind her hand
meanwhile this other brother
gets fed up with all the bull
he starts talking about
he wants to reach

his destination & this
is why niggas don't own shit
after saying this
he turned his head
to the future
out the window
& tapped the briefcase
he did own

Bus Stop V

by now bruised eye gin
who ain't nobody's mama
is shaking hands with folks
talking about
its been fun
white T-shirted muscles
cuts the crap for a minute
sincerely warns her
to be careful
them streets is dangerous
she weaves her way
up to the front
of the bus
but instead of getting off
she starts messing with
watutsi calling her
watutsi bitch
& she gets some laughs
from that
but watutsi laughing too
steadily telling bruised eye gin
we all africans
but gin
who ain't nobody's mama
just keeps laughing
saying all loud
fuck you
i'm from chicago

Encounter With a Young Brother

do you want me to slap you
preadolescent voice cracking
school hallways marked up
ghetto style calligraphy
do you want me to slap you
he asked again
angled with buoyant confidence
how he imagined his daddy
might ask his momma
mannish and unafraid of anger
and sad death rank in his
g.i. joe idea of love

The Fairytale Version:
Poem for Donald

it's the closest thing st louis had
to hip
so we went there
to eat brown rice & tofu
to make the day normal somehow
to leave the morphine aroma
& rotting flesh behind.
it was july
sweat dripped from the bricks
& squeezed streets going only one way
but in my memory it was cold
like the breath of god
sighing.
you wore a leather coat into the heat
moving in a slow deliberateness to the car
cousin steve drove thru streets that demanded
you talk about riding an old bicycle
right over there or walking in
dusky shadows playing miles & parker
thru your head
your mother alive then
& brew & kools cigarettes & canned vegetables
as a middle class symbol
& stereophonic component sets
& it was you then
clean shaven & childless
on the mantle
the photo of the boy really
old enough to call himself a man
in the sailor suit bought for his first trip
to the navy.
then in another twenty years
it was you again
in a motorhome heading east,
spread on my cut-off jeans

a man of forever shaped like the u.s.
to wake up each morning [in] a different place
to remember myself fourteen
to remember henry miller
tropic of cancer read by a river
in mexico near acapulco
to be able to hang out & feel myself
a child of the word & earth
when you were still daddy.
& you were pa that night
you stopped the motorhome
the only name we'd ever called
the elephant vehicle you'd park
on a south central l.a. street one day
& call your home
you were pa that night on the shoulder
of the road in the colorado mountains
the radio was static
we heard hillbilly song
a starved voice sang 'bout
some gal named kimi-sue
the name of my baby sister
lit the blank stars & caressed
the blackness around us
& you were father in arizona
cutting a watermelon for snack
in the crest of some rock statues
that grew from the mute earth
apparitions of resistance
where we carved our names
so we could always be there.
you were not daddy pa or father
that dying day we stood outside
the only macrobiotic restaurant we could find
on a street really nothing like haight st.

but reminded me of it anyway
you never knew we stole some of your pot
candi started calling it pot time we drove
over the golden gate bridge pulling out of
her sixties index retrophrases like
meeting a connection & bread
all codes from some other life
so we stole some of your weed & called
it pot in golden gate park
the breeze sang janis joplin
when we were quickly high for
it didn't take long then
we giggled & decided to say
we were stoned
man
we were kids wanting another generation's
neurosis
to not have to atone for disco & blackula
flicks played with two others
in grand old derelict movie palaces
on broadway in downtown l.a.
you were no daddy on the street
in st. louis in july not quite
twenty years later
but you were donald
asking me to help you
out of that suffocating coat.
you'd hardly finished your food.
we stood waiting for stevie
to bring the car around
the two block walk to it
was too tiring for you
& we looked at some kids in punk hairdos
you laughing that we'd finally found the hippies.
refusing to sit down
donald said
leaning on my shoulders
& the weight of him was like the feel
of pictures of me & my sisters
at four, five, or six in those old photos

hair in plaits
white T-shirts on if saturdays
or itchy dresses hair in bows if sundays
all leaning on each other's shoulders
perfectly balanced
it was like that
donald was leaning on my shoulder
i heard him say
let's stay like this
a little while
hanging out in the sunshine
just being cool
& it was a plea & a wish & a pleasure
to stand there with you
& live a wish come true
& maybe that's the key to having
your wishes granted immediately
you've got to keep them simple
& intangible.

Desire: Waiting for Rain

when your hand kneads my flesh again
all i forget to feel will rush tears
across this droughted mountain that is
my face/
the taste of you may choke me
i've eaten day barren sailed concrete licked shut
ruptured skin danced in monthly blood & winced
as well-intentioned brothers called me
black queen
queen to match a king — oh come now
dethrone that delusion
i would rather be held than adored
oh find me a nontoxic grape
roll it over my nipples
look at them
such hussies standing up straight
commandeering a kiss — i can't stand this
the bed is unbalanced
& love strings you will hear
they are exiled angels
crying in my vagina
wanting to be human again

All the Work is Not Undone

women i've known
so many kitchens
front room spaces
babies and lit ranges
singing along 'bout some man
as aretha do wail
in a time there was
a music called soul
a woman called queen
folks talked about her
like she was they cousin
or somebody
assigning to her
nicknames like retha & re-re
all of us attuned
to the statistical pain
locked up in soledad prisons
overcrowded with arsenio hall's brothers

First Take Before Sunrise

sweet tongue sifting stained glass over
dust tracks down a road
that ain't georgia
this time of dark morning
this is the face i give for scarification/unbathed
this is the teeth i use in plural disagreement
of a people long ways from shore
this is the ear/no
these is the ear i want to hear sound slight as gesture
bellowing way down in my belly baby
          way down in my belly
bellowing way down
in this disquieting morning i breathe
an act outside my will
strangely lifelike

Another Morning

a red sea of ambrosia is my god's nectar
& my god's anonymity wails in tongues
pawned in a dawn of promises & trains
shanking underground & desire & need
sweat under armpits & i smell streets
& sad morning rises like baptismal mist
from the steamy holy water in which
we try not to drown & close
to floating is the saddest kind of survival

On Self-Healing

1.

without regret walk onto the islands of your many fears
relax there in a mud bath of absolute fertility
don't think of lovers of his voice of phone calls unreturned
of the end of the world as you imagine it would come
in tentative sunshine wilting the edges of a brave spider plant

think instead of water of the middle passage of yourself
chained below a slave ship's deck
think instead of a grief far greater than your own
of a yogic posture you have yet to achieve
of war. any war. then breathe deep. then deeper still.

2.

be dance/
naked/
satin rooms/
mirrors/
be dancer in a satin room
dance naked in front of mirrors

loving and healing is the same act of devotion
loving and healing is the same act of devotion
list all the things that hold you to this earth
picture the emotion
now go back
retrace your steps cross everything off the list and as
you do recite a prayer you learned from childhood that has long
since lost meaning

3.

now pretend you are dead.
think now of someone who should have loved you & didn't
now that you're dead

and it doesn't matter
forgive them.
think now of your most severe self-betrayal
now that you are dead
and it doesn't matter
forgive yourself.

living and dying is the same act of devotion
living and dying is the same act of devotion

as is being healed.   as is healing.
as is being loved.   as is loving.
breathe deep.   then deeper still.

4.
we forgive ourselves our godlessness
we forgive ourselves our angers
each on our own terms
each in our own turn

Tangled History

I am not a river flowing red thru ancestral homelands
this tinselless metropolis got hollywood hung from polluted
hillsides imitating mountains not holy or magic but
corporate hustles stagnant in white boy dollars
prancing in tight jeans singing i heard it thru
the grapevine in commercial animations/

            remember sundance rings
            on a moon sent
            night all
            the people
            dance naked
            in a catfish fry
            house party
            & we still
            claim ourselves
            to be the
            only real thing
            & the only
            real thing
            claims itself in us
            applaud
            the mythic
            people who
            will fly again
            like legend holds
            from new age
            cotton fields

vo doo ain't no new st. laurent scent
thirty second spot breathing foul air in our faces
plastered in blood-red lipstick
leering a white girl come
on the premise envy creates desire
& desire sales/no voo doo ain't been bottled & sold
its the shit we live from bill to pill
the hustle we go thru to make ourselves real

is how we maintain equilibrium in a place
castrated black bodies seek revenge & ghosts
of antebellum white houses dressed in whips
spikes & george washington wigs run
in fear from burning plantations
i say voo doo and black magic spirit hustles
is ancient arts i learned while slow grinding rubs
wooed me from snake pit brinks back to the center
of a music we learned once culture was not
bought   repackaged   &   sold back to us/

                    mountain me
                    in bamboo tongues
                    i want
                    to sing orgasms
                    to listening
                    winds
                    to everyone
                    who ever felt
                    the drums
                    timekeeping
                    in they toes
                    who know
                    the generic
                    prayer
                    know the curses
                    & praise poems
                    & saints
                    & words
                    that record
                    what we will
                    not allow
                    ourselves
                    to lose
                    memory
                    of

Darrell Stover

Dash

We are that dash in African-American
There are those of us pulled to the right to dwell as Americans
and those of us pulled to the left to dwell as Africans
The choice is conscious
But as that dash we are challenged
Our allegiances in daily dalliances called to question constantly
as we face each other in the mirror of the past, present
        and future
What we were, are and will be on the world's stage
Acting the role of the upper right key on the typewriter of life
Playwrights all as we create the play that portrays conditions
and resolutions climaxing in our own versions of what us is
        and ain't
The plot twist is to become double-agents
Master spies of Dubois' double-consciousness
Interchange freely on both sides of the dash between African
        and American
I see you voting in numbers unimaginable
Electing officials you see are your saviors
I see you standing on the bridge of history very wary of a people
whose intentions have always been suspect
I see you uniting with other people of color globally
in a struggle for retribution
I see you as specialists of the back and forth motion of give-
and-take dialogue so essential to future parity
I see you listening, hand on chin, eyes squinched in deep
        thought
Putting aside the art of put-down to stop together into a picture
framed as masterpiece
The masterstroke on a canvas that reflects contrast but
        completeness

Weaving, working inside and outside of the system
Not and of
Amazed at the successes that come not with being on either side
But by being the dash itself
A dash of this
A dash of that
And finding that you are more than some single demarcation
Doubly destined to be the differences on the world's stage
Take on both roles and play them to their fullest
There is no conflict between you and you
You are us
We are you
Don't dash our hopes and dreams
Dash our differences
Dashing to the finish line
The trophy
Us all attaining the highest level of existence
Now dash
Dash
Dash on!

Never Die in Bahia

(for Patricia)

Eshu laughs at the raven on your chest
You probably thought you've danced your last Carnival
Bright REDS and YELLOWS jiggle/walk the boulevards
Drums bang BLUE splashes to settle in your hips
But Yemenja's sea breeze you are to breathe no more
Unless
Unless of course
You wish to trade lies with the orishas
And see who makes who chuckle
Tell you what
When you last left Rio
There were no people on the beach
Where were they that morning, afternoon and soft, YELLOW
    evening?
Had they all arrived at your funeral too soon?
A GREEN and ORANGE frog you never ate awaits an answer
Sleep will never greet your eyes in death
Not here
Not when nightlife screams BLACK
And you've seen stranger things here than in your dreams
Who wants to see an endless dream
When they can see this
An old, legless man dances the steps of a
younger man with a woman whose beauty has
never appeared on this sphere before
Her beauty was not only in her smile
But in the way she wore a multi-hued skirt
Draping a figure godly in its aura
Sinful in its sensuality
A flash
A man
Athletic fine
Romantic intellect leaves you crying
Has now taken her place

The old man is now an older woman
Strobing life light to you as your
eyes open on an empty beach
Waves wash up the smells and colors of the freshest bouquets
Contemplate death and you die
The Tropic of Celebration is where that frog lives
And it knows life is a Carnival!
She wants to know do you.

Metro Lover

10:14 PM at Metro Center she
departs leaving Metro Lover
for his Orange Line adventure.
They had just met sharing
poetry for a cause — the cause
to give shelter and sustenance
to homeless women. They had
watched the passage of people
as they entered and exited
the subway system. Drawn to
one another by creative de-
sires, hearts, smiles, and
tale-swapping, passion's doors
were opened. They had watched,
she especially, as a family
unit consisting of two young
sons, a mother and a father
entered the system. The boys
gave the only transfer ma-
chine a workout driven by
child energy and inquisitive-
ness. Metro Lover watched
these two young powerhouses
as they used the Metro's hand-
rails for Monkey bars and ar-
gued whether the subway doors
went do-do or pin-ping be-
fore they closed. The young-
est eventually agreeing with
the oldest — do-do it was.
Their actions reminded Metro
Lover of a poem shared earlier
in the evening in which a
poetess praised her young
nephews as heroes with their
own adventures to write
and likened their approach to

tornados and thunderstorms.
As the Metro dooew-dooewed
out of Landover, Metro Lover
walked looking forward to
being on the other end of
the phone of feel with she
of beautiful spirit, mind
and bod.

Poem for Jay Bias

Large hearts dribble from our eyes pumping a solemn refrain
We have shed our last tears in last week's headlines
The news is no different with the TV off or on
Another soul has been sent on its way
Why remains an unanswered question for families, friends
    and children
No longer petrified by death yet cradled, heaving in the arms of
    one another

Basketball trophies replenish memories
Unworn athletic shoes and still pressed suits
Wear miraged images that touch a deeper core
The door knocked twice by a collector of souls has a grim polish
Cold howls fill the night to frame the silence of a family
    in mourning

Maybe the first time was a fluke
But the second does not allow for easy dismissal
Put the two together and you get pain
You also get real worried
The statistics
          Damn the statistics

            OUR BOYS

            OUR MEN

            OUR SEED

Are spilling their lives in a cryptic message we can
no longer leave undeciphered

         No Longer Leave

         Unchallenged

         Unchecked

         Unchanged.

Divine — at the Go-Go

One dark hole attached to a
　she-stallion that upon entry
　　rides like a rhinocerous

Brasilia beats rapidly
　roaring through to the
　　inner core of my mind

I soar with the eagle
　glide with the vulture
　　and flutter at peace with
　　　the dove

Love loses once it tastes the
　smile your libido wears; there
　　can be no greater lust. There
　　can only be the raw sting on the
　　　centers of pleasure

Measured doses of exposure are
　suggested like too much peyote
　　you enjoy only once then forget
　　　you exist, hanging onto nothing
　　　　except the last pleasure which will
　　　　　be your constant companion in bliss

Strange, how you never come
　How you never knock at Legba's door
　　Is he not there for all men who have
　　　looked upon you? Why then is he not there
　　　　for you? Maybe he knows that your soul is not
　　　　　for sale and in your presence his would indeed
　　　　　be forfeit

No, you do not dance
　You ritualize some ancient
　　homage to other worldly spirits

No, you follow some lullaby all
  your own which casts a webbed spell
    over male widows of the night whose
      dark journeys are rewarded at the spread
        of you.

Coltrane Poem

Want to write me a Coltrane poem
A poem that hits stars
Shattering into rains
Of sound coming
Down all around
Shouts, screams
Bebop yells
Bohemian
Black
Blows

BEYOND

Want to write us a Coltrane poem
A poem snatching hearts
Into a Love Supreme
Cooperative
Collective of
Our favorite things
Chillin'
Absolute Cool
Profound Cool
Out

THERE

Want to write a Coltrane poem
A poem sending "thank you's"
To you whenever wherever
You are played in brain
In the great on and   on

Take us

Undefined

The long shadow of winter
  Portrayed Funk to be the sun
    High in the sky, an arrival of
      Metro at Takoma Park, two hawks
        Flying over Landover — one smallish
          Sparrow hawk pestering a larger, immature
          Red shouldered hawk, and a quarter of a century
          Old Black man reminiscing on herb.

Oh! And All This — For Gwendolyn Brooks who has been like a burst of spring on the Washington Metropolitan poetry scene

Brown-oranges
    Red
        Yellow-greens
            Laying lightly
                in view

Pulled by rays' warmth
    Time has come
    On twigs brightly
            in view

Wind swayed youth
    Bud again
        Pasteled peeps of spring
            in view

Bare bark
  Given to
    Greening layers
        Placed plant life airish
            in view

Feel anew
        These colors slightly
        Burst
          All over again
            in view

Bonesongs

Who stole my voodoo?
                By the time the comet came back again
Who stole my voodoo?
                When we were visited by AIDS my friend
Who stole my voodoo?
                Africa's children do know
Who stole my voodoo?
                The beat of our bonesongs grows
Who stole my voodoo?
                Middle Passage hear my cries!
Who stole my voodoo?
                Bones beat blues gods arise
                Bones Beat Blues Gods Arise

BONES
     BEAT
          BLUES GODS
            ARISE!

Genesis

Men don't belong here
Why do you think they
Call it Mother Earth?
And who is Adam?
Sometimes the feeling
I don't belong rings
From someplace else
What if I told you
Women were here first?

And Whales Way Off Track

(for Greenpeace)

So many say nothing about the atrocities
I see nothing but blood on my hands shining
For I do not die aboard ships going down
Animals know nothing of nuclear Armageddon

   Just clubs and harpoons and Nature telling us something

I DIED–Lament on Leaving Takoma

Metro Lover for us all
Touched the third rail
                    Not METAL TINGLIN' the gone
     Singeing the system of five senses
     A loneliness lingers when a lover leaves
      Electrocution proceeds
       Hear my brain boilin'
        Taste my melted eyes on my cheeks
        Slurped down past a nose
          Now numb to BBQ's, bakeries and
          Death row executions
            Only exile will tell the tale of
             The title's five green letters on a white page
            No more mimed mockingbirds spelled at
             Midnight in Azalea City Historic District
             When lightnin' bugs flash stops
               A female leaves eating the heart of another lover

Party Over Here and There, Y'all

From the Party Over Here in the Sewer It Came
Cops in Search of it
Disappearing Into the Metro Dooew-Dooew

Whereupon Funk Was Heard Within the Go-Go
  Brother Blues Returned Cuttin' the Rug
    With Metro Lover in Green
    Listenin' to Black Classical Music
        Chantin'
    Don't Forget that Gospel, Y'all

    High Unto Our Ancestors Who
    Smile/Cry
  Each Time a Voice is Raised in Outrage and Protest
  To scream the Truth
  Stingin' Like Sonia

  Slicin' Like Farrakhan

Poet/Griots Supplying Slingshots
  As the Sheep Look Up
    Spittin' the Fire that has Burned in Our Souls & Hearts
      For Oh So Long
        The Real Party Will Just Be Startin'
          Let The Turntable Rotate and Relate
            For What Goes Around Has Come Around
            Let the Actions Be Swift, Unmerciful
            And as Jazz Improvised

            dooewdooewdewtdewt
            dooewdooewdewdewt tch tch

        DOOEWDOOEWDEWDEWT
        DOOEWDOOEWDEWDEWT TCH!

Mariah L. Richardson

English as a Second Language

my "black" english
used to roll off my tongue
rhythmically
like a heavy rain
with its synchronized fashion
with romance that
I was not eeeeeeven aware of.

"Hey, like I be thinkin
wid my black self and
shiiiid . . . . I be wondrin
why them teachers
be sayin that
I cain't talk
when my words
are electric   like me."

Thoughts be forming
themselves in my
mouth
and it be like music
my own self
dripping like honey
in sunshine

But it had to be
spoken in secret,
in the privacy of my home
and in school I learned
that you caint be not
doing nothing
cause that's a
double negative.

223

Now,
my english is proper
and polished
but, I cannot hold
a decent black conversation
without stammering
in search of words.

Maisha

Encounter

With eyes as dreamy as a midnight swim
Close and touching is his personality
With a build that shows the consciousness
    in him
Magnetic is his vibrant energy
Smooth is his walk
Gentle and caressing is his talk
Teaching and passing on a much desired need
Focusing on each recipient to try and succeed
His smile, "Ummm," quite expressive
    As he observes and relates
With a refreshing sensitivity
    One that understands and communicates
His idea of love is not to suffocate
For he hates the questioning deal
To see him friendship is to appreciate
    He finds no need in strictly sex-appeal
As it appears
    for the sisters to hear
You'll find yourself in a line I'm sure
Not first, second or last to be,
    but each one feeling secure
This brother is Kool with his naturalness
So to approach him is easy and Free
Meeting him, you'd be quite impressed
With his sweet sincerity.

Marcus Mosiah Garvey: The Whirlwind and the Storm

Proud and gallant — you stand tall
Sure and outspoken for us all
You saw the light
The flame of your people
Your words of knowledge and   wisdom ignited and awakened
You were chosen to perform a miracle
That has left the oppressors shaken
For you gathered the scattered sons
and daughters of Afrika under one international banner

ONE GOD, ONE AIM, ONE DESTINY

That was the battle call for the consciousness in me
Though your adversaries attempted
to douse the flaming spirit of truth in you
Your thunderous roars of "Afrika for the Afrikans"
are echoed through and through
Having no fear of man, in you
assures our victory
Waving our flag of colors . . . so high
We know the call is unity

RED, BLACK, and GREEN

THE BLOOD, THE PEOPLE, THE LAND

You preached and prophesied in the name of blackness
The redemption of the Afrikan
Though many have tried
to cast you aside
with their devilish schemes and lies

They bit off their tongue
'Cause your work has just begun
we feel the power, the energy
Of all our ancestors in the fight for

                         Liberty

The Trump

I knew him
And he was good for me
I, even better for him
Upper hand
Thumbs down
Momma said, don't settle
I knew him again
And some in between
He was better
I, the best for him
Sure thin?
Pass, momma said
I knew him once more
Obliging others by and by
He was at his best
Bid, momma said
I, failed to follow suit
       RENEGE

Visions

They gather in clusters
Chit-chatting
Bearing their souls in lies
That would be truth
What should have been
If only —
Daytime dreams
For nightmares of reality
No one's life is as good as mine
So when I understand the words of silence
Between the words of praise
I know it's hell (for them too)
Brown bags with gourmet taste
Gold bands displayed as rare diamonds and gems
Like a rainbow after the storm
What a price to pay
Lunch time between nine and five
Ladies of leisure
Woman with girlish dreams
Too old or too late
What should have been
If only —

Jennifer Smith

On One Sister Being Responsive to Some Jive Ass Rap

run it down to me babe,
he crooned.
tell papa what it's all about.

& she did.

a nine-year-old.
a three-year-old.
a grocery list.
a disconnect electric notice.
a 50-hour work week.
a part-time weekend gig.
a $600 rent payment.
a car that never funs.
a handy man to fuck
    twice a week.
a special man to love
    on holidays.

    now run it down to me babe,
    she hummed.
    tell mama what it's all about.

Debate

said i was a crazy
mixed-up fool

i said i was saving all
my sanity for me

said i was bitter
angry unjustified
writing radical
black poetry

i said i was just sharpening
my pencil point

said i was stupid
believing a world
could change

i said i was printing
new signs to be posted
any day now

said i was anti-everything

i said i was pro-anti-opposite

said i . . .

i said . . .

Black Art

mama said i always did crave
sweets, plain white paper
number two pencils and
good good cuttin scissors
smuggled outta
government supply rooms
via daddy's accordion briefcase

& i recall withstanding
early silences
& teasings
of having not
listened to enough of the
godfather, four tops &
p-funk to earn the
title: hip
to cause rhythm
& rock hatred of
black roots: jazz & blues

no sir ree, i loved love them
misty marvelous tunes pumpin
outta the basement
crashing spinning popping
45's until somebody
hollered down the steps
commandin that i turn them
old ass records off

but who could speak in such a way
of yardbird, the duke, of holiday?

i answered as i always did
always do do
brand me an L-7 if you may
but no unorthodox negroes
done forgotten the way
of originality

A Poem for Unspoken Voices

he beat her/
beat her
beyond the savagery of
iron-hard knuckles
    pounding
    punching
    splintering
her skull
her bones

he ripped her spirit
punched out her eyes
(so she could not see)
her lips where
her nose use to be

he beat her
when supper wasn't seasoned
to his taste
he served her up
hot steamed
blueblack flesh

he beat her
when she spoke out of turn
or spoke-at-all
or smiled
or frowned
his hands/his fingers
    choking
    suffocating
    crushing
her soul
her silent-pleading
her long fought fight

For All the "Think-They-Conscious" Writers Who Applauded Wilson Goode at a Conference Celebrating Black Writing

is this aaanotha MOVE poem?
anotha poem to be read at readings/
publication parties to be marketed
to brothers/sisters who think
cultural aesthetic the correct/only
response to white oppression?

is this aaanotha MOVE poem
for anotha book of poetry/essays/
documentaries to be sold for profit?

yes, there is money to be made off
the torching of them dreadhead
back-to-nature niggers over
there on osage avenue
by bourgeoisie negroes pim
ping the continent pim
ping the cause

ask any bookseller
ask any philly tourguide

or is this a poem to cause you to squirm
in yo seat/strip you naked/shame you/
skin you to the bone/gut your spirit/
make you slam yo soul up against the wall
ask yourself where the hell you were
on May 13, 1985 when 14 black
men women children were eaten by flame
in a house C-4 bombed by the state police?

or is this a poem written to say
"oh isn't it a shame"
aaanotha poem demanding
        no retribution
        no justice for
birdie & ramona africa?

no, this ain't just aaanotha MOVE poem
to be politely digested with reception/
handshakes/autographs to follow

no, this poem is free is a free MOVE poem
whether you ask for it or not

We Workers

we spend eight hours
on our feet/sittin in an
ole uncomfortable chair/
bendin/stretchin
countin the seconds til five
cheatin at break time
attachin one half hour to the
15 minutes alloted our
personal/bodily needs
for 1800 seconds of the
24 hour day
we are self-crowned
slicksisters

we gossip on client-charged
calls long-distance
steal postage from the
pitney-bowes meters &
count with preciseness
just how long the office
alcoholic is overdue
& debate the usual
"he's extra-late" game
we've learned to
play for dismal
conversation

on fridays we collect
our pay &
come saturday mornings
write-out our bills
sleep through sunday worship
from saturday night partying
& wake mondays begging
fridays to come quickly
so we can dance
to repeat

we live our lives with
the predictableness of
our periods
no need to
think about it

think about it

Chima Uchendu

An Untitled Love Poem

Oh, how I recall the strangeness
in the mystery
and the mystery also
in the strangeness
on that premier meeting.
Cupid fed my emotions with passion fodder —
of beauty, grace, charm and BLACK.

Friendship for a while . . .

Then behold!

The naked reality inevitable.
Gentle ruthlessness — momentary madness.
Which manifest in lovers
after the demystification.

Oh, sweet mystery,

                    return.

Alan Spears

Period

To gain consciousness
women bleed.
But what sort of menstrual cycle
does a race need?

Dreadlocks and Other Assumptions

Somewhere,
along the way to the middle class,
all that checked ambition became knotted.
Things hatred sprouted.
Things rejection prompted.
Things integration allowed.

They cannot be;
Combed out,
greased under,
lacquered smooth,
bombarded thin, or
plastered with poisonous lye
to limp straight and die.

Like a black European lost in the "new world."
Choking on the venomous bile of self-deception
                              deprecation
                                destruction.

My hair,
a by-product of a natural function,
reworks twisted assumptions,
in knotted rebellious lint consumption,
causing barbers to dysfunction.

Watch me,
I am this dreaded disruption.

Of Kerouac and Talk Shows

Before Ted Koppel married Oprah Winfrey,
and took over the nation via the t.v.
Jack Kerouac was drunk on *Firing Line*.
And wasn't his irreverence fine!

Buckley looking six months dead,
his back placed at an impossible angle
into a reclining chair,

asked Jack about the Beats,
and being a Beat American,
about being a Beat American, maan!
About being a Beat American and about
a thing they called Vietnam.

He asked Kerouac about Big America
stomping on the Vietcong.
And did Beat America
think it was right or wrong?
                              Maan!

And the question trickled out of his square square mouth
like convoluted ketchup, on and on,
and on,
          and on . . .
Buckley's self-importance growing about his head like a fern.
The divine talk show host
and his thorny crown,
the weight of which pushed him down,
                              down.

Further into that chair.

And Kerouac, never past his prime
placed the reason behind the rhyme,
And maan! How he blew everybody's mind,
by being drunk on *Firing Line*.

The Right Reverend?

No *black man*
should have hair like that
unless he is accompanying James Brown on stage,
                                            or to jail . . .

His bellicosity
is as great and gross as his belly.

And he remains proof of the fact
that nothingness emanates
from the "Void"
of black political leadership, our lost legacy.

The dweebish nephew to the King.
Near last on a list of inheritors
of a 1963 dream speech.
Proof, conclusive, that we took a wrong turn
after we got to the mountain top!

Our new sovereign be default.
De' fault of USACIAFBI assassins . . .

To whom I say:

            "Thank you America.
            I will take your racism.
            But I cannot stomach reverend al."

Makeshift Jesus

You want to tell them . . .
when they come knocking at your door,
or
tramping down the dirt road of a small southern town
to sit and sing
for hours
'neath the revivalist tent . . .

Where these negroes appear so contented
they make you *ill*
with jealous intellectual rage
against their naiveté . . .

You want to tell them . . .

That the long winding suffering of man
will never end
because god is a practical joker.
Keen on physical and psychic torture . . .

And in the pain of this isolation
                              so rough,

the love of Jesus
is
never,
        ever
                    enough . . . .

Poetry and Other Self-Inflicted Wounds

Men experience love
through division and conquest.
You may not like it,
but the truth is irrefutable.
See it in the eyes of the lovelorn male.
His affection declared forever
in immovable heaps and mounds,
Lancelotian fits and starts,
battles and wars,
poetry and other self-inflicted wounds.
The note pad and pencil
maintained discreetly at the bedside
record the score.

But you are wrong to think
that it has ever been about getting over.
Rather,
our behavior comes from
having watched too many English war movies
when we were young.
They instilled a rigid sense of chivalry
and *noblesse oblige*
which required that one volunteer remain behind
when the ammunition had run out,
when the reinforcements had been turned back,
and the heathens were about to over run the last wall.
You see,
a senseless massacre
was better than a sensible retreat on any day.

And if it was a woman's pitiable lot
to lay still and "think of England"
as her lover moved inside her.
It was his dreadful labor

to read the pained expressions on the face below
and wonder if she had ever loved him at all?

If you insist the two burdens are incomparable
then I will quickly yield.
But despite all evidence to the contrary,
you would be wrong to think that men don't feel.

She Need Not Know — an indirect approach for Kris Miller.

If I tell everyone in the world
except you.
Were I to sing out
like the man in the soft drink commercials, or
run an ad in the daily paper.
If I wrote you love letters in the sand
after the beaches had been closed.
Or sent a valentine to your old address.
Then,
you need not hear directly from me.
(It will come to your attention sooner or later)

You will know that I love you.

While waiting in the express line to pay for your groceries
you might read some innuendo
telling of my great affection for you
(Still, I have not said it).
I could learn Zulu or Xhosa
and leave strange clicking noises on your answering machine.
Would you work to get the message?

If one day the clouds spell out your name,
or the hedges have trimmed to heart shapes
on the neighboring lawn . . .
When you hear your face described
within the lines of a love poem . . .

If I tell everyone you ever met
how wonderful you are.
Were I made King of the universe
and proclaimed you my favorite star.

Then,
you need not hear from me a thing,
and still, somehow, you'd know.

This strangely silent black man
is the one who loves you so.

Embrace

The sound of the word has texture,
like the ruffling of her shirt
in my hands.
Fingertips of the left
massaging shoulders.
The palm of the right
pressed into the small of her back.

Forehead to forehead.

Lips brushed against lips,
though not yet joined to form a kiss . . .

The temperature of a body multiplied by two.
I could melt into you.

Afrikan Culture

Young men,
blacker than Black,
embracing Afrikan culture.
Africa, the place they know
is somewhere east of Philly or D.C.

Young men
blacker than thou!
Fighting "the powers that be"
are more confused than a body has a right to be.
Fighting for their right
to buy and consume.
Or to be bought and be consumed.

Young black men,
often with hearts and minds of Gold.
And so often,
the gold chains and ear rings to match.
Reject everything and create so little in return.

Save for Malcolm X, on a t-shirt.

Martin Luther King, on a t-shirt.

Slave mothers and fathers, all on t-shirts.

A litany of "Blackness."
More nigger iconography.

We "practice" being black,
and are not yet very good at it.

Detachment

Whirl infinitely in ellipses.
Let all languages be foreign.

Move in slow motion
unplug your telltalevision
which has left your retina dangling
like an un-u-said extension chord.

Scale infinitely higher in patterns
let all motion be your language
as you plug into your poetry
let your conscience be your jury.

The tongue wagging "Hello"
from the bottom of your throat, the place
where those guttural bass sounds
kom frum . . .

Watch infinitely in cycles
of on again off again, walk and don't walk.
Avoid the specific
as you embrace the discursive.
And hide behind your telltalevision
when you re-sight your latest bombs
(They could call it poetry but dey won't!).

Style infinitely in stages.
In NASA rocket ship divorce rages . . .

and then,
when you have separation . . .
with "whitey up deah on de moon," n' all dat!

Spin pretty
like a beautiful black dancer,
bow to the audience,

and fly away

Bios in Brief

Yao Bhoke Ahoto: is a resident of the District of Columbia.

Akili: is a member of the Nommo Posse and Subterra Sounds. His book of poems *Makantagara* was published in 1991. His poetry has previously appeared in the *D.C. City Paper*.

Susan Anderson: Susan began writing poetry at the age of 14. Her work has been published in *The Antioch Review*, *The Black Scholar*, *Electrum*, *rara avis*, *The Massachusetts Review*, *Freedomways*, and *5 A.M.* Her unpublished manuscript *Salvaging the Dreams* is in search of a publisher. Currently, she lives in Los Angeles with her husband and son, Langston.

Toni D. Blackman: is a recent graduate of Howard University in Washington, D.C. Her work has previously appeared in *JANUS: The Howard University Literary Journal* and *Omowe Journal*.

Valerie Clarke: is a resident of Washington, D.C.

Kenneth Carroll: is a resident of the Metropolitan area and a cornerstone of the Washington, D.C. poetry community. Kenneth is rumored to have placed a poetical hex on George Bush, Dan Quayle, and the legacy of J. Edgar Hoover.

Michelle T. Clinton: hails from Santa Monica, California. She has published a book of poetry entitled *High Blood/Pressure* (West End Press, 1987) and served as the editor of *Invocation LA*, an anthology of multicultural poetry (West End Press, 1989). Her work has appeared in *Gargoyle*, *The Black Scholar*, *Enclitic*, and *Muse!*

Wanda Coleman: is a native of Los Angeles. Her books *Mad Dog Black Lady* (1979), *Images* (1983) and *Heavy Daughter Blues* (poems & stories 1966-1986) appear via Black Sparrow Press. She was the recipient of a literary grant from the National Endowment for the Arts, 1981-82; Her first book of fiction *A War of Eyes and Other Stories* was published by Black Sparrow in the fall of 1988. She received the Woman's Building's 7th Annual Vesta Award in writing in 1988. Her 6th book from Black Sparrow Press, *African Sleeping Sickness: Stories and Poems* was published in October of 1990.

Meri Nana-Ama Danquah: is a native of the west African country Ghana. A recent transplant to the D.C. area from Los Angeles, Meri has an extensive background as a performance artist, poet, and dancer. She is currently editing an anthology of poems, essays, and photographs regarding the state of African Americans and race relations in the United States.

Patricia Fields: is a resident of Temple Hills, Maryland. Her work has previously appeared in *Black Reflections*.

Brian G. Gilmore: was born and raised in Washington, D.C. A writer of poetry and fiction, Dr. Gilmore's work has appeared in *Obsidian II, The Side Bar,* and *The Unity Line*. His first collection of poems is entitled *Elvis Presley is Alive and Well and Living in Harlem*, and is due out in 1991 from Third World Press.

Melvin E. Lewis: has been published in a number of anthologies including: *1989 American Anthology of Midwestern Poetry*, and *NOMMO: A Literary Legacy of Black Chicago (1967-1987)*. Melvin Lewis' articles, poetry, and interviews, have appeared in the *Afro-Hispanic Review, Black Panther Paper, Black X- Press, Chicago Illini, Cumbaya, Dial-a-Poem, Chicago!, Direct Line, Lucky Star, New Sense, Obsidian, Obsidian II, Oba Songs, Presence Africaine* (Paris), *Revelry, Urban Focus,* and the *WDCU Jazz 90 Program Guide*. Melvin Lewis was the 1987 recipient of the "Significant Illinois Poet Award."

Philip Lewis (Henderson): resides in the Washington, D.C. Metropolitan area when not traveling the world. Philip recently published a collection of poems entitled *A Reflection* (Black Coffee Press, 1990). His work has appeared in *Dark Future, Black Coffee Review,* and *Black Ice*.

Bernard Harris, Jr.: hails from Seattle, Washington. His poem "I'm the-Mailhandler" achieved wide acclaim. Bernard's work has previously appeared in the *Seattle Postal Dispatch*.

Reuben Jackson: is a poetry and music enthusiast who believes that poems should be as "exciting and sensual as . . . a Marvin Gaye ballad." His book, *fingering the keys*, published by Gut Punch Press in 1991, was selected by Joseph Brodsky as winner of the Columbia Prize for a book of poems published in the Washington metropolitan area. Reuben has previously been published in *Chelsea, Indiana Review, Lip Service, Washington Review, The Black American Literature Forum, Visions, T.W.I., The Christian Science Monitor, City Paper* (Washington, D.C.), and *Folio*.

Maisha: is a graduate of Virginia State University (Petersburg, VA). She began writing poetry in 1980 and has published her work in *Ujamaa Drum*.

Keith Antar Mason: is a poet and playwright from Santa Monica, California. His poetry has appeared in *Shattersheet, The Anthology of St. Louis Black Poets,* and *Harbinger*.

Kim Nault: currently resides on the West Coast. Her poetry has previously appeared in *Paradox* and *Scars* fanzines.

Christopher Nickelson: was the 1990 recipient of the John A. Wright Poetry Award from the Afro-American Resource Center at Howard University. He desires one day to own a goldfish named "Arthur."

Akilah Nayo Oliver: is a writer and teacher in Los Angeles. Her poetry has appeared in *Harbinger* (L.A. Festival & Beyond Baroque, 1990), *Invocation L.A.* (West End Press, 1989), *Tax* (UCLA, 1989), *Full Circle Nine Anthology* (Guild Press, 1988), and *The Otherwise Room Anthology* (Southwestern Illinois University Press, 1981). She has performed her poetry at the Midnight Special Bookstore (Santa Monica), Poetcentric Lounge,

KXLU, KPOO, and KPFA radio. Akilah Nayo Oliver was the 1991 recipient of the California Arts Council Artist in Residence Grant.

Michelle Parkerson: is a writer and independent film/video producer living in Washington, D.C. Her work has appeared in *Heresies, Callaloo, Sinister Wisdom, The New York Native, Essence Magazine, The Washington Blade, Black Film Review, The Independent,* and other publications. She has performed her poetry at the Folger Shakespeare Library (Washington, D.C.), Harlem's Cotton Club, and the Painted Bride Art Center (Philadelphia). Michelle Parkerson has produced four films including a documentary on the black women's a capella group Sweet Honey in the Rock entitled *Gotta Make This Journey: Sweet Honey in the Rock* (1983). Michelle Parkerson is the author of *Waiting Rooms* (Common Ground Press, 1984). She is currently working on a manuscript entitled *Public Love.*

Rabia Rayford: has been described as the "High Priestess" of black poetry. Her performances combine elements of dance and theatre to create a compelling visual image. Her first book of poetry is entitled, *Yes! We are Colorful!!! A Celebration* (Dancing Lion Press, 1990). Rabia Rayford currently lives in Washington, D.C. with her two children.

Mariah L. Richardson: describes herself as a recent transplant to southern California from St. Louis, Missouri. Her work has appeared in *Word-walkers Anthology, Catalyst #7, Essence,* and the L.A. Festival's anthology, *Harbinger.*

Sakinah: is a poet, world traveller, jewelry maker, and educator. She currently resides in the District of Columbia and is working on an untitled manuscript of poetry.

Tanya Seale: is a graduate of Clark University in Worcester, Massachusetts.

Jennifer E. Smith: is a poet and a writer living in Washington, D.C. Her poetry and fiction have appeared in *Black American Literature Forum, Obsidian II, Catalyst, Essence, Et Cetera, About Time, Blind Alleys, Black Arts Bulletin, Colorlines, Griot, PressTime, Moving Out,* and *Appalachian Heritage.* She is coordinator of the University of the District of Columbia Poetry Series and editor and publisher of the *Black Arts Bulletin.* Jennifer is the winner of the 1991 Mount Vernon College Poetry Festival, and author of *D.C. Jazz & Blues,* a collection of poetry.

Kweli Smith: describes herself as a "Performance Artist, Poet, and Educator." She has been featured at the Kennedy Center for the Performing Arts, Sanctuary Theatre, the Bethune Museum Archives, and the Smithsonian's Anacostia Museum. Kweli Smith is a resident of Washington, D.C. She has published a collection of her poetry entitled *Slavesong: The Art of Singing.* Kweli Smith's poetry has previously appeared in *Three Apples Fell,* and *Black Mother and Daughter Anthology* (Beacon Press).

Alan Spears: A graduate of Clark University in Worcester, Massachusetts, Alan began writing poetry in 1986. His work has previously appeared in *Un-e-brijd: The Clark University Journal of the Arts* (Summer 1986). Alan is a long time resident of the District of Columbia, and wishes that he were a better soccer player!

Darrell Darius Stover: Darrell "The Man in the Green Hat" Stover is a native Washingtonian and a senior editor for Cambridge Scientific Abstracts of Bethesda, MD. Darrell is the director of The Spoken Word, a poetry performance ensemble. His first collection of poetry *Record of the Green Hat Chronicles Volume One* (MELO — Metro Lover Lives Press) was published in 1988. Darrell Stover's work has previously appeared in *Black Explosion, Drumbeat, Drum Voices, Uncut Funk, Positive Energy Newsletter*, and the *University of Maryland at College Park Black Alumni Newsletter*.

Natasha Tarpley: is a student at Harvard College in Cambridge, Massachusetts. Throughout 1991, Natasha gathered material for *Raising Up the New Bones*, an anthology of poetry by black college students to be published sometime in the near future.

Kim Taylor: is a resident of the District of Columbia.

Chima Uchendu: graduated from Howard University Law School in 1989.

Jennifer Lisa Vest: is a graduate student in the Department of History at Howard University. She is a member of Daughters of the Dream, a black womens poetry collective based in Washington, D.C., and Women of Mixed Heritage based in Berkeley, California.

White Deer Woman: is a poet and activist who has worked extensively toward Native American liberation. Her poems have appeared in *Bomb Magazine* (New York, Spring 1986), and *Moccasin Line*.

Austin F. Wooten: is a member of the Howard University Alumni Association, a fan of chess, tennis and physical fitness.

(Continued from acknowledgements page)

"Sisters," "Name Change," and "Wouldn't it Be a Shame," by Rabia Rayford from her *Yes! We're Colorful!!! A Celebration*, Dancing Lion Press, 1990. Reprinted by permission of the author.

"Doors 16," "Doors 17," "Doors 18," and "Doors 19" by Melvin E. lewis have appeared in *The Griot* (Fall 1991).

"Doors 20" by Melvin E. Lewis has appeared in *The Willow Review* (April 1991).

"Shit Talk on the Venice Boulevard Bus Heading East One Summer's Night," by Akilah Nayo Oliver has previously appeared in *Invocation L.A.*, West End Press, 1988.

"Metro Love," "Coltrane Poem," "Undefined," "Oh! And All This," "Bonesongs," "Genesis," "And Whales Way Off Track," "I Died," and "Party Over Here & There Y'all" by Darrell Stover from his *Record of the Green Hat Chronicles Volume One*, MELOLIPS (Metro Lover Lives Press), 1988. Reprinted by permission of the author.

"Black Art" and "We Workers" by Jennifer E. Smith have appeared in *Obsidian II*.

"Black Art" by Jennifer E. Smith has also appeared in her collection, *D.C. Jazz & Blues*. Reprinted by permission of the author.

Paths of Urban Transformation

The European City
in Transition

Edited by Frank Eckardt
and Dieter Hassenpflug

Vol. 5

PETER LANG

Frankfurt am Main · Berlin · Bern · Bruxelles · New York · Oxford · Wien

Frank Eckardt (ed.)

Paths of
Urban Transformation

PETER LANG
Europäischer Verlag der Wissenschaften

Bibliographic Information published by Die Deutsche Bibliothek
Die Deutsche Bibliothek lists this publication in the Deutsche Nationalbibliografie; detailed bibliographic data is available in the internet at <http://dnb.ddb.de>.

This publication has been realized by the support
of the European Commission
and the Deutsche Forschungsgesellschaft.

Photo: Frank Eckardt

ISSN 1619-375X
ISBN 3-631-52211-8
US-ISBN 0-8204-9820-3

© Peter Lang GmbH
Europäischer Verlag der Wissenschaften
Frankfurt am Main 2005
All rights reserved.

Printed in Germany 1 2   4 5 6 7

www.peterlang.de

The European Cities in Transition Series

Cities are a mirror of society and a motor of change. Especially the challenges produced by the growing interconnection of people and places find their spatial organisation in the world's metropolis. Globalization shapes new forms of economy, culture and social life and it comes all together in the historically grown European city. The increasing of mobility and communication brings forward the key questions of urban life again: How can the heritages of a European city been transmitted to a city in times of profound changes? What does it mean for political, cultural, social and architectural decision makers to act in an urban setting transformed by major societal trends?

The "European Cities in Transition Series" aims at publishing answers from all disciplines that are dedicated to find theoretical and practical solutions for the European City under the circumstances of the globalization and the unification of Europe. Edited by Dieter Hassenpflug and Frank Eckardt who both work at the Bauhaus-Universität Weimar, the tradition of the first Bauhaus is remembered: The Bauhaus architects like Mies van der Rohe and Walter Gropius have been searching for adequate solutions for the city of modernity. Today, this spirit has to be brought in, again. The post-national age requires new approaches for understanding the European city. Bringing together the findings of research of scientists, city planers and architectures, the series will focus on different aspects of the current transition of urban life.

First volume: Consumption and the Post-Industrial City
Second volume: Urbanism and Globalization
Third volume: City Images and Urban Regeneration
Forth volume: The City and the Region
Fifth volume: Paths of Urban Transformation

Contents

Contributors

Ileana Hapenciuc Blum is an architect and a researcher at INSA Lyon and the University of Architecture and Urbanism "Ion Mincu" of Bucharest. She is currently working on her PhD thesis on urban regeneration and the renewal of institutional practices concerning the urban development of Bucharest. Her research interests include urban models and their impact on urban actors practices, EU conditions for the enlargement to the Eastern Europe and their impact on the urban actors practices at a local level. Contact: ileanka@yahoo.com

Ognjen Čaldarović is a full professor of sociology at the University of Zagreb, Faculty of Philosophy, Department of Sociology. He teaches *Urban Sociology, Contemporary Sociological Theories, and Sociology of Risk*. He was invited to many universities to lecture in Europe and in America. He has published ca 80 professional papers and several books and research publications. Major publications include: Urban sociology: Social Theory and the Urban Question (1985), Contemporary Society and Urbanization (1987), Energy and Society (1991), Social Theory and Hazardous Life: Risks and Contemporary Society (1995), How to Live with Technical Risks (1997). Contact: ognjen.caldarovic@ffzg.hr.

Luan Deda is an urban designer and development planner for Alan Baxter & Associates, London. He completed his MSc studies in London on Urban Economic Development and Housing Studies focusing to Tirana's household economics and development challenges during the transition period. Luan has previously been part of Co-PLAN, Institute for Habitat Development, which is a leading research and consultancy organisation in Albania and partly in the Balkans. He has contributed in several publications such as 'Housing Change in East and Central Europe: Integration or Fragmentation' 2004, throughout this period. Contact: luandedamail@yahoo.co.uk

Frank Eckardt is Junior Professor for the Sociology of globalization and is working as an urban sociologist at the European Urban Studies programme of the Bauhaus-Universität Weimar, where he is the local organizer of the "European Cities in Transition Conference" Series. He has finished his PhD at the University of Kassel in political science. Recent publication: "Soziologie der Stadt" (2004).
Contact: Frank.Eckardt@archit.uni-weimar.de

Marjan Hočevar, Assist. Prof. holds a full-time position at the University of Ljubljana, Faculty of Social Sciences, Center for Urban and Environmental Studies. His research and teaching activities are linked to spatiosociological subjects. His main research domain is territoriality, especially the processes of transformation of cities and contemporary urban phenomena in the circumstances of globalization. His Slovenian and international published references are focused on thematizing of spatial networks, trends of dehierarchization of European urban systems and on changing roles of city centers as influenced by individualization of life styles. He is coordinator of the thematic group TG06 Local/Global sociology at the ISA (International Sociological Organization), and is also a member of the International research committee for Urban and Regional Research (ISA, RC21). Contact: marjan.hocevar@fdv.uni-lj.si

Györgyi Ignits is research associate at the Tocqueville Research Center (Budapest). She graduated from the University of Budapest in 2003. His research interests are in social history, history of mentality, political sociology of local governments, and sociology of local communities. She has both qualitative and quantitative research experience.

Anna Karwinska, a sociologist, is a lecturer and Academic Fellow at Krakow's University of Economics. She is a chair of the Department of Sociology and currently the vide-Dean of the Economics and International Relations Faculty. Her research interests lie in the urban problems and the culture of cities. She has published widely in these fields in Poland and abroad, she also presents her work at many inter-national conferences. After publishing a book on urban social development she got habilitation in sociology from Silesian University, Katowice. Anna Karwinska teaches several courses in sociology and she was a visiting professor at Grand Valley State University ,Allendale, Michigan. Contact: karwinsa@ae.krakow.pl

Drago Kos, Associate Professor of social ecology and urban sociology at Faculty of social sciences University of Ljubljana. He is head of the research Center for Urban and Environmental Studies. Member of several expert teams who evaluated ecological hazardous projects such as waste disposals, highway constructions, industrial plants, etc. Recent publications include Sociology for Urban Planners (Ljubljana, 2002), Reform of Local Government in Slovenia (Budapest 2000), Ljubljana - Encyclopedia of Urban Cultures (Danbury, 2002). Contact: Drago.Kos@fdv.uni-lj.si

Vera Marin is a Ph.D. candidate of both Ion Mincu University of Architecture and Urban Planning in Bucharest and Institut d'Urbanisme in Lyon, working on the topic of housing policies – focusing on the current situation of large real estates built during the communist regime. She combines the theoretical approach (as a young researcher and as a

teaching assistant at Ion Mincu University) with a practical one (as a president of ATU – an NGO of young urban planners - and as a team member in various urban planning projects).
Contact: veraurbanplanning@yahoo.com

Elidor Mehilli is writting a thesis at Cornell University that analyzes the cultural politics and the architectural development under the socialist regime in post-war Albania. His interests focus on the intersection of politics and visual culture and the histories of cities.
Contact: em92@cornell.edu

Konrad Miciukiewicz is a is a Ph.D. candidate in sociology at the Adam Mickiewicz University in Poznań and at the European University Viadrina in Frankfurt (Oder). He is currently working on his thesis on the transformation of urban public spaces in Eastern European cities.
Contact: kmiciukiewicz@poczta.onet.pl.

Olga Mrinska is Lecturer in Regional Development/ Policy at the Department of Geography, Kyiv National Taras Shevchenko University and Deputy Ukraine Programme Manager of the Department for International Development of the United Kingdom based in Kyiv. She wrote her PhD thesis at the Institute of Geography of the National Academy of Sciences of Ukraine on EU regional policy and relevance of its ex-perience to Ukraine. Among latest publications are contributions to the books 'Subnational Data Requirements for Fiscal Decentralization' (2003) and 'Structural Transformations in Ukrainian Economy: Regional Aspects' (2003). Contact: omrinska@gala.net

Martin Ouředníček is lecturer in Social Geography at the Department of Social Geography and Regional Development of the Charles University in Prague. In 2002 he completed his PhD thesis "Urbanisation Processes in Prague Urban Region". His research interests include the urban and settlement geography in post-socialist countries, (sub)urbanisation and suburban development and its impact on social environment of urban regions. Contact: slamak@natur.cuni.cz

Maciej Smętkowski is an Assistant and a Ph. D candidate at Centre for European Regional and Local Studies, Warsaw University. He is also a Member of Board of Regional Studies Association – Polish Section. His interests cover urban and economic geography, instruments for supporting regional and local development, foreign capital in process of economic development. The chapter in this volume is a part of his Ph. D thesis based on research carried out as part of a project "Metropolis-

Region: New Relations in Information Economy" funded by the State Committee for Scientific Research. Contact: m.smetkowski@uw.edu.pl

Gábor Soós is the managing director of the Tocqueville Research Center (Budapest, www.t-rc.org). His publications focus on local politics, civil society, local elites, metropolitan governance, and public administration reforms. He is the project director of the Indicators of Local Democratic Governance Project, a multi-year, international re-search on local democracy in Central and Eastern Europe.

Akos Szepvolgyi is research fellow at the Centre for Regional Studies, Hugarian Academy of Sciences. In 2000 he completed his master degree on regional geography. He is currently completing his PhD thesis on regional aspects of the information society. His research interests include the information society, intelligent regions, knowledge management and social inequalities. Contact: szepvol@rkk.hu

Enkeleida Tahiraj has a background on Contemporary European Studies (MA-University of Sussex, UK) and Social Policy (PhD – University of York, UK), and is currently working as the director of Nash Albanian Studies Programme at the School of Slavonic and East European Studies, University College London. She was a fellow at EUREX 2001 and contributed in the subsequent forthcoming book publication. At SSEES/UCL she is part of an exiting team that has initiated a seminar series on 'Cities in CEE'.
Contact: E.Tahiraj@ssees.ucl.ac.uk

Jana Temelová is a PhD candidate in urban geography at Charles University in Prague, Department of Social Geography and Regional Development. She is currently working on her thesis focused on the role of real estate, in particular high profile buildings, in city promotion and physical revitalization of inner city. Contact: jana.temelova@centrum.cz

Franc Trček is an Assistant Professor at University of Ljubljana, Faculty of Social Sciences. His current research is concerned with the socio-spatial implications of informatization. He is the author of publications on the problem of socio-spatial informatization among which: "Community-net in South and East Europe" (Ed., 2003), "Glocal localities" (Eds. with M. Hocevar 2002), "Attitudes Towards Subnational and Supranational Regional Networking: The Case of Slovenian Istria" (with M. Hocevar, 1999), "Territorial cultures and global impacts" (with Z. Milinar, 1998). Contact: franc.trcek@guest.arnes.si

Matjaž Uršič is a researcher at University of Ljubljana, Faculty of Social Sciences. He is member of Center for Urban and Environmental Studies. His research interests focus on urban systems, with particular reference to transformations due to processes of suburbanisation, deurbanisation and reurbanisation. Publications include Urban Spaces of Consumption (Ljubljana, 2003), Compact and Spread City – Global Networks and Local Differences (Salzburg, 2002), he is the co-author (with Franc Trček) of Gift Economies and the Transformation of Regional Networking (Vienna, 2001). Contact: matjaz.ursic2@guest.arnes.si

Yani Valkanov has degrees in architecture from UACEG, Sofia, Bulgaria and urban planning & housing policy from University of Lincoln, UK. He is currently working in Sofproject-Master plan – a municipal planning organisation, responsible for the development and implementation of the new master plan of the city of Sofia. His research interests include socialist cities' urban spatial structure, suburbanisation, brownfield regeneration, industrial zone planning and design, etc. He is a visiting lecturer in UACEG, Sofia and Free University, Varna.
Contact: yvalkanov@architect.bg

Elena Vesselinov, Ph.D. Her research and teaching interests are in the areas of urban sociology, housing, immigration and globalization. A central focus of her academic research is the interrelation between processes of social and spatial inequality. Her dissertation research examines housing inequality in the contexts of post-communist market transition and economic globalization. Contact: Vesselin@gwm.sc.edu

Lubica Vitkova is an Associate Professor at the Slovak University of Technology in Bratislava, Faculty of Architecture and has been working there in the field of Urban Planning and Urban Design since 1991. In 1990 she was a planner at the Department of Main Architect of the City of Bratislava. She was a project leader of 7 research projects. She is the project leader of the running research project "Grand Commercial Investments and Urban Structure of the Towns", She is involved in the international research project ECOCITY "Urban Development towards Appropriate Structures for Sustainable Transport" SPECTRA Centre. She wrote a textbook Urban Economics, STU Bratislava 2001. She is also active as an architect and urban designer.
Contact: vitkova@fa.stuba.sk

Paths of Urban Transformation
(Introduction)   *Frank Eckardt*

Studying cities is all about studying changes. The motivation for urban sociology from its very beginning can be traced down to the experience of a visible change in the city. It is not by accident that the point of departure for a sociological interest in urban life is the explosive manner of industrialization and the mass movement from the countryside to the urban. This was the situation when Georg Simmel, during his walks through the rapidly growing, overcrowded inner-city of 19th century Berlin, asked himself how the changes of the German capital influence the mental life of the urbanites. This was even more the motif of the Chicago School at the beginning of the 20th century, trying to reflect on the patterns of urban life in an overcoming geography in the eyes of the researchers. And nowadays, the situation in the 21st century impressively calls for our attention towards the hyper growth of mega-cities in the so-called Non-OECD world where cities, as populated as entire European nations and as fast growing as never before in human history, provoke outstanding political, social and economic challenges.

While we have a seemingly profound theoretical reflection underpinned with a rich body of empirical research on the developments towards a modern city, it is obvious that urban research is still not guided by a framework that derives from the changes at the end of 20th century. A general debate on how to deal with the changes occurring in urban development has left two alternatives: first, the city is seen not only as a product of change but also defined as being constituted of constant mutations. Thus, continuity is not seen as the opposite of change but both terms become synonyms of each other. This thinking leads to massive analytical problems as the profound category of "space" is no longer linked to the second key dimension of social science which is "time". Apparently, urban scholars tend to be much more sensitive to spatial dimensions of societal phenomena, as the time oriented perspective of analysis seems to be overwhelming in the general discourse on social science. In practice, urban theories have either had no particular interest in reflecting on the time related pattern of urban development or have framed their work rather poorly into debates on "modernity" or "postmodernity". Ed Soja, with his claim to put "space first," gives the space (over time) preference an elaborated concept of a "postmodern" view on the relationship between both fundamental categories of urban studies. This attempt to outline the timeless "post-modern geographies" (Soja 1988) of contemporary urbanity brings up new questions. Postmodernization can thus be understood as not em-bedded into a real historical development and becomes only a step forward in the theoretical framework (from the Chicago to the LA School, for example).

A second, history-oriented solution to reflect on the changed relationship between time and space relates back to a rather old approach of linking the two. Urban studies in this perspective often do not differ much from the classical view of historical work. In this regard, urban research has often not taken the long standing debate of historians into account. Rather, without being influenced by concepts of the linguistic turn in history, urban scholars tend to present their view on urban development as a traditional narration. Many works can be read/ cited to follow a dramaturgical line of representation with a line of narration wherein starting points, tensions ("crisis") and the arrival of a certain situation are crucial elements of representation. As historians have pointed out, narratives line beginnings and ends to construct some kind of sense for both the reader and the researcher. Whether it is imaginable to explore new ways of binding urban research into a time related structure of research and analysis is rather doubtful. Hayden White points to the fact that the "authority of the narration relates to the authority of the reality", but that every historical representations leaves at least two ways of telling the "plot" (White 1990, 33). Paul Ricœur (1984-1988) has been more profound in making considerations against the background of a wider philosophical theoretical framing in his three volumes on "Time and Narration". His main argument is that the time concept allows reproducing the structure of the events. Narratives reflect the linguistic dimension of time, and time is incorporated into the human language. In this way, not only language gives a symbolic meaning to historical events, but historical realities are also produced by their symbolic relation to human beings. In this way, Ricœur re-establishes "events" as major foci of historical research and thereby produces a firm contradiction to philosophies on history which define time in periods. Convincingly, he shows that those historical analyses (using Braudel's work on the *longue durée* of the Mediterranean world, 151-160) which try to avoid narrative structures by not paying attention to events and instead follow periodical approaches actually construct themselves as narrations. As a consequence, fictional elements are intrinsically needed to write narratives and cannot be left out since narrations do not reproduce an anonymous (and past) time but reflect the time-based embedding of both reader and historian. Time is aporetic, and there will always remain a friction between phenomenological and experienced time on one side and developing and cosmological time on the other. Time comes suddenly and remains hidden; it comes "shock-wise" to our consciousness as Walter Benjamin puts it.

For Ricœur, time finally remains a subject not to be researched in its very meaning. Urban studies cannot leave/ depart from this statement without considering its significance for the relationship to space. The "authority of reality" is also at stake with regard to its spatial dimension. Urban scholars like Lewis Mumford have underlined the significance of cities in history as such, but after the linguistic turn in history, a wider re-lecture of the classical assumptions on the role of cities in history can no longer only be "worked out" and addressed by case studies on single "historical places". Reflexive urban studies has to allow a differential construction of the narratives, take into account the way in which urban studies "invent history" and acknowledge the fact that changes can only be "told" alongside events. As this might be seen as a treat to any kind of an operationalising urban research, it is in fact a plea for a self-reflection of urban scholars on some basic points of attention. It leads to an examination of the language of urban studies and their use of metaphors, fictional elements, narrative structures and representations of experienced/total time. The urban scholar lives the city with all its events, memories, relationships, stories, pictures and symbols as well.

Narrating urban change, however, can use this incompleteness of analysis to identify important events and other elements necessary to let the authority of reality enter the imagination of the scholar as much as possible. Key concepts are mostly linked to one or the other kind of identified "turning", qualitative leaps, interruptions and discontinuity. In each case, it remains open to discussion whether continuity and change are in such a proportion that one of the two is seen as dominating. As Robert Beauregard has already questioned, this conception of urban life based on dual and antagonistic concepts leads to a limited scope of analytical, political and planning alternatives (1993). In reality, the urban complexity often leaves a hard challenge for the writer to tell a novelty which is looked at from the inside and when the "local" does not appear to be such big news at all. Confronted with the request for legitimacy of research and for many other reasons, urban studies work with the narrative structure from a certain point A to a more recent point B.

II.

This book could easily bear the title "A Decade of Urban Transformation", "Post-socialist Cities" or something alike. There is more than a gentle hesitation as to whether the recent state of transformation in cities addressed in this book still allows to rebind them to what was once "socialist" or under "communist rule". While it might have been adequate to reflect on the actual change in the loose framework of "cities after socialism" (Andrusz, Harloe and Szelenyi 1996), urban analysis can no longer only refer to the concept of post-socialism and transformation theory. Political, economical and social evidence clearly speaks against this. In 2004, many of the former post-socialist countries and cities have entered the European Union and others are soon due to be part of it. Other major discourses like globalization theories question the further dominance of the "post-socialism" approach to analyse life in the cities concerned and labelled as such.

In line with Ricœur, urban studies would necessarily reflect on the events and relevant actors which give the direction of research a starting point. In general, these selected points and persons of historical development are framed by two concepts only little sensible to both: modernity and transformation. While modernity stresses the importance of the processes of industrialization and societal changes in their run starting in the 18th century, transformation nominates a rather political and economic change in the 20th century. In a narrowed perspective, transformation is linked to the end of the socialist regimes in East and Central Europe. As this book samples case studies from those cities and countries normally viewed as part of the "post-communist" world, a further consideration on the very concept of "transformation" and its relationship to modernity should be taken into account. Urban studies cannot be seen disconnected from the overall debate in social science about these main forms of societal development.

15 years after the Fall of the Berlin Wall and the changes in most parts of the post-socialist countries, the first argument against the sampling of case studies under the common denominator "post-socialist cities" would be that there is little or no comparative level anymore (if there was at all) by simply referring to the bygone form of a regime which claimed to be socialist. A more fruitful comparison could be opened up by a thematic approach wherein West European cases would also be suitable and deliver a specific "urban" dimension otherwise overlapped by the occupancy with the concern of the national level of politics. This argument holds ground and certainly points to a research strategy that will produce important insights. Nevertheless, to what extent factors such as the socialist "heritage" and the national state of transition do not limit a purely urban comparison, remains an open question. On the other hand, it can be also said that the concentration on "post-socialist" cities creates an artificial basis of comparison as the process of transformation does not allow putting countries as diverse as Albania and Estonia, Poland and Croatia, into one category. In fact, this book wants to have a closer look at the state of transition but rejects the conceptual basis of a sort of intrinsic continuum which fixes cities and states down on a line between "totally transformed" and "only little changed" with all kinds of grey inbetween. As it has often been said before, this perspective on transformation suggests a certain path with a more or less well defined ending (western style, European Union compatible) and a dark starting point. Instead, transformation here is not seen as following a certain pattern of

change *alinea recta* but the cities of East and Central Europe are in a state with different times of transformation. Political, economical, social and cultural changes do not evolve separately, but they can be embedded into a specific local situation wherein one aspect of societal development is more outspoken in a condition of change than another. Cities in East and Central Europe thus follow their particular way of transition, and that is why, theoretically, we have to acknowledge a wider range of paths of urban transformation (see also Zapf 1996).

On the other hand, theory would be helpless, if one would consider transformation to be purely particular. Accepting the (partly unfinished) collapse of the Soviet-led block at the end of the eighties as one "event" which would allow asking the question of an intrinsic logic of development for those cities now opened up to the globalizing world, leads to the Hegelian request to consider "the final purpose of research of transformation" (Hopfmann and Wolf 2001). Transformation can be defined as a process that is significantly different than "social change" and modernity in certain ways: First of all, it is a politically perceived way of transition and thus reacts to the intention of actors. Secondly, transformation processes affect all levels and aspects of society. In this way, much literature on transformation suffers from the reluctance to take other than political or economical processes into account. As Polanyi (2001), in his earlier book on "The Great Transformation," worked out the consequences of the emergence of the bourgeois/civic society for all other parts, transformation research requires a holistic approach encapturing different societal layers. Thirdly, transformation research has to be regarded as a process which can reach a certain "end" but which remains open with regard to its outcome (Mayntz 1998). In this sense, many traditional approaches (like Habermas 1990) which suggest a conversion from "socialism to market economy/capitalism" and a "catch up race" with western democracy should be reconsidered seriously (Reißig 1998).

III.

Besides the ambitious intention to cover "society" as such, researching transformation with a theoretical ambition faces two particular difficulties. First, transformation research aims at formulating a theoretical approach which has lost significance with the so called end of ideology. In general, the everyday life of science is dominated by middle range theories which have some loose contact to a wider debate on certain issues, but which allow to outline methodological strategies of a limited time and resource budget. This is clearly not the case with a theoretical ambition which intends to testify whether "transformation" is still a valuable concept in understanding changes in the concerned cities. Secondly, methodologies deriving from limited fields of transformation operating with middle or short range theories have not delivered a specific profile of research (Schmid/Weihrich 2001). Model forming has been used to overcome the regionalizatlon of transformation, common to the sampling of case studies. Although this book too does not deliver an innovative methodological strategy in this sense, modelling has also not been regarded to fulfil the intention of the transformation research defined above. Models are used to have a systematic comparison with a principally limited number of factors that can be taken into account as producing evident influence under different circumstances (Schmid 1996, 265). In essence, modelling in social science allows recognizing a factor in one examined situation as being of importance and which lacks the same significance in another model case. In an ideal research condition, both models approximate each other and thereby a progress in theory can be formulated, as a critic on the knowledge *ex ante* becomes possible.

A pre-condition to progress in transformation research is a certain theoretical clarity about the paradigm integrated in the larger analytical framework. This would require a decisive point of departure regarding competing approaches which can be worked out to outweigh their evidence in explaining a general mode of transformation (Müller 2001). A principle discussion remains whether a "city" as such would offer to be a model for use in this neo-Popperian design of knowledge generation. On first sight, cities vary unimaginably so that only general factors like density, heterogeneity and (high) number (Wirth 1938) would allow us to limit the outlines of a city-based comparative research. With these preconditions, research could easily bring in two factors measurable on a timely perspective signifying the relevance of a competing paradigm. In practice, however, two cities as ideal as considered here cannot be found. Further limitation and constraint to the selection of comparable case studies might be seen as a way-out for the dilemma in this *in vivo* research. But a closer look disillusions this approach as the Wirth factors for urban life are not at all clear and comparable. What a high number of inhabitants is, can differ extremely in various national contexts if one does not look at this variable in a static or ontological way. European cities are often, in comparison to mega-cities in the rest of the world, only of a small size. However, nobody would question that European cities can be considered to embody much of what we normally would regard as being "urban", with an economic welfare, social cohesion and cultural values (Jayne 2005). If one, therefore, leaves the methodological approach of model forming behind, it is difficult to think of an adequate framework for researching cities in transformation even until now, and especially due to the "post-socialist" changes in East and Central European states. In comparative studies on the sectoral transfer of institutions in East Germany, the term "path dependency" has been established to link the micro and meso level of processes in different economic sectors (Lehmbruch 1998). These studies have the advantage of working with a limited and more or less defined "policy domain" which one cannot trace to the question of the "urban;" where other operative terms like "issue area", "arena", "policy community" would not cover the whole range of societal aspects one usually has in mind while talking about the city. A solution here might be to have sectors defined in cities to make them comparable. The outcome, however, for innovating knowledge on the macro-level of urban society is limited in its range of explanations.

IV.

Today, transformation theories have achieved a certain age of maturity. After neo-liberal approaches in line with a modernization discourse have put particularities aside (and thereby concluded with "regional studies"), a "second generation of theories" has entered the debate in social science (Bönker, Müller and Pickel 2002). A wider acceptance of cross-disciplinary approaches can be observed and, with the inclusion of many different aspects of transformation societies, the complexity and dif-ference in time horizons of these processes becomes increasingly visible: Neither the focus on the state (dominant in analysis of the political transformation), nor on the market (as in the classical Hayekian dilemma left to the economic transformation discourse) has been dis-solved to make way for a new – sociological ? – paradigm; however society as such has gained attention. Eisenstadt's theory of "multiple mo-dernities" (2002, see also Sachsenmeier 2002) has been also received and used as a fruitful concept to explain the so-called "post-socialist crisis" (Müller 1998), not foreseen and unexplainable by the rigorous first generation of transformation theories. Especially, the resurrection of nationalism has been a major challenge to the hitherto theoretisation of transformation. With particular attention to the concept of collective identities (Spohn 2002, Jackson 2004), a historical-sociological ap-proach, with the inclusion of an analysis of the relationship between de-velopmental trajectories and interrelated social structures and social actors, seems to address the most powerful societal paths of trans-formation until now.

The urban focus, thus, needs to be redirected to a theoretical framework that encounters the new openness of transformation theories and which also reflects the variety of levels, macro-meso-micro relationships, in-stitutions of different sizes and range, (im)balances of power, fluidity and continuity of societal structures and networks, local absent and global present societal actors in the city. Territoriality, however, has only been discussed indirectly in theories of multiple modernities. Cultural differences, in the widest sense, have been addressed by Eisenstadt as being part of the outer-European regions (Allardt 2002). Besides the question whether this concept remains valuable for addressing the differences between national and urban cultures in East and West European cities, the very term of modernity does not reflect the obvious changes that are occurring world-wide. One could point to the technological innovation causing (or allowing) new forms of social and geographical behaviour and thus producing new landscapes of power, society and culture. Modernization has become different in its character. Consequences of modernity are unintended, unplanned and beyond the national framework. Modernity has become, in the words of authors like Ulrich Beck and others, reflexive (Beck 1998). With the promotion of a "second modernity," the research agenda has also shifted towards other forms of "making (world) society". And finally the debate on the (cultural) dimension of globalization questions the concept of a re-definition of modernity in a sense that there are several competing but territorially limited modernities. With regard to the transformation theory, we can see that East and Central European cities are not simply transforming from one system to another but are caught in a globalizing process that overlaps, constrains, fosters and hinders those aspects of transformation addressed by the classical transformation theory, i.e. the establishment of a market economy and a liberal democracy.

Research on "post-socialist cities" therefore remains not only confronted with questions like how far transformation has reached, what has been achieved and where are the obstacles. It is becoming increasingly doubtful if the observed changes are due to transformation any longer. How much – instead of how far – is transformation shaping the life world of the cities in East and Central Europe? The counter-assumption and the alternative theoretical framework of analysis is globalization, while both concepts remain to be discussed with their relationship to modernity. A first hypothesis for future research could define these relationships as devolving from a modern society to a globalizing/reflexive city via a transformed state and market.

References:

Allart, E. (2002) The Questional Blessings of the Modernization Concept. In: Adamski, W.; Machonin, P.; Zapf. W. (eds.) Structural Change and Modernization in Post-Socialist Societies. Hamburg: Krämer.

Andrusz, G.; Harloe, M. and Szelenyi, I. (eds.) (1996) Cities after Socialism: Urban and Regional Change and Conflict in Post-Socialist Societies. Oxford: Blackwell.

Beck, U. (1998) Democracies Without Enemies. Cambridge: Polity Press.

Beauregard, R. A. (1993) Descendants of Ascendant Cities and Other Urban Dualities. In: Journal of Urban Affairs. No. 3, 217-229.

Bönker, F.; Müller, K. and Picle, A. (2002) Cross-Disciplinary Approaches to Post-Communist Transformation: Context and Agenda. In: Bönker, F.; Müller, K. and Picle, A. (eds.) Post-Communist Transformation and the Social Science. Cross-Disciplinary Approaches. Lanham et al.: Rowman & Littlefield.

Eisenstadt, S. N. (2002) Multiple Modernities. New Brunswick: Transaction.

Greskovits, B. (2002) The Path-Dependency of Transitology. In: Bönker, F.; Müller, K. and Picle, A. (eds) Post-Communist Transformation and the Social Science. Cross-Disciplinary Approaches. Lanham et al.: Rowman & Littlefield.

Habermas, J. (1990) Die nachholende Revolution. Frankfurt: Suhrkamp.

Hopfmann, A.; Wolf, M. (2001) Was heißt und zu welchem Ende betreibt man Transformationsforschung? In: Hopfmann, A.; Wolf, M. (eds.) Transformationstheorie – Stand, Defizite, Perspektiven. Münster: LIT.

Illner, M. (2003) Devolution of Government in Ex-Communist Countries: Some Explanatory Frameworks. In: Baldersheim, H.; Illner, M. And Wollmann, H. (eds.) Local Democracy in Post-Communist Europe. Opladen: Leske+Budrich.

Jackson, L. (2004) Nationality, Citizenship and Identity. In: Bradshaw, M. and Stenning, A. (eds.) East Central Europe and the Former Soviet Union. The Post-Socialist States. Harlow. Pearson.

Jayne, M. (ed.) (2005) Small cities: Urban Experience Beyond the Metropolis. London: Routledge.

Juchler, J. (2002) Is „Modernization" Enough? In: Adamski, W.; Machonin, P.; Zapf. W. (eds.) Structural Change and Modernization in Post-Socialist Societies. Hamburg: Krämer.

Lehmbruch, G. (1998) Zwischen Institutionentransfer und Eigendynamik: Sektorale Transformationspfade und ihre Bestimmungsgründe. In: Czada, R. and Lehmbruch, G. (eds.) Transformationspfade in Ostdeutschland. Beiträge zur sektoralen Vereinigungspolitik.

Mayntz,. R. (1998) Soziale Diskunitäten: Erscheinungsformen und Ursachen,. In: Hierholzer, K. and Wittmann, H.-G. (eds) Phasensprünge und Stetigkeit in der natürlichen und kulturellen Welt. Stuttgart: Wissenschaftliche Verlagsgesellschaft.

Müller, K. (ed.) (1998) Postsozialistische Krisen. Opladen: Leske+Budrich.

-, (2001) Konkurrierende Paradigmen der Transformation. In: Hopfmann, A.; Wolf, M. (eds.) Transformationstheorie – Stand, Defizite, Perspektiven. Münster: LIT.

Polanyi, K. (2001) The Great Transformation. Boston: Beacon Press.

Pickel, A. (2001) Transformationspolitik, Transformationstheorie und die Rolle der Sozialwissenschaften. In: Hopfmann, A.; Wolf, M. (eds.) Transformationstheorie – Stand, Defizite, Perspektiven. Münster: LIT.

-, and True, J. (2002) Global, Transnational. and National Change Mechanisms: Bridging International and Comparative Approaches to Post-Communist Transformation. In: Bönker, F.; Müller, K. and Picle, A. (eds.) Post-Communist Transformation and the Social Science. Cross-Disciplinary Approaches. Lanham et al.: Rowman & Littlefield.

Reißig, R. (1998) Transformationsforschung: Gewinne, Desiderate und Perspektiven. In: Politische Vierteljahresschrift, 2, 301-328.

Ricœur, P. (1984-1988) Time and Narration. Three volumes. Chicago University Press.

Sachsenmeier, D. (2002) Reflections on multiple modernities. Leiden: Brill.

Schmid, M. (1996) Rationalität und Theoriebildung. Studien zu Karl Poppers Methodologie der Sozialwissenschaften. Amsterdam: Rodopi.

-,   and Weihrich, M. (2001) Die Wende und ihre Theorien – eine modellogische Kritik der soziologischen Transformationsforschung. In: Hopfmann, A.; Wolf, M. (eds.) Transformationstheorie – Stand, Defizite, Perspektiven. Münster: LIT.

Soja, E. (1988) Postmodern Geographies: the Reassertion of Space in Critical Social Theory. London: Verso.

Spohn, W. (2002) European East-West Integration, Nation-building and National Identities: The Reconstruction of German-Polish Relations. Frankfurt/Oder: FIT.

Stenniing, A. (2004) Urban Change and the Localities. In: Bradshaw, M. and Stenning, A. (eds.) East Central Europe and the Former Soviet Union. The Post-Socialist States. Harlow et al.: Pearson.

White, H. (1990) Die Bedeutung der Form. Erzählstrukturen in der Geschichts-schreibung.

Wirth, L. (1938) Urbanism as a Way of Life. In: American Journal of Sociology 44, 1-24

Zapf, W. (1996) Die Modernisierungstheorie und unterschiedliche Pfade der gesell-schaftlichen Entwicklung. In: Leviathan, 1, 63-77

Effects of transition to a knowledge-based society on the Hungarian regional development

Ákos Szépvölgyi

It is a widely accepted both in the academic community and among practitioners that we are moving towards a knowledge- and information-based economy. It represents a quite new period both in the economic and social development, and in the co-operation of involved countries.

Co-operation of economic corporations has been increasing since the first decades of the 20th century, due to the mutual economic benefits arising from co-operation. These horizontal forms of collaboration among firms that working in the same sectors is still developing, but all the same vertical co-operations of different spatial levels come to the front (Kocsis – Szabó 2000). In our view, these co-operations seems to be in close connection with the diffusion of information and communication technologies. These technologies were emerged in the early nineties when the new and widespread infrustructural development made the integration of different economic and social activities possible (Gáspár 1999).

The promotion of these co-operations can originate in the potential of flexibility and continuous adaptation to market processes. Competitiveness of a spatial unit can be increased either directly, through economic collaborations or indirecly, through educational, cultural and other social processes. That is why these processes may change the economic and social mechanisms, as well as the characteristics of regional and urban development. In this way, the economic and social cooperation become more intensive as compared to previous decades, and the regional competitiveness and innovation ability turned into new directions.

For this reason, the Hungarian regional science – in line with international tendencies – has a growing interest in studying spatial relations of this phenomenon. Its focal point is that human resources and resource-based economic processes are pushing into the background, while the knowledge- and information-intensive economic and social networks are coming to the front of economic and social processes.

We suppose in this study that the new economic and social mechanisms may change the regional competitiveness and restructure the spatial differences of Hungarian regions and their centres. However, it will be the case only, if the above mentioned technical and human infrastructural preconditions are given.

This paper is aimed at describing the effects of transition to a knowledge-based economy on the "traditional" inequalities of seven Hungarian regions. To reach this goal we applied two basic methods for investigations. The first method involves the assessment of national[1] e-readiness i.e. to establish how ready a society to benefit from the in-formation technology is. The second one is the comparison of competitiveness of the seven Hungarian regions and their centres by con-structing a coherent, general index of comparison.

In principle, in this paper we try to find answer to the following question: Do these new processes strengthen the cohesion among and within Hungarian regions in the present state of their development?

E-readiness of Hungary

The development of the knowledge- and information-based economy is partly based on information and communication technologies. However, ICT environment is a necessary, but not sufficient condition for the successful development of a knowledge-based economy (Mako et al 2003). Therefore, a short statistical review of PC penetration, Internet access and Internet costs seems to be very important to establish the e-readiness of Hungary.

The most widely used building element of the information infrastructure is computer availability. The number of computers available in Hungary is continuously growing. However, it is still low, amounting 9 PCs/1000 capita being about 25% of the EU average. Data on the basic information and communication infrastructure of the seven Hungarian regions (Fig. 1) are shown in Table 1.

Figure 1: Regions and their centres in Hungary

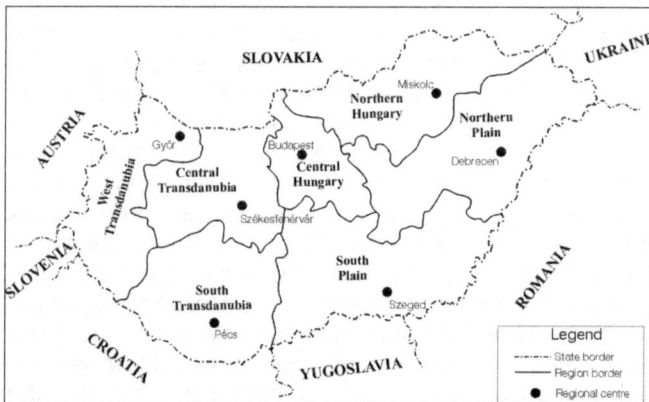

Source: edited by the author

---

[1] E-readiness assessments are only available at national level, because there has been only aggregated data of the Hungarian Central Statistical Agency with no spatial decomposition.

Table 1: Modern information and communications facilities in households by regions (% of households)

Regions	Internet access	PC	Cable television	Wired phone	Mobile phone
Central Hungary	6.9	19.7	62.4	79.4	24.5
Central Transdanubia	5.6	15.5	56.6	75.9	15.2
West Transdanubia	5.4	15.0	51.1	78.4	16.3
South Transdanubia	2.6	12.8	49.2	68.3	11.4
Northern Hungary	2.0	13.1	43.4	67.8	11.5
Northern Plain	3.5	11.3	24.7	62.7	10.8
South Plain	3.0	10.8	33.4	65.0	11.7
Average	4.8	14.4	40.3	71.8	17.0

Source: Hungarian Central Statistical Agency, Budapest 2002.

The level of Internet access shows a quite similar picture. The 68 Internet Service Providers have more than 500000 subscribers (about 5% of total population) in 2003, being higher of 41% as compared to 2001.

There are perceptible differences in the type of Internet connections among the existing communication channels if we compare Hungary to EU. The telephony and telecommunications infrastructure is of outstanding importance in Hungary. It is the main channel for computer communications with a share of 92%. Nevertheless, this is the slowest way of data transfer. The broadband penetration is below 1% in Hungary. These figures are 35% and 40%, respectively, in the EU countries.

The costs of Internet access are different even in the EU countries. Sweden, Finland and Ireland have most favourable positions: the Internet costs in these countries are below the EU average (Fig. 2). In these countries, the costs are one fourth of the Hungarian tariff (highest in EU and AC). The relatively high access costs are impeding the widespread use of Internet in Hungary.

Figure 2: Costs of Internet access in 2000 (EU average =100)

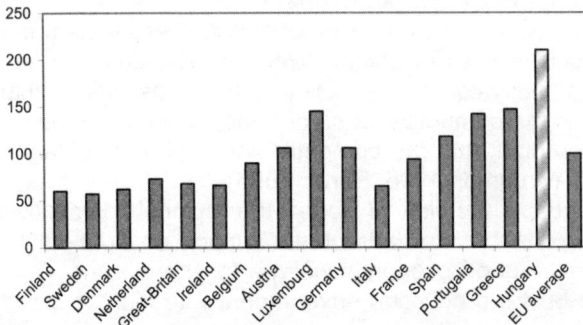

Source: European Survey of Information Society Projects and Actions, Brussels, 2000.

Over the last couple of years a number of 'e-readiness' assessment tools have been developed. These tools use wide variation of measuring methods with widely varying results (Comparison of E-Readiness... 2001). They analyse not only the abovementioned infrastructure, but the access, applications and services, the enablers (policy, privacy, security and ubiquity), the e-business climate and the human capital and awareness, as well. Thus, so they give a rather complete picture about e-readiness.

IDC-World Times created one of the well-known e-readiness rankings. Its results show that Hungary is in the 29th position among the 55 investigated countries. This result can be explained by the continuous shortfall of competition in the field of infrastructural development and the lack of aligned governmental strategy in the second half of the last decade[2]. Financial Times published another interesting ranking in 2001 for the OECD countries (Marsh 2001). Hungary seizes a very good (6th) position in this survey, by going before - among others - Japan, Germany or UK. The induction points out that this position is rooted from economic opening (for example majority of foreign share in processing industry). Finally, the Economic Intelligence Unit and the Pyramid Research also created their rankings aligning the surveyed countries. Hungary goes to the third group (from four), which means that the country had been classified into e-economy followers along with the CEE countries and other half-peripheral Asian and South American countries.

Some indicators and some of the above rankings show positive change and quite good position. However, Hungary still does not seem to be ready to adapt new conditions. In spite of current situation, adaptation of the country may improve in the near future. The government created and started many programs to achieve this goal in the past three years. In view of this processes, analysis of spatial differences seems to be of high importance.

Regional and urban competitiveness

Competitiveness receives growing attention. Researchers are often concerned about the loss of competitiveness. The desire to improve competitiveness motivates many policy actions, as well. What is mostly referred to is the competitiveness of firms, nations or other spatial units. We should remark that the competitiveness of firms differs from that of spatial units (Krugman 1996; Porter 1996).

This study adopts the view of Porter: the regional competitiveness is the ability of regions to foster, attract and support economic activity in order to ensure quite good economic welfare for the citizens. Competitive regions have built a production environment with high accessibility. It per-

---

[2] Source: IDC-World Information Society Index; www.worldpaper.com

petuates and attracts new production factors, and results in a fostering economy. These factors include skilled labour, innovative entrepreneurs and footloose capital. Success in attracting these factors creates external economies, such as agglomeration and localisation benefits, that further enhance the economic fortune of a region.

Based on this approach a great number of regional studies were published on competitiveness in the last decade (Freeman 1990; Krugman 1995). A common feature of these studies is that they tend to concentrate on some restricted aspects of competitiveness rather than providing an overall and coherent, general index. Moreover, there have been only few attempts for incorporating knowledge-based businesses as factors of spatial competitiveness. Therefore, in constructing the index we integrated and completed the results of the comparison of competitiveness across regions, including the indicator of knowledge-based businesses, created by Phil Cooke.

The investigated indicators were (i) business density, knowledge-based businesses[3] and employment rate as input measures, (ii) investments as an output measure, together with (iii) VAT and unemployment rate as outcome measures.

In this work, we balanced the indicators as above to ensure their comparability. For this reason, the three groups of indicators had equal weights. In a similar way, the individual indicators within groups also had equal weights. The weighting changes neither the information content of the indicators, nor their correlations. In this way, we can calculate the competitiveness index. It is important to note that the indicator value of 100 refers to the whole country (national average).

Table 2 shows the competitiveness indexes calculated for seven Hungarian regions (for legends Fig. 1 is referred).

Table 2: Indexes of regional competitiveness (Hungary=100)

	HU	CTD	NTD	CHU	STD	NHU	NP	SP
Business density	11,1	10,6	11,1	15,7	10,2	7,9	8,1	9,5
Investment	33,3	34,1	44,0	48,6	22,2	24,5	22,7	19,3
VAT	16,7	10,5	15,3	21,5	13,8	13,9	13,3	13,6
Employment	11,1	12,3	12,8	12,7	10,5	9,7	9,7	11,0
Unemployment rate	16,7	22,1	22,7	22,1	12,2	11,2	12,2	17,6
Knowledge-based economy	11,1	6,8	6,6	17,7	7,2	6,6	6,8	6,8
Competitiveness index	100	96,4	112,4	138,3	76,0	73,7	72,8	77,8

---

[3] To measure it, we followed the definition of OECD (1999) covering all high technology manufacturing and knowledge-based services. To classify the businesses, we used the nomenclature of KSH (Hungarian Central Statistical Agency) which allows aggregated comparison.

Comparison of the regional and the urban indexes makes possible to show the position of each region and the regional centres in the country. Using this concept, this section aims to introduce the main characteristics of spatial competitiveness in the investigated regions and cities.
The competitiveness indexes of regions show visible differences. The values for the investigated regions range from 72.8 to 138.3, which indicate their position within Hungary. Thus, four regions show great disadvantages over the country, and only three of them have competitive advantages in general terms.
The most important result of our investigation is that only two indexes, namely investments and employment exhibit great correlate with the competitiveness index at regional level. This means that regions of high level of investments and employment tend to be more competitive.
Not only the regions, but also the surveyed cities show obvious differences in the competitiveness index (Table 3). However, all cities possess significant competitive advantages over the country. Thus, the economic competitiveness in the investigated regions weakly correlates with the concentration of knowledge-based businesses.

Table 3: Competitiveness indexes of selected cities (Hungary=100)

	HU	Szfvár	Győr	Budapest	Pécs	Miskolc	Debr.	Szeged
Business density	11,1	16,9	16,2	18,7	15,3	11,2	12,2	14,3
Investment	33,3	39,4	18,6	48,6	11,7	18,7	19,0	19,3
VAT	16,7	54,4	77,8	79,9	61,1	54,4	57,2	62,0
Employment	11,1	13,7	13,2	13,4	11,3	10,0	11,0	11,4
Unemployment rate	16,7	36,6	36,6	38,1	29,7	16,4	23,2	25,7
Knowledge-based economy	11,1	13,1	10,6	22,5	9,8	8,6	9,4	12,4
Competitiveness index	100	174,1	173,0	221,2	138,9	119,3	132,1	145,2

Legend: Szfvár = Székesfehérvár; Debr. = Debrecen

The aggregated competitiveness indexes for the surveyed cities vary from 119.3 to 221.2. It indicates that the differences in competitiveness are more significant at city level than at regional level.
Analysis of data in Table 3 revealed some interesting differences at city level, as well. In Székesfehérvár, the role of knowledge-based businesses having basic influence on the competitiveness index is not as strong as that of economic capacity. However, it does not necessarily mean a disadvantage, because the high concentration of investments and the low level of unemployment may counterbalance it. Quite similar situation can be observed in Győr (one of the well-developed cities of Hungary), where the low role of knowledge-based businesses is counterbalanced by the high level of VAT payment and the low level of unemployment. On the contrary, a quite developed knowledge-based business sector was found in Szeged. Here the third level education repre-

sents a dominant force, but the other investigated sub-indexes (business density and employment) shows that economic capacity of Szeged is quite underdeveloped.

Data presented in this work illustrate that position of some regions greatly differs from that of its centre, while others have relatively good positions for the whole region. Comparing the positions of regions and the cities in national scale, Central Hungary, Western-Hungary and Central-Transdanubia have the most favourable positions. These regions seem to have the most competitive centres. On the other hand, a quite competitive city, like Szeged is a centre of an underdeveloped region. Southern-Plain together with Northern-Plain and Northern-Hungary seem to be underdeveloped and non-competitive regions. Actually, they can be regarded as peripheral regions of the country. Therefore, in terms of regional competitiveness, mobilisation of internal resources (such as the growth potential of their centre) seems to be of crucial importance.

Conclusions

This work gives an overview on the present situation of knowledge- and information - based economy in Hungary, and on its effects to inter- and intraregional economic cohesion, as well. We summarize the most important findings of our study as follows:

The present technological and social readiness seems to be un-satisfactory in Hungary for adapting new processes. In spite of the quite dynamic development and some new governmental programs, the lack of readiness sets back the spreading of knowledge- and information-based economic sectors.

Analysis of spatial effects of these processes shows that the regional concentration of information-intensive enterprises does not coincide with regional economic performance in all cases. The traditional economic indexes do not influence definitely the spreading and development of information-intensive sectors. Some other factors like third level education and research and development capacities may stimulate the development, e.g. by facilitating the establishment of spin-off companies.

The powerful economic concentration seems to be in typical future. The high competitiveness indexes of regional centres refer to it. The spill-over effects of well-developed regional centres still do not prevail. Moreover, the information-intensive activities do not mean real tension even in the local economies.

Our results confirmed that the number of knowledge-intensive enterprises is not the only decisive factor in Hungary in terms economic competitiveness. Other factors like investment, unemployment and business density have crucial roles, as well.

To sum it up: development of knowledge- and information-intensive economic activities does not increase inter- and intra-regional cohesion in

Hungary for the time being. The new working organisations and novel collaboration methods did not decrease the differences in the spatial development of the country up to now.

References:
Comparison of E-Readiness Assessment Models. Final draft, v. 2.13, 14 March 2001. www.bridges.org
Cooke, Ph.; Clifton, N.; Huggins, R. (2001) Competitiveness and the Knowledge Economy: the UK in Global, Regional and Local Context. Cardiff: Institute for Advanced Studies – University of Wales, 22.
Freeman, C. (1990) Economics of Innovation. (International Library of Critical Writings in Economics) Brookfield (USA): Edwards Elger.
Gáspár, B. (1999) A számítógépes hálózatok hatása a gazdasági életre. PhD dolgozat, BKE, Budapest.
Kocsis, É.; Szabó, K. (2000) A posztmodern vállalat. Tanulás és hálózatosodás az új gazdaságban. Oktatási Minisztérium, Budapest.
Krugman, P. (1995) Development, Geography and economic development. MIT Press, Cambridge, UK.
Krugman, P. (1996) Making Sense of the Competitiveness Debate, Oxford Review of Econonomic Policy, No.2.
Makó, Cs.; Illéssy, M.; Szépvölgyi, Á.; Tamási, P. (2003) Technology, Economy and Diversity in the Periphery. Wokpackage 5. – Regional Integration. Draft.
Marsch, P. (2001) New Millennium's winners and losers. Financial Times, 19th October.
Porter, M.E. (1996) Competitive advantage, agglomeration economies, and regional policy. International Regional Science Review. 1-2.

New Relationships between the Metropolis and the Region in Information Economy: Warsaw Metropolitan Region – A Case Study[1]

Maciej Smętkowski

The paper describes the impact of the metropolisation process on regional development. In its initial part, examples of the world city network are provided, along with selected theoretical concepts explaining this phenomenon. Further, the metropolisation process is described, followed by the description of the model of changes occurring in the relations between the metropolis and the region. Subsequently, the author examines the hypothesis that the interrelationships between the metropolis and the region are becoming relatively weaker, therefore the hinterland plays a decreasing role in the metropolis development process. This, in turn, leads to the marginalisation of the surrounding region and an increase of disparities in the level of development between the core (metropolis) and the periphery (hinterland). The paper focuses on the Warsaw metropolitan region and the following phenomena: internationalisation of economic activity, changes in the regional migration patterns and the polarisation process within the metropolitan region related to contemporary metropolisation processes, which can nowadays be observed in Poland.

1. The metropolisation process

Contemporary economy is more and more frequently dubbed "information economy", particularly in highly developed countries. This is due to the increasing role of information in production and management processes (Cf. Castells 1989). Information is becoming a production factor, in addition to the traditional ones: land, labour and capital. The competitiveness of enterprises and territorial systems depends on the creation of new knowledge, access to, and processing of information. The issue of competitiveness should be seen in the global context, since openness to flows of information and capital, as well as internationalisation of labour market, driven by the operations of transational corporations, is becoming a feature of contemporary economy (Cf. e.g. Gorzelak, Jałowiecki, 2000). Metropolises, by taking over management and control functions of the global economy, are becoming centres of economic development (in lieu of urban and industrial agglomerations[2] in in-

---

[1] Research financed by the State Committee for Scientific Research (KBN) as part of grant no. 2 H02C 016 23.
[2] Unlike the concept of agglomeration, use of the term „metropolis", firstly, signals the functional approach in delineating its range (the metropolitan area), contrary to the morphological approach (related to land use), which is used most frequently in the case of agglomeration. Secondly, the significance of the service sector in the city's

33

dustrial economy). Kukliński (2000) observes that it is metropolises, *"core centres of the information society's global space"*, that are the main carriers of globalisation processes, in addition to transnational corporations. Numerous examples in evidence of the formation of a world city network can be found, as well as new theoretical concepts explaining this phenomenon, which may be seen as a confirmation of the increasing role of the metropolis[3].

1.1. Selected examples confirming the formation of a world city network

Contemporary urban development processes are of a unique nature and are often referred to as "megalopolisation", since the population is more and more strongly concentrated in multi-million cities and the surrounding urban complexes. The world's nineteen largest urban complexes have either exceeded or are approaching a population of ten million. Besides these mega-cities, the number of cities with a population in excess of one million is growing steadily. There were 227 such cities in 1997, with nearly two thirds of them situated in developing countries (Cf. Scott 2000).

Nonetheless, it seems that the essence of the metropolisation process is not an increase in the population living in huge urban complexes (especially in view of the fact that the process is observable mainly in developing countries). Here, the aforementioned concentration of the control functions of global economy is the decisive factor, as well as an increased intensity and significance of relations between metropolises (Cf. Sassen 2000). On the one hand, a multi-centre world city network is emerging, and on the other – strongly integrated regional subsystems of cities (e.g. Randstad Holland). The existence of a world city network would not be possible without an extremely efficient network of transport connections and telecommunication links. Rimmer (2000) writes about the fourth "revolution in logistics", which may be summarised as the existence of a new, dense, multi-layer transport network, comprising fast but not very capacious connections between the exchange centres – the road network along with traffic control and satellite monitoring systems, as well as telecommunication and aviation networks. Huge cities, connecting the regional (national) economic environment with the global economy function as hubs in this network. As a result, these huge cities – metropolises – become attractive locations for transnational corporations

---

economy is emphasised, as opposed to industry, which used to play a leading part in urban and industrial agglomerations.

[3] Many examples are provided by studies within Globalization and World City Study Group and Network (GAWOC) http://www.lbro.ac.uk

and companies offering specialised services in a global dimension, as well as centres of the global capital market.

What factors are required so that a city could be called a metropolis? Many authors agree with the opinion that metropolises are cities which have been able to create a suitable environment for innovation, bringing together economic, technological, institutional and social relations for the development of the information sector. Jałowiecki (2000, p.33; after Bassand, 1994) outlined the conditions necessary in this respect. The most frequently adopted criterion of the metropolitan character of a city is the population around one million. Other factors include:

- a well-developed service sector (mainly institutions and services related to financial services, mass-media, telecommunications, management of the economy, science and research, art, culture, as well as public administration);
- potential for innovation (institutions related to the generation and processing of information: universities, research institutes, laboratories);
- distinctive character of the location (cultural and architecture assets, etc.).

1.2. The world city network – a theoretical approach

It has been mentioned above that intense interrelationships within the world city network and links between this network and certain sectors of the respective national economies constitute characteristic features of metropolises. Thinking of huge cities as a complementary network and distinguishing world cities can be attributed to Friedmann[4] (quoted after Soja, 2000: pp.219-221), who was the first to formulate the world city hypothesis. The key assertions of the hypothesis were the following:

- the form and the scope of the city's integration with the global economy and the functions attributed to the city in the global division of labour determine all structural changes occurring in this city;
- the biggest cities are used by international capital as basic hubs of spatial organisation of production and as sales markets. The capital is concentrated mainly in world cities. The resultant network of relationships leads to the emergence of a hierarchical network of world cities;
- global control functions are reflected in the structure and dynamics of the production sector and in the employment structure of the cities (the service sector will be the main source of employment);
- world cities are the targets of both domestic and international migration;
- the emergence of world cities leads to spatial and social polarisation and entails social costs, which are impossible to bear, notably by developing countries.

---

[4] J. Friedmann, 1986, The world city hypothesis, Development and Change no. 17(1).

The advancement of globalisation processes has led to the formulation of the world city hypothesis and transforming it into the concept of the global city. This concept was developed by Sassen (1991), who perceived the strategic role of huge cities in the conditions of spatial deconcentration of capital and production, with simultaneously increasing global integration. In addition to the traditional roles of huge global cities – global trade and banking - she added new ones, namely:

- cities as decision centres of the global economy;
- cities as key locations of companies offering specialised services (FIRE)[5], which superseded the production sector;
- cities as leading locations of high-tech industries and generators of innovation;
- cities as sales markets for state-of-the-art products and innovations.

This model of the global city is built around six hypotheses (Sassen, 2000). Firstly, geographic deconcentration of business activity, coupled with the increasing integration of various types of activity, is the main factor responsible for the growing importance of central functions (relating to management, coordination, service and finance). These central functions are becoming so complex and intricate that huge enterprises outsource them to specialised service companies, dealing with such types of activity as accounting, legal services, public relations, IT and telecommunications. Owing to the specific character of such specialised services, they need a suitable information environment that only large cities can offer. At the same time, the more services are outsourced by enterprises, the more freely they can choose locations for their offices, as they do not need an advanced information environment, unlike service companies. On the other hand, service companies providing global services have to open their branch offices in big cities, which leads to an enhanced exchange within the world city network. As a result, the number of qualified specialists and innovative enterprises in huge cities is growing, which produces increased social and economic inequalities and polarisation of urban space.

Castells' space of flows theory (1998) can be seen as a generalisation of the global city theory; it is the product of the author's many years of research on social space. The basic tenet of his theory is the assertion that contemporary society is organised around flows: of capital, information, perceptions, sounds and symbols. According to Castells, these flows no longer form a part of the society's organisation, but constitute a process that has pervaded the economy, politics and space. The new form of space, which controls and shapes the network society: the space of flows,

---

[5] FIRE (finance, insurance and real estate).

can be regarded as a material manifestation of these processes. This space consists of three layers (Castells, 1998, p. 412-416):

- **the first (technical) layer is made up by the network of electronic flows;**

The network of flows is a new form of space, in which no location exists until it is defined by flows. This does not mean that locations no longer exist; it means that their significance depends on the network. The structure of the space of flows is not determined by locations, but by a network of interrelationships.

- **the second (spatial) layer is made up of flow hubs;**

Even though the flow space is based on electronic networks, it connects specific locations. Some of them are huge exchange hubs performing an overriding and coordinating role, while other hubs in the network perform functions organising the local environment. The world city network is hierarchical in nature. Global financial centres can serve as an example of a network of flows. Apart from global cities at the pinnacle of the network's hierarchy, there exist hubs of continental, national and regional economies, through which they connect with the global network. These hubs must ensure an adequate technical infrastructure, a well-developed service sector, qualified personnel and a suitable living environment.

- **the third (social) layer is made up of the spatial organisation of the elites controlling the network.**

The metropolitan class is also a part of the space of flows (Jałowiecki, 2000); it comprises specialists whose main asset is knowledge. The metropolitan class is cosmopolitan, while the masses are local. This class has specific spatial requirements and a distinct lifestyle. Its members, owing to their knowledge and the resulting good financial standing, lead cosmopolitan lifestyles, try to keep up with the global trends in fashion, including technology (cellular phones, Internet, etc.). Its representatives travel a lot, live in luxurious conditions and enjoy sophisticated entertainments. At the same time, this class is in control of global flows and thereby has a decisive influence on the process shaping the face of the economy, society and space.

2. The metropolis – the region relationship

An analysis of the impact of the metropolisation process on regional development invites several questions helping to structure these considerations. The questions are the following: what is the impact of the metropolitan process on the regional environment (hinterland) of huge cities ? Which processes will prevail: spread effects or backwash effects concerning the development resources ?[6] And, ultimately, will it lead to levelling the disparities in the development level between the city and the region or to the polarisation of development ?

2.1. The regional aspect of the metropolisation process

Another aspect of the metropolisation process (less researched, unlike the processes of the concentration of the central functions in cities and the process of the emergence of a world city network, discussed above) is the change of the relations between huge metropolises and their regional environment (hinterland). Many authors formulate the hypothesis that the regional environment is functionally less and less indispensable for metropolises (Cf. e.g. Castells 1998, Gorzelak 2000a, Jałowiecki 2000, Kunzmann 1998, Sassen, 1991). Castells (1998, pp. 405-410) quotes the metropolitan region of the Pearl River Delta in China as an example of an increasing significance of global interrelationships, with simultaneous weakening of local interactions (which, in his opinion, will lead to the emergence of a new form of urbanisation). This region is not a conurbation, as it is characterised by the lack of continuity between urban and suburban areas; big cities and clusters of industrial plants are dispersed and separated by poorly developed rural areas. The region's skeleton is formed by fast transport and telecommunication connections between those centres and excellent connections with the world city network via huge airports and sea harbours. The centres making up the region are dependent on its environment practically only for potable water.

In this context, Jałowiecki's definition of metropolisation (1999 p. 29) should be evoked: metropolisation is *"the final stage of urbanisation, consisting in the transformation of urban space and change of the relations between the central city and its direct environment and in a non-discrete way of using urban space. It is manifested by a weakening or severing of the city's economic ties with its regional hinterland and replacing them with contacts with other continental or global metropolises".* This leads to the polarisation of development, that is, a continuous strengthening of the centres and marginalisation of the regional hinterland, whose role is becoming limited to providing residential and recreational functions for the dwellers of the metropolis. At the same time, the author observes that the formation of metropolises and the metropolisation process does not mean an end of cities or urbanisation processes. Urbanisation is continuing, albeit dominated by metropolisation. The metropolisation process

---

[6] These notions are used in the growth poles theory to describe relations between the centre and the periphery. For instance, A.O. Hirschman distinguished positive, trickling-down effects of infiltration and negative polarisation effects. On the other hand, Myrdal distinguished centrifugal, progressive spread effects and centripetal backwash effects (quoted after: Grzeszczak, 1998).

causes changes in the entire social and urban texture not only in the metropolis, but also in the regions dependent on the metropolis.

To sum up, it should be emphasised that the notion of metropolisation can be understood as having two meanings, viz.:

- the formation of a multi-centre network of huge cities – metropolises having global functions;
- the process of diminishing the dependence of metropolises on their regional hinterland, replaced by contacts as part of a multi-centre, global city network.

2.2. New interrelationships between the city and the region

In light of the above definition, the new development paradigm and hypotheses put forward in the literature of the subject worldwide, the following evolutionary model of the relations between metropolises in the regional and global context may be proposed (Cf. Gorzelak 2000b).

In industrial economy, the relations between the city and the surrounding region were relatively strong. The region provided simple resources: unqualified labour in the form of daily shuttle migration (using railway transport), food products (intensive cash crops production in the city's alimentary zone), raw materials for production and construction plants located in the city. In return, the agglomeration provided its hinterland with income from work, processed products (shopping in the city) as well as higher-level services (healthcare, culture, tertiary education, etc.). The regional environment was dominated by the city, which exploited its resources to propel its economy. Nonetheless, the agglomeration was highly dependent on its regional hinterland. The stronger it was, the higher was the status of a given city.

At the same time, relations between the city and the global economy in industrial civilisation were largely restricted to the exchange of industrial goods. On the one hand, the city exported processed industrial goods, and on the other – it imported the needed raw materials and semi-products and augmented its sales market by imported consumer goods. The city's competitiveness was determined by its available resources of labour, raw materials and energy, production and office space as well as mass transport, fusing the agglomeration into a functional whole. Municipal authorities could influence the city's competitiveness using traditional policy instruments, such as various reliefs in local taxes and levies, as well as co-financing and grants awarded to preferential activities.

In information economy, the relations between the metropolis and the region have become relatively weaker. Other assets and resources, which could not be found in the regional environment, have become indispensable for the development of the metropolis. Therefore, the role of the hinterland has been limited to the provision of qualified labour (most frequently educated in the city itself) in the form of weekly shuttle migration or permanent migration, as well as environmental assets: potable water, recreational space, etc. On the other hand, the region has become the recipient of increasingly stronger negative stimuli generated by the metropolis. Cheaper and more remotely located areas have become attractive locations for the development of technical infrastructure which is unwanted in the city (e.g. waste disposal sites), transport and transmission infrastructure (which often leads to the fragmentation of the regional space), for distribution centres, traditional labour- and resource-intensive production sectors, as well as residential and recreational housing (frequently in the form of gated communities). Nonetheless, the significance of the regional environment for the metropolis, which developed more vigorous contacts with other huge cities, has diminished. Resources which were previously provided to the city by the region, have started to be supplied from other sources (e.g. foods) or have lost their significance (e.g. raw materials). This does not mean that the processes of exploiting the region by the metropolis have entirely terminated, but that their significance for the metropolis has diminished. A rapid development of the metropolis, if its spatial range and impact is limited, is bound to lead to the marginalisation of its regional environment.

In information economy, cities compete for capital and innovative sectors of economic activity. They struggle to create an attractive environment for the operation of huge transnational conglomerates. In this respect, quality-related location factors play a larger role, e.g. qualified labour, possibilities for cooperation in production and reliable infrastructure. Metropolises, striving to increase its competitiveness on the international scene using the existing indigenous potential, pursue a policy od developing global or continental functions at the expense of other functions (e.g. by providing support to scientific and research institutes and strengthening hubs in the transport systems). They strive to develop both "hard" and "soft" location factors. On the one hand, cities enhance their accessibility and improve infrastructure standards, trying to attract international institutions and investors. On the other hand, municipal authorities initiate large investment projects in order to improve the city's aesthetic assets and sponsor events aimed to attract world famous guests (Kunzmann,1998). In this way, they demonstrate their cultural achievements and attract qualified labour. If those initiatives prove to be successful, the city becomes a metropolis – a hub focusing global information and capital flows (including human capital). In information economy, the concentration of such flows (often having an intangible nature) has become more important than material exchange of goods and attracting mass-scale labour (factors which played a crucial part in the development of urban and industrial agglomerations).

Figure 1: Relationships between the city and the region in industrial and information economy

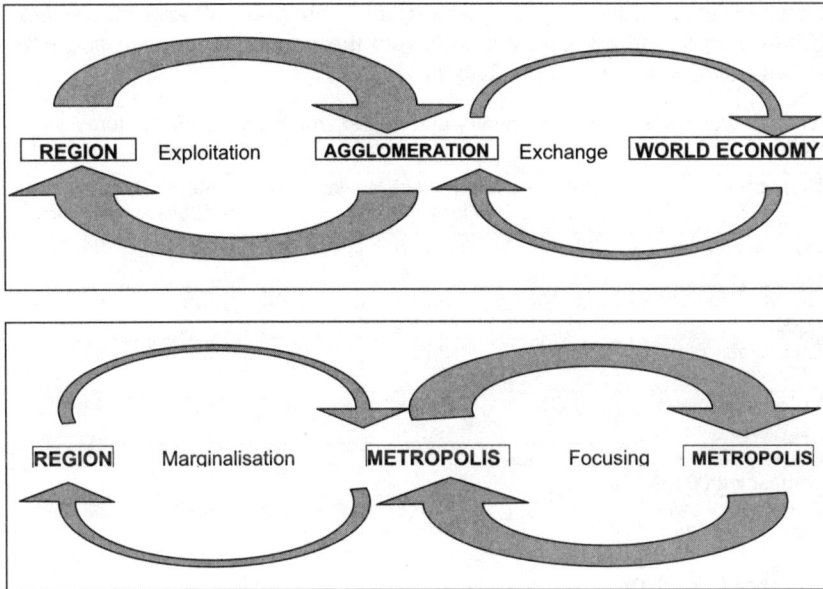

REGION Exploitation AGGLOMERATION Exchange WORLD ECONOMY

REGION Marginalisation METROPOLIS Focusing METROPOLIS

3. Metropolisation in Poland

Metropolisation processes and the related transformation of the interrelationships between the city and the region are more and more noticeable in Poland. Warsaw can serve as an good example; it, owing to its capital city status, is well suited to play a role in the European network of metropolises. This part of the paper provides overall characteristics of Warsaw and describes the internationalisation process of the city's economy, changes in the regional migration patterns, as well as spread and backwash effects observable in the city-the region perspective and the resultant polarisation of development processes in the Warsaw metropolitan region.

3.1 Warsaw vis à vis the country and the region

In 2001, Warsaw's population totalled 1.615 million, i.e. represented 4.2 per cent of the population of Poland. If we take into account the city's metropolitan area, inhabited by 800,000 people, this share will grow to 6.2 per cent. The size of the Warsaw labour market corresponds to the city's demographic potential, with average earnings (approximately EUR 750) twice as high as the national average. The lack of any clear demographic dominance of the capital is offset by its economic, scientific and service potential (Tab.1). Seen in the regional context, Warsaw can be regarded as the indisputable centre, a place of residence of every third inhabitant of the region, concentrating between 50 and 80 per cent (depending on the adopted indicators) of the economic, service and R&D potential of the entire region (Tab.1).

Table 1: Warsaw vis à vis the country and the Mazowieckie voivodship [province] in 2001

Wskaźnik	Poland	Mazowieckie voivodship	Warsaw	Poland = 100%	Mazowieckie = 100%
Population ('000)	38 641	5 075	1 610	4,2%	31,7%
Urban population ('000)	23 847	3 264	1610	6,8%	49,3%
Employed ('000)	14 670	2 309	761	5,2%	33,0%
- of which market services	2 334	849	377	16,2%	44,4%
Commercial law companies ('000)	177,1	48,6	38	21,5%	78,2%
Commercial law companies with foreign shareholdings ('000)	45,8	15,8	13,0	28,4%	82,3%
Foreign investments over 1 mln USD	2397	661	464	19,4%	70,2%
Employed in R&D ('000)	123,8	33,9	28,0	22,6%	82,6%
Expenditure on R&D (mln PLN)	4 858	2 141	1 682	34,6%	78,6%
Number of higher schools	344	80	62	18,0%	77,5%
Number of students ('000)	1 719	333	255	14,8%	76,6%
Seats in fixed cinemas ('000)	231	40	26	11,3%	65,0%
Tourist accommodated ('000)	45 946	3 392	1 029	2,2%	30,3%
- of which foreign tourists ('000)	3 151	667	429	13,6%	64,3%

Source: based on CSO (Central Statistical Office) and Polish Agency for Foreign Investment data

Map 1: Warsaw and its spheres of influence in the context of Poland's administrative division

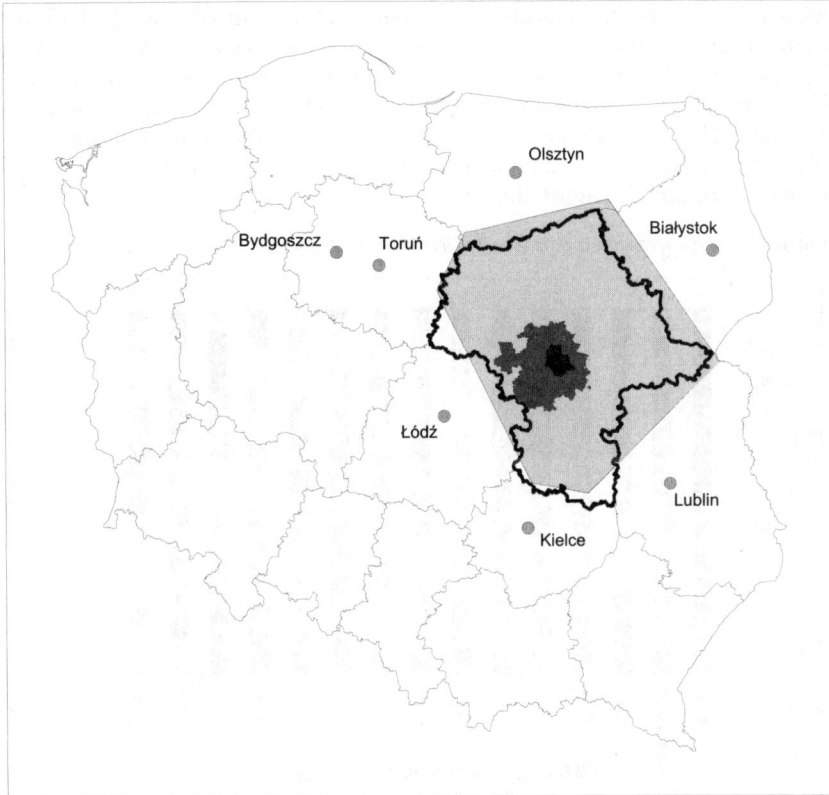

Warsaw

Metropolitan area*

border of voivodships

Mazowieckie voivodship

Capital cities of neighboring voivodships

Warsaw metropolitan region**

* metropolitan area marked by synthetic indicator consists of: migration balance, companies with foreign shareholdings and number of enterprises registered in REGON

** metropolitan region marked out on the basis of Reilly's law (1931)

As a result, a marked dichotomy between Warsaw and the remaining part of the Mazowieckie voivodship [province], which heavily depends on the centre, particularly with regard to economy, is clearly discernible.

This is easily visible in the structure of the labour market in the Warsaw metropolitan region. What is particularly striking is the concentration of jobs in the financial, insurance and tourist sectors in Warsaw (70-80 per cent of all employed). In the remaining markets services, Warsaw also has an over 50 per cent share in the regional labour market. On the other hand, the capital's significance in the industrial sector is much smaller. In the case of production processing as well as energy, water and gas supply, the position of the remaining towns of the region and of the direct vicinity of Warsaw is rather strong.

Figure 2: Employment structure in the Warsaw metropolitan region in 1999

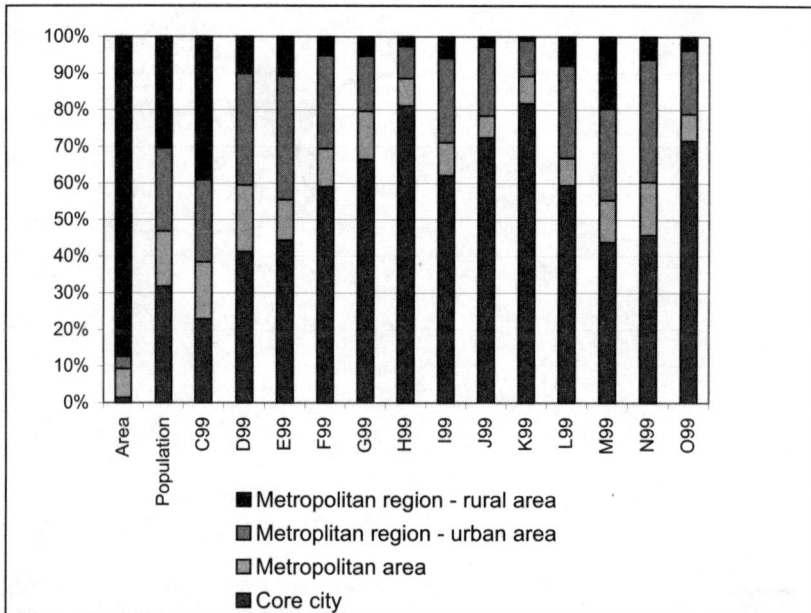

C - Mining and quarrying
D - Manufacturing
E - Power, gas and water supply
F - Construction
G - Trade and Repairs
H - Hotels and restaurants
I - Transport, storage and communication
J - Financial intermediation
K - Real estate and business activities
L - Public administration
M - Education
N - Health care and social security
O - Community, social and personal services

3.2 Internationalisation of the urban economy
Foreign capital

The last 10 years were characterised by a growing influx of foreign investment to Poland. Altogether, foreign investors have invested over USD 65 billion as direct investments (FDI), and a considerable portion of these funds has been invested in Warsaw. In 2001, there were registered approximately 13 thousand companies with foreign shareholdings, including 464 investors who invested sums in excess of USD 1 million.

In the years 1994-2001, the share of companies with foreign shareholdings in the total number of business entities registered in Warsaw increased from 4.2 per cent to 5.3 per cent. Additionally, the growth dynamics was nearly twice as high as that of other entities. Taking into account commercial law companies only[7], in 2001 the share of foreign companies was 34.5 per cent (an increase by 3.7 percentage points as compared to 1994). In this case, also the growth dynamics was higher, albeit only in the 1994-1997 period.

Table 2: Number of companies with foreign shareholdings registered in Warsaw

Specification	1994	1998	2001	1994 - 1997	1997 - 2001	1994 - 2001
Number of enterprises	148837	219525	247363	47%	13%	66%
Number of commercial law companies	20175	29978	37751	49%	26%	87%
Number of companies with foreign shareholdings	6210	10467	13035	69%	25%	110%
% of all enterprises	4.2%	4.8%	5.3%	-	-	-
% of commercial law companies	30.8%	34.9%	34.5%			

Source: author's own calculations using CSO data

Tourism

Simultaneously, in the years 1994-1997 Warsaw saw a boost in the hotel sector, which offered in all 14 thousand beds in 2001 (a 60 per cent increase as compared to 1994). The number of hotels grew considerably, mainly lower-standard ones (although those with a standard of over 3* were built, too). In 2002, several new top quality facilities were completed. At the same time, the number of hotel guests increased by approximately 20 per cent. This increase, however, was generated mainly

---

[7] Under Polish regulations, entities with foreign shareholdings must be registered in the form of a commercial law company.

by Polish guests, while the number of foreign guests stayed at a relatively unchanged level. Nonetheless, in the last four years the dynamics of incoming tourism was higher; foreign guests accounted for 58 per cent of all those using hotel accommodation.

Table 3: Development of the hotel sector in Warsaw

Specification	1994	1998	2001	1994-1997	1997-2001	1994-2001
Number of hotels	26	30	49	15.4%	63.3%	88.5%
-hotels of minimum 3* standard	17	23	25	35.3%	8.7%	47.1%
Beds	9033	10292	14723	13.9%	43.1%	63.0%
Guests	843380	925891	1003602	9.8%	8.4%	19.0%
- Poles	267337	394589	418210	47.6%	6.0%	56.4%
- foreigners	576043	531302	585392	-7.8%	10.2%	1.6%

Source: author's own calculations using CSO data

As compared with the changes in the number of hotel guests, the traffic in the Warsaw airport has considerably increased. The number of checked passengers increased from 2.1 million in 1993 to 4.7 million in 2001, i.e. by 120 per cent. The prevailing share of this traffic was generated by international flights (86%). Comparing these data with the number of border checks by the airport passport services, we can estimate the number of foreigners in air traffic in 2001 at 48 per cent.

Tertiarisation of Warsaw's economy
Internationalisation of Warsaw's economy was also connected with changes in the employment structure. In the years 1995-1999, the labour markets in Poland's major cities underwent significant changes. Particularly visible was the decline in the number of those employed in the industrial and construction sectors. In this context, Warsaw, retaining the majority of jobs in industry and construction, was an exception[8]. In the same period, the major cities saw an increase in the number of jobs in the service sector, most notably Warsaw and Poznan – by approximately 15 per cent. Nevertheless, in all such cities the number of employed in the service sector per one employed in industry increased, the highest figure being recorded in Warsaw (2.8).

---

[8] This paradox may be explained in several ways: firstly, the number of the employed was in this case measured using the workplace method, and not by actual employment; secondly, since the Warsaw industry had a relatively favourable structure (small share of traditional heavy industry sectors, high share of modern sectors), there was no need for such a deep restructuring process as in the other surveyed cities; and, thirdly, its restructuring processes were the fastest, and completed before 1995.

Table 3: Changes in the employment structure in the largest Polish cities.

City	Employed in industry and construction		Employed in services		Employed in services per 1 employed in industry	
	in 1999 ('000)	change in the years 1995-1999 in %	in 1999 ('000)	change in the years 1995-1999 in %	in 1995	in 1999
Poland	4402.8	-3.4 %	7017.8	10.2 %	1.40	1.59
Warsaw	207.9	-0.9 %	580.0	14.4 %	2.41	2.79
Krakow	100.9	-10.3 %	183.0	8.3 %	1.50	1.81
Wroclaw	70.2	-11.0 %	145.0	7.7 %	1.70	2.06
Poznan	78.7	-11.5 %	164.7	15.0 %	1.61	2.09
Tri-city	81.5	-15.0 %	161.7	1.5 %	1.66	1.98
Lodz	81.5	-19.4 %	146.6	1.0 %	1.43	1.80

Source: author's own calculations using CSO data

Innovation introduced by enterprises

The survey of 246 randomly selected production enterprises located in the Warsaw metropolitan area, carried out in 2003, indicated that 82 per cent of them in the past two years introduced innovation concerning processes, products or organisation. Among the most frequently quoted sources for the implemented innovations (of 12 possible choices), there were: the enterprise's own resources and support from the capital group, information from clients or competitors, as well as fairs and conferences. For each source, the respondents were asked to specify its location. As a result of the survey, it was found out that the large share of information which was the driver for innovation originated from other areas of the country (31 per cent). Despite its considerable research and development capability, Warsaw was at the similar level as the source of information (33 per cent). Less importantly, foreign sources of information about innovation had a smaller impact (19 per cent). At the same time, the metropolitan region and the Warsaw metropolitan area independently generated 11 and 6 per cent information, respectively. As compared with their potential, this was a relatively good result.

Spread effects of development processes

An analysis of the spatial distribution of companies with foreign shareholdings may indicate to what extent the manifestations of the internalisation of Warsaw' economy influenced the surrounding region. Based on such an analysis, it can be said that the spatial range of the spreading of the Warsaw metropolis was limited. The activity of foreign investors was restricted to an area of 30-40 km in diameter from the city's administrative boundaries, delineated by Warsaw's main by-pass road (national roads no. 50 and 62). On the other hand, a considerable part of the metropolitan region remained an "uncharted territory" for foreign investors. In this respect, the role of main national and regional roads for the capital diffusion process could be distinctly visible.

Map 2: Registered companies with foreign shareholdings in Warsaw metropolitan region in 2001.

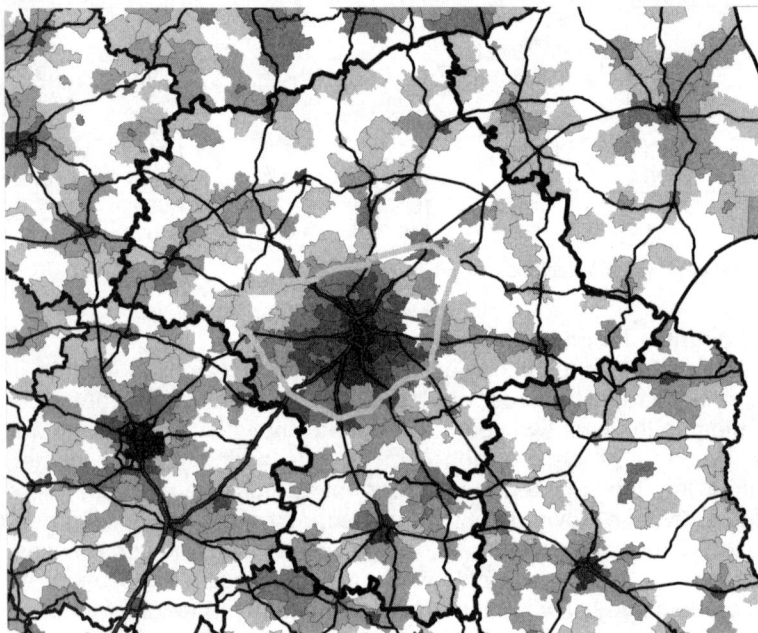

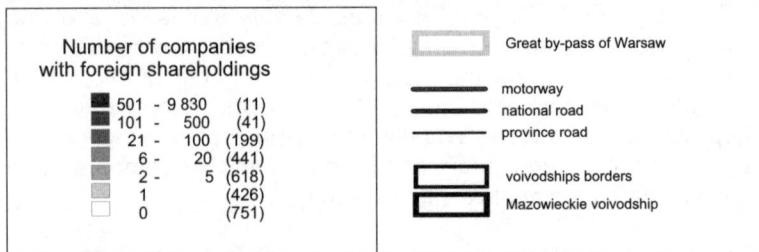

Number of companies with foreign shareholdings

501 - 9 830	(11)
101 - 500	(41)
21 - 100	(199)
6 - 20	(441)
2 - 5	(618)
1	(426)
0	(751)

Great by-pass of Warsaw

motorway
national road
province road

voivodships borders
Mazowieckie voivodship

3.3 Migration in the Warsaw metropolitan region

After 1989, the intensity of permanent internal migration in Poland was significantly reduced. On the other hand, suburbanisation processes in the vicinity of the largest Polish cities, non-existent before, have become distinctly observable. An analysis of the changes in the population and the balance of migration in six largest Polish cities and their surroundings in the years 1994-1999 indicates that suburbanisation process were particularly well visible in Warsaw and Poznan and, to a lesser degree, in the Tri-City (Gdansk-Gdynia-Sopot), manifested by an increased number of inhabitants within a radius 30 km from the city, especially in the belt of municipalities surrounding the city, with a simultaneous decrease of the urban population.

Commuting

In addition to decreased intensity of permanent migration in the initial phase of the Polish transformation, the scale of commuting was also reduced. It is difficult, however, to accurately assess how this observation related to the Warsaw labour market.

In the years 1964-1983, about 20 per cent of those employed in the socialised (state) economy commuted to Warsaw, mostly in the form of shuttle migration within the Warsaw agglomeration, directly targeted at the region's capital (97 per cent in 1973 and 90 per cent in 1983). About 50 to 70 thousand people, i.e. 9 per cent of those employed in the agglomeration, commuted to Warsaw city-agglomeration from locations situated at a larger distance (Potrykowska 1983, GUS 1986, 1990).

After 1989, no comprehensive research has been carried out in Poland concerning commuting. Nonetheless, based on the preliminary findings from a survey of 246 randomly selected enterprises, it can be said that the labour market in this sector is still largely confined to the Warsaw metropolitan area. About 95 per cent of executives and 86 per cent of other staff live and work in the Warsaw metropolitan area. The scale of com-muting from longer distances was higher in the case of staff at other than executive positions; about 14 per cent of them commuted from beyond the metropolitan area (including 7 per cent from other voivod-ships than Mazowieckie), against 5 per cent of executives (including 3 per cent from other regions of the country).

Table 4: Place of residence of those employed in enterprises located in the Warsaw metropolitan area

Location of the company / Place of residence	Warsaw and metropolitan area (N=246)		Warsaw (N=186)		Metropolitan area (N=80)	
	Executives	Other staff	Executives	Other staff	Executives	Other staff
Warsaw	68%	56%	77%	70%	40%	21%
Metropolitan area (excluding Warsaw)	27%	30%	20%	21%	47%	55%
Mazowieckie voivodship (excluding Warsaw metropolitan area)	2%	7%	1%	4%	6%	14%
Poland (excluding Mazowieckie voivodship)	3%	7%	2%	5%	7%	10%

Source: author's own calculations based on research results

Spread and backwash effects processes

The map showing the balance of migration in the Warsaw metropolitan area indicates that there has been an inflow of population to municipalities situated in the vicinity of Warsaw. Most probably, this is due to the outflow of population from the capital. Also, the outflow of population from peripherally located rural municipalities situated in the northern and eastern part of the metropolitan region, and to a lesser extent in the southern region, most probably targeted at the metropolitan region.

Map 3. Balance of migration in the Warsaw metropolitan region in the years 1994 - 2000.

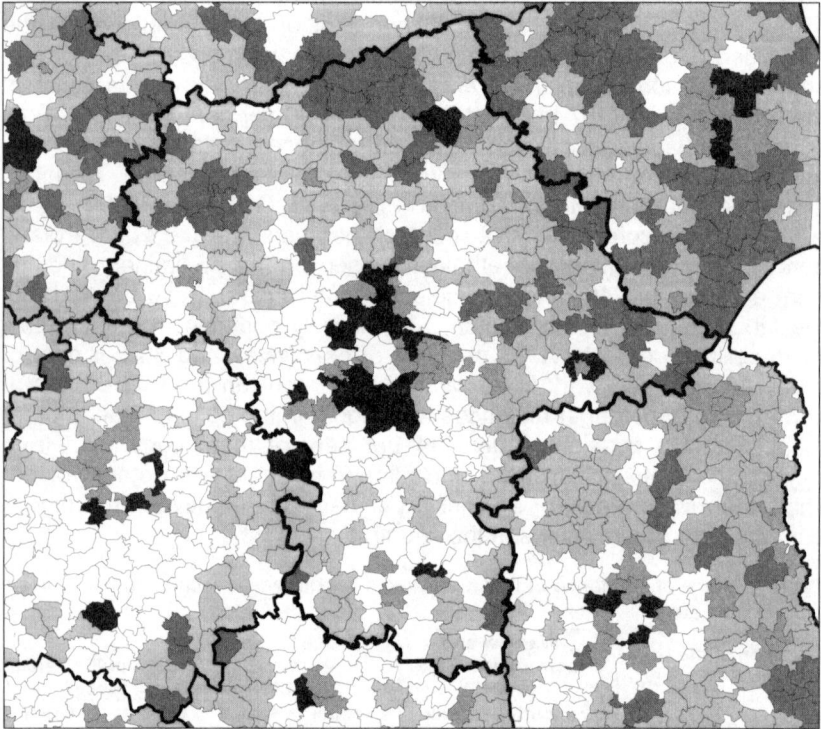

Migration balance in years 1994-2000
in promils

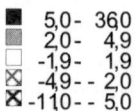

- 5,0 - 360
- 2,0 - 4,9
- -1,9 - 1,9
- -4,9 - -2,0
- -110 - -5,0

3.4 Polarisation of growth processes in the Warsaw metropolitan region

The change of the development model in Poland after 1989 has undoubtedly contributed to changes in the spatial relationships of Warsaw and, as a result, has affected regional development processes. In the years 1994-2002, an evolution of internal disparities within the Warsaw metropolitan region could be observed[9]. This period can be divided into two phases: the years 1994-1998 and the years 1998-2002. In the former, two processes were most distinctly visible: the formation of a belt of poorest municipalities around the centre of the metropolitan region and a rapid increase in the stratification of incomes between the centre and the periphery of the region. In the latter period, the main changes on the map of municipalities' own revenues along with the share in state taxes per capita included a dilution of the belt of poorest municipalities around Warsaw, decelerated pace of differences in incomes between the centre and the periphery, slight expansion of the area of richest municipalities situated in close proximity to Warsaw (incorporated in its metropolitan area) and a lasting stagnation of the majority of municipalities situated on the fringe of the metropolitan area, in addition to a relatively improved situation in some of the district towns.

To sum up, it should be observed that the development polarisation processes which emerged in the years 1994-1998, were to some extent weakened, while the years 1998-2002 saw a simultaneous expansion of the area situated within the zone of Warsaw's positive impact. On the other hand, the situation of municipalities located far from the regional centre was deteriorating steadily, which in consequence has led to the deepening of intraregional disparities in the development level.

Conclusions

Based on the information concerning the essential processes shaping Warsaw's spatial relationships and discussed above, it can be observed that:

- the recent years saw a gradual increase in the intensity of links connecting Warsaw with its external environment, both foreign and domestic, through the influx of foreign capital, tourists (including business) as well as the transfer of information about innovation. This could indirectly point to the city's internal weakness, related to the lack of capital resources and an insufficient generation of innovations. In addition, those resources cannot be supplied to the city from its regional hinterland, which is evidenced, for example, by the

---

[9] In order to measure the differences in the development level of the Warsaw metropolitan area, own revenues of municipalities plus their share in the state taxes (PIT and CIT) were measured per capita.

commuting of executives to Warsaw: according to business survey, they commute more frequently from cities situated outside the Warsaw metropolitan region than from the metropolitan region (excluding metropolitan area);

- In the relations between the city and its regional environment, a distinct dichotomy between the area situated in direct proximity to Warsaw and the area lying at the periphery of the metropolitan region could be observed. The spreading of the capital's development processes in the form of the inflow of capital and population, as well as an increased intensity of two-way commuting was confined to a 30-40 km zone from the city boundaries, could be seen. On the other hand, this was coupled by an outflow of employees (most probably those best educated) from the region's periphery to the centre. At the same time, the scale of daily commuting to Warsaw by less qualified employees from the metropolitan region has slightly increased in the recent years;
- As a result of the observable processes, differences in the development level between the centre and the periphery of the metropolitan region were increasing, although the dynamics of this process was decelerating, due to the gradual expansion of the sphere of Warsaw's positive impact.

These observations are based on a number of stronger or weaker premises, which undoubtedly – at least in some aspects – call for further research in order to be fully validated. Furthermore, at this stage of research, it is too early to relate the research findings to the model of the changing interrelationships between the metropolis and the region, connected with the shift from industrial to information economy, discussed above.

References:
Castells, M. (1989) The informational city, Blackwell, Oxford.
-,   (1998) The Information Age: Economy, Society and Culture – The Rise of Network Society volume 2, Blackwell, Oxford.
Gorzelak, G.; Jałowiecki, B. (2000) Konkurencyjność regionów (A Competitiveness of the Regions), Kwartalnik SRiL nr 1, EUROREG, Warsaw.
Gorzelak, G. (2000a) The regional dimension of Polish Transformation: Seven Years Later. In: Gorzelak, G.; Ehrlich, E.; Faltan, L.; Illner, M. (Eds.) Central Europe in Transition: Towards EU Membership, RSA Polish Section, Warsaw.
-,   (2000b) Potencjalne ośrodki wzrostu w województwie mazowieckim i ich miejsce w strategii rozwoju województwa (The Potential Growth Poles in Mazowieckie Voivodship and its Position in Strategy of the Voivodship), Kwartalnik SRiL nr 8, EUROREG, Warsaw.
Grzeszczak, J. (1999) Bieguny wzrostu a formy przestrzeni spolaryzowanej (The Growth Poles and the Forms of Polaristaion Space) , Prace Geograficzne Nr 173, Warsaw.

GUS (Central Statistical Office) (1986, 1990) Rocznik Statystyki Pracy (Yearbook of Labour Statistic), Warszawa.

Jałowiecki, B. (1999) Metropolie (Metrpolises), Wydawnictwo Wyższej Szkoły Finansów i Zarządzania, Białystok.

-, (2000) Społeczna przestrzeń metropolii (A Social Space of Metrpolis), Wydawnictwo Naukowe Scholar, Warsaw.

Kukliński, A.; Kołodziejski, J.; Markowski, T. Dziemianowicz, W. (Eds.), (2000) Globalizacja polskich metropolii (Globalisation of Polish Metropolis), EUROREG, Warsaw.

Kunzmann, K. R. (1998) World city regions in Europe: Structural change and future challenges. In: Lo, F.; Yeung, Y. (Eds.), Globalisation and the world large cities, UN University Press, Tokyo – New York – Paris.

Lo, F. Yeung, Y. (Eds.) (1998) Globalisation and the world large cities, UN University Press, Tokyo – New York – Paris.

Potrykowska, A. (1983) Współzależność między dojazdami do pracy a strukturą społeczną i demograficzną regionu miejskiego Warszawy w latach 1950-1973 (A Correlation between Commuting and Social and Demographic Structure of Warsaw City Region in Years 1950-1973), Dokumentacja Geograficzna, IGiPZ PAN, Warsaw.

Reilly, W.J. (1931) The Law of Retail Gravitation, New York.

Rimmer, P. J. (1998) Transport and telecommunications among world cities. In:. Lo, F.; Yeung, Y. (Eds.) Globalization and the world of large cities, UN University Press, Tokyo – New York – Paris.

Sassen, S. (1991) The global city, Princetown University Press.

-, (2000a) Cities in a world economy, Pine Forge Press.

-, (2000b) Global City and Global City-Regions: A comparison, [in:] Scott A. J. (Ed.) Global City-Regions: trends, theory, policy, Oxford University Press, Oxford.

Scott, A. J. (Ed.) (2000) Global City-Regions: trends, theory, policy, Oxford University Press, Oxford.

Soja, E. W. (2000) Posmetropolis – critical studies of cities and regions, Blackwell Publishers Ltd, Oxford

Patterns of urbanization and the question of multiculturalism and territorialization: an example in transitional society (Croatia)

Ognjen Čaldarović

1. Introduction
Multiculturalism and territoriality are interconnected issues and topics in social sciences. The search for a territory is so typical for any cultural, ethnic or any other denoted agglomeration (or unity) of people that even in the modern society "searching" for a territory. This is rather typical for many countries with a long history of immigration (territorialization of ethnicities) and it is not yet so typical for ex-socialist societies or transitional societies what the Croatian society represents too.

But, with the changes that started to occur approaching the end of the 1980s in most of the previously socialist societies (now called societies in transition or simply "ex-socialist" or "post-socialist" societies) and in Croatia as well, the idea of „normalness" or normality of the existence of social differentiation and social segregation as a consequence of migrations – territorializations and therefore "ethnic territorialization", as opposed to the non-existence in previous times, have completely influenced and changed the institutional way of looking at that phenomenon, the way of thinking, behavior and social practices, and thus the institutional basis for the establishment of new patterns of social differentiation and segregation (Čaldarović, 1991). This new situation opens many questions including the ones concerning problems of social integration, the way how to achieve it in an increasingly disintegrated and fragmented society (Čaldarović, 1989.), which methods and institutional factors and organizations should be engaged "to stimulate" social integration and what kind of new ways and patterns of integration should be expected in the future.

In this paper we discuss major aspects of this new territorialization of ethnicities (Čaldarović, 1987.), new segregation patterns and new problems of social integration concerning multiculturalism and territorialized expressions of differences which could be seen as different "styles", habits or simply "ways of life" oriented to show "the difference", or in more symbolic way – a right to show the particularities, the differences, and a right to make it in a legitimized way.

2. Major ideas and concepts
In sociology, several concepts are common for the description and explanation as well as for the research on social differentiation and segregation (Derek, Urry, eds., 1985.). One concept - social differentiation - describes the situation where the differences between groups, strata or individuals in a society are classified "as normal", and then inevitably

registered, but the pattern of this differentiation is usually represented on a horizontal level which means that no hierarchy is involved, no super ordination and no subordination between groups and members in a society. In other words, there is *no systematic pattern, backed by current ideology and practice* in a given society that will inevitably place a member of the society in a socially different position from another - above or below the others. In this case, there are no systematic "social forces" behind a certain type of differentiation and the perceived and established differences in several breakdowns and thresholds are more or less explained as normal and expected (Čaldarović, 1987.).

On the other hand, social segregation or social stratification (residential segregation) as a research tool and concept for the investigation and explanation of the unequal distribution of social groups, strata and individuals in a society has much stronger political and social connotations, because it denotes the process in which various social groups, strata or individuals are placed in different positions on a vertical scale. This means that questions of inequality or lack of egalitarian distribution are practically applied and exemplified. This pattern of unequal representation of various classes or strata, groups or even individuals in the social structure of any society is present everywhere, but the explanations for the forces which have brought to this situation vary. For example, in the long history of social urban ecological studies, especially in the Chicago School of Sociology (Čaldarović, 1985a.), the unequal representation of various social strata in cities (better to say in the society as a whole!) has been explained as, for example, a "clustering of similarities" - groupings of representatives of various nations, various types of individuals, groups or ethnicities in a certain part of a city as an inevitable consequence of "similarities in their lifestyle", cultural practices and the "natural drive" to come closer to each other. This "clustering of similarities" could be also labeled "a natural segregation" (R. Park also used the expression "natural areas") due to the fact that - presumably - it does not involve any pattern of external social force or institutional ar-rangement to intervene into the natural grouping of people in a certain part of a city.

In the history of urban studies in the former socialist societies, for example, social segregation was explained as an „unfair", unjust, and unequal representation of social strata in the society. But, where does unequal distribution come from in formally equal societies (French, Hamilton, 1979.)? Thus, social segregation or social stratification must always include hierarchy, a vertical division between members, groups and strata in a society, which means that there is a pattern to that kind of distribution which is usually backed by the current ideology and actual practices in the respective society. In sociology an interesting concept of social justice (Harvey, 1975) is usually linked with notions of equal, fair or just distribution of amenities, goods, politics, culture, etc. - practices and freedoms to be applied in the society. In other words, in former socialist societies, ideas and practices of social life based on equity are to be implemented in models of socialism/communism and political practices in these societies in general (Badcock, 1984). "Socialist values", expressed as general as well as specific values of society, must be provided and distributed properly among all members in the society. One of the operationalizations of just distribution in this field was the principle of e-qual wages or the application of the reasonably acceptable ratio between the lowest and the highest wage (say, 1:3). In the field of culture and policy, there should be just and equal distribution, in order to give equal chances and equal opportunities to all members of a given society for cultural expression and participation in the cultural life, as well as to ensure equal grounds for political participation. Yet, apart from the many ways to question the possibilities of how to apply these principles, some of the greatest problems concerning this model were the criteria of distribution and the subjects of distribution, as well as the decision making procedures needed to reach the proclaimed goals.

The functioning of that model is even more interesting if one attempts to discuss the equal distribution of various social groups, strata or even classes in the inevitably unequal conditions of urban living in cities and regions (Čaldarović, 1975; 1985a.). Equal conditions for life, provided for all strata, groups or members in a society are very rarely found to be the same for all members (citizens) of a society. Various social groups, strata or - if we use the more modern expression - territorialized ethnicities (Čaldarović, 1989; Čaldarović, 1985b.) are experiencing unequal quality of life, due to living conditions, due to the inevitable differences between places, regions and territories, or - if we apply this idea to the patterns of territorial segregation - various strata in the society are "unequally" represented in different parts of cities and regions. In former socialist societies this inequality was one of the major research project targets in urban sociology due to the fact that there was an inevitable gap between the ideological principles of governing the society (equality for all members, equal conditions for life in the urban environment) and the actual practices, including urbanization and urban patterns of life. In other words, researches (especially in urban sociology) usually discovered through their investigations and survey the existence of social segregation in space as well as other inequalities between strata, groups and individuals in a given society (Burns et al., 1981.).

Summarizing the major shifts which occurred in today's post-socialist or transitional societies, we might say that a general shift from the "melting pot" ideas toward "up-rooting" and "ethnic revival", as well as a shift from a "non-segregation" ideas to the formation of territorialized ethnicities could be registered.

We should remind the reader that – usually – common features of ethnicity are: collective name, a shared myth on common descend, a common past (real facts usually combined with political and mythical construction), distinctive shared culture – conceptualized as a media, legitimization of a given political order, etc., shared solidarity feelings, feeling of belonging, shared (collective) identities (primordial, essential, crude-soft, ambivalent, traditional-modern, open-closed, total and exclusive, etc.), territory as an "attachment", and common and collective memories, values and symbols. In Croatian society – to come closer to the ground – major variables for social integration are the following: regional background, language, religion, cultural traits, interest, specific destiny of a person (refugees from the same area, expellees, etc.)

3. How to understand ethnicity and territoriality in a multicultural perspective?

One of the ideas concerning ethnicity emphasizes the idea that ethnicity is a *"given fact"* concept where ideas on ethnicity are usually based on: different historical reasons, common background of a group of people, on the existence of a community (*Gemeinschaft* and *Gesellschaf*). Social integration, as a "second part" of the territorialization concept, could be operationalized in the following variables: territory, group(s) of people, wider environment (local society, global society), formal and informal rules and networks of conduct, complex developmental process in time embedded in a concrete dynamic social context mostly determined by external conditions and the dynamics of the local context.

First types of local communities had been primarily strongly connected to a territory as a practical accomplishment of "their success", their rights for a possession of certain region, part of the country or a country as a whole. It is interesting that in the Chicago School of Sociology major analytical concepts concerning the idea of the community were very vaguely defined - as a very local unit or a very large unit, as a local community in its entirety, as a neighborhood (unit), as a certain part of a city, as a whole city or, even as a society in its entirety. Also, major socio-ecological concepts applied to the migrations of groups of people which had been then developed are very instructive for the contemporary discussion on the territoriality, multiculturalism and the meaning of territorialized ethnicities: (1) invasion (of a territory), (2) competition (of different migrant /ethnic/ groups to conceive a certain territory (part of a city, for example), (3) conflict ("open" and obvious competition between different migrant groups), (4) accommodation (of different groups to a certain territory) and (5) assimilation (of different groups to certain territories). It is also interesting to mention concepts of "natural" and "moral" areas and types of social order which are then expected in different areas of the city: people of the "higher similarity" should tend to settle in certain parts (territories) of the city.

Well, after so many years and so many transformations of societies, is it true that territoriality is less and less important aspect of social integration and human communities, as well as less and less important concept in social sciences? Are modern societies more and more "de-territorialized"? Is it correct to say that social integration in modern societies is more and more de-territorialized, fragmented, segmented, partial, specified, trans-boundary, international, cosmopolitan or just "symbolic"? In modern social theory there is an ongoing discussion, especially among urban sociologists on the concepts of individualization (or "de-collectivization"), detachment of social groups from the territory that could mean that territory, as an explanatory concept is less and less important? Major point of discussion, if we are to follow this kind of explanations, is to try to understand an ethnic *identity* as an inscriptive characteristic of an individual - it is "chosen" later (someone is born in one ethnic community, but he/she can choose or accept a nation; or, someone "must" be of a certain ethnic affiliation due to the fact that he or she was born in one ethnic environment, by the parents belonging to a certain ethnic group).

The second approach could be connected with "*social construction*" ideas that are usually based on feelings, perception, cognition, myths on a certain ethnic groups (and territory - long-lasting, genuine, natural, "clean", closed, "the only one", a "defended community" etc.). It is therefore socially contextualized, in most of the cases independent from the features on the current social life, and dominated by many inter-vening situational factors (i. e."refugee identity", "pragmatic ethnic identity", "technical ethnic identity", etc.). Different historical and temporal dimensions like the "roots", "common time", and actual social context also dominate it.

The results of ethnic territorialization as well as ethnic emphasis usually influence also specific processes in social groups like social fragmentation (the people are recognized mostly through their fragmented roles), social segmentation (the people are recognized through their segmented roles, as well as through social territorialization (residential segregation) of some social groups in a society (for example Roma people, Croats from Janjevo, etc.)

Due to the fact that there is no specific *appearance* in ethnic behavior", we must rely on a hypothesis that the need to emphasize an ethnic difference in a post-socialist society do have some specific objectives and that they are usually hidden and/or latent, and manifest or "functional" for different purposes. It means that an emphasis on ethnicity as an important social factor in a society does have many "functions" and do serve many social needs. The most important *potential functions* of manifest and latent functions of ethnicity are to establish, underline, and functionalize a difference (between people, i.e. between different ethnic affiliations, between different ethnic groups), to secure and document a difference (on which real grounds are we really different?), to supplement and back potential other dimensions of difference, to reorient the discussion to a common field, to organize a "defend structure" from a larger society, to survive in a hostile environment (a war situation), to provide e-vidence for the existence of "one nation, one culture, one state" and to bring about to the nation-state ideas, to secure the power in the hands of the existing elite based on mythical grounds, etc.

We might even talk about some general functions of an emphasis of ethnic dimensions in a certain society - to hide the real state of affairs (in a given country), to back and resist insecurity caused by globalization, redistribution, and privatization.

4. The development of the quest for ethnic affiliation/belonging and territorialization in a post-socialist society

Major hypothesis should rely on a fact that in the former socialist so-cieties, minorities and ethnic groupings had existed, but had not been (enough) recognized, institutionalized and legitimized. It means that an effective *cultural diversity management (management of cultural diversity)*- multi-culturalism, inter-culturalism, trans-culturalism, cultural plu-ralism etc. had not been efficiently applied in the current practices of an everyday life. Due to that fact, these dimensions had been "hidden" or had been placed under the carpet and – suddenly, after the break with socialist regimes, started to be one of the major issues.

Contextual historical perspective in the Croatian society, as an example of a transitional society will show that a certain change does happen through many years – from an egalitarian society to a society where ethnic differentiation and separation started to be almost the most im-portant issues in social representations. In this sense, ethnicity was (is) identified with nationality where a great shift was done: minorities should to be established with all their rights. The egalitarian syndrome – as an implicit political idea in former socialist societies, with an echo "no ethnic problems" had been transformed into much more stratified society.

In a complicated structure of the former Yugoslavia, major problems *(1975-1985)* started to be more and more influencing current life of people. One of the aspects was a generalized (more or less) feelings of being "exploited" (cheated) almost by all (different) members of social (ethnic) groups in the country by the "others" (whoever). Based on different historical overestimations some real facts and indicators on the unequalness of all in the society had been presented and that in this sense made a basis for social protests and discomfort. We might men-tion also possible denial of cultural, social, political, religious, etc. rights of some social groups together with economic problems and deprivation as well as rising differences in the economic level of development which influenced the rhetoric of local politicians and national (republican) leaders. Nevertheless, from a unified, equal society, post-socialist society became increasingly differentiated and fragmented. As mentioned earlier, the dissolution of socialist societies after 1990. (Simmie, Dekleva, 1991.) has brought about some other features of social segregation, as well as the emergence of some new features of the same phenomenon. Let us briefly summarize the most important ones.

Post-socialist societies are getting more fragmented (differentiated, segregated, stratified) on the basis of wealth (economy), political affiliation (various political parties - from the left to the extreme right), social standard of living, ethnic and regional origins. This accelerated fragmentation is so compressed in time that it does not leave any room for slow social adaptation for many members in these societies. The common picture of a post-socialist society today would be fragmented into many layers. Something we could call "the old middle class" - has dropped to the lower levels of the social structure pyramid and a new social strata (something that might be called "new upper middle class") has risen which, as a general rule, creates the picture of a social structure pyramid that has a very thin top and a very large base, thus making the difference from bottom to top very big. These fragmentations include: an ethnic fragmentation to the ones who make up the majority (usually the "prime nation" in a country) and minority groups (members); a very clear division between rich and poor members of a society; the ones who belong to the ruling or the opposition parties. Therefore, in the 1990s, we can talk about post-socialist societies primarily as fragmented societies - from the idea that "we are all equal" to the idea "we are inevitably unequal" - due to our success, individual differences, abilities, etc., from the idea that "we all believe in one party" (the "rightness" of the features of one society), to the idea that we belong to various political parties, various ethnic groups which are now institutionalized, legitimized and, in many cases, territorialized, from the idea that "we all share the same values in the society", to the appearance of completely disparate and opposed value systems expressed and practiced by members of various religious, political, ethnic and even regionally affiliated groups.

Post-socialist societies are also getting more and more disintegrated. As an inevitable consequence of economic, social and political fragmentations, former types of social integration in socialist societies are lost. Due to the facts that there are no one-party systems anymore, that, in principle, there are no efficient mechanisms for social care for the newly arisen "misfits" and that people witness a sudden rise and fall of certain members of the society, there is a widely dispersed perception and cognition that a unified, the type of the-society-we-all-live-in does not exist anymore. They are actually several societies existing parallel in one society - one comprises the rich, another the poor, members of some societies are prosperous, others are not, etc. Social disintegration as a result of fragmentation has been the constant feature in all post-socialist societies throughout the 1990s.

Growing social fragmentation and disintegration have also brought about the abandonment of the concept (and actual practice) of the egalitarian syndrome that was studied, for example, by the Croatian sociologist Josip Županov. In short, that syndrome in the previous Yugoslav society and most probably in most of the ex-socialist societies had been the most important unifying force of the people in a given society. "We are all equal" and "we want to be equal whether rich or poor" - that was probably the most important popular belief and feeling connected with this syndrome. It could be said that the former Yugoslav society did have an ideology as well as a social practice based on these ideas that promote - at least on the theoretical and ideological levels - the general equality between members of the society. It is important to see that the egalitarian syndrome has been transformed into something we would call "normality of differences". This opens up a very important question: what are the integration forces today in post-socialist societies, if we take into account that the growing differentiation is not yet perceived in the society as normal, equal and - more important - "fair"?

Post-socialist societies are getting increasingly conflictive. Conflict between members of various ethnic groups, political groups, groups belonging to different economic strata, groups working in different areas, between the rich and the poor, etc., as opposed to presumed consensus, is becoming the new reality of the previously allegedly peaceful and unconflictive (consensual) socialist societies.

There is a tremendous change in the organizational, institutional and ideological arrangements of post-socialist societies. New political parties, new economic practices, new patterns of differentiation and new social policies have brought about the formation of a new perception of social structure in general. The structure of a given post-socialist society is constantly changing which also promotes the feeling of uncertainty, helplessness and the lack of optimism for the future in the eyes of the ordinary citizen. The state of anomie (E. Durkheim) and/or the state labeled frequently as a "lack of rule of law" sends a clear message: get what you can as quick as possible while it lasts.

5. Some specific Features of the Croatian Situation

Some special features of the important social, political as well as urban changes in Croatia during 1990s include, among other things, the following.

- *Increased differentiation* between people, groups and strata in the society is starting to be perceived and understood - as we mentioned earlier - as a "new normality" and new reality for members of society that they must adopt and adapt to;
- *Growing fragmentation* in the society has brought about to the emergence of new social strata (e.g. the so-called "new rich"), as well as the dissolution of something we might call "old middle (socialist) class";
- The *consequences of war* in Croatia (1991-1995) as well as the more or less direct or indirect inevitable consequences of the war on the territories of Slovenia and Bosnia and Herzegovina (Čaldarović, et. al. 1992.) have also brought about:

1. *Mass migration* of displaced persons, refugees and of all people who were frightened and wanted to get out of the war zones. This mass migration ended mostly in bigger cities, and especially in Zagreb, which is the biggest city in the country;

2. *War activities*, in many cases organized as a technique for "ethnic cleansing" ("cleaning the territory" from members of one ethnic group, in order to populate it only with members of the other ethnic group) brought about new territorial patterns of population grouping, new types of territorial segregation and, on the one hand, heavy concentration of population in some areas, and on the other hand, the vacating of some other areas (parts) of the country.

3. *Areas* populated mostly by only one ethnic group can be found increasingly in bigger cities, which document the fact that principles of residential ethnic segregation are actively intervening into the distribution of population in a society. This new form of concentration of people, or territorialization (the term "new post-socialist teritorialization" can be used) was stimulated by the war in former Yugoslavia. One of the widespread images of the war - mainly a consequence of the newly invented war technique of ethnic cleansing - was that it was a war between nationalities, between people belonging to different ethnic groups. As a consequence of ethnic cleansing, people migrate to territories where they can find "their people" only, people of the same ethnic or even regional background. In this sense, some bigger city areas, especially Zagreb, are moving towards clear residential segregation on ethnic and regional basis. It is not only interesting, but also a social fact that has been legitimized due to the previously mentioned general change in the political and ideological arrangements of the society. In other words, residential segregation is now a legitimate fact in Croatia, no longer a side effect of some, say, uncontrolled processes or occasional grouping of certain social strata in specific parts of the city. In a broader sense, one could even talk about the global ethnicization of society.

4. *Migrations*, which can be called "selective types of migrations", have brought about the rise of conflict between the old settlers and new-comers, which is often reflected as the conflict between members of two ethnic (regional) groups. These conflicts are then transferred to the younger generation, producing the popular image that there are specific conflicts between the young who stem from different ethnic or regional backgrounds.

5. As one of the results of the war in Croatia, a *specific conflict* which influences the relationship between various groups in the society has arisen between the groups we might call "war profiteers" and "war losers". In some cases war profiteers are identified with some ethnic groups, which makes the situation more complicated due to the effect of generalization and identification of all members of one ethnic group with the members of one or the other profitable group in the society in general. This also has a strong reflection on the young generation. This type of conflict can be also mirrored as the conflict between the rich and the poor members of society, many times also strengthened by the popular belief that some groups (the rich) are privileged by the ruling party and some are not. Some ethnic groups are therefore often i-dentified with a certain popular belief and others are not. This is also re-flected in the young generation which strengthens the popular prejudice about the "qualities" of the young belonging to one or another ethnic group (due to the fact of the overall popular identification with the social status of their fathers or mothers).

Some earlier, broader processes that influenced urban patterns and distribution of population and housing situation were the following:

1. The construction of mass housing units in the 1960s and 1970s can be viewed as the concentrated housing of population on relatively small plots. The type of population in „new settlements" was generally heterogeneous and the effect on social segregation was - to some extent - „positive".

2. The loss of population from the center of the city (Szelenyi, 1987.) is also relevant for the discussion of social segregation in space and for the problems of integration of different social strata in social space of a city. In the case of Zagreb in general, the loss of population was only marginally the result of suburbanisation, but rather of many intervening factors such as the death of the older generation, the break-ing of pattern of subletting apartments and the conversion of housing into office space. The emptying of the city center in the 1960s and 1970s caused the rapid development of slums and the birth of ideas for „city re-habilitation", "city renovation" or "urban regeneration".

3. „City renewal" was also an important development in the 1960s and 1970s as well as in the 1980s that had a strong impact on the

changes in the social composition of the population. The „city renewal" movement could also be seen as a rehabilitation of the city's social structure through different processes such as construction of housing units in the city center, which would house „new" inhabitants, i.e. a new social structure. The general impact on the structure of the city center was positive because it created a „new" and „better" social structure of inhabitants and halted the spread of slums. However, the intensity of construction in the city center was not so great and the changes in the composition of the population were mostly marginal.

6. Conclusion: Types of ethnic social construction in a post-socialist society: tentative typology

The described processes are still moving ahead with an unclear final result. We might mention here several factors contributing to the social construction of ethnicity as a specific typology and as an example of social fragmentation in the society, like - "real ethnicity" (based on history, social perception, religion etc., combined with myths, values, ideas, etc.), "imagined ethnicity" (based also on myths etc., but also on potential role, functions, religion, history, social roles, potential "members" and social evidence to acquire some advantages in a given social context), "technical" (practical, pragmatic, "survival") ethnicity of a strictly functional, temporary, restricted nature, and based on the necessity to choose ethnic affiliation (to survive in the war) and which might be typical for a refugee identity. And, final hypothesis: in a post-socialist society the lack of major features of civil society are still preventing the dissolution of ethnic questions as "independent", decisive, and with great political potential. In a longer run, the development of civil society could be a small guarantee that ethnic (national, etc.) questions should not be anymore percepted as the most important questions in the society.

References:
Badcock, B. (1984) Unfairly Structured Cities. London: Basic Blackwell.
Brčić, C.; Čaldarović, O. (1998) Položaj mladih u Dubravi (Zagreb): socijalna integracija i dezintegracija ("The Position of Youth in Dubrava (Zagreb): Social Integration and Disintegration"). Migration Themes 14(1-2), 65-79.
Burns, T.; Čaldarović, O.; Kregar, J.; Sekulić, D.; Woodward, A. (1981) Citizen Participation in Housing Management and Local Community Development: The Case of Yugoslavia. The University of Uppsala, Sweden.
Čaldarović, O. (1975a) Neki pokazatelji prostorne socijalne diferencijacije i socijalne segregacije stanovništva Zagreba 1971 ("Some Data on Spatial Social Differentiation and Social Segregation of Zagreb Population in 1971"). Revija za sociologiju (IV)4, 58-66.
Čaldarović, O.; Richter, M. (1975b) Sociološka studija južne Dubrave /Zagreb/ (*Sociological Study of the South Dubrava /Zagreb/*). Zagreb: Urbanistički zavod Zagreba.

Čaldarović, O. (1985a) Urbana sociologija: socijalna teorija i urbano pitanje (*Urban Sociology: Social Theory and the Urban Question*). Zagreb: Globus.

Čaldarović, O. (1985b) Teritorijalizacija etniciteta i problemi socijalne integracije ("Territorialization of Ethnicities and Problems of Social Integration*")*. Pogledi, 2:155-166.

Čaldarović, O. (1987) Suvremeno društvo i urbanizacija (*Contemporary Society and Urbanization*). Zagreb: Školska knjiga.

Čaldarović, O. (1989) Društvena dioba prostora (*Social Fragmentation of Space*). Zagreb: Sociološko društvo Hrvatske.

Čaldarović, O. (1991) "Socialist Urbanisation and Social Segregation". In: Simmie, J.; Dekleva, J. (eds.) (1991), 131-143.

Čaldarović, O.; Mesić, M.; Štulhofer, A. (eds.) (1992). Sociology and War: Social Consequences of War in Croatia 1991-1992. Zagreb: Croatian Sociological Association.

Čaldarović, O. (1997) "Residential Segregation and Integration: The Case of Zagreb (Dubrava)". In: Švob, M.; Held, J.; hrsg. Jugend zwischen Ausgrenzung und Integration. Zagreb: Institute for Migrations and Ethnic Studies, 101-107.

Derek, G., Urry, J. (eds.) (1985) Social Relations and Spatial Structures. New York: St. Martin's Press.

French, R. A.; Hamilton, I.E. (eds.) (1979). The Socialist City. Spatial Structures and Urban Policy. Sussex: J. Wiley and Sons.

Harvey, D. (1975) Social Justice and the City. London: E. Arnold.

Musil, J. (1980) "Urbanization in Socialist Countries". International Journal of Sociology (X) 2-3.

Simmie, J.; Dekleva, J. (eds.) (1991). Yugoslavia in Turmoil: After Self-Management. London and New York: Pinter Publishers.

Transformation of Łódź: Seeking for a New Region

Konrad Miciukiewicz

This paper examines the processes of transformation that have been taking place in the Polish city Łódź and its urban region since 1989. Łódź, as a socialist industrial monoculture, finds the system transformation very difficult to handle. Since the textile industry (which was strategic for the whole region) collapsed, Łódź and its satellite cities fell in economic crisis; as a result the regional network of economical and social relations has been ruptured. All the cities must find their own strategies of redevelopment. The main objective of this paper is to catch the processes of Łódź's urban restructuring which determine the city's way of transition from a socialist center of textile industry to a polymorphic and diverse European city involved in a network of various national and transnational connections. There are three stages of region's development pointed out in the analysis: 1) 1989 – 1997: conservation of Piotrkowska St. (city's main historical and commercial street) and disurbanization stage - building suburban shopping malls and growth of suburban housing; 2) 1998 to present: inner city revival - foreign and domestic investment in the city center (office buildings, and inner city shopping galleries), renewal and gentrification of several central blocks of streets, the beginning of centripetal movement of inhabitants; 3) projects for the future: the creation of Warsaw–Łódź "Duopolis" – new fast railway route and highway, suburban housing and the new major Polish airport in the heart of the new agglomeration.

Łódź has been the most rapidly growing city in the Polish history. The beginning of the intensive growth was connected with selecting the small town for the industrial settlement in 1821. At this time, Łódź was polulated by 762 people; by the end of XIX century the city had over 300,000 inhabittants. The spatial and architectural landscape of the city has been formed in the XIX century, in the end of which Łódź and its region became the center of textile industry. The urban system of the second Polish city (800,000 inhabitants) has been shaped by narrow streets and apartment houses built on the small parcels, with the huge textile factories and residences of their owners spread all around the core city.

The economy of Łódź and its metropolitan area (containing several big satellite cities: Pabianice (76,000), Zgierz (60,0000), Ozorków (22,000), Aleksandrów Łódzki (20,000) and Konstantynów Łódzki (18,000)) was very like an open system with numerous international connections and multinational investment. Most of industries have been founded with foreign capital, so the city has become the place of multicultural tradition, especially German, Russian and Jewish. After 1945 the contacts of

Łódź's with the Western Europe much decreased, but thanks to keeping strong relationships with the eastern markets the city was still expanding[1] and held its important position in textile industry.

1. 1989 – 1998: economic crisis and disurbanization of the city

In 1989 started the biggest crisis in the city's history. Łódź, being one of postcommunist industrial monocultures, finds the system transformation very difficult to handle. The city was regarded as one of the biggest urban losers in the Polish transformation. Just as many other monofunctional industry centers in Poland, including "one plant towns" (Blazyca, Heffner and Helińska-Hughes 2002: 265) and the most problematic Polish industrial region – Upper Silesia, the Łódź metropolitan region experienced and still experiences a serious post-1989 decline. Since the textile industry collapsed as a consequence of the loss eastern sales markets (mainly Russia and former communist block) and low attractiveness of the textile products on the national market, the city and its region[2] have been having very big problems to adapt to capitalist economy.

The whole Łódź region (administrative *Łódź Voivodship*) has been classified in the last group of Polish provinces as the regression region, whose indices were lower than the national average in all fields (Głębocki and Rogacki 2002)[3]. The economic significance of the region was systematically decreasing in the 90ties. Most of industry restructuring programs undertaken by the local and national authorities[4] failed to overcome the regional crisis (Markowski i Stawasz 1997). The restructuring funds received from the central government were on a very

---

[1] The last intensive industry development program in the city was held in the 70-ties. In this period 40 new factories were built,130 old ones were modernized and 37 were relocated from the central to the new industrial zones located on the outskirts of the city. (Marczyńska-Witczak 1996). The partial degglomeration of industry was followed by renewal and modernization of the inner city, including location new blocks-of-flats in the historical center.

[2] the satellite cities' economies were based on the textile industry even stronger than Łódź's economy was.

[3] Głębocki and Rogacki distinguished four groups of Polish regions due to level of development: 1) regions of intensive development (Pomerania, Kujawy-Pomerania and Wielkopolska), 2) regions of moderate development (Mazovia, West Pomerania, Lubuska Land and Lower Silesia), 3) regions of poor development (Silesia, Warmia-Mazuria and Opole), and 4) regions of regression (Łódź, Lublin, Małopolska, Podkarpacie, Podlasie and Świętokrzyska Land).

[4] Starting from 1989 the state's capacities to regulate socio-economic situation in Polish regions have dramatically fallen. One hand, the state had not the sufficient funds for modernization and restructuration of the industries in the regions. On the other, the central administrative authorities were not prepared for supporting the regions in the conditions different than socialist central planning, as well as most of the competences of various, both central and local, institutions were ill-defined.

low level, what reflected the priorities of the state, which allocated most of regional aid funds in restructuring of the heavy industries, especially mine industry in Upper Silesia. On the other hand, Łódź and the satellite cities do not posses any internal resources, which could be used for the regional restructuring and economic growth – they are not attractive for tourists, have neither natural resources and nor strong national companies (Stawasz 2002). The region lacks the local solidarity and common undertakings. The regional network of social and economic relations, which was built on cooperation between textile industries, has been ruptured. Łódź and surrounding satellite cities must now find their own strategies for empowering of the local production system and building polyfunctional economic structures.

The economic crisis in Łódź and its region in the 90ties was even more serious, because the foreign investors avoided the city when locating their regional branches. The second Polish city was ranked barely at the 10th position in the urban foreign investment ranking[5] (Stawasz 2002). During the first years of transformation the only big investments in the city were hypermarkets, shopping malls and petrol stations. People said mockingly, that there was not possible to produce goods in Łódź anymore, only to sell. There was no foreign or domestic companies, which would generate jobs for the people (mainly women[6]) who lost the job as a result of reduction of employment or closing the of textile industries. As the result, the unemployment rate in the 90ties was very high ranging from 11% to 19%, which was the highest rate noted in the highly urbanized areas. Therefore, the transformation in Łódź economy induced changes in social sphere and marked social inequalities in income, which have also a spatial dimension. Huge enclaves of poverty are spread through the whole city, including the representational quarters in the historical center (Grotowska-Leder 1998).

---

[5] In the ranking of Polish cities due to economic development and attractiveness for foreign investors constructed by Sawicka (Sawicka 1998) Łódź was located on the 8th position with 1,2 companies with foreign capital for 1000 inhabitants (1. Warsaw: 5.9/1000, 2. Poznań 2,6/1000). Sawicka constructed also a synthetic ranking considering 22 partial indexes such as labor market index, level of development, health and social services index, living condition index, etc. In this ranking Łódź was located the 9th position behind 1. Poznań, 2. Warsaw, 3. Katowice, 4. Kraków, 5. Wrocław, 6. Gdańsk, 7. Lublin, and 8. Szczecin.

[6] Women have much more suffered from post-1989 unemployment on the national scale, but the extent of unemployment of formerly working women in Łódź is much higher than the Polish average. Most of the women who lost the jobs in the textile industries were low- and semiskilled workers, and have low chances for being re-employed. They have also received much less help from the state (which has offered them almost no re-qualification funds) in comparison to former miners and other heavy industry workers in Upper Silesia, who had formed very strong labor unions, thus being particularly important in the political terms.

Łódź has been facing also serious demographic problems. Due to economic crisis after 1989 many people decided to leave Łódź searching for work in other regions. The city has been put at the risk of massive disurbanization. The low birth rate, which passed '0' in 1985 and reached -6,7‰ in 1996 (the lowest among big Polish cities) cannot be compensated by the migration flows[7] any more (Michalski and Nowakowska 1998). The loss of population cannot be also interpreted as a consequence of suburbanization, because the metropolitan region as a whole has been suffering from depopulation. During last 15 years Łódź's population decreased almost by 50 thousand from 847,000 in 1985 to 803,000 in 1999 (Patriarcha 2002).[8]

At the same time the core city started to loose the metropolitan functions in favor of suburban areas. The most of new small companies, which produce more than a half of the city income, have been located on the outskirts, while buildings of closed factories in the centre remained empty. In the Łódź suburbs appeared several shopping malls, which took over most of the merchandise flow. The whole centre fell in a process of degradation. The only revitalized area was the main commercial and representational Piotrkowska Str., where conservation works were concentrated, but the rest of the centre remained degraded. Economical crisis and neglected urban structure made the city less and less attractive to live. The conducted surveys have shown, that Łódź is one of the last big cities where the Poles would like to move in, it is also one of the last ones in terms of identification of the inhabitants with their city.

2. 1998 to present: the beginning of inner city revival

Increasing external flow of the inhabitants outside the inner city and successive loss of the metropolitan functions have put Łódź at risk of reduction to the city of a medium scale. Łódź experiences very intensively one of the biggest problem that are all post-communist societies recently faced with: how to create material structures for the capitalist economy? This problem must be linked, however, with the second one – how to "reconstruct urban space as lived space"? (Delanty and Jones 2002: 459) Therefore, two questions have become the most important in the attempts to preserve the city from further disurbanization: 1) how to improve the urban system in order to adapt the form of the city to the new economic conditions, and 2) how to preserve local identity and express the real needs of local people at the same time. This part of the paper

---

[7] The migration balance in Łódź fell from +598 in 1990 to -145 in 1996 (Obraniak 1998).
[8] If this trend remains, the city can lose the next couple of thousands inhabitants in the forthcoming years. Due to the research conducted by Stawasz, the population of Łódź might be reduced even by 100,000 people by the year 2020 (Stawasz 2002).

refs to two urbanistic projects which have been held in the center of Łódź from 1998: The south frontage of Piłsudskiego Ave., and Commercial Centre "Manufaktura".

2.1. The south frontage of Piłsudskiego Avenue

New Piłsudskiego Avenue frontage is located in the heart of the city, close to the elegant Piotrkowska Str. The architectural aggregate, which constructs the frontage occupies two entire blocks of streets (from Piorkowska Str. to Kilińskiego Str.) – the space which was totally abandoned for 20 years after demolishing several historic apartment houses in the 70s due to realization of unfinished socialistic centre rebuilding programme[9]. Five buildings (one just next to another) were constructed in this architectural gap (four completely new and one adapted factory building): office building of BZWBK bank, 2) cinema multiplex Silver Screen and 3) Hotel Ibis (occupying one block of streetes), 4) editorial office of "Gazeta Wyborcza" and 5) shopping centre „Galeria Łódzka".

The decision to let the multinational corporations in the very centre of the city was seen by many as a serious threat to local identity. On the one hand, it was a chance to start the urban revival and bring back the metropolitan functions to the centre due to big international investments. On the other, there was a possibility that the qualitative *social use value* of the space could become rationalized and organized in favor of the *exchange value* (Kazemian 1991). Using Manuel Castells' terms, new frontage was meant to become a *space of flows* (where the global capitalistic structures are reproduced), which he finds contradictory to *space of places* (where local cultural orders reproduce themselves, ensuring endurance of the historically rooted societies) (Castells 2001). In Castells' view, within the *space of flows*, created by delocalized and a-historic architecture (mainly office and service), symbolic relations between the city space and its inhabitants disintegrate. Historical societies – he says – need the space of meeting and interaction within the place - the space of places.

In Castells' division, the new frontage in Łódź, due to the functions of its buildings would be located in the *space of flows*. Five new buildings were constructed to house five types of flows: 1) financial flows (the bank), 2) flows of images (the cinema multiplex), 2) tourist flows (the hotel), 4) information flows (editorial office) and 5) merchandise flows (the shopping gallery). However, using Castells' category of *space of flows* (understood as a space of delocalized architecture) to describe the new Łódź frontage cannot be held valid after we look at the new buildings more closely. Only the first three can fall into this distinction: the mo-

---

[9] Due to the project from the 70s in these blocks of streets huge blocks-of-flats should appear as a continuation of the settlement built from the southern side.

dernistic, reflective glass WBK office building, Silver Screen, and Ibis Hotel have been designed according to the standard construction patterns functioning in other countries.

The other two buildings are different. The editorial office of "Gazeta Wyborcza" is located in the old Prussian, renovated and reconstructed factory building with a new addition. The editorial office, which is a historic building adapted to fulfilling new functions, makes reference to industrial architecture, one of the two basic architectural identities of the 19th century Łódź. It does not create a homogenious and ahistoric space, as Castells would like, but opens possibilities for uncovering a varied, multicultural tradition. The editorial office of "Gazeta Wyborcza", which fulfills the function of a local node of the global information flows, at the same time is an expression of regional architecture and stands as "the resistance movement to the homogenizing forces of global capitalism" (Frampton 1985).

The most interesting, however, of these buildings is probably shopping centre "Galeria Łódzka" (the biggest of them which occupies the whole block of streets). The idea of building the huge shopping gallery in the centre caused numerous doubts. Most shopping malls, which are built on the suburbs are turned back to the city and totally isolated from surroundings, are one of the most important factors of increasing disurbanization of cities (Majewski 2003). The idea of "Galeria Łódzka" is just opposite. German company ECE, who owns the center, builds its galleries in city centres in the way so they could fit to the local inner city atmosphere. ECE pays much attention to making its projects harmonious with the cultural landscape of the city engaging local architects and using high-quality architectural designs. The „Galeria Łódzka" building opens itself for the street space through its big shop windows. It makes also reference to two of the local identities: 1) industrial factory identity – through red brick selections and the shape of the windows, and 2) traditional Łodź frontage – through the elevation division into narrow segments shaped the same as historic apartment houses.

2.2. "Manufaktura"

Participation of foreign companies in the forms of returning local Łódź identities appears most clearly during the construction of recreational-cultural center "Manufaktura" (previously named Nowy Świat) which is planned to be opened in 2005. The new center will be located in the historic Izrael Poznanski's industrial site at Zachodnia Str., which is now rebuilt by the French company Apsys. This project is the biggest town-planning undertaking in Eastern Europe of this kind. The area of 27 hectares, probably the largest in the country urban construction site, will house a center including cinema multiplex, giant discoteque, 20 restaurants, 250 shops, fairground, several art galleries, 3 museums, 3 fashion houses and fashion promotion center.

"Manufaktura" is to be a city within the city, Łódź in miniature. The historic site contains not only industrial buildings; it has its own transport system with streets and cable cars. Construction works are aimed at revitalizing and restoring the town-like character of this industrial aggregate. Apsys wants to give names to the streets and reactivate the cable car in order to develop the new centre's public transport. The most interesting is idea of creation a market place, which in fact Łódź doesn't have being a 19th century city built on a scheme of perpendicular streets. The new market place, which is planned to be bigger than the Warsaw's Old Market, will be surrounded with thematic streets symbolizing cities of the similar history and cities commercially connected.

The idea of creating the market is meant to be a key contribution of "Manufaktura" to a civic development. On the one hand, it will become (together with planned parks and squares) a new public space in the city, a space of meeting and social interaction for inhabitants of Łódź and its region. On the other, this market, joining the historic buildings with elements of contemporary architecture, could be understood as an "art of communication" (Zuziak 1996). The very essential for the idea of the market in "Manufaktura" is the thematization of surrounding streets. The very unusual theme park proposed by Apsys in "Manufaktura", is based on a theme of the housing city itself. The themed streets which themes refer to the atmosphere of European cities (ex. Lyon, Stuttgart) connected with Łódź, are aimed to symbolize city's European proveniences, economic ties and multicultural roots. The market in Łódź surrounded by European-themed streets, brings the notion of Łódź as an European city, which, after years of isolation, returns to the map of integrating Europe.

2.3. Signs of economic revival
The last two years have brought also the first positive signs for restructuring of Łódź's economy. The city seems to have come back on the Polish investment map. The most important investment is contracted to be built on the northern side of Piłsudskiego Ave. just in front of 'Galeria Łódzka'. Philips is going to relocate its European Financial Center the from Ireland and Holland, offering 700 office jobs in Łódź. The city is also becoming the Eastern European center of the household goods industries, while Merloni Indersit and Bosh-Siemens are enlarging the existing factories and building the new ones (*Polityka* 2004). Gillette is closing its factories in Germany and the UK in order to open the new ones in Poland. Łódź, which has been depicted as the best investment allocation city in Poland in the McKinsey annual report, is becoming more attractive for the domestic investors as well. Two biggest internet banks - mBank and MultiBank - chosen Łódź as the place for their head-

quarters. Polish mobile phone operators, national telecommunication company TP S.A and banks locate their call centers here. Why?

The inhabitants of Łódź can work for 30% less money than the companies would have to pay the employees in Warsaw. They are ready to accept worse work conditions and have lower expectations; they are more determined and more loyal to their employers. There are lots of low- and semiskilled workers, who lost the jobs in the textile industry, and many high-qualified unemployed young people, who have just graduate from the third biggest university in the country. Paradoxically, the high unemployment rate (19,2%) and the low average salary have became the city's social capital.[10] Łódź's authorities believe in the synergic effect – that the existing investors will pull in the new ones. There is a chance for the economic restructuring in Łódź, but at the moment it is very hard to formulate any prognosis for the longer run. The city of Łódź, more than many other Eastern European is now a crossroads: its socialist features are fading, but is not yet clear where it is heading for (Szelenyi 1996). Many former economic structures have already disappeared or are now decaying rapidly, the new ones are just emerging. The question, if the city is capable of joining the Eastern European urban development axis or will be degraded to the status of provincial middle size city, is still open.

3. Project for the future: the idea of establishing Warsaw-Łódź "Duopolis"

The attention of Łódź city councilmen and architects focuses now around the urban planning idea for linking Łódź and Warsaw into one city – "Duopolis Poland" (Czekalski 1998, *Dziennik Łódzki* 2002, Krajewski 2002, Liszewski 1998, Szul 1998, *The Warsaw Voice* 2002). In the first stage of the project, transport integration is planned (fast railway, motorway, a new airport); in later stages, spatial integration would be built by developing a highly urbanized region between two largest Polish cities. Warsaw and Łódź are already separated by a dense settlement belt with

---

[10] The average salary in Łódź is 1.950 PLN, while in Wasaw is 3.680 PLN (national average – 2.300 PLN). Both unskilled labors in the new factories and the qualified office staff are low paid. If for example Philips had opened its Financial Center in Warsaw, it would have paid the employees 20 – 40 % more. At the same time the Philips employees in Łódź earn about 8 times less than their colleagues in Eindhoven working on the same positions. It must be said also that over 90% workers of the Philips Center in Łódź have graduated the university at the M.A. level, while almost half of the Dutch workers have only secondary school education. The other problem is, that the new jobs were generated mostly in industry and are not followed by the transfer of the advanced technologies. There is a high risk, that these investments have only temporary character. Most of the newly located factories could be easily moved further east, when the average salaries in Poland and the city itself reach the higher level.

medium-size cities, inhabited by 3 million people. The metropolitan areas of Warsaw (2.5 mln inhabitants) and Łódź (1.5 mln people) together with this settlement belt would create a 7 mln metropolis of the economic and cultural potential largest in Poland. As the authors of the project "Duopolis Poland" forecast, the metropolis could become the strongest centre of economic growth in central Europe, at the same time counterbalancing Prague (2 mln), Budapest (3 mln), and Berlin (5 mln).

Overlooked for many years by investors, suffering from economic recession since 1989, Łódź is interested in the project far more than Warsaw. The success of the project would give it an opportunity to find its new place in the differentiated network of regional and European economic ties. It could become part of a significant European centre. Yet, the integration can also be attractive for Warsaw, even if now it has the unchallenged position of the centre of Polish economy. Its demographic and economic potential is too small to give it a competitive advantage among the cities of integrating Europe. Cities and regions are nowadays the most active participants of economic processes, so such functional spatial system of complementary potentials of Warsaw and Łódź would stimulate development not only of the region but also the Polish economy as a whole.

The idea of linking Warsaw and Łódź, 120 km away, originates in the middle of the twentieth century, especially in the 60s and 70s when the doctrine of belt development was promoted in Europe; the idea later dropped as unfeasible economically. The economic and political transformation and European Union accession providing structural funds have revived the idea of integrating the two cities. The project received its present shape in 1997 and since then local authorities of Łódź and Warsaw have been consulting it. Letters of intention have been signed by their respective mayors (Marek Czekalski, Krzysztof Panas in Łódź and Wojciech Kozak, Marcin Święcicki in Warsaw).

3.1. Integration of transport

The starting phase for the Duopolis project will be focused on the transport intergation of Warsaw and Łódź, which should make the time of transit between the two cities by road and rail two times shorter. Fast road connection will be constructed independently of the agreements. In the national motorway construction plan Łódź is the most important transportation centre in the country, being located south of the crossing of A2 and A1 motorways. North of the city will run A2 - the east-west motorway, Polish section of the transport corridor Paris-Berlin-Moscow – which will connect Łódź with Warsaw in 2010. In the same year, the city section of A1 – north–south motorway – will be completed connecting southern districts of Łódź with Warsaw.

To establish fast rail connection between the city centres of Warsaw and Łódź a new link must be constructed as the transeuropean corridor N II bypasses Łódź in the north (Friedberg 2001). Now it takes 100 minutes to get from the station of Łódź Fabryczna to the station of Warszawa Centralna. It is far too long for 10 000 people[11] commuting from Łódź to Warsaw, and consequently hinders the labor market integration. With the planned IC connection, in which the new track would permit the speed of 250 kmph, it would take 45-55 minutes to get from one main station to the other and 55-70 minutes to get from Łódź to Warsaw airport (Janiszewski, Kwaśkiewicz and Lisowski 2001). The project is estimated at 3 billion PLN and would build the first experimental connection of High Speed Railway (KDP) in Poland, making use of European Union structural funds for up to 80% of its cost.

And finally but perhaps most importantly, the project on which the success of "Duopolis Poland" depends most is the construction of a new airport located between Warsaw and Łódź. In 2020 Warsaw must have a new airport as the capacity of Okęcie is running out.[12] If the location of Rawa-Skierniewice (in the middle of the way between two cities) is chosen, the centre of the new Łódź-Warsaw metropolis will have a large transcontinental airport which will eventually take over from Okęcie the functions of Poland's main airport. It would be situated between the A2 motorway and NII railway corridor and the High Speed Railway connecting Warsaw and Łódź, near the crossing of A1 and A2 in Stryków. Easy access to the airport from different parts of the country would also facilitate urbanization of the new Metropolis' centre and the belt separating the two cities now.

---

[11] In the situation when the Polish State Railway suffers from the falling number of passengers, the number of passengers in this connection has increased by 80% in the years 2000-2003. Of course there is an increase in the number of car commuters, so the rail transport on this line is going to grow and be profitable. The construction of High Speed Train line, the only one in Poland, could be a chance for restructuring the heavily indebted Polish State Railway.

[12] Poland's main airport, Okęcie south of Warsaw, is already working much above its capacity. The capital's authorities have decided to build a new terminal at Okęcie, which would for some time solve the problem of too much traffic at the Warsaw airport. The air transport analyses show, however, that in 2015 Okęcie will lose its capacity, so a new airport is an absolute must. By the end of 2004 the final decision must be made on the location and character of the new airport – whether it will remain Poland's main airport or be an additional one for Warsaw. One of the proposed locations for Okęcie 2 – Poland's main airport – is the area between Skierniewice and Rawa Mazowiecka, the central point in the planned "Duopolis Poland" (other locations chosen in the national pre-selection are: Modlin, Mszczonów and Sochaczew).

3.2. Spatial integration

The authors of the Duopolis Poland project assume that the new airport in Skierniewice together with the road and rail infrastructure will attract investors to the Warsaw-Łódź metropolitan area, suburbanizing it and gradually unifying spatially the two cities. The forested area along the new transportation tracts on the line Łódź-airport-Warsaw will become attractive housing areas, providing easy access to both the two cities and natural resources. The authors of the project, however, hope mostly for building around the Skierniewice airport and the crossing of the two motorways: A1 and A2. Three European transportation corridors: Paris-Moscow, the Baltic-the Adriatic, Via Baltica, cross there, so the site could become central Europe's logistical center and a giant shopping mall. Details of the construction plans for the airport area are not known yet, but the authors of the project count on the office and technological parks to be set up there. In the vicinity of the new airport Poland's first edge city could be situated.

3.3. Revitalising the centre

Spatial integration of Warsaw and Łódź within the Duopolis accounts not only for the linear suburbanization of the region but also, and perhaps mainly, for rehabilitating and revitalisating of the centres of the two connected cities. One of the most significant assumptions of the project is the creation in each city of "metropolitan gates" – multifunctional commercial centres that would be set up in the areas surrounding the railway stations of Łódź Fabryczna and Warszawa Centralna (connected by the High Speed Trains). Actually, Warszawa Centralna has already been surrounded with a business commercial centre. In Łódź, on the other hand, the postindustrial site around the station has not been used and is very neglected.

The authors of the project suggest that the rundown, closed down, post-industrial site can be turned into Łódź metropolitan gate, „Łódź Portal". If successful, the project would change the old power plant, warehouses, and disused rail infrastructure into a commercial business centre pro-viding office space, conference centre, shopping space. This vast, un-used area, between Sienkiewicza, Narutowicza, Rydza-Śmigłego and Tuwima streets is still viewed as one of the most important development sites in the city's structure. The city's main street, Piotrkowska, Uni-versity's main building, and the city's main offices are very close, so the site seems ideal for the city's future business centre.

The city authorities' efforts to develop „Łódź Portal" concentrate now on clearing the site and finding investors for public-private undertakings. The city administration, looking for new office spaces, could be parti-cularly involved in the first investments. Łódź University also shows a lot of interest in the space of the future "Portal", because its rectorate is located next to the Łódź Fabryczna station. There are plans for locating there a new university mini-district, with new administration spaces and class-rooms. There is also a possibility of building a big office and conference centre for servicing the offset program introduced by Lockheed Martin which would be held by Łódź University and University of Texas in Austin.[13]

One proposal on developing the space, by Jacek Ferdzyn, relates the urban structure to the historic site and plans adaptations of some beautiful industrial buildings still on the site of the old power plant, where the Museum of Art could be located. The street plan, however, would be changed to create a new network, to facilitate traffic and create additional access to the facades of the new buildings. The plan includes also construction of some new road connections (with the tunnel under the railway as an extention of Targowa Str.) and the station of underground railway connecting Łódź Fabryczna and Łódź Kaliska (Ferdzyn 2002).

In the first stage the author of the project proposes concentrating on clearing the sites and reconstructing the streets in order to improve the transport system around the station. In the next one, the historic stations would be rebuilt in the way that its railway functions would be fulfilled only in the first floor. The rest of the building would be reserved for administration spaces for the city council and merchandise spaces. Later the clearing of the terrain would be continued and next block of streets after several divisions would be prepared. Adaptation of the rest of the buildings and construction of the new ones would depend on the private investors, but with a possibility of co-financing of conservation of the historic buildings, which could house some cultural institutions, from the city founds and structural EU founds.

Conclusions

The biggest problem of the „Duopolis Poland" project is that due to financial situation of the country the establishment of metropolitan community in the nearest future has small chances of realization. It faces the wave of press criticism, being often regarded as unrealizable project and a typical example of wishful thinking of the local elites, inherited from their predecessors working in the times of the grate socialist development plans. It seems still to be the very distinctive for Eastern Europe, that many, often very spectacular urban projects end their life on the declarative phase. Warsaw-Łódź "Duopolis" project could face the same destiny. However, the integration of two biggest Polish cities will happen spontaneously. At least some of the goals could be achieved in

---

[13]As one of offset revenues connected to buying F-16 by Polish Army, the American producer Lockheed Martin offered the transfer of technologies worth 150 mln USD and further 100 mln USD for the realization of the whole undertaking.

the next few years time. The crucial factor for the success of integration of Łódź and Warsaw today is the choice of Skierniewice as the location of the new major Polish airport. If the airport is located between two cities, the perspectives of creating "Duoplis Poland" and introducing massive urban revitalization of Łódź will become real.

The integration with Warsaw seems to be the only solution for improving the economy in Łódź. The realization of Duopolis project would give also the chance for urban redevelopment, with a special reference to adaptation of historic industrial buildings and bringing back varied metropolitan functions to neglected city centre. Examples of the new realized urban projects in the city center (New South Frontage of Piłsudskiego Ave. and commercial centre "Manufaktura") can be interpreted as the signs of the beginning of the inner city revitalization. The possibilities linked the present wave of foreign investments in Łódź and the Duopolis project could bring further changes.

The most important of them would be re-introducing the idea of open city. The processing of re-opening Łódź can be understood in three contexts. In the first one, Łódź would regain its international ties becoming open for its multicultural tradition and varied European relationships. In the second sense, the city due to integration with Warsaw would be opened for becoming a part new regional structure. In the third and probably the most important one, the city would open its abandoned and fenced industrial spaces to the inhabitants. The former factories may become the most important public spaces in the city, the spatial manifestation for local public sphere where the local identities could be maintained and reconstructed.

References:
Blazyca, G.; Heffner, K.; Helińska-Hughes, E. (2002) 'Poland – Can Regional Policy Meet the Challenge of Regional Problems?'. In: European Urban and Regional Studies 9 (3).
Castells, M. (2001) The Rise of the Network Society. Oxford - Malden: Blackwell Publishers.
Czekalski, M. (1998) 'Łódź Warszawa razem w Europie i w Świecie', in: VII Konwersatorium Unii Metropolii Polskich: wspólnota metropolitarna Łódź & Warszawa. Kolej, autostrada, lotnisko. Łódź, 6th of September 1998.
Delanty, G; Jones P.R. (2002) 'European Identity and Architecture'. In: European Journal of Social Theory 5 (4).
Dziennik Łódzki (2002) 'Politycy i marzyciele' (Saturday, 14th of December).
Ferdzyn, J. (2002) Portal Łódzki. (architect's documentation).
Frampton, K. (1985) 'Critical regionalism: speculations on an architecture of resistance'. In: Johnson, C. (ed.) The City in Conflict. London: Mansell.
Friedberg, J. (2001) 'Koncepcja integracji transportowej metropolii Warszawy i Łodzi: główne aspekty strategii przygotowania i realizacji przedsięwzięcia'. In: Konsylium Unii Metropolii Polskich. Warsaw, 23rd of November 2001.

Głębocki, B.; Rogacki, H. (2002) 'Regions of Growth and Stagnation in Poland: Changes in Agriculture, Industry and International Markets'. In: European Urban and Regional Studies 9 (3).

Grotowska-Leder, J. (1998) 'Łódzkie enklawy biedy'. In: Warzywoda-Kruszyńska (ed.) Żyć i pracować w enklawach biedy (Klimaty Łódzkie). Łódź: Agencja Projektowo-Wydawnicza ANaGRAF.

Janiszewski, A.; Kwaśkiewicz, J.; Lisowski, K. (2001) 'Wstępna koncepcja szybkiego połączenia kolejowego Łódź – Warszawa'. In: Konsylium Unii Metropolii Polskich. Warsaw, 12th of November 2001.

Kazemian, R. (1991) Urban Renewal Planning versus Local Values: a Study of Modern Urban Policy and Renewal Processes and of their Impact on a Local Community (Case of Grone Gatan in Göteborg). Göteborg: Chalmers University of Technology.

Krajewski, S. (2002) 'Wnioski konsylium N°1 Portal Łódzki'. In: Konsylium Unii Metropolii Polskich. Łódź, 15th of February 2002.

Liszewski, S. (1998) 'Łódź –centrum nowego regionu'. In Michalski, W. (ed.) Najnowsze problemy transformacji aglomeracji łódzkiej. Łódź: Łódzkie Towarzystwo Naukowe.

Majewski, J. S. (2003) 'Nowa pierzeja w Łodzi'. Architektura, n°8, 2003.

Marczyńska-Witczak (1996) 'Zmiany struktury gospodarczej Łodzi'. In: Transformacja społeczno-gospodarcza Łodzi na tle regionu. Łódź: PTG.

Markowski T.; Stawasz, D. (1997) 'Łódź i region – przyczyny upadku i rozwoju'. In: Gorzelak G. (ed.) Studia regionalne i lokalne, no. 19, Warsaw: EIRRiL UW.

Michalski, W.; Nowakowska, B. (1998) 'Ludność w przestrzeni miasta'. In: Michalski, W. (ed.) Najnowsze problemy transformacji aglomeracji łódzkiej. Łódź: Łódzkie Towarzystwo Naukowe.

Obraniak, W. (1998) Migracje ludności w województwie łódzkim w latach 1975-1996. Łódź: Łódzki Urząd Statystyczny.

Patriarcha W. (2002) 'Strategy for Łódź on the Eve of European integration', paper presented at the conference "Łódź & European Integration". Łódź 2002.

Polityka (2004) 'Łódź na Fali' (n° 13 (2445).

Sawicka, D. (1998) 'Łódź na tle największych aglomeracji miejskich'. In: Michalski, W. (ed.) Najnowsze problemy transformacji aglomeracji łódzkiej. Łódź: Łódzkie Towarzystwo Naukowe.

Stawasz, D. (2002) Współczesne uwarunkowania rozwoju polskich regionów. Łódź: Wydawnictwo Uniwersytetu Łódzkiego.

Szelenyi, I. (1996) 'Cities under Socialism - and After'. In: Andrusz, G.; Harloe, M.; Szelenyi, I. (eds.) Cities after Socialism. Urban and Regional Change and Conflict in Post-Socialist Societies. Oxford: Blackwell Publishers.

Szul, R. (1998) 'Integracja Warszawy i Łodzi'. In: VII Konwersatorium Unii Metropolii Polskich.

The Warsaw Voice (2002) 'Urban Spawl' (April 28 May 2002 N° 17/18).

Zuziak, Z. (1996) 'Managing Historic Cities: New Challenges for Urban Planning'. In: Chatterji, M.; Domański, R. (eds.) Urban and Regional Images in Countries in Transition. Warsaw: Wydawnictwo Naukowe PWN.

High Profile Buildings:
Help-mates in international and local competition
The case of Prague

Jana Temelová

1 Introduction

In response to globalization urban, regional and national entities compete with each other driven by the ambition of an effectual integration and participation in international production. In return they hope for influx of capital, creation of new jobs and generation of wealth. The mode on which nowadays world operates obviously brings considerable consequences for economic, social as well as physical development of contemporary cities. The increasing interconnection of the world economic system creates social, economic and spatial inequalities among cities as well as within cities (Hall, 1998).

Various assets from cultural resources to economic success stories happened to play more or less prominent role in aspirations of cities, regions and nations to make a mark in wider international arena. Apparently architectural artefacts got involved in struggle for place recognition too. Many urban scholars have argued that urban governors employ qualities of built environment in city-marketing and image-building strategies (Greenberg, 2003; Hubbard, 1995; Zukin, 1995). In the context of international competition certain kind of buildings apparently picks up a prominent position in place-promotional and image-building efforts of cities. The first objective of this paper thus becomes to explore what kind of contemporary buildings these are; in particular to what kind of contemporary buildings public decision makers attach the prime importance in international marketing of Prague. I chose to call these structures *high profile buildings* since I suppose that governors believe in their power to shape a favourable image and by promoting them they hope to raise the international profile of the city (with desirable impacts on local economy, quality of social life, physical value of urban space etc.).

The competition takes place not only on global scale but strikes also entities at lower levels of spatial order and thus rivalry and uneven development within cities occurs (Hall, 1998; Stanback, 1995). Approaching buildings as physical assistants in internationally oriented marketing practices of urban governments poses a question whether the buildings that appeal to the challenges posed on cities by global competition may strengthen the position of particular neighbourhoods in intra-urban competition as well. Therefore my second objective will be to investigate the effects of high profile buildings on local attractiveness of the neighbourhoods in which they are set.

In short within the scope of this paper I will address the following two research questions:

- What kind of contemporary buildings is recognized by governments at local, regional and national level as worth showing-off when it comes to international promotion of Prague?

- What is the possible effect of high profile buildings on local attractiveness of their neighbourhoods?

2. Cities in competition, urban regeneration and the role of built environment

The global competition for capital, resources and jobs has become a discussed theme among urban scholars as well as growing policy concern of urban practitioners. As Castells (1996) outlined in his concept of network society the internationalised urban hierarchy is unstable and thus a subject to fierce inter-city competition. The competitiveness at global scale prompts local, regional and central governments (and companies alike) to fight for a favourable position in internationalized economy in hope for prosperity and economic affluence. Accordingly Thronley (2002) pointed out that many city leaders nowadays hold the attitude that taking a proactive role and promoting their cities is essential to keep up with the ongoing competition.

Castells and Hall (1994) argued that image creation happened to constitute an essential basis for successful competition. Also Zukin (1997) pointed out that image making is a key element of international competition among cities. She brought forward that cities in the transition from industrial to service based production "emphasise their *symbolic economy* in both material alternations that ´upscale` the built environment and symbolic representations focusing on image" (Zukin, 1997, p. 206).

Since physical structures enable to carry symbolic forms and cues they acquire an operative role in image creation and place marketing. In the concept of *buildings as signs* Haila (1997) suggested that the investment to prestigious and landmark structures represents one of the promotional and image-making tools, which is used by both private and public investors. She distinguished three types of sign buildings: *trophy buildings*, referring to Zukin (1991), give name, fame and prestige to their owners, *exclusive buildings* aim to exclude and segment the market and at last *image buildings* promote a favourable investment climate in order to attract foreign investors (Haila, 1997). Similarly it is appropriate to appeal to Zukin's (1991) idea of *signature (trophy) buildings*. In her words "signature or trophy buildings link the cultural value of architecture with the economic value of land and buildings" (Zukin, 1991, p. 45). Although neither signature and trophy nor image buildings directly produce money they are supposed to have an indirect effect on profit making by creating a flourishing image of companies or places. They can serve as "means of enhancing commercial success" for adjacent building development (office, shopping, residential, entertainment) and in long-term run they can support generating of investment by making places more noticeable and by attracting outside activities (Logan and Molotch, 1997, p. 311). The Guggenheim museum in Bilbao represents a well-known example of prestige-like project, which happened to symbolize an economic regeneration of declining industrial Basque region. Nowadays, especially in South East Asia the spectacular high-rise structures re-present a common tool of city's progressive image as emergent world cores.

The notion of buildings as feasible marketing tools should not be seen in isolation from more general trends in governance of Western cities. Harvey (1989b) proposed that as a consequence of changes in global e-conomy a shift from *managerial* practices (provision of services and benefits to local population) to *entrepreneurial* strategies focusing on local economic development and speculative projects carried on by public-private partnerships has emerged in urban governance since the recession in 1970s. It has been pointed out quite clearly that physical en-vironment and creation of new urban landscapes represent important in-struments in city marketing and entrepreneurial practices of cities. Harvey (1989a, p. 91-92) emphasized that nowadays cities and places seem "to take much more care to create a positive and high quality image of place, and have sought an architecture and forms of urban de-sign that respond to such need." The creation of spectacular urban land-scape thus became a means to attract capital as well as affluent people (Harvey, 1989a). Alike Hubbard (1995, p. 244) remarked that „promotion of environmental quality is just one of the strategies used by urban governors in an attempt to make the city more attractive to potential in-vestors". He offered an example of Birmingham where the city council pledged itself to continual environmental improvements since the local representatives believed that "an attractive environment will improve the quality of life for the city's residents as well as stimulate investment" (Hubbard, 1995, p. 246).

A lot of debate concerning the improvement of city image and production of new urban landscapes appears in relation to pro-growth local eco-nomic strategies adopted by many industrial cities as a response to de-cay. Drawing upon the work of Loftman and Nevin (1995, 1996) the de-velopment and promotion of *prestige projects* has become a key com-ponent of urban regeneration initiative in Britain (and beyond) in 1980s and 1990s. Local governments as well as urban development cor-porations saw prestige projects as essential mechanisms for physical re-generation of declining urban areas and as important city promotion de-

vices in inter-urban competition (Loftman and Nevin, 1995). The up-
grading of physical environment and improvement of urban design have
been not once recognized as planning devices to reach the en-
hancement of neighbourhoods and to bring about the local economic re-
generation (Gospodini, 2002; Hubbard, 1995). The statement basically
leans on assumption that the physical upgrading might trigger off a range
of chain reactions and bring about a wider improvement of social and e-
conomic situation (Loftman and Nevin, 1995; Smyth, 1994).
In the same way as signature or image buildings also high profile
buildings get a word in portraying places as attractive for investment, for
tourism or for living. I assume that also in the case of Prague public re-
presentatives believe in favourable agency of architectural structures in
city promotion and accordingly advertise certain buildings in urban
guides and promotional brochures. However only a few structures from
the pool of contemporary construction come up to suit this purpose; what
kind of buildings they are remains to be explored further in the paper. Al-
though it is obviously hard to extract a "pure" agency of one building from
the net of factors, forces and actors that effect the area attractiveness I
believe that a meaningful connection between the location of high profile
building and the position of neighbourhood within the intra-urban
hierarchy can be found.

3. Methodological approach

Selection of high profile buildings
Which contemporary buildings were recognized as important for pro-
motion of Prague and therefore chosen by appropriate decision makers
to advertise the capital in the international arena? Though I admit that
various paths through which physical structures embrace a high profile
label may exist in this paper I selected the high profile items of built en-
vironment according to their occurrence in capital-marketing materials
produced by relevant public authorities. I took into account promotional
materials produced at three administrative levels, namely at local (city),
regional (region) and national (state). I ought to emphasize that
governmental bodies or institutions needed to be the agents promoting
and advertising the buildings. Since I aimed to pick up those con-
temporary structures which were regarded as significant especially in re-
lation to outward promotion of the capital, it means those targeting pri-
marily tourists, business community and other people coming from out-
side the country the availability of marketing materials in English
language was required.
As to the advertised buildings I introduced several restrictions concerning
their attributes (type of construction, location, year of completion) as well

as the mode and frequency of their occurrence in capital-marketing materials:

- New constructions.
- Located within administrative boundaries of Prague.
- Completed after 1990 (including).
- Buildings promoted as decoys, attractions, points of interest. Not only function, but also the physical structure which houses it represents a value to be advertised.
- Building appeared in more than one promotional material.

Measuring local attractiveness
The reviewing of promotional material provided me with three high profile buildings in Prague:

- office building Dancing House (Tančící dům)
- commercial centre Golden Angel (Zlatý Anděl)
- TV tower Žižkov

For further investigation regarding the effects of high profile buildings on area attractiveness I decided to pick up the commercial centre Golden Angel. I find the building the most suitable for this purpose since it is located in formerly industrial inner city neighbourhood which has been experiencing a significant redevelopment in the recent years (Dancing House is located in the traditionally attractive city centre; TV tower is in inner city residential area yet its foundation during socialism and completion already 12 years ago make the inquiry into its impacts rather complicated). The indicators I selected to examine effects of Golden Angel on neighbourhood attractiveness are twofold:

- **Property market indicators** (trends, most-preferred locations). I discussed the trends in rental and sale prices of residential and office real estate in Prague over the last 5 years with the particular interest in reporting neighbourhood. I further added the information on popularity of particular districts and areas as to the demand for office premises and residential units. The limited availability of detail-structured real estate data represented the main restriction of the chosen approach.

- **New development projects** (influx of real-estate investors, construction activity). I considered the follow-up investments in real estate (new development projects) in the neighbourhood as another relevant measure of local gravity.

4. What makes a contemporary building the high profile building?
The selection of high profile buildings in Prague based on the buildings' occurrence in promotional materials produced by governmental bodies

on local, regional and national level resulted in a sample of three buildings. Presumably thanks to their advertising potential these buildings were employed by decision makers in believe that they help to enhance global profile, attractiveness and competitiveness of the capital. I expect that a particular set of features makes high profile buildings especially apt for advertising of contemporary cities. Drawing on the examples of high profile buildings identified in Prague I will now pay attention to some of their attributes which I find rather distinct and at the same shared by all of them.

High profile function

In the concept of transformation from *managerialism* to *entrepreneurialism* Harvey (1989b, 1988) proposed that entrepreneurially thinking urban governments emphasise the city's advantages for production of goods and services by stimulating the invention and application of new technologies, they seek to attract consumers by enhancing the quality of life (investment in culture, environmental upgrading) and they focus on infrastructural provision for control and command functions by investing in transport, communications and adequate office space. *Table 1* introduces the building types and primary functions (activities) that high profile buildings selected in Prague accommodate. The overview indicates that buildings maintaining promotion for the capital relate to the purposes of advanced services and communication, the realms depicted by Harvey (1989b) as relevant for urban entrepreneurialism.

Table 1: Building types and functions of high profile buildings in Prague

Name of building	Building type	Function
Dancing House	office building	professional services (financial)
Golden Angel	office and shopping centre	professional services (mixed) and retail
TV Tower Zizkov	TV transmitter	communication, broadcasting

Dancing House is an office building owned by insurance company Nationale–Netherlanden (a member of multinational financial corporation ING Group) and rented to multinational management consulting company Accenture. Beside the spectrum of retail facilities, commercial complex Golden Angel gathers offices of several companies operating in advanced services sector, including ING Group head office (owner of Golden Angel) and other financial and legal firms. TV and radio transmitter in Zizkov constitutes a part of infrastructure serving to the needs of telecommunications and broadcasting.

Landmark architecture

A wide range of physical structures accommodates high profile functions but obviously no all of them deserve the label high profile buildings. To produce some kind of symbolical message in the sense depicted by Zukin (1991) in the concept of *signature buildings* clearly poses certain challenges on symbolic and architectural expression of buildings. Haila (1997) described *image buildings* as landmarks, visible signs that lend to a city the appearance of global city. The notion of *landmarks* formulated by Lynch (1960) appears to be helpful in approaching the contextual distinctiveness of buildings. According to him the key physical feature of landmarks as the most visually significant elements creating the city image is their singularity, "some aspect that is unique or memorable in the context" (Lynch, 1960, p. 78). I will show that the selected high profile buildings in Prague fit to greater or lesser extent the idea of visual distinctiveness. Mainly through the visual and contextual efficiency in urban physical space the high profile buildings represent a particular kind of landmarks symbolizing contemporary epoch.

Dancing House designed by a world-known architect Frank Gehry (in cooperation with locally based Vlado Milunic) represents the best example of post-modern architecture in Prague which is still rare in the Czech environment (see *photo 1*). The two playful towers reminding of a dancing couple gave the building its characteristic name. The glaring expression of contemporary architecture made the Dancing House very recognizable in its local historical context.

Photo 1: Office building Dancing House in Prague

Source: www.pis.cz

The structure of Golden Angel designed by another celebrity architect Jean Nouvel (in cooperation with local architectural firm A 8000) represents an extraordinary building set in a former industrial Prague's neighbourhood (see *photo 2*). The glass facade with a motif of angel inspired by both the historic name of place and Wim Wenders' film *Wings of desire* is the most eye-catching feature of the whole complex. The image of angel is accompanied by fragments of poetry which come from the texts of famous authors strongly linked to Prague.

Photo 2: Commercial centre Golden Angel in Prague

Photo by author

The TV tower in Zizkov is at its 216 metres the tallest building in Prague and thanks to its visibility from far away a true landmark of the city (see *photo 3*). Many consider the futuristic high-rise structure as one of the capital's most emphatic dominates.

Photo 3: The TV transmitter Zizkov in Prague

Source: http://www.radio.cz/en/article/33525

Attracting attention – gaining publicity

Most of the contemporary constructions are rather average, do not lean out from the main stream and thus not many discussions accompany their rise. On the other hand global competition challenges to contest for recognition and calls for projects provoking international attention. Harvey (1989a) assigned a greater importance to advertising and media in the growth dynamics of capitalism particularly due to their ability to manipulate tastes and desires through images. I suppose that the achievement of building in city marketing largely depends also on publicity surrounding the whole project. To be seen means to get involved into public debates and discussions, to be present in newspapers, magazines or on TV shows.

A variety of building-related factors may support a desirable publicity and spread of awareness. The high profile function and activities taking place in venue may provide one of the decoys and sources of public interest. As top envoys of contemporary built environment high profile buildings appear on pages of architectural journals and monographs and their architects often win architectural awards. Moreover the participation of a world-famous architect helps to target the focus of local as well as international scene. In the case of Guggenheim Museum in Bilbao Rauen (2001) pointed out that the involvement of a prestige architect with international reputation (Frank Gehry) was one of the essential elements in focusing world attention towards the city. Architects of two high profile buildings in Prague, Frank Gehry and Jean Nouvel, belong to globally active designers who leave their signatures on landscapes of cities all over the world. Their names lend credibility, prestige and publicity to their clients as well as to the projects. The engagement of top-class architects earned a great deal of publicity and popularity surrounding Dancing House and Golden Angel and I believe that it added to international visibility of Prague too.

To situate a modern building in prestige or somehow exceptional area and thus create a contrast to local context can be an intended answer to the challenge of a place as well as a source of public polemics leading to presence in media. Especially the projects located in historically significant sites tend to appear controversial. Dancing House has become a part of an open debate for its exposed location in heritage conservation area. Even before the opening the structure attracted a considerable share of opponents who criticised its extravagance and impropriety for the character of historical neighbourhood. Although not in the historical core the domination of high-rise TV tower over the Prague's cityscape was not accepted smoothly either. Already in the initial phase the project raised many negative reactions criticizing almost everything; the purpose, the appearance, the location as well as the harmful effect of electromagnetic radiation emitting from the transmitter. After the political turn in 1989 many people even claimed a demolition of the unfinished dominant.

What remains important in regard to city marketing is that distinct buildings moreover designed by architects of global fame help to focus the public interest. As popular targets of media high profile buildings contribute to worldwide publicity and spread awareness of a place. After all even people who have never visited the city have some kind of virtual perception of it from the advertised buildings.

5. Golden Angel and Smíchov Area

Remarkable structure penetrates industrial neighbourhood

The office and shopping centre Golden Angel is located on the junction Anděl which forms the central part of inner city neighbourhood Smíchov. Since the beginning of the 19th century Smíchov had been developing as an important industrial base of Prague. Until recently it could had been described as a traditional inner city working class neighbourhood facing the lack of investment, deterioration of housing stock and concentration of population with lower social status.

Figure 1: Position of Smíchov (dark dot) and city centre (grey spot) within Prague

As an effect of deindustrialization heavy industry moved out from the inner city and left behind a large amount of empty property. Providing an excellent location in close proximity to the city centre supported by a good transport connection Anděl area certainly had a lot to offer. Accordingly already in early 1990s ING Real Estate expressed the interest in land at Anděl junction and eventually entered the neglected neighbourhood with a project of office and shopping complex Golden Angel.

The project history dates back to the year 1990 when a deal between ING Real Estate and Municipal Council of Prague 5 was signed. The ING Corporation pledged to draw up an urban and economic development plan of Smíchov in exchange for an exclusive right to property at Anděl. A year later ING representatives brought forward a development strategy drew up by a French architect Jean Nouvel. He has proposed a new complex of buildings in working class Smíchov with the core of Golden Angel, a keynote building in revitalization of the neighbourhood. The strategy was approved by local authorities and in 1996 the property was sold to ING Group. Completed in the year 2000 Golden Angel became the pioneering project in the area. Indeed the local authority of Prague 5 who has been aiming at revitalization of central Smíchov acknowledged shortly after the completion that Golden Angel was an impulse toward transforming Smíchov into the first among the Prague's secondary city centres (Úřad Městské části Praha 5, 2000).

Real estate market and construction boom at Anděl
As a result of spatial decentralization of commercial development the locations in inner and outer circle of Prague have seen a growing interest of occupiers since the mid 1990s. Although the city centre has remained attractive the main interest of investors and tenants shifted to non-central areas of Prague where the projects compete with the centrally located schemes by offering high quality space at lower prices. Especially Prague 4 (Pankrác) and Prague 5 (Anděl and Nové Butovice) are becoming more attractive; in the year 2003 the majority of development activities has been concentrated there (CB Richard Ellis, 2003; Jones Lang LaSalle, 2003). The area surrounding the metro station Anděl is experiencing a construction boom thanks to several projects of office blocks, shopping malls and entertainment facilities located there. The mayor of local municipality Milan Jančík stated that the large-scale construction changes taking place in Anděl raised the interest of entre-preneurs in renting commercial spaces in municipal ownership (Houdková, 2003).

Figure 2 offers an insight into the trend in rental band in office sector in Prague and in Smíchov (Anděl) between the years 2000 and 2003. The average price level has been more or less stabilized in Smíchov over the reporting period while the overall trend in Prague showed a moderate decline between the last two years. The two rental trends point to a re-latively high attractiveness of Smíchov as to the demand for office premises in Prague.

Figure 2: Prime rental band in office sector in Prague and in Smíchov (IV.Q, 2000 - 2003)

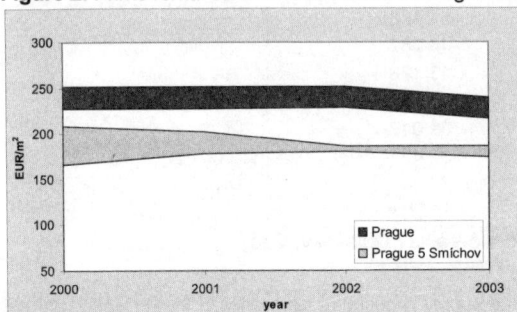

Source: Elaborated from data of Jones Lang LaSalle

Figure 3 demonstrates another important rental trend in Smíchov office market and thus the growth of the lower bound of rental band together with the converging tendency of curves representing lower and upper boundary of the rental band. Since the rents of office premises are primarily influenced by location and quality of offered space the described trend may signify an increasing gravity of Smíchov as a location for companies as well as a growing supply of high-quality office premises. Obviously the first and the second interpretation support each other.

Figure 3: Prime rental band in office sector in Prague 5 Smíchov (quarters, 2000 - 2003)

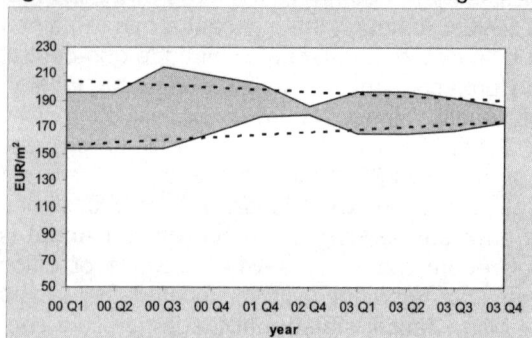

Source: Elaborated from data of Jones Lang LaSalle

Alike in the office market also the trends in residential property affirm that the highest prices are to be found in the city centre however some sections of Prague 5 and Prague 6 are comparable (Bricker, 2004). A selection of the first ten municipal districts of Prague by average sale price of a square meter of flat in the year 2003 is shown in *Table 2*.

Table 2: Average prices of flats in selected municipal districts in Prague (June 2003)

Rank	Municipal district	Price (CZK/m^2)
1.	*Malá Strana*	85 467
2.	*Nové Město*	59 231
3.	*Vinohrady*	51 468
4.	*Dejvice*	44 787
5.	*Břevnov*	43 123
6.	**Smíchov**	**41 234**
7.	*Žižkov*	39 012
8.	*Vokovice*	37 421
9.	*Holešovice*	36 242
10.	*Strašnice*	36 231

Source: LN, ČVUT - team of Doc.Ing.Václav Dolanský, Csc.
       In: Urbánek V. (2003).

Note: Listed prices represent average supply prices of all categories of flats in Czech market. Therefore the real prices of particular flats may significantly differ from the listed values.

Smíchov occupies a front position after the city centre and the traditional high status neighbourhoods. Obviously the prices are very much affected by the structure of flats in supply so that the areas having a large share of villa apartments are likely to belong to the expensive locations (e.g. Dejvice, Břevnov). Considering that Smíchov represents a neighbourhood here the working-class type of housing dominates (though it has villas too) the neighbourhood can be regarded as a relatively expensive one. It is very much in line with the opinion that as to the sale prices of flats the former sharp boundary is blurring and the attractive territory of Malá Strana is expanding towards Smíchov (Beňová, 2001).

By the same token the economic weekly Ekonom (2001) suggested that the construction bustle in Smíchov brings along the betterment of real estate in the area. According to the weekly the market price of an older 3-bedroom flat of 70 m^2 increased by about 40 % between the years 1999 and 2001. Likewise the sale price trend in Smíchov residential sector between the end of 2002 and the beginning of 2004 has a tendency of a steady increase.

Nowadays Smíchov belongs to one of the most significantly and the most dynamically developing parts of Prague. Zlatý Anděl represents the pioneering but not the last project taking place in central Smíchov. Since the year 2000 several other commercial developments mostly financed by foreign investors have emerged on sites of abandoned industrial complexes (see *Figure 4*). Two years ago a French developer finished a new cultural and shopping centre Nový Smíchov. The first stage of several-phased project of office, shopping and entertainment complex Anděl Business Center has been completed nearby while the following two phases are on the way. The other two developments of office, residential and shopping facilities are under construction (Anděl Park and Anděl Gate).

Figure 4: New developments in Anděl area

1 Zlatý Anděl
2 Nový Smíchov
3 Anděl City
4 Anděl Gate
5 Anděl Park

6. Conclusion

The purpose of this paper was to discuss what kind of contemporary buildings is employed by local, regional and national authorities in external promotion of Prague. Further I was interested if these buildings, which I chose to call high profile, help to establish a stronger position of their neighbourhoods in locally based intra-urban competition. I framed the idea of high profile buildings into the context of global competition and the theoretical assumption regarding the role of buildings in city promotion and urban regeneration.

By examining three contemporary constructions selected in Prague I tried to suggest some characteristics which may be important for the role that high profile buildings fill for capitals in the international marketplace. The three cases indicated that these buildings share some common features regarding the activities they accommodate and the architectural form they capture. Firstly high profile buildings gather functions which seem to be important for the mode on which nowadays world operates (office space, communication). Secondly the visual distinctiveness in local setting seems to be one of the more pervasive characteristics of selected high profile structures. Thanks to these two features and with them interrelated issues (e.g. global architect, controversial manner, architectural expression) high profile buildings tend to focus local and international interest. I believe that publicity surrounding the construction and afterwards existence of high profile buildings represents a significant factor in maintaining the international image and visibility of cities.

The selected case of commercial centre Golden Angel showed that this pioneering project provided a sign of certainty to follow-up investors in the neighbourhood. The trigger off development resulted in capitalizing of real estate values as well as in enhancement of area attractiveness for both commercial and residential sector. In this case the allocation of high profile building to inner city served not only as an advertisement of Prague in global marketplace but also as a promotion of neighbourhood's comparative advantage within the urban area.

Since I carried my investigation only in one city on the examples of a few buildings (one building respectively) I do not claim that the above mentioned conclusions are necessarily valid in general terms. The effect of high profile buildings on area attractiveness is surely conditioned by a range of factors including the potential of the area and its previous gravity, quality of new project, institutional context, etc. Similarly the measurement of local gravity asks for more comprehensive and detailed indicators. Thus the previous ideas represent only the example of possible effects of a certain kind of buildings in a particular context.

References:

Beňová, B. (2001) "Globalizace má mnoho podob", MF DNES, 22nd October.

Bricker, M. K. (2004) "Right places, right time", The Prague Post Online, 19th February, http://www.praguepost.com (on 03.03. 2004).

Castells, M. (1996) The Rise of the Network Society, Blackwell, Cambridge.

Castells, M.; Hall, P. (1994) Technopoles of the World. The making of twenty-first-century industrial complexes, Routledge, London and New York.

Cb Richard, Ellis (2003) Prague Property. CB Richard Ellis, Market Index Brief, 2nd Quarter.

Ekonom (2001) "Obchodní a zábavní centrum Nový Smíchov", Ekonom iHNed.cz, 6th December, http://ekonom.ihned.cz (on 16.03.2004).

Gospodini, A. (2002) "European cities in competition and the new "uses" of urban design", Journal of Urban Design, v. 7, n. 1, 59 – 73.

Greenberg, M. (2003) "The limits of branding: the World trade center, fiscal crisis and the marketing of recovery", International Journal of Urban and Regional Research, v. 27, n. 2, 386 – 416.

Haila, A. (1997) "The Neglected Builder of Global Cities". In: Källtorp, O.; Elander; I.; Ericson, O.; Franzén, M. (eds.) Cities in Transformation – Transformation in Cities. Social and Symbolic Change of Urban Space. Avebury, Hampshire, 51 – 64.

Hall, T. (1998) Urban Geography, Routledge, London.

Harvey, D. (1989a) The Condition of Postmodernity. An Enquiry into the Origins of Cultural Change, Basil Blackwell, Cambridge.

Harvey, D. (1989b) "From Managerialism to Entrepreneurialism: the Transformation in Urban Governance in Late Capitalism", Geografiska Annaler, v. 71B, n. 1, 3 – 17.

Harvey, D. (1988) "Voodoo Cities", New Statesman & Society, v. 1, n. 17 (30 September), 33-35.

Houdková, M. (2003) "Zájem o nebytové prostory v okolí Anděla v Praze 5 je veliký", Reality.iHNed.cz, 4th July, http://reality.ihned.cz (on 16.03. 2004).

Hubbard, P. (1995) "Urban Design and Local Economic Development. A case study in Birmingham", Cities, v. 12, n. 4, 243 – 251.

Jones Lang LaSalle (2003) Prague City Profile, Jones Lang LaSalle, March 2003.

Loftman, P.; Nevin, B. (1996) "Going for growth: prestige projects in three British cities", Urban Studies, v. 33, n. 6, 991 – 1019.

Loftman, P.; Nevin B. (1995) "Prestige projects and urban regeneration in the 1980s and 1990s: a review of benefits and limitations", Planning Practice and Research, v. 10, n. 3/4, 219 – 315.

Logan, J.R.; Molotch, H.L. (1997) "The City as a Growth Machine". In: Fainstein, S.S.; Campbell, S (eds.) Readings in Urban Theory, Blackwell Publishers, Oxford, 291 – 337.

Lynch, K. (1960) The Image of the City, The M.I.T. Press, Cambridge (Mass.).

Rauen, M. (2001) Reflection on the Space of Flows: the Guggenheim Museum Bilbao", Journal of Arts Management, Law & Society, v. 30, n. 4, 283 – 301.

Smyth, H. (1994) Marketing City. The Role of Flagship Developments in Urban Regeneration, E & Fn Spon, London.

Stanback, T. M. (1995) „Putting City-Suburb Competition in Perspective" In: Brotchie, J.; Batty, M.; Blakely, E.; Hall, P.; Newton, P. (eds.) Cities in Competition, Longman Australia, Melbourne.

Thornley, A. (2002) "Urban Regeneration and Sports Stadia", European Planning Studies, v. 10, n. 7, 813 – 818.

Urbánek, V. (2003) "Průměrné ceny bytů v Kč/m2 v Praze – dlouhodobé srovnání", Zpravodaj.cz- internetový ekonomický deník, 9th July, http://www.zpravodaj.cz, (on 22.03.2004).

Úřad Městské části Praha 5 (2000) „Představujeme Vám Zlatý Anděl", Pražská pětka, n. 10, Úřad Městské části Praha 5, http://www.prazskapetka.cz (on 28.03.2004).

Zukin, S. (1997) "Cultural Strategies and Urban Identities: Remarking Public Space in New York". In: Källtorp, O.; Elander, I.; Ericson, O.; Franzén, M. (eds.) Cities in Transformation – Transformation in Cities. Social and Symbolic Change of Urban Space, Avebury, Hampshire, 205 -217.

Zukin, S. (1995) The Cultures of Cities, Blackwell Publishers, Oxford.

Zukin, S. (1991) Landscapes of Power: From Detroit to Disney World, University of California Press, Berkley and Los Angeles.

Sources:
http://praha5.cz
www.czechtourism.com
www.czechtourservice.com
www.czecot.com
www.ingrealestate.cz
www.navalarch.com
www.pis.cz
www.prague-photos.com
www.pragueguide.com
www.praha3.cz
www.radio.cz
www.tower.cz

Online and printed promotional materials of the following institutions: Prague Information Service, Czech Tourist Authority, Ministry of Foreign Affairs.

Urban Regeneration in a Post-Communist City.
The Case of Bucharest.

Ileana Hapenciuc Blum

Introduction

Bucharest, the capital of Romania, a city with more than two millions inhabitants is located at the outskirts of the European economic space. Nevertheless, it is apparently facing similar problems as the Western European cities: decay of inner urban space and deterioration in the social, economic, political and finance fabric of the city. In spite of the apparent similarity in the forms of manifestation of these phenomena, their substance is different.

The "urban regeneration", the "urban project", the "image of the city" are today some of the most debated subjects in the general context of the urban development. In the Western countries, the urban actors' interest in urban regeneration is converted into political willingness to react to an urban area in crisis. In these countries the urban regeneration represents a theoretical, operational and political framework (often called into question, though) designed to cope with the urban space in crisis.

In Bucharest there aren't available any urban policies which should facilitate long-term large-scale urban operations, whereas operational urbanism follows the laws of the market and especially the demands of private investors. Nevertheless, the city keeps developing, the urbanization process continues, even if apparently far from a coherent development of the entire city. The Romanian society, which has abandoned communism (for 13 years, now) is about to re-coagulate into a civil society, but is still dominated by informal rules inherited from the past.

Where could the analysis of this city begin? What paradigm could help us understand its development? What part can the Occidental concept of "urban regeneration" play for the study of the present urban development of Bucharest, being aware that a confrontation with the European economy and cities is inherent?

To provide an answer to these questions, in the first part we are going to present the specificity of the urban context and the interaction between the urban actors in action today in Bucharest. To this end, following a short historical presentation of the city's development, we will present a large-scale urban project which left a mark on the urban configuration. During the communist regime this large-scale urban project affected hundreds of hectares in the city of Bucharest, whereas after the fall of the communism in 1989 it witnessed an attempt to trigger a process of "urban regeneration", in the Western sense. We are going to highlight the characteristics of the urban actors' interactions so as to put them in relation with the new sociospatial transformations in the city. This first part represents the conclusions of the research we have undertaken for our Master's Degree in 2002. In the second part we shall advance some hypothesis concerning the questions formulated previously.

We are going to examine the various effects that the globalization of the economy and the European reintegration have on Bucharest, a city in transition.

We shall look beyond the areas in obvious crisis and we will examine the urban regeneration of Bucharest, seen as an articulation between a fragmented territory and a flow of activities. From this point of view, the city's territory will be analysed as a mosaic of fragments supporting the flow of activities. By this analysis we intend to review the possible roles of the Western theoretical and operational models in the current urban development of Bucharest.

First part

A historical outline

Bucharest did not appear as the capital of the country. Its historical development was greatly indebted to its geographical position, located at the crossroads of the old transcontinental trade routes and at the junction of different cultural areas. The city started out as a coagulation of several small communities from the area, and in the absence of the surrounding walls, it kept on extending by the agglutination of others. This is the reason why until late in the 19th century, the city had a structure characterized by an articulation of territorial units corresponding to communities, connected by green spaces or waste grounds. The various influences Bucharest underwent throughout its history also left their mark on the contrasting character of the urban fragmentation.

Attested by documents going back to 1459, Bucharest became the capital of Walachia in 1659, the capital of the United Principalities of Walachia and Moldavia in 1859, and the capital of Romania in 1881.

Beginning with the second half of the 19th century, after the union of the Romanian Principalities (1859), and the gaining of the independence (1877), that put an end to more than 300 years of Turkish domination, Bucharest turned to the European political and cultural models. It became an important node in the Western States' economic expansion to the East, a commercial and banking centre, a cosmopolitan city, attracting the businessmen, tradesmen and craftsmen from Austria, Germany, France, Italy, Russia, Greece and Turkey.

Until late in the 19th century, the urban structure remained almost unchanged, in the sense that the street network and the parceling plan made visible the configuration from the 18th century, as it was represented in the oldest available plan of the city. On this structure, the

19th century's architecture with a strong French influence was implanted, and by the end of the same century large boulevards were opened up by the example of Haussman's Paris.

The systematization plan, which for the first time raised the issue of a global development of the city - became operational in 1921. However, the city kept on changing, even if very slowly. The lack of the great development projects in the 19th century didn't hinder the city's modernization, but this process was due rather to the slow adaptation[1] of the urban structure to the new needs of the society.

After 1918, following the Great Union, the enlarged Romania engaged in a fast process of industrialization. As a result of this process, in only 12 years the number of production, commercial and transport companies as well as that of financial and banking establishments in Bucharest doubled. At the same time, the number of inhabitants and lodgings (accommodations, residences) also doubled. The evolution of the city was based on the modern urbanism of the time, which led to the creation of new districts and new industrial parks, the development of the parks and the lakes in the Northern part of the city, the opening of new traffic arteries and the construction of modern buildings.

After 1948, the communist regime came to power in Romania and shortly afterwards it turned into a totalitarian one. Between 1948 and 1950 the State confiscated private property (Nationalization of Private Assets).

As far as Bucharest is concerned, starting with the Seventies the urban restructuring of the inner city became a central priority of the communist regime's public policies. This urban restructuring made a clean sweep of 500 hectares in the center and afterwards, they had the new Civic Centre rebuilt in the same place. This new center included the House of the Republic and the boulevard called at the time "Victory of Socialism" with the adjacent buildings: the seats of the ministries, the Grand Opera House, the National Library and other stores and residences. The Civic Center was uncompleted by the fall of Communism in December 1989.

After the fall of Communism, the country engaged in a process of transition towards the State of Law. Romania presented its candidacy for EU membership in 1995.[2] This candidacy also involves the observance

---

[1] The transformation of the ancient medieval city was the result of public administration's intervention by two methods. Firstly, the City Council initiated public urban operations, having relative amplitude, which modified partially the urban structure's configuration – the opening of the new boulevards. Secondly, the management and the control of private initiative concerning construction were introduced by the urban legislation that had continuous and diffuse effects on the city's urban fabric. These two aspects represented complementary facets of the public administration's urban policy in Bucharest. (Lascu, 1977)

[2] Romania presented its candidacy for the EU membership on June 22, 1995. The negotiations began on February 15, 2000.

of the Copenhagen criteria[3] (according to the Council Decision of March 30, 1998 concerning the principles, priorities, intermediate objectives and conditions of the partnership for Romania's integration).

Urban development in Bucharest. Present status.

The urban development in Romania is at the borderline between the former system of socialist planning – featuring a very strong hierarchy, at the top of which was the chief of the State – and a new system characterized by the emergence of new actors, in which the private initiative is at the starting point of most of the urban projects.

We place the current urban development at the borderline between these two systems because in spite of the formal change that occurred after the fall of Communism, at the level of the official institutions, we can still distinguish some important constants which persisted in the informal practices of the urban actors.

In order to illustrate this matter, as a case study we have considered a great urban operation that transformed Bucharest. The size of the operations allowed the involvement of all major urban actors (at local and State level). For this reason to which we may add the ideological movements, the political and legislative reforms occurred at the time, we've been brought to consider the analysis of these actors' interaction as a significant element for the comprehension of the projects which followed one after the other in the inner city of Bucharest. Our analysis comprises two distinct phases:

(1) Before 1989. As a whole, the intervention in the Eighties had as its objective the creation of the city's Civic Center. It came within the framework of the operations of urban renewal (demolishing and rebuilding). In Romania, the operations of urban renewal were based on a particular ideological logic preaching the demolition in order to promote the ideas of the political power in place and to break away from the traditional structure. The result of this policy was the creation of a morphological and social fracture of the urban fabric.

(2) After 1989. The existence of this fracture in the capital's inner city aroused the interest of the professionals, as well as of the political power, and an international contest was organized in 1996 (the Bucharest 2000 Contest) to suggest a solution for the development of this area, and especially for the non built land. That contest was the only attempt to initiate the working out of a project for this territory.

---

[3] Stable institutions guaranteeing the democracy, the rule of the law, the respect of the human rights, the respect and the protection of the minorities, the existence of a viable market economy, as well as the capacity to face the competing pressure of the market forces inside the European Union, and in particular, subscribing to the objectives of the political, economic and monetary Union.

The contest required an answer concerning the urban design. The winning project suggested a principle for the morphological regeneration of Bucharest's urban fabric. According to a statement of Romanian's Prime Minister at that time, the institutional and legal frameworks necessary for the implementation of the solutions suggested by the contest were to be created thereafter. The organization of this contest followed the Western strategies of urban marketing[4].

Although the claimed objective of "Bucharest 2000" was the economical revival and the social and urban regeneration of the inner city, the steps which were to follow never came into being. Therefore, this phase could be characterized by the impossibility to unblock the implementation of the contest's results.

Today there isn't available any Master Plan for the urban and economical development of the "Bucharest 2000" area, as defined by the contest. Therefore, the consequences are visible:

In the Southern part of the inner city, in the Civic Center's area:
Dozens of hectares of wasted grounds and several unfinished buildings, belonging mostly to the State, remain blocked in the inner city since 1990.[5]

With regard to the social aspect, the most serious consequence is the extent of the relocations and the traumas suffered by the population: approximately 40 000 inhabitants were dislocated from the demolished districts. The rural population's migration to Bucharest (as workforce in the socialist industry) had serious impact on its social structure. An important consequence was the forgetting of the city's past.

While in the rest of the city:
Fearing the legal claims related to the matter of the land's ownership, the building companies have supported construction projects in other available areas of the city, as well as the creation of new satellite districts.

An important economic indicator, the construction of office building shows an increased concentration of this type of buildings in the northern

---

[4]The "urban marketing" translated by the strategy of the projects' sale is strongly related to the creation of a public image of the metropole, seducing for the investors, and this process of creation of image requires a reflexion on a local culture, an inheritance or even a territorial identity (Ascher, 1995).

[5] It concerns: wide demolished areas which look similar to wasted lands, and which do not keep any trace of the old streets or allotments (today, they are still undeveloped areas); uncompleted building sites, such as the National Library and The Opera House; apartment buildings partially used for offices and banks; the House of the Republic, today the Palace of the Parliament; the former Boulevard of the Victory of Socialism, today the "Unirii" Boulevard (3 km long); small enclaves belonging to the old urban fabric protected at present by the law.

part of the city. According to a Colliers International report, the demand for class A office space remains high in Bucharest. However, even if during the period 2001-2002 the supply of quality office space increased, the rents remained rather high compared to the rest of the East European countries. In Bucharest the rents for office space were 40% up to 60% higher than in Prague and Budapest. In 2001, the rents ranged between 20-24 USD/m^2/month for class A office space and 15-18 USD/m^2/month for class B but the report estimated that in the next two years the rents will stabilize at rates comparable to other European markets. According to the same report, the office construction is continuing in the North side of the city, which has become by far the most developed area due to the city's business center and to the number of luxury residences premises are to be found there. Nevertheless, the demand for office space in the Central part of Bucharest remains high, but it focuses on the Northern part of the inner city. The area which made the subject of "Bucharest 2000" (located in Central-southern Bucharest) is perceived as an area lacking potential for future development due to the State's ownership – perceived as a drawback for investors.

The report predicts an increasing demand for large office buildings. In this context, the dozens of blocked hectares in the southern part of the inner city have a serious effect on the rents' level and on the city's urban structure, which witnesses the densification of its more accessible areas and the neglection of others.

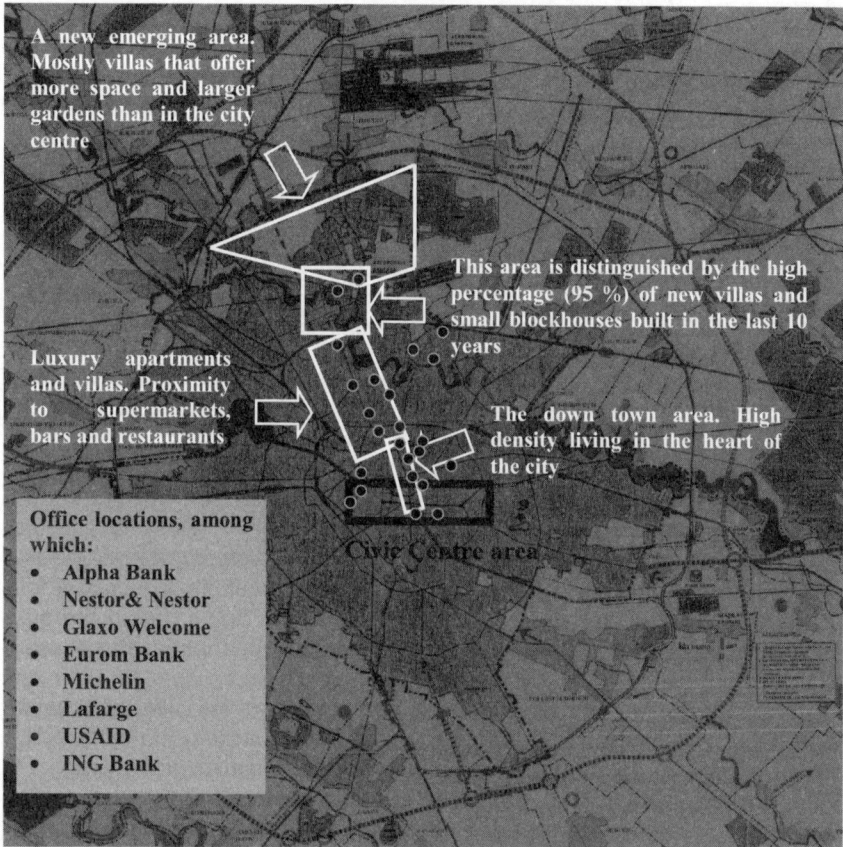

A new emerging area. Mostly villas that offer more space and larger gardens than in the city centre

This area is distinguished by the high percentage (95 %) of new villas and small blockhouses built in the last 10 years

Luxury apartments and villas. Proximity to supermarkets, bars and restaurants

The down town area. High density living in the heart of the city

Office locations, among which:
- Alpha Bank
- Nestor& Nestor
- Glaxo Welcome
- Eurom Bank
- Michelin
- Lafarge
- USAID
- ING Bank

Civic Centre area

Some points of view in order to identify the blockages in the regeneration of the Bucharest's inner center.

The passivity of the State

Over the 1977-1989 period, the urban actors belonged to a pyramidal official system, with a strong hierarchy imposed from the top, characterized by the lack of horizontal communication, and by the lack of decision-making power for those situated at the bottom of the hierarchy, limited to stick to their professional roles. Within the framework of the Totalitarian State this system managed to mobilize all human and economical resources to accomplish the objectives stated by the chief of the state, the main promoter of the project.

This official mechanism and its institutions have promoted an informal system of relations, which left a serious mark on the social practices (Mungiu-Pippidi, 2000). This informal system could be described in point of its most important features: dispersal of the actors, top-down relations, lack of confidence in the laws, the development of relations typical for the "status groups"[6].

During the 1990-2000 period, the urban actors fell under an official system about to be decentralized and transformed, characterized by a loose "hierarchy", due to an unstable period of transition to the de-ocratic state. This period can be characterized by a proliferation of the decision-making powers, opinions and roles.

The urban actors, which didn't belong to a strong hierarchy anymore, got involved in this project for variable periods of time to pursue their own interest. This informal system can be described by characteristics of which the most relevant for our study are as follows: continuance of the actors' dispersal, the short, unstable relations, disregard for the law, and survival of the previously created "status groups". The stake of the times that followed the fall of Communism was a reformation of practices. Nevertheless, this reformation had to be done within a society affected for a long time by a totalitarian system and which consequently, continued to maintain an informal system of relations.

If we compare the characteristics of the informal systems at each phase, we will notice that the effects of the informal relations existing before 1989 became the causes of the informal relations noted during the subsequent period, and this greatly contributed to obstruction of the practices' reformation.

After 1989, these informal relations have catalysed the corruption within the public administration (Mungiu-Pippidi, 2000). Lacking the culture of a participatory democracy, the population didn't penalize these practices. The decentralization only increased the uncertainty of the decisions and roles within the framework of a legislative system that still needs to be improved.

The nature of the inherited informal relations determined the survival of the ancient practices, which acted like a pattern in the urban actors' interactions. More, this pattern proved particularly powerful for major actors, such as the public institutions (the local and the central public administration).

---

[6]The development of a hereditary status group is generally a hereditary form of appropriation of privileges by an organization or by qualified individuals. [...] The status groups are often created by the property classes. Every status society lives according to conventions that regulate the lifestyle and therefore creates an irrational model of economic consume, restricts the free market by a monopolistic appropriation, and the individual's earning power. Max Weber, 1978, Economy and society, University of California Press, Berkeley and Los Angeles, London, p. 306.

The effects induced by the absence of urban policies after the fall of Communism

The current balance of forces is unstable. The Agency "Bucharest 2000", founded as the main initiator, referee and institution in charge with the application of the contest's solutions, isn't in fact operational. As far as the urban projects located in the inner city are concerned, the public actors remain yet the main decision-makers. In the absence of any public policies concerning the development of the area, they have the power to promote projects that often come against the objectives stated on the occasion of the contest.

The urban-planners involved in the contest's organization have continued to hold sometimes influential positions in the public administration's staff, but they turned their professional activity especially to the private sector. As the private sector is the main initiator of investments in Bucharest, the current urban projects are small-area isolated operations that aim a fast economic efficiency. The urban-planners, which advocate a sustainable urban development, express their opinions only in the specialized publications, for the moment.

The Romanian society is still about to coagulate into a civil society able to express its opinions and penalize the decision-makers on occasions others than those of the elections.

First part's conclusions:

If we compare the patterns of actors' interactions as well as their socio-spatial consequences throughout these two phases, we will identify several reasons for these blockages:

1. The survival of several patterns in the actors' interactions.
2. The lack of the urban policies as a framework generated by democratic practices.
3. The lack of means of actions – urban planning methods and tools developed in the respect of a "strategical urban management so as to face the complexity and the incertitude of contemporary urban dynamics" (Ascher, 1995).

We would like to emphasise that whether in the presence of an authoritarian referee, or in the absence of any long-term urban project, the effects of the urban actors' action resulted in a sociospatial fracture of the urban fabric. As a consequence, the inner city area concerned by the international contest is now off the market, while the investments are directed to more accessible areas, which increase the city's fragmentation.

Second part

Fragmented territory and flow of activities.

In this second part we are going to turn our attention from the inner center to the entire city. It is from this point of view that we shall examine the urban regeneration in Bucharest.

The study of the urban projects in the Western countries reveals that they are frequently experiencing repeated blockages and resumptions of the operations. However, in order to understand the nature of these blockages, we must look beyond the specific urban regeneration operations and analyse the general context of the urban development. This context, as well as its economical, social and spatial characteristics, changes from one region to another throughout Europe.

At the end of 20th century, the fall of Communism in the East European countries and the world economy's globalisation have generated fundamental transformations all over the world. Besides their general impact, these phenomena induced particular effects according to the local specificity.

The Global Economy, Network society and urban transformations.

In the European city[7], regarded as a "compact city", urban fracture has a negative connotation, as it corresponds to the social and territorial dispersal, which are the main features of the "diffuse city". In this context, the urban renewal in Europe tries to establish connections between the urban fragments through urban regeneration policies[8].

In the context of the "compact city" model, the opposition between fragmentation and continuity is the subject of lively debates. Yet, in spite of the announced death of the city (Choay, 1994), the urban fabric keeps showing signs of vitality and renewal. Several authors[9] intended to go beyond the rigid opposition between center/periphery and inside/outside the city.

---

[7]With the meaning of European City as Leon Krier has formulated it in "The Reconstruction of the European City" in 1980.

[8] The European Commission stated that a sustainable city is a compact city. (Villes et développement durable. Principes d'action et enjeux des politiques urbaines du développement durable. 28.08.02)

http://www.urbanisme.equipement.gouv.fr/cdu/accueil/bibliographies/devdurable/sommaire.htm

[9] In Switzerland, the research led by André Corboz (1983, 2001), historian of Architecture and Urbanism. In France, the publications of Gabriel Dupuy (1991), the research initiated by the PCA (Plan construction et architecture), at the MELTT (Ministère de l'équipement, du logement, des transports et du tourisme), under the direction of G. Dubois-Taine. Also, Stefano Boeri (1998, 2000) and Rem Koolhaas (1995, 2000).

Among them, Stefano Boeri[10] considers that most of urban crisis symptoms are linguistic. That is, the concepts we use (such as megalopolis, diffuse city or emerging city) help us to describe but not to explain urban transformations. What we need in his opinion is not another vocabulary, but "another paradigm in the conceptualisation of the urban phenomenon". He criticises the so-called "zenithal paradigm" (Boeri, 1998) re-founded in the Sixties – which is the view from above of several specialised layers representing two-dimensional descriptions of society, of the territory's economic and institutional relations. He considers that this view from above overlooks the real meaning of the contemporary urban phenomenon. The multi-dimensional tensions between space and society are not visible in the outlines of the zenithal analysis, so they require a "lateral thinking", able to reveal the various levels at which they occur.

The network concept[11] has emerged as a support of a new paradigm for the conceptualisation of urban structure. Manuel Castells regards the network society as the social structure typical for the Information Age[12]. The major metropolitan centers in the world function like nodes in the global economy's network. However, this network is not reduced to the major metropoles because global economy is also based on other emergent regional centers.

Facing the Information Age, the European cities experience important transformations. For the understanding of these transformations Castells proposes two new forms of time and space: "timeless time" and "space of flows" which coexist with the old forms of space and time. Time is compressed thanks to the new technologies of communications. The space of flows refers to the technological possibility of organising simultaneous social practices apart from the geographical contiguity. In this way, he highlights the dynamics of the existing relations between the nodes and conceives places as the geographical support for the nodes.

---

[10] Stefano Boeri, architect, co-founded Multiplicity, a research group in Milan, with Maddalena Bregani, John Palmesino, Francesco Jodice, and Giovanni La Varra. One of theirs projects, USE (Uncertain States of Europe, 2000) examines in 24 case studies the radical changes taking place in Europe's urban and rural environment as a result of political, social and economic developments.

[11] The network concept allows a different look on the organisation of the urban space and an alternative to the urban zoning, based on the Athens Charter of 1933. G. Dupuy mentions Ildefonso Cerda, Frank Lloyd Wright et Maurice François Rouge as initiators of this concept.

[12] By Information Age Castells refers to "a technological paradigm constituted around microelectronics-based information/communication technologies, and genetic engineering. It replaces/subsumes the technological paradigm of the Industrial Age, organized primarily around the production and distribution of energy." (Castells, 2000).

The space of flows is a changing space articulated by connections be-tween the centres of production and consume.

In the metropoles connected to the global economy network, these new forms of time and space determine important transformations, among which the most visible is the emergence of the business center as the driving force behind the metropole's economy. The business center is a node of telecommunication infrastructures, urban services and flows of capital to which it may be added tourist and cultural services. This busi-ness center is based on the existence of a technocratic-managerial-po-litical elite that creates exclusive spaces that are belonging to an inter-national recognizable lifestyle. The development of this "Informational City" ensures the metropole's connectivity at local and international level. The emergence of the Informational City, which for Castells is synonymous with the Global City, determines an imbalance reflected by the strong polarisation of employment at the top of the social groups' hierarchy and the serious impoverishment of the other social cathe-gories. The dramatic gaps between the social conditions of the various groups inhabiting the same city finally transform it into a Dual City.

According to Castells, the management of this transition to the global city amounts to the articulation between the economic functions moving to-wards the global economy (which express themselves by the develop-ment of the space of flows) and the local culture and society (which ex-press their identity by the rehabilitation of the traditional space of places).

Reinterpreting Bucharest in the light of the contemporary urban transformations

The fall of Communism marked for the countries of the old communist bloc the beginning of a process of transformation into an economic ap-pendix of the North. In other words, even if the admission process in the EU continues with varying speed for all these countries, the economy's globalisation, which easily transgressed the official borders, didn't take much to make felt its effects.

As far as Bucharest is concerned, Romania's largest and most developed city needed to prove competitive in the process of connecting to the rest of the world. But bringing this city and its society up-to-date had to be done at a speed that spread confusion in the society and in its inhabitants' mental representations of the urban space.

In Bucharest, we can already perceive the gap announced by Castells, between the development of the activities ensuring the city's connection to the international networks and the activities ensuring the local culture's preserval. This gap was widened by the economical and political re-quirements that must be met by the country in the integration process into the EU. As the changes induced by this institutional process have occurred too fast to be assimilated by the Romanian society, the local forces have appeared as forces of resistance and inertia. In this context, the Dual City is the city which is divided between the forces of economic progress and the forces loyal to the ancient socialist labour culture according to which any competition and free initiative was non-existent. On the political level, The Dual City is also divided between the liberal forces and the conservative ones, which hold the largest share of the resources and power (the latter were identified in the first part of our analysis as the "status groups"). Bucharest is also the city of great contrasts in the living standards of its inhabitants.

Due to the morphological characteristics crystallised during its historical evolution, the space of places in Bucharest appears fragmented. The Eighties totalitarian interventions accentuated this fragmentation. However, this urban patchwork, made up of stratified fragments witnessing the Phanariot city, the French 19th century influence, the modernist city of the Thirties, to which it was added lately the Communist Civic Center, forges the specific image of Bucharest among the other metropoles. The urban-planners delimited a hundred of "protected areas" scattered throughout the city, representing urban areas which have acquired a strong character and morphological coherence during their historical evolution. This abundance of protected areas will remain however a simple effort of collecting precious debris if the urban policy doesn't consider connecting them by flows of activities. The absence of such a policy which should have functioned as a framework for the urban operations initiated after "Bucharest 2000", has proven one of the main reasons for the suspension of these operations.

The concentration of the space of economic flows in the north side of Bucharest accentuates its Dual City character. The emergence of the business center in the north of the city generates social and spatial segregation. Indeed, the north side gathers the international airport, the international companies' headquarters and the best residential areas, and therefore it is the location most sought after by the new managerial-technocratic-political elite. The building density in the north of the inner city increases, the existing buildings are improved, and new districts are created in the northern suburbs, near lakes and forests. These are the visible effects of the transition to Castells' Informational City.

If we return to the network concept in order to conceptualize Bucharest's urban structure, we will need to highlight its sociospatial centers of production and consume and the relations created between them. In Bucharest, the functioning of the network presents an imbalance caused by the overload of some nodes and the neglecting of others. The economic and institutional flows are concentrated in the North, so they do not circulate through the city. In order to avoid degradation, the space of places must function as a geographical support for the flows, as an "exchanger", according to Castells.

In the space of flows' analysis, the concept of "lateral thinking" proposed by Stefano Boeri turns out to be an essential tool. The classical "zenithal analysis" highlights only the areas in obvious crisis such as the historical core, the suburbs or the wastelands, which are the subject of the urban regeneration operations in the European city. Yet, the nodes of the urban network are placed at various levels and the connections can be multi-dimensional and fluctuating. Therefore, the flows of activities' analysis needs a "lateral" glance coming from the inhabited space which is fragmentary and which reverses the hierarchies imposed by the means of such institutionalised values like common heritage and pro-tected areas.

Some hypothesis for the Bucharest's urban analysis and urban regeneration

A first hypothesis is that the analysis of the contemporary space of places in Bucharest should go beyond the traditional conception according to which the urban fabric's fractures are generating urban frag-mentation. Urban fragmentation is a fact that characterises the city whe-ther compact or diffuse. The historical core or the suburbs are areas that compose the urban patchwork, each having its own special character. The hierarchies and the connections created between these urban areas are unstable, because they are established according to these areas' ca-pacity to accommodate and impel the flow of activities, which is fluc-tuating by its nature. In other words, the space of places should be de-veloped according to its potential to become an "exchanger" for the space of flows.

However, when it occurs exclusively as a result of the private investors' action, the urban renewal might stand in opposition to the local interests and culture. In relation to this observation, we shall formulate the second hypothesis:

In Bucharest, the creation of an urban policy is extremely necessary. This policy should use Bucharest's economical and political connection to the most-developed European metropoles network, so as to make the local specificity act as a lever, and thus determine an enhancement of the city's international influence. Within this framework, the urban re-generation policy of Bucharest as a metropole and capital of the country should determine the creation of connections between the space of places and the flow of activities.

Some reflections concerning the urban models' possible role in Romania

In spite of Romania's not being a EU member yet, the country's opening to the West, which occurred right after the fall of Communism, in 1989, had an immediate effect as it exposed the country to the influence of the processes which occur on a worldwide scale. As a consequence, the world economy's globalisation and the free flow of information had a strong influence on the activities and the lifestyles in the Romanian post-communist society. The political actions undertaken by the Romanian institutions are supervised by international organisations, such as the EU and the IMF, which formulate various requirements in order to determine the Romanian democracy's consolidation. Indeed, Romania might have the opportunity to short-circuit stages already experienced by the Western countries. One of the effects could be a change in the government's practices in Bucharest and the creation of the urban policies. On the other hand, we wonder about the efficiency of any public policies that emerge only as a formal response to such requirements.

In this political context, our interest goes to the international urban development models that are today subject to debates. Although urban development is much too complex to be captured by models, they can be used as tools for creating paradigms of the urban development. As we examine the possible role of these models for the comprehension and the regeneration of urban structure in Bucharest, we should emphasise that urban regeneration as it is defined and applied in the North Europe countries cannot represent a model in itself for the case of Bucharest. However, the study of the Western theoretical and operational framework might provide some clues, concerning the theoretical and operational framework of the urban development in Bucharest.

References:
Ascher, F. (1995) Métapolis ou l'avenir des villes. Ed Odile Jacob: Paris, 346.
Boer, S. (1998) Eclectic atlases: Four possible ways of seeing city. DAIDALOS 69/70, 102-113.
Castells, M. (1993) European Cities, the Informational Society and the Global Economy. In: Journal of Economic and Social Geography, No.4.
Castells, M. (1998) The education of city planners in the informational age. In: Berkeley Planning Journal 12, 25-31.
Castells, M. (2000) Materials for an exploratory theory of the network society. In: British Journal of Sociology, Vol.No. 51 Issue No.1 (january/march), 5-24.
Chaline, C. (1999) La régénération urbaine, PUF, coll Que sais-je ?, Paris, 127.
Colliers International (2001) Real Estate Review 2001-Romania.
Corboz, A. (2001)(1983) Le territoire comme palimpseste et autres essais, Ed.de l'Imprimeur, Besançon, 281.
Dubois-Taine, G.; Chalas, Y. (1997) La ville émergente, éd. de L'Aube, St-Etienne, 279.
Dupuy, G. (1991) L'urbanisme des réseaux: Theories et Methodes, Armand Colin, Paris, 198.
Grillet-Aubert, A. (2003) De la typomorphologie à la ville diffuse: Notes sur les Notes pour un programme de recherche de Stefano Boeri, dans Les Cahiers de la recherche architecturale et urbaine no. 11. Sur quelques theories du XXe siècle. 63-75

Giurescu C. Dinu (1990) The razing of Romania's past, World Monuments Fundation, London, 68

Glaser P., Jaklin T. (1998) The catalogue of the Romanian-German architecture workshop Bucharest 2000, summer 1998. Braunschweig: Ed Apelhaus Verlag, 95.

Hapenciuc Blum, I. (2002) Influence du jeu des acteurs sur la forme urbaine. Le cas des grandes opérations urbaines en centre-ville de Bucarest, 1977-2000. Mémoire DEA (Master's Degree). INSA- Lyon,121.

Harhoiu, D. (1997) Bucuresti, un oras intre orient si occident (Bucharest, a city between Orient and Occident), Ed Simetria, Bucuresti, 135.

Koolhaas, R., Boeri, S., Kwinter, S. [et al.] (2001), Mutations, Ed. ACTAR Bordeaux: arc en rêve centre d'architecture, 800.

Krier, L. (1980) The reconstruction of the European City. In: "Leon Krier : Drawings", Archives d'Architecture Moderne, Brussels, pp. xxv-xxxi. Revised version in "Architectural Design", Vol. 54 (1984) Nov./Dec. 16-22.

Lascu, N. (1997) Legislatie si dezvoltare urbana. Bucuresti 1831-1952 (Legislation and urban development. Bucharest 1831-1952), PhD Thesis. IAIM Bucarest, 382.

Mungiu, A. (1995) Romanii dupa 1989 (Romanians after 1989), Humanitas, Bucuresti, 326.

Mungiu-Pippidi, A. (2002) Politica dupa comunism (The politics after communism), Humanitas, Bucuresti, 279.

Rauen, M. (2001) Reflections on the space of flows: The Guggenheim museum Bilbao, Journal of Arts Management, Law & Society; Vol. 30 Issue 4, 18.

Roncayolo, M. (2002) Lectures de villes. Formes et temps. Ed. Parenthèses, Marseille, 386.

The Case of Commercial Investments in Bratislava region (Slovak republic)

Lubica Vitkova

Construction of the grand commercial investments without any particular conception draft has a great impact to deteriorating of functional efficiency and environmental qualities of cities and their surroundings. There is also an influence to the quality of their spatial and functional structures.

The goal of the paper is to give an overview of commercial investments problems in Bratislava (as the capital of the Slovak Republic) and its surroundings. The study is oriented to the basic types of commercial investments (office, business, residential, leisure, industrial) and their allocation on the level of region, town and its zones. The paper analyses recent and predicted trends in allocating of different functional type from the points of view: requirements of the market, traffic optimalisation within the town, region and character of urban fabric and surroundings.

The present situation of market space in the Slovak Republic and especially in Bratislava region is very interesting. The preferences of segments of the commercial investments, their capacities and the preferences of location are quickly changing. The close distance between Bratislava and Vienna plays important role.

The preference of "self – organising" tendency of commercial facilities is also considered as a problem in contemporary Slovak conditions. (The problematic is not appropriately overlooked on the level of "public sector".) There are also many difficulties of integration (unintegrated forms) of the commercial investments especially into the urban fabric of the city and its surroundings.

The paper presents the case of commercial investment in Bratislava in introduction and following periods:

- Bratislava in a wide context - characteristic of the town and region
- View in the past - situation of the starting point from which the market got in the area after 50 years
- The present day - analyses of the market operations in the area of the town and region
- Future - strategy of development /master plan of the town/

Bratislava in a wide context - characteristic of the town and region
The capital of the Slovak republic Bratislava is an administrative, economic, industrial and cultural center of the country. It is situated in the center of Europe. From the south it border on Hungary and from the west on Austria republic.

The location of the town in the European context has a strategic importance. Bratislava lies close to the border of Austria, Hungary and Czech republic. So the town is the entrance between east and west. Bratislava is important transport intersection. In its territory come across seven main road lines and several railway lines of freight and personal railway transport. The harbor in Danube fulfill important role too. It connect town with Black See and canal Rhine - Mohan and with the counties lying along Danube. Airport is situated nine kilometers far from the city center.

The capital of the Slovak republic is the part of the region Vienna – Györ – Bratislava. This region is one of the most perspective regions in Europe by the studies of European Union. Bratislava has the highest purchase power in the Slovak republic. The number of its inhabitants increase during the day to 640 000 people (trough incoming workers and guests).

Table 1: Comparison Bratislava with other middle European towns

Town	Surface area (km²)	The number of inhabitants
Bratislava	367,5	447 345
Budapest	525,2	1 775 000
Prague	496,2	1 181 126
Warsaw	494,3	1 610 471
Vienna	415,0	1 615 438

Present day - analyses of the market operation in the area of the town and region

Development in the region
Development in the region during the last thirteen years has several characteristic periods of evolution with following indications
- Sub-urbanization trend /which runs all over in several waves
- Moving a part of inhabitants from the city to the country side
- The retail facilities of big capacity are establishing outside of the city
- Development of entrepreneurial activities in the periphery of the town and also in the countryside /particular industrial parks/
- Multilateral function development of smaller towns near Bratislava – transformation of country side, village satellites to multi function self service structures
- Large penetrative investments come to inner city structure

For Bratislava region is typical uniform allocation of commercial investment all types, forms, sizes and digress of concentrations.

Table 2: Location of new commercial activities in the region - countryside

Kind of new commercial activities in the region - countryside	Structure of the village	Periphery of the town and village	Countryside
Retail, services, gastronomy			
Small facilities	+		
Shopping centre	Supermarkets	Shopping centers, hypermarkets	Design Outlet
Car store	+	+	+
Car – second hand store		+	+
Mc. Donalds		+	+
Lodging			
Hotels	+	+	+
Guests house	+	+	
Works facilities 3. – 4. sectors			
offices	+		
business parks		+	+
technological parks		+	+
commercial television		+	+
Industrial and enterprise activities			
craft production	+		
small production facilities	+	+	
industry park			+
store area	+	+	+
gardening	+	+	+

Source: Own Resource

Table 3: Impact of the commercial investment to the urban fabric and countryside

Kind of new commercial activities in the region – countryside	Strange element in the village, small towns and country side	Symbiosis with environment	Accent to architecture design in countryside
Retail, services, gastronomy			
Small facilities		+	
Shopping centres	+		+
Car store	+		+
Car – second hand store	+		+
Mc. Donald's	+		+
Lodging			
Hotels	+	+	+
Guests house	+	+	
Works facilities 3. – 4. sectors			
offices	+		
business parks	+		+
technological parks	+		+
commercial television			+
Industrial and enterprise activities			
craft production		+	
small production facilities	+	+	
industry park	+		+
store area	+	+	+
gardening		+	

Source: Own Resource

Mutual action of Bratislava and Vienna

It is not possible to explore Bratislava and Bratislava region without following mutual action of Bratislava and Vienna.

The border opening and deletion of iron curtain between Slovakia and Austria signify boom for both towns and their regions. For expansion of commercial investment the area which lies between Bratislava and Vienna is particularly important.

Economic revive and growth has two main periods

- The first period was characteristic by the growth of shopping centers capacities in regional level
- The second period is characteristic by the growth of entrepreneurial facilities in countryside

The growth of shopping centers capacities in regional level

Vienna started to grow up their regional Shopping Center South and other centers in the periphery as the reaction to the expansion of foreign shoppers from Slovakia, Hungary, Czech republic. It protected in this way its inner city from attack of traffic.

Than shopping centers started to move more closer to the border with Slovak and Hungary. Design Outlet near Parendorf lies 25 kilometers from Bratislava.

The same effort we can see in the Slovak site of the boundary. But it has different background. The Austrian shoppers are attractive for Bratislava. The investors try to attract them to the city. In December 2000 there was opened new Shopping Centre Aupark as the initiative of private investor and as a magnet for foreigner shoppers. The Shopping centre offer concentrated supply of branded goods. But this idea does not work in this way. The centre attracts domestic people.

The growth of entrepreneurial facilities in countryside

In present day entrepreneurial facilities are allocated in the area between Vienna and Bratislava, Vienna and Gyor primarily on green meadow and along the main transit routes, which connected these towns. Villages fight among themselves for allocation of this kind of commercial investment up to industrial parks. They wish to have these facilities close their boundary. Entrepreneurial facilities have also tendency to develop themselves near the state borders.

If we compare Bratislava and Vienna region we can see some differences. While in the Bratislava region we can see even (uniform) allocation of commercial investment in whole area, in the Vienna region exist more sharp differences of hierarchy of the territory. There are areas with powerful economy – with economy expansion (upper said territory), but there are also areas, which have typical countryside character with recreation and agricultural functions.

Development inside the town Bratislava
Development in Bratislava during the last thirteen years has several characteristic periods of evolution:
- The first step: construction of the headquarters of the banks (mainly as the high-rise buildings or reconstruction of existing buildings in the inner city)
- The second step: development of shopping centres and hypermarkets primarily in the periphery
- The third step: expansions of the offices in the town (mainly in the inner city structures)
- The fourth step: to the city is returning development of the housing investment
- The fifth step: arrangement of the great commercial projects with multi function use (in inner city structures)

For Bratislava, as the town with the long tradition of the outside expansion and destruction of big part of historical structures, is very important to pay attention to development of their inner urban fabric. This is the reason, why the new commercial investment is monitoring carefully also from this point of view.

Phenomenon of shopping centres and hypermarkets
Bratislava has the highest purchase power in the Slovak Republic. But the Slovak market is relatively small. Evolution of the market started three years later than in the surrounding post - socialist countries in the year 1999. But the next development of shopping investment is enormous.
The present Bratislava retail-trade sector has general tendency towards concentration. Concentration follows through accretion of the floor rate of shopping units and also through concentration of shopping centres and hypermarkets on the few areas in the town.

Bratislava has:
- ten hypermarkets (fife of them were built as a separate building, five of them are integrated to the shopping centre,
- six sopping centres,
- tree buildings of BAUMAX,
- IKEA

The construction form of the shopping centres developed. The firs one was built as the simple ground floor building integrated shopping units by way of the open arcade and open parking places. One of the latest is the typical shopping centre with mall and other uses in several levels with

underground garage. The structure of the complexes combines space for work, relaxation, shopping and accommodation.
The goal is to integrate shopping centres to the urban fabric - to the system of streets and squares. Reduce the number of separate large unites in periphery.

The characteristics of the biggest units are following:

Table 4: Characteristics of the biggest units

Shopping unit	Capacity of the shops	Other function	Location
Shopping park Soravia			Periphery
Danubia Shopping Centre	30 000 m²		Periphery of dwelling area - district Petrzalka
Polus City Centre	38 000 m²	Sport and entertainment facilities - 12000 m² Offices	Centre of the district Bratislava III
Aupark Shopping Centre	26 000 m²	Sport and entertainment facilities - 16500 m²	Border of inner city
Avion Shopping Centre + IKEA	35 000 m² 22 000 m²	Sport and entertainment facilities - 16500 m²	Periphery

Source: Own Resource

Development of Office in Bratislava
Foreign companies prefer Bratislava as the capital to other Slovak cities. Most companies want to be closed to their suppliers, the same, as they want to be in contact with the competition. Those companies looking for experience in their expansion eastwards have their seats in Bratislava.

Reconstruction was first carried out on representative, historical objects. The present is marked by construction of individual buildings-system of buildings, while the future is in the grips of constructing multi-functional zones. One of the firs multi- functional complexes in Bratislava was Polus City Centre. The centre combines administrative spaces and a shopping mall and with sport and entertainment facilities - cinema multiplex. The parking is situated in underground level. The principles "the city within city" is a way to express combining individual units into a functioning whole. The positive of this centre is also its location. The centre lies on the east axes of Bratislava, which connects suburbs on the east with Bratislava centre. Polus City Centre is also accessible by trams and buses lines.

Urban design and integration with the surrounding space is suitable too. Polus Centre forms the main street (axes) and a small square in front of the entrance to the shopping and office part of the complex.
What is typical for the present office market in Bratislava?

Visibility: "to see and be seen" is the view of strong company that knows its price.
Accessibility: The basic indicator is accessibility via the mass transport and proximity of major roads connected to adequate parking space.
Location: The linkage of administrative centres generates interest in other to locate their activities to an area with a high potential for development.

Some problems of Bratislava resulting from market activity
Almost exclusive participation of private capital on new upbuilding is possible to consider for most fundamental changes of new period. This one and other factors, namely economical, logistical or marketing contexts have radically changed investor conduct in the territory. New upbuilding results for last years have positive, but unfortunately also negative manifestations.

Recently the most disputable investments are so-called large constructions. Among them are administrative complexes (namely high-rise objects), shopping centers and large business units built on our town periphery. To objectionable upbuilding from the regional development viewpoint also belongs suburban "luxurious" residential quarter development. They are oftentimes so-called notional projects, which are built for the profit.

Development strategy of listed investments can't be in any case only the matter of private investors, because majority of them has marked consequences on:
- urbanistic town structure,
- region, and
- traffic relations.

These investment locations in the town or agglomeration mean the demand to realise all its consequences on town image creation and given territory operation. These buildings have effect not only on aesthetic quality of urban surroundings but radically change its functional and operational relations. They evoke increased traffic demands namely, which influences also more distant surroundings, and inhabitant conduct models in its scope outlast.

To main reasons of negative market activity on urbanistic structure of our towns belongs:
- Absence of conceptional urbanistic solution to town development.
- Market capacity absolutization.
- Market principle misunderstanding.

The report centrally focuses on recent condition analysis in our towns, namely from the viewpoint of public administration unpreparedness on market activity in the territory, and therefore also incapability to exploit its potential positively. It emphasises principles of public and private sector positive co-operation.

References:
Brian,J. (2003) Slovak real estate market opens door to foreigners
Toft, C. (2003) Property prices on the rice

Inhabiting the Outskirts of Bucharest
"Old" Socialist Housing Estates versus "New" Capitalist Suburbia
Developments

Vera Marin

A. Introduction
In this article, we propose a query on the current situation of the dwellings placed outside Bucharest's city core. The huge majority of these dwellings are apartments in pre-fabricated blocks of flats built during the communist regime. Since 1990, some other types of dwellings have appeared as a result of individual initiative or as real estate development of private firms.

This paper also investigates the urban planner's quest for trustful answers: the "grand ensemble" model has failed; the "north-American suburbia" model finds critics all around the world. What attitude to choose concerning the future of inhabiting at the edges of Bucharest? Is the Brownian movement of the individual initiative the most reliable formula, the most adaptable one?

Our assumption is that the situations of inhabiting the periphery of Bucharest today (in the blocks of flats or in the recent developments with individual housing) are unfair with the dwelling users (rich or poor): the welfare of the residents did not and does not come first. In the communist years, the political ideology imposed the large prefabricated real estates (built almost exclusively by the State) as being the only way of living "correctly" in the city. Nowadays, the logic of profit exploits the reaction of the people against the collective housing in such a way that the offer is still reduced to very few not high-quality options.

The starting point of this paper was a query about the current situation of the dwellings placed outside Bucharest's city core – the "material" in between the city centre and the surrounding territory. As already mentioned, a high percentage (around 80%) of the population of Bucharest live in collective housing buildings. Since 1990, other types of dwellings have emerged, and even though they are less important in number, they are still very important when considering the diversity of inhabiting the periphery. For these "new" typologies that have appeared after the fall of the communist regime, this paper takes into consideration two main tendencies: the so-called *residential parks*, placed especially in the northern part of the city and the *individual initiatives* that show up here and there with an extraordinary dynamism, in an urban fabric less well structured.

121

We have tried to find some possible interpretations of the existing situation of dwelling in the periphery. We emphasise the two opposite logic that have driven the construction of these dwellings: the socialist model (from the '60 to the '80) and the free-market model after 1990. The decision making process concerning the housing sector in Romania will be a frame for our analysis. The urban strategy for the city of Bucharest is another important issue to be considered (references to the city of Bucharest General Urban Plan[1] and to the General Urban Plans for the surrounding local communities)

B. Description of three main situations of inhabiting the edges of the city *and general context of their making*

B.1. "Old" socialist housing estates
Logic of formation
The communist regime imposed the nationalisation of private property, as well as it started the construction – along with filling some of the bombed areas – of collective dwellings. These were more appropriate to the egalitarian aspirations of the communist society, which declared that workers should have access to a decent home and that such accommodations should be all the same, to prevent discrepancies arising between the members of society. Professor Zahariade considers that, proven also by the official documents of the period, the programmatic idea of the *socialist city* was opposed to the *capitalist city*, the latter being the product of the chaotic development of a society based on exploitation, exhibiting scandalous *differences between centre and periphery* - the most obvious expression of social inequality. Consequently, as it is clearly stated in the official documents, the inherited urban form is obsolete, and the architects' task is to find a new form of the city, structurally tuned to the socialist life-style, and to *gradually erase the traces of the old society*. The *socialist city* was to glorify the collectivism of the social life, with no social segregation. (Zahariade 2003)

In order to understand how the city of Bucharest grew in the socialist years and, moreover, how this affected its whole structure, we shall refer to a scheme of Bucharest made by Derer (1982) in the '80, which contains the main dwelling categories. The plan also shows the areas of so-called "cheap dwellings" from before the WW2 or immediately after. They are single family houses, each one on its own private piece of land, but showing some features of rural dwelling (the courtyard used as vegetables garden and the presence of domestic animals). (figure 1)

---

[1] General Urban Plan for the Municipality of Bucharest, adopted through Local Government decision, 2000

After Zahariade (2003), the professionals' position during the communist regime was a delicate one: "since the early 1950s and until 1989, the dwelling is placed under the sign of maximum economic efficiency; hence the favourite target was that of standardised design. Although before the WW2, low-cost housing existed as a preoccupation both for politicians and architects; Romanian modernism was not concerned at all with this issue (its focus was on aesthetics). That is why, unlike what happened in other neighbouring countries (as Poland, the Czechoslovakia, Hungary, etc., where remarkable studies and low-cost housing developments have been achieved) one can say that, in Romania, the real rationalist culture of the dwelling is elaborated in the "design institutes" (especially IPCT), during the Communist period. It finally aims at a modular co-ordination between the designers and the producers of building materials and equipment, theoretically easier in a strongly planned economy (the reality did not confirm this hypothesis)

Figure 1: different typologies for dwellings in Bucharest - 1982

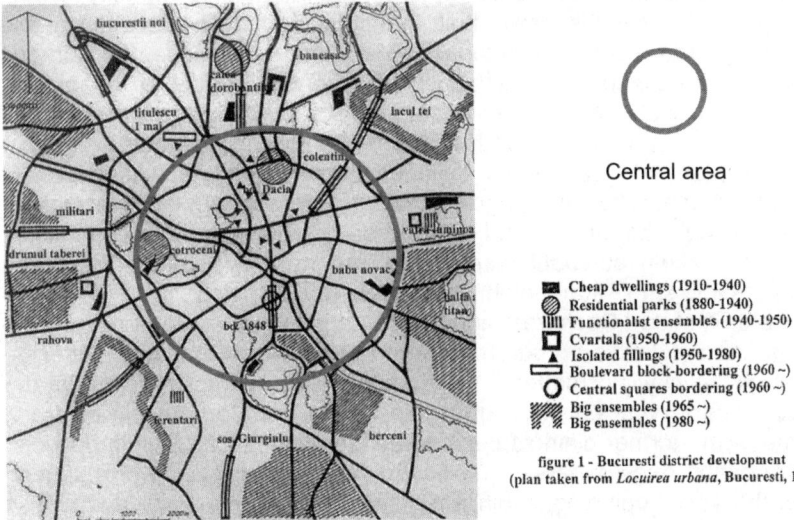

Central area

☒ Cheap dwellings (1910-1940)
◉ Residential parks (1880-1940)
▥ Functionalist ensembles (1940-1950)
☐ Cvartals (1950-1960)
▲ Isolated fillings (1950-1980)
▭ Boulevard block-bordering (1960 ~)
○ Central squares bordering (1960 ~)
▨ Big ensembles (1965 ~)
▧ Big ensembles (1980 ~)

figure 1 - Bucuresti district development
(plan taken from *Locuirea urbana*, Bucuresti, 1982)

A chronological approach is helpful for situating the housing districts in the reality of Bucharest. The social migrations of the time led to a major change in the social structure of the city. Now it is almost impossible to define Bucharest without considering the mass of these housing ensembles impinge on the whole city. After Teodorescu's chronology "the first to appear were the cvartal and soon after, the microraion, respecting the Soviet socialist realism style. The architecture of these collective dwellings follows the line of the traditional city scale, balancing the public and the private space. Apartments had one or two small rooms, and they

included a kitchen and sanitary facilities. The front yard was in close con-
nection to the adjoining street and main facades were quite imposing.
The backyard was either used in a traditional way (such as drying
laundry or playground for children) or – if being made of the precinct
itself - became a small park, which has turned in time into a quite en-
joyable area (as now, trees and bushes define their character). However,
all schemes lack a preoccupation for the service areas, which are basi-
cally non-existent, with the exception of some *cvartals* that have shops at
the ground-floor level." (Teodorescu 2002)

At the end of the Stalinist period, the 1960s brought along a relaxation to
some extent, which affected all areas of existence, be it political, social,
economical etc. In architecture, there was a certain opening towards the
Western type of rationalist urbanism, effectively promoted through the
principles of the Athens Charter. Functionalist blocks – but housing
mainly flats and not the other functions proposed by Le Corbusier in his
Unité d'Habitation – were built in the peripheral zones of the city, on the
free grounds near the newly built industrial areas. The location at the
periphery had some advantages. First, one could use the already
created infrastructure of the industry for service supply of the blocks.
Second, the distance between home and workplace was relatively short,
therefore transport was eased. In the beginning, the districts were rea-
sonably planned: the correct distance between blocks was kept, ac-
cording to the rationalist principles to provide sunlight and ventilation.
Soon enough though, around 1975, there was a new idea coming up:
why not making our boulevards more important by flanking them with
rows of blocks, ten floors high. Even more unfortunately, the 1977 earth-
quake devastated Bucharest and the damages were a good enough rea-
son to start a devised program of demolishing which eventually affected
most of the city, no matter if necessary or not. It was a dictatorial de-
cision. The fervent construction of blocks did not stop, on the contrary.
Some of the former districts became denser with blocks built in between
the previous ones, whereas the new dwelling complexes were planned
from the very beginning within a denser urban frame – which was also
"helped" by a law passed in 1980 introducing the need to define the
perimeter of cities. Not only that the architecture of the blocks them-
selves had a lot to suffer from the standardised design, where main prio-
rity [was] a minimal use of materials, but the residual space between the
buildings, as well as the services in the areas, were not properly con-
sidered in the planning of the districts. First, the apartments had to ob-
serve the main rule: "[they] should not contribute to waste of resources
through 'over-dimensioning' and 'over-finishing'." (Teodorescu 2002)
Such schemes were carried on until 1989, when the communist regime
fell. Concrete shells of unfinished blocks remained unfinished for some

time. In a short while, some of them were acquired by various companies to be turned mainly into offices building.

"Old" socialist housing estates - the situation nowadays

"One could hardly find a more representative architectural symbol of the totalitarian regimes in Eastern Europe, than the 'block of flats'. Its omnipresent image, as negative as possible, engenders today a visceral rejection of the collective dwelling in general. The material and the expressive poverty, the huge scale and the terrifying uniformity, and last but not least, their disastrous state greatly explains this situation." (Ghenciulescu 2003)

The communist housing estates are generally rejected by the public opinion and this is not an unexpected fact: built in the '60, or in the '70 or even more for those which were built in the '80, small or big ensembles are in a very difficult situation today. They face many different problems, some related to the building itself and to the urban setting, some to the infrastructure and some to the general functioning in the recent years. Although a number of local studies have been undertaken, the overall state of Romania's housing stock has not yet been surveyed, and the cost of repair, remodeling, refurbishment and renovation remains unknown. There is no national work program to rectify the obvious structural or qualitative defects of the housing stock. Furthermore, the challenge for housing appears to be compounded by the poor condition of the infrastructure that services housing - for example, the utility services, including energy and water distribution, district heating systems, sewage and refuge collection. Given the economic hardships of the past ten years, it is not surprising that only a nominal amount of public or private funds have been invested in the housing stock in general. The vast majority are very poorly insulated, causing major discomfort and endangering health and even life in both the heat of summer and cold of winter.

A very large part of Romania's housing (70% of the urban stock) consists of apartment blocks constructed by the State in a prefabricated building system. Through privatization, the vast majority of these apartments have been sold into private ownership, a measure which enjoyed widespread support at the time, reflecting the population's strong preference for owning their home. Consequently, the public ownership of the blocks was fragmented into multiple ownerships within condominiums. Gradually, a very limited proportion (3% in the year 2000) remained in public ownership for the cases where tenants were unable or unwilling to buy. The handling of building work, payments for utility services, and other matters of common interest to condominium residents depends on the effectiveness of their homeowners' associations which varies considerably since a firm legal basis is currently being set-up.

After meeting their everyday living costs, few households owning apartments have sufficient disposable income left to contribute to the costs of cyclical maintenance and minor repairs; and even fewer can save for major repairs to their buildings. As a consequence, the general condition of the apartment blocks can be expected to deteriorate, rendering an increasing number unfit for habitation. There are households (typically older people on fixed pensions) who cannot afford even to meet their heating and other utility bills and their tenure can only be maintained if the State-owned utility companies are subsidized and tolerate arrears. Although the ownership of an apartment represents a real financial asset, the general lack of maintenance and repair can easily imply a significant risk for any potential private investor, making it relatively difficult for homeowners to raise mortgages in a poorly developed financial market. There is also little or no public funding available for homeowners.

The nowadays reality of peripheral multi-family housing estates is one of a poor condition, grey, dull and sad. However, the apparent uniformity can be further analyzed only to discover a certain variety of situations and responses.

B.2. "New" capitalist suburbia developments
After 1990: the free-market model
In his contribution to the book "Cities after Socialism", S. C. Pickvance (1996: 232) speaks about the positive and the negative aspects that the contemporary societies have to face in Central and Eastern Europe. He assumes that while both positive and negative legacies of the past exist, the former being stronger than the latter and acting as obstacles to dramatic change. It is rather difficult to explain the last ten years of urban development at Bucharest's edges. The general frame was given by an extremely changeable legal environment and also by the incredible dynamic of land property market. As Ghenciulescu argues, the structure of the change was given by the "transgression of some laws primarily regarded as interdictions, and not as rules based on social consensus. In this sense, the cultural area circumscribing the city of Bucharest has traditionally witnessed such instances of transgression. On the other hand, the evolution from a totalitarian regime to a society with normal rules, explains to a large extent the explosion of individual initiatives, the present impossibility of controlling urban growth and the lack of a global project. After 1990, the fall of the regime equated to the disappearance of absolute control and to the explosion of urban life, with an intensity proportional to the paralysis characteristic of the previous period. The num-

ber of the constructions drastically decreased as compared to the socialist epoch and the state came to play practically no role in the request and execution of those buildings. If the number of new constructions with permanent character is still a reduced one, space transformation and grabbing tried to compensate for everything that had not been possible before. The urban reflexes frozen for the past 50 years started to surface again, even if in a disconcerting manner. Practically determined only by the rules of profitability and lacking any type of planning, the first years after the fall of the communist regime were "crazy" years. The background was a total incoherence and inefficiency of the laws concerning the construction and protection fields." (Ghenciulescu 2003)

We can speak about a frenetic development, in some aspects similar to the pioneers' adventures in the Far West of the 18th century America. Prices that changed in the nick of time from 0,50 Euro to 10 Euro per square meter (and still increasing for well equipped and already populated areas) do demonstrate this fact. Both newly built individual houses and the private firms' residential micro-ensembles are created in a conquest spirit. The road infrastructure which has been underdeveloped for decades, has even more difficulties now in trying to keep up with the speed of single family houses construction.

The so-called "residential parks"
A dedicated issue of *Arhitext Design* Magazine (3/2001) was entitled "*Residential Parks*" and the articles published at that time were a signal that a new phenomenon was starting to occur and, along with it, new and not well defined notions. "*Parcuri rezidentiale*" is a direct translation from English fast introduced in the common vocabulary.

"An attempt of clarification was made by considering the two words that are associated in this expression: 'park' and 'residential'. The first word brings over the idea of 'garden cities', and the second one sends us to the functional zoning approach, where 'residential' is the main function which defines a certain zone. In the case of these ensembles, the zone is defined through the function, but also through the common physical features of the buildings: developments (made at the same moment with same materials and probably employing the same architect) that include a various number of single family, low rise, individual houses. The zoning principles are about control and protection of a certain area that is not to be troubled by some other functions. So is the case for the so called residential parks." (Marin 2001) It is possible that the term of "residential ensembles" is more appropriated in naming the grouping of single family houses, on a private property piece of land, divided into equal plots that assure an efficient use of land and a controlled way of bringing the necessary infrastructure for communal services. There is a unity in style and in dimensions of these houses – and only the interior is sometimes customised.

Is it a false name for a new reality? Is it a local hybridisation of an imported model? Internet commercial sites show that "residential parks" around the world are quite different from what we may see in the North of Bucharest especially as for proportion between the built areas and the green areas. The beautiful images of the western web-sites show the residential function is sometimes completed by the "leisure" function, and in these cases, golf fields, shipping facilities, clubs and sport centres are in the core of the developments. Some examples present a fabulous natural setting, individual houses hidden behind rich vegetation.

If the high and impenetrable fence is a characteristic feature of some "residential parks" in the United States, then the gated community may also be defined as a residential park? "The texture of life in gated communities, on the whole, is a smooth, bland texture, strikingly uniform despite the effort to separate the communities into categories: "prestige communities" and "lifestyle communities", mainly situated around golf courses and marinas, make up the vast majority of the surveyed places. 'Security Zone Communities' created by traffic barricades within existing urban areas are more embattled and middle class. But nearly all the gated community dwellers are affluent corporate executives, tanned, fit and dressed in chinos, polo and golf sweaters. Some are retired; others are empty-nest professional couples... what these people want is not community but privacy and security. No matter how affluent they are, they dread the world outside the gates – crime is an obsession, despite the absence of any credible threat... " (Blakely, Snyder 1997) In the north of Bucharest there are big concrete fences, electronic devices, and private guards who become very frightening for those who want to take pictures. It seems then that the new developments in the North of Bucharest have similarities with the American middle class gated communities.

We assume that the general use of "residential parks" as the name for the new suburbia developments in the North of Bucharest has been chosen mainly for commercial reasons. Though they are all called "residential parks", they are not all the same: the criteria for a typology could be first of all related to the dimensions. They vary from a group of around ten units (of course that the units are always named "villas"), to more than one hundred single family houses. Other criteria could be the level of equipment with common facilities which are described with a lot of pride in the commercial brochures: the majority of the "residential parks" have protection and security services, maintenance of the internal streets, a control point (beside the entrance gate) or control centre (when it is placed in the centre of the development). 'Green Paradise', which is situated at half an hour of driving from the centre of Bucharest (but placed outside Bucharest's administrative territory), has the richest offer from the common facilities point of view. Still as a future investment stage, there will be a club with a restaurant, two tennis fields and a football one, a kindergarten and a retailing shop. Last but not least, the set of criteria related to the urban composition and the architecture (aesthetic vocabulary, layout design, building materials), though they may be less objectively considered, they are extremely important to define the different types of residential ensembles. Unfortunately, criticizing their architecture, one author characterized them as a "more and more crowded collections of architectural non-senses - many villas scattered in luxury ensembles of the "residential-parks" or in what is considered to be, for some abstruse psycho-sociologic reasons, the new chic-suburbs". (Zahariade 2002) Our assumption is that the real problem comes, in most of the cases, from the fact that the architecture doesn't belong to the place. The references are some commercial catalogues or the series on TV. There is no interpretation of the site: they could be "implanted" anywhere as long as there is some equipped land and a road to lead there.

A winner of an essay competition wrote few years ago: "[...] the American Village landed near the city of Bucharest as the star ship Enterprise from the Star Trek movie. It is the product of the global cyber-culture, sold at a very good price like in a commercial for a phone card. The project manipulates our most intimate dreams about welfare, comfort and social status – building up in a sophisticated shape, the evasion from the unbearable prison of the reality. It creates for us a new cultural identity, a poor one, based on profit and cash flow." (Caciuc 2001)

A specific case:
Does the National Housing Agency build "residential parks"?
Another strange category of dwellings at the edges of Bucharest is the "Henri Coanda" ensemble built by the National Housing Agency. Besides the new blocks of flats (looking and functioning strikingly similar to the blocks of flats built during the communist regime), NHA also proposes ensembles of single family houses. The registering process for obtaining a house in the "Henri Coanda" development follows rules related to the ability of the family to pay the instalments. As we can see from the NHA web-site, the list of clients for the single family houses, also defined as 'villas', are public figures from the political sphere or the media sphere.

This fact raises some questions on the objectives that NHA has for residential developments like this one.

In the middle of the '90s, the housing policy shifted from using government funding to bring down the price of housing to using it to stimulate new construction output. A new government program launched the National Housing Agency in September 1999. The Agency is supposed to provide Romanians with decent housing, and the program to relaunch new housing construction is the Agency's first activity to this end.[2] NHA acts through a central administration and branches throughout Romania. Each year, NHA management has to report to Parliament on its activities. The NHA represents cooperation between the State, the commercial banks, and the potential clients for new homes. It proposes housing-related financial products for the Romanian market and manages their use as packages. It also acts as a consultant: compiling technical, economic, legal and financial reports on aspects of home-ownership."[3]

The images presented in the recent exhibition at the Ministry of Construction, Transport and Tourism have shown a very large development plan, mixing single family houses with few multi-storey buildings with flats for subsidized renting to young families. A possible argument for the high prices of the 'villas' is the need to compensate the expenses for building these apartments that count as social housing. We may consider as some other 'compensation' the fact that the land was very cheap: the local authority is supposed to allocate the equipped land on which the NHA builds the social housing but also the 'not-so-social' individual houses.

The tools for improving the dwelling at the periphery are very limited nowadays. In this context, we consider that it is rather incorrect that the National Housing Agency behaves like a private investment firm. This way of acting decreases the chances to a more diversified "collection" of dwelling types for inhabiting the periphery.

---

[2] Financial resources for the program come from an international credit of US$ 300 million granted to the Romanian Government, which will be transferred to the Agency as a State budget allocation. Apart from public subsidies, the Agency's income will derive mostly from interest on loans, bank deposits and government bonds. The Agency is also allowed to issue medium - and long term bonds, guaranteed by the State.
[3] COUNTRY PROFILES ON THE HOUSING SECTOR: ROMANIA, Economic Commission for Europe, Geneva, UNITED NATIONS, New York and Geneva, 2001

The individual initiative

Our initial intention was to present the individual initiative as the 'hope' for inhabiting the edges of Bucharest. Some longer and more focused trips to the periphery of Bucharest brought some doubts: the variety is impressive, the dynamic is amazing and both the energy and the will to build are enormous. Unfortunately, good architecture is an exception to the rule; in a very reduced proportion we find the relatively modest 'inserts' in the semi-urban fabric from before the WW2. The majority of the newly built individual houses are excessively big and the exterior decoration is a non-sense (from an architect's point of view, a very subjective one). Usually, these new houses replace demolished cheap dwellings built before the WW2 or in the first decades of the communist regime. In these areas of "mahala"[4], one street atmosphere changes rapidly when the critical mass of old houses are replaced in this way. There is an important difference in scale between the old houses and the new ones. The same parcel surface is used more intensively, very often much beyond the allowance provided by urban regulations.

In many cases, the house is built without employing an architect, in some others, even if an architect had signed a project, the realisation did not respect the provisions of the project. In order to establish a typology of the houses which are the recent results of the individual initiative, one important criteria seems to be the architect client's profile. Generally speaking, there are two types of clients: those who want to impose their will (the ones who know better because their own home is at stake) and the ones, less numerous, who invest some trust in the architecture as a profession.

The first category needs the architect to sign the project for the building authorisation; the architect is supposed to draw the house of the client's dreams. The dialogue between the architect and the client is very difficult. After Zahariade, the explanation may be that "the most common client is the upstart, the new social stratum of rich clients who want luxurious, representative villas. Theoretically, the villa has always been a privileged building-type, a site of expressive experiments. Not in our present architectural landscape: it was quite difficult to identify those examples where interesting architectural ideas and expressions, reflections on space, light and materials could have developed, suffocated as they are by the big number of unspeakable buildings... there is a discrepancy (sometimes irreconcilable) between the cultural references of the architect and the ones of the client. If the references of the architect are

---

[4] Turkish word for "neighbourhood" that is still used in Romania to name a peripheral area composed of modest dwellings

generally foreseeable, the post-Communist client is more unexpected: his taste goes directly to the House of the People (huge, opaque, over decorated, artificial, stiff, absurd), perfectly tuned with the client's dictatorial behaviour." (Zahariade 2002)

Opposed to the first category, "the good client" is the person that "builds-up" a project with the architect, identifying together the solutions that apply to his/her specific needs and to the characteristics of the place. It is not an easy challenge for the architect, especially when the client tries to escape the nightmare of the communist housing areas through a healing brought by the architect's creative fantasy. Falling in the extreme of over-decoration and over-dimensioning is sometimes a danger for the architects also who, for decades, have had to restrain their skills to standard plans and for whom the client was, most of the time, an abstraction.

C. Searching for explanations
Urban planning for Bucharest outskirts

For the dwellings placed or to be placed in the peripheral areas of Bucharest, the General Urban Plan of Bucharest provides zoning for residential uses and identifies vacant land for housing construction. The urban regulations that accompany the Plan supply detailed provisions for the type of housing construction to be built (density, height, distances, etc.). The building authorization process entails the prerequisite of infrastructure for every construction project. The General Urban Plan for each area contains clear provisions for each case of undeveloped land, demanding the following: an obligation to connect to the existing networks; individual solutions (for water, sewerage) where there are no networks (with the obligation to connect later if such are built); an obligation on the developer to extend or to increase the capacity of existing public networks (in the case of larger developments).

Generally speaking, the nowadays urban planning refers mainly to urban regulations and therefore it has little to do with strategic planning. The control of the city is relatively frozen through the General Urban Plan that establishes the land uses and the built densities on the basis of multiple analysis concerning mainly the physical context (the social and economic analysis are also present, but the integration of different disciplines and professions is usually a difficult process). Another important problem is that the regulations of the General Urban Plan can be changed through a Zone Urban Plan – at a more detailed scale for a certain area. In this case, the alleged flexibility of the general master plan is rather its weakness as long as these detailed urban plans are commissioned by the investor/promoter to private urban planning studios, they will inevitably speak for the private interests, rather than for the public one. Unfortunately, this issue (which should be recognised by the civil society and which should be the core of the professionals' debates) has become the general norm and it presents already a strong inertia to possible changes that may occur. And since the public-private partnerships are still a dream, there are no examples of advantageous arrangements between the residential ensembles promoters and the local public authority. A developer of a so called "residential park" must very often overcome extremely difficult obstacles. As for the individual initiative, the authorization process is, in most cases, long and costly.

Economics: housing real estate market for Bucharest outskirts

The housing market in Romania has emerged immediately after the start of transition to a market economy. It received a strong impetus from the mass privatization of housing and the restitution of urban land which is still in process, due to the very complicated situations for the official documents. So the market has continued to develop rapidly and we can speak now about a fluid market (unstable in some aspects), offering a wide range of prices and amenities. Most transactions involved the privatization of existing dwellings in the communist blocks of flats or their resale, and not newly constructed units (for example, only about 36,000 new units were finished in 1995, yet there were approximately 170,000 transactions during that year - representing about 2% of the total stock).[5]

The environment for housing finance is now steadily improving (both in institutional and macroeconomic terms), but we have to take into consideration that it started from a very low base; and there is still a rudimentary market-based housing finance system in Romania. [6]

Private land for residential construction can be acquired through market transfers and through the restitution of former property rights on plots of up to 300 sqm in rural and 150 sqm in urban areas. For the residential ensembles promoters, an important constraint is the difficulty of consolidating large parcels of land. Public land can be obtained only from the State or local administrations: through public tender, in accordance with the provisions of the urban development plans; and also without tendering, where the land is leased for public purposes (including social housing). The minimum leasing price is decreed by the local council, to recover the market price of the land and the infrastructure costs over 25 years. Land leased for housing purposes should not exceed, in urban

---

[5] COUNTRY PROFILES ON THE HOUSING SECTOR: ROMANIA, Economic Commission for Europe, Geneva, UNITED NATIONS, New York and Geneva, 2001
[6] During the year 2003, supposedly caused by a more relaxed credit market, the prices for the apartments in the pre-fabricated blocks of flats went very high compared to the situation of one year ago.

areas, 300 sqm for a single family house; 200 sqm for a house with two storeys, 150 sqm for a collective housing unit with maximum 6 dwellings. Larger projects have a higher risk of property because of the restitution process that brings over claim disputes (about 70% of all titles issued since 1990 were being contested in court afterwards). Titles issued up to 1999 do not contain information on precise location and tax payments. Cadastre registering is incomplete, since there is no legal obligation to register land transfers and 50 years ago private land was transferred to the public domain and most of the registers have been lost. Therefore new claims to a piece of land cannot be ruled out and buying land involves risks.

Legal frame: ownership rights
The UNECE Report -The Country Profile on the Housing Sector on Romania shows that the sequences of legal framework refer mainly to the privatization of State-owned dwellings and further construction work on uncompleted blocks. More recent legislative documents contribute to the clarification of the restitution process for nationalized dwellings of the '50, as well as the social and other rental housing, or the regulation of the urban development process. Still in a very impressive dynamic, there are legislative documents concerning the financial aspects of the housing sector, the taxation (housing-related coverage is found in several acts) and also some related legislation (the finance of local public administration; the local public finance; the organization of real estate agents' activity). The legislation for the thermal insulation of the existing building stock and the promotion of thermal energy conservation is an ongoing process.

The legislative mechanisms and instruments are market-economy oriented and were created within a short period of time. There are certain general defects which need to be rectified: the big number of legislative documents relating to land, the implementation of the new system of property registration that is slow. Regarding the functioning of the housing estates built during the communist regime, although the legal framework for homeowners' associations (HOAs) was approved in 1996, there appears to be a general ignorance of their advantages among the new owners (in spite of several modifications and simplification of the law, the universal creation of properly functioning HOAs is far from being complete). In short, the success in passing legislation which empowers action is not matched by legislative or other measures which ensure its implementation.

Social strata for Bucharest outskirts

For the communist housing estates, a significant chart in a World Bank report shows that around 1970, the people who migrated from the rural areas to towns constituted a major percentage of the total migrations around the country, and interestingly enough "the migration rates [...] were highest among those between twenty and twenty-four", plus that "60 percent of those arriving in urban areas were between fifteen and twenty-nine years old." This means that nowadays the majority of the population residing in the peripheral ensembles of Bucharest, built during the communist years, are the first generation to live in the city. Their present age range from 45 to more than 60 years old. They continue to live in blocks of flats in these districts, as the housing stock has hardly been improved after 1989. Their neighbours – the people born in Bucharest - are the ones who had their homes demolished in the modernisation process of the city.

The apartments are very crowded: the first generation who arrived to the city in the '60 dwell with their children (the second generation in the city), among whom many also have children themselves (the third generation). Due to the discrepancy between the average revenue and the price of an apartment, we can find quite often, three generations of a family in the same apartment. The tensions brought over by the crowding are juxtaposed to the hardships of the daily life, which – in its turn – is due to the transition towards a market economy and democratic society.

It is difficult to appreciate the proportion of newly built single family dwellings which are inhabited by the fortunate families that could escape the communist housing apartments. There is no data, no survey available on the issue of residential mobility. From the empirical observation, it seems that young families, when they afford, buy apartments in the blocks of flats. Building a house at the periphery of the city is more of a case or successful professionals in their forties.

Games of interest for Bucharest outskirts

It is rather difficult to project a general picture of interest groups regarding the different dwelling categories at the periphery of Bucharest. A complete analysis is far beyond the limits of the present paper. What becomes clear is that the transition brought over a kind of Brownian movement and that the inertia of the ancient regime now mixes with the new rules of the game – in a very interesting, often surprising way. Different urban actors are in a rapid learning process. Each actor's part in the general play will become more stable in time along with the European Union norms and constraints.

This article considers that the position of the central administration with regard to the housing strategy has to be considered on the principle that the Romanian Government has a very significant role in developing and maintaining a suitable framework for encouraging, facilitating and helping direct private investment into housing so as to solve the various problems. The Government has become increasingly active in the formulation of a housing policy, and has taken various initiatives in housing issues. It is essential to identify the objectives of Romania's housing policy. There is no shortage of strategies, policies and legislation in which aspirations for the country's future housing are set out; and, yet, these aspirations have produced only a few concrete objectives or practical measures. The National Housing Agency has given shape to the governmental initiatives, which do appear to be beneficial, but in a very narrow area. There is a danger that this success might distract attention from all the other issues not yet being addressed, leading to complacency by those in authority, and the public who are keen to see real progress, which in turn might prevent action until it is too late.

Judging by the size of budget allocations, housing is neither a national nor a local political priority. This reflects the attention being given to more urgent and politically sensitive issues, and the tight budgetary policies necessary if EU applicants such as Romania are to comply with the Maastricht criteria. More significantly, the prevailing view in official circles – at least at the national level – appears to be that the only major housing problem requiring government intervention is the need to "kick-start" the market in house purchases: all else can be left to market forces.

The construction of new social housing is currently negligible. This can be attributed to the lack of public funding, or to the general idea of the political representatives that there is no actual need for more social housing and that there are more important issues on the political agenda. Nonetheless, there are signs of tension which will resurrect the need for building social housing: not least a growing number of evictions and increasing homelessness (caused by the retrocession process), but also the mismatch between households and their living space, or between households' income and the increasingly difficult access to buying a home.

Despite the relatively low level of direct budget allocations for housing, considerable public resources can actually be seen to flow indirectly into housing. This takes a variety of forms. Some reflect the fact that not all areas are market-oriented: as for example real expenditure in subsidizing utility services; or the costs of artificially low public rents, or the State land provided free for development (NHA). More hidden is the relatively unrecognized enormous depreciating asset value of the country's housing stock due to insufficient investment in maintenance and repair - a loss for both state and private owners. This again reflects the lack of appreciation of market values which would come from a well-established market

The strategy for public investment in housing in other countries usually tries to stimulate investment among parts of the population who otherwise would not invest in housing (aide à la pierre), or to provide housing (or services) to those who are not in a position to afford suitable housing (services) in the market (aide à la personne). In Romania, in contrast, the main focus of current public expenditure is the National Housing Agency, whose activities apparently do not concentrate on those areas most in need of government investment.

D. Conclusion
Tendencies for inhabiting Bucharest periphery

The communist housing estates: steps towards ghetto-isation?
A number of major problems have been identified in connection with the apartment blocks. One fundamental issue is that there has been no survey of these physical conditions, and therefore there is no firm knowledge of their scale and extent, or of their rectification costs".[7] Unless these issues are addressed, Romania faces the prospect of emerging ghettos of poorer households literally trapped as owners or tenants of unsuitable properties that they cannot afford to maintain. Many households are investing money in improving their own apartments. However, investing in the jointly-owned building structure or utility infrastructure is often impossible because either some resident households cannot afford to contribute or because cooperation within the homeowners' as-sociation, if any, is poorly developed. The situation is being exacerbated as the people who would normally afford to contribute are moving out of the apartments to purchase newer and/or better quality properties. This can be seen as the first stage of a social polarization, which will lead to an increasing concentration of poorer households in these apartment blocks.

The newly built dwellings: a difficult free-market context
Since the free housing market in Romania is not yet well developed, it is not surprising to find that the new market generated construction is limited (even for the city of Bucharest). There are two categories of

---

[7] COUNTRY PROFILES ON THE HOUSING SECTOR: ROMANIA, Economic Commission for Europe, Geneva, UNITED NATIONS, New York and Geneva, 2001

problems to be considered for the newly built dwellings: the selling price (which limits accessibility to a relatively small portion of the population) and the variable building quality (including the architecture and the relation of these new houses with the rest of the city).

The price is the result of the general socio-economic context of transition and negotiation to join the European Union. It is governed partly by the inefficiencies associated with obtaining serviced building sites (urban planning conditions, housing real estate market conditions, legal frame...), and partly by the cost of finance (financial frame), materials and construction. As for the building materials, the efforts made to introduce innovative building methods and materials to produce new homes at lower costs have not been generally welcomed by potential customers (possible explanations we can find in a conservationist attitude, or may be in the disillusionment with system-building methods used for apartment blocks in the 1960s).

The search for quality should start from questioning the principles to which these dwellings answer. In our opinion, both the old communist housing estates and the new residential parks have a common feature: a severe lack of urbanity which can be explained through a deficient connection to the city centre, especially from the people's representation point of view. For the socialist blocks of flats areas, this cutting-out was the result of the modern urban planning (grand ensemble − autonomous area with elementary facilities included). For the new residential parks, the isolation is a purpose in itself: Being more like 'gated communities', these developments answer to the recently established real estate market.

How to tell right from wrong?
Distributed in small standardised apartments or persuaded to spend their money on "villas" in a highly dense gated community − is from our point of view taking advantage of the fact that there is a severe lack of "good references". The common people, rich or poor, do not have examples of various housing typologies: it is either the grey block of flats, or the individual house produced by a recently established developer who buys cheaper land in the "suburbia". What reference has someone who has lived all his life (born in the '60) and who only knew the apartment in the block of flats? Some of these people struggle to escape the small, the grey and the uniformity and when they built their own house, they will fall in the other extreme of over dimensioning and over decoration. And if we refer to the architects' education (built up during the communist regime), how prepared are they to propose various different types of homes?

The communist blocks of flats were the answer to functionalist theory of zoning mixed with the specific constrains in a totalitarian society. People were told that living in an apartment in a great ensemble is the modern and the correct way to live in the 20th century. After the fall of the communist regime, people started dreaming of a house like in the American movies: the suburbia became the model to wish for. Both models were imported – and they have both been used in opposition to the previous period: the collective housing was "better" than the bourgeoisie style of living; the individual house with the green patch of grass in front of the entrance door is the opposite of the tiny superposed boxes in the blocks of flats.

The critique of the functionalist housing estate model was very little known by the Romanian architects and urban planners due to the isolation of the country especially towards the end of the communist regime. Even so, as Zahariade (2003) explains, "in the second half of the 70s the architects start to question the quasi-mandatory lack of differentiation and try to propose other types of dwellings, sociologically substantiated, for different life-styles, based on the idea to graft on the collective dwellings the qualities of the individual houses (on the model of low-rise high-density developments, or what the French architectural culture calls *habitat intermédiaire*). Unfortunately it was too late, and lots of projects and studies (part of them designed in collaboration with the School of Architecture in Bucharest) remain in the drawers, or are lost in the archives of the design institutes, not able to navigate through the thicker and thicker 'forest' of the bureaucratic mechanism of 'official approval'.[8]

The critique of the American suburbia and especially of the 'gated community" model is related to concepts like 'urbanity' and 'civility' - the irruption of these terms in the urban planning corpus of knowledge corresponds to the nostalgia for the 'real city': "[...] in the United States, some 3 million residences with some 8.4 million people are now situated behind the gates, some of them staffed with twenty-four-hour guards and patrolled by private security forces, some relying on electronically operated gates [...] for centuries, American moralists have fretted about the fragmenting of the community – even as most of them tolerated or even celebrated the market feeding that fragmentation." (Blakely, Snyder 1997) Urbanity is called upon like the quality inherent for having the city that has been lost after WW2. Starting from the 1980, the urbanity will be looked for either through rehabilitation strategies, either through social and economic efforts for rehabilitating big or small ensembles. In the

---

[8] Especially during the last two Communist decades, we can see a peculiar "mush-rooming" of the official bodies in charge with the control and approval of the projects.

French context (Choay, Merlin 2000) of the 1990, the term 'urbanity' is often associated to 'civility'. Together, they constitute fundamental values to which the urban societies tend to adjust through regulations. If urbanity qualifies at the same time the modern urban citizen and his space, civility raises the issue of behaviour which governs a social code. The word urbanity itself comes from the latin urbanitas (life in Rome, then, by extension, moral quality of what belongs to the city). More recently, it is also used as synonym for a refined urban ambience. At a superior abstraction degree, if we try to define "what makes a city", the idea of social interaction is fundamental. All economic activities have to come in contact with the customers – and the customers prefer to have many services concentrated in a relatively reduced area. A central-city location is essential for the success of services, commerce, culture activities. In this way, the urbanity of a settlement appears as the manner of organising the space in order to facilitate and to multiply to the maximum all forms of interaction between partners.

After Marcus Zepf (2001), there are three ways of considering the concept of urbanity: the social urbanity, the spatial urbanity and the politico-administrative one. The author refers to this concept as to a barometer for the aggregation level of a city. The ingredients that are supposed to be aggregated are social, spatial, political, economical phenomena. If considered as an operative concept, 'urbanity' leads to the analysis of the aggregation level of a place. The social urbanity relies on the heterogeneity and on the density of social groups, on the development of a security feeling due to a kind of social informal control, on a dialogue between the public sphere and the private sphere. This dialogue creates a behaviour code that encourages the communication and the need for socialisation. The spatial urbanity is about the possibility of distinguishing the built spaces from the 'empty' spaces. At an architectural level, the spatial urbanity is linked to the capacity of a façade to 'speak' about the relation between the public space and the private space: its composition and the degree of its apertures that allow the contact, the exchange of information between the private and the public sphere. The spatial urbanity is also related to the genius loci, to the history of a certain place. There is a strong link between the spatial and the social configuration of a place in time; from this point of view, the urbanity is obviously influenced by the utilisation rhythms of an urban space.

Is this concept a possible way of telling right from wrong? The challenges of transforming it into an operative concept are related to the evaluation of the potential and of the realities of an urban space: the spatial discontinuity, the territorial paradoxes may be observed and analysed considering this concept which contains elements that speak about the history of the urban space. The presence of these elements forces us to think of the collective urban memory and in this way it "forces" us to take into consideration all urban levels: the social, the spatial, the political and the economical one.

Our hope is that, in time, inhabitants' expectations will rise on the basis of various living experiences, and also on the basis of the increasing professional knowledge of the other stake-holders who are already present or who will arrive in the field of housing.

References:
Blakely, E.; Snyder, M. G. (1997) Fortress America – Gated Communities in the United States. Washington: Brooking Institution Press / Lincoln Institute of Land Policy.
Caciuc, C. (2001) The American City from Bucharest – in Invitation to a Debate. In: Arhitext Design, No. 3/2001, 23.
Choay, F. ; Merlin P. (2000) Dictionnaire de l'urbanisme et de l'aménagement, Presses Universitaires de France, 3rd Edition, 167.
Derer, P. (1982) Locuirea Urbana. Bucuresti: Ed Tehnica.
Ghenciulescu, S. (2003) Everyone's space, someone's space, No One's Space. In: Lost in Space. Bucharest: New Europe College.
Marin, V. (2001) Parcuri rezidentiale, un termen nou pentru un nou mod de locuire?. In: Arhitext Design, No. 3/2001, 23.
Pickvance, C G (1996) Enviromental and Housing Movements after Socialism: The cases of Budapest and Moscow. In: Andrusz, G.; Harloe, M.; Szelenyi, I. (eds) (1996) Cities after Socialism, urban and regional change and conflict in post-socialist societies. Blackwell. 232.
Teodorescu, I. (2002) Improving quality of life in the neighbourhood - Community centres as means for housing districts rehabilitation – the case of Bucharest. Bucharest: New Europe College.
Zahariade, A. M. (2002) Puzzle, rubicube or "roadside picnic"?, presentation paper for the International Union of Architects Congress, Viena,October 10th 2002.
Zahariade, A. M. (2003) The dwelling and the socialist city. In: "Two Books, The Communist Dream & Dacia 1300 – Fragments of an architectural landscape". Simetria.
Zepf, M. (2001) Les paradigmes de l'espace public. In : Toussant, J.Y., Zimmerman M. (ed) (2001) User, Observer, Programmer et Fabriquer l'Espace Public, Lausanne : PPUR, Collection des Sciences Appliquées. 173-183.

New suburban development in the Post-socialist city: the case of Prague

Martin Ouředníček

Introduction

The development of urban systems in European countries is currently relatively stable lacking clear dominance of one urbanisation process (Champion 2001). While during the period of industrialisation number of urban systems were characteristic by population concentration and during post-war years prevailed deconcentration (suburbanisation), spatial processes of population and their activities are nowadays less evident. However, there exists in the post-socialist cities of East-Central European countries one common feature of urban development, which is suburbanisation or more generally suburban development. The strongest migration flows from the cores of large cities to the adjacent suburban zones can be observed in many post-socialist countries. There is comparable (or even stronger) trend of the stretching commercial activities within suburban areas of large cities.

Since the fall of Iron Curtain there has been published big amount of works dealing with urbanisation processes in countries of East-Central Europe during the communist era (Enyedi 1996; Sjöberg 1999; Szelényi 1996; Tammaru 2001; Weclawowicz 1992 etc.). Recently prevail articles and books more concentrated on the study of transformation development in post-socialist cities (Kovács 1999; Musil, 1993, Ott 2001; Ruoppila/Kåhrik 2003; Sailer-Fliege 1999; Sýkora 1999; Sýkora/ Čermák 1998; Timár/Váradi 2001; Vendina 1997; Weclawowicz 1998; Wiegandt 2000 etc.). Publications directly dedicated to research of suburbanisation or suburban development are relatively scarce (Kok/Kovács 1999; Tammaru 2001; Timár/Váradi 2001) or are written in domicile languages (in Czech for example Mulíček 1999; Ouředníček 2003; Ptáček 1997; Sýkora ed. 2002 etc.).

The paper seeks to describe and evaluate processes changing the suburban zone of post-socialist cities on the case of Prague. Main stress is put on investigation of residential suburbanisation and on changes in social environment of suburban settlement. The paper first describes differences between processes of suburban growth and briefly outlines three periods of Prague's urban development with particular stress on deconcentration processes, suburban development and suburbanisation. The paper concludes with discussion of negative and positive features, which can change physical and social environment of suburban zone of Prague Urban Region.

Suburbanisation and other xy-urbanisations

In the recent geographical literature four key processes of urban development are stated – urbanisation, suburbanisation, counter-urbanisation and reurbanisation. These processes are thought as consequent stages of urban development and they are defined on the base of population growth/decline of core and periphery (suburban zone) of metropolitan regions. Theory associated with four stages of urban development was one of the most influential paradigms of urban studies in 1980s and 1990s (Hall/Hay 1980; van den Berg et al 1982; Cheshire/Hay 1989; Cheshire 1995, Champion 2001). Many other authors tried to describe phases or stages of urban development using similar or successive models. Among them we cannot omit Fielding's (1982) urbanisation versus counter-urbanisation and Geyer's and Kontuly's theory of differential urbanisation (Geyer 1996; Geyer/Kontuly 1993, 1996, 2003; TESG 2003). Today it is clear, that theory of stages of urban development is insufficient for description of complexity of urban development in Europe. Firstly, it seems to be obvious that sequence of particular stages of urbanisation processes doesn't fit well neither for description of current urban development nor generally for changes in urban systems in European countries in the past. Secondly, model of stages of urban development is acceptable for cities, which went through intensive Industrial development but is less valuable for administrative, service and other non-industrial cities. It is apparent for example from empirical analysis of British authors (Cheshire/Hay 1989; Cheshire 1995), whose study covered more than 200 of metropolitan areas (functional urban regions – FUR). However, no single FUR went through complete cycle of consequent stages. Even more, only a small amount of FURs (18 per cent), all of them entirely industrial cities, went through at least half of defined cycle. Empirical verification of theoretical models is not persuasive enough in the case of 189 metropolitan regions from 14 countries investigated by van den Berg's group (1982). Similarly, results of retrospective analyses (TESG 2003) aimed on verification of theory of differential urbanisation could be perceived rather in contradiction with theoretical model of proposed theory.

There is no doubt that xy-urbanisations mentioned by van den Berg and others are still the most important processes of urban development in Europe. On the other hand it must be noted, that these processes are not consequent stages but rather kinds of urban development. Although we are aware these particular urbanisation processes are mutually interrelated, two or more of them can (and they do) coexist within one urban system or urban region. In my opinion, seeking for new cycles of urban development or attempts to apply characteristics of any xy-urbanisation processes to the current situation is not a perspective approach. Suburbanisation is today dominant process in the East-Central European countries. However, it is obvious, that at the same time other (though less intensive) urbanisation processes also go on. To support this idea, we can bring wide evidence of scientific works dealing with processes of counterurbanisation, gentrification, reurbanisation and other shaping urban environment of post-socialist cities.

To summarize contribution of works dealing with stages of urban development it is right to say that either empirical analyses or description of reasons and consequences of xy-urbanisations are useful materials for deepening our knowledge about urbanisation processes. On the other hand, the main disadvantage of proposed theoretical models is narrow view on urbanisation processes concerned only relation of population growth of core and periphery of metropolitan regions. The substantial body of xy-urbanisations can be expressed only with use of additional qualitative characteristics. Among them there are of great importance migration characteristics such as structure of source destination, motivation or reasons of migration, social and demographic structure of migrants (Fisher 2003; Ford 1999; Halliday/Coombes 1995; Lindgren 2003; Tammaru 2001). Attempts toward categorization or purification of terminology (Halfacree 2001) in the case of xy-urbanisations are useful for understanding reasons and consequences of urbanisation processes. This paper doesn't include accurate definitions of all urbanisation processes, but for the purpose of theme being discussed there will be presented basic approach to define urbanisation processes and deeper "purification" of suburbanisation process.

If we accept division of settlement (or environment) to the three different types – urban, suburban and rural – and overlooking blurred boundaries within rural-urban continuum, we can summarize migration directions in following table:

Table 1: Types of migration processes (in brackets terms used by Fisher 2003)

Environment		In-migration to		
		Urban	Suburban	Rural
Out-migration from	Urban	Intra-urban or Inter-city migration	Suburbanisation (Suburbanisation)	Deurbanisation (Counterurbanisation)
	Suburban	Reurbanisation	Tangential migration (Population retention)	Deurbanisation (Counterurbanisation)
	Rural	Urbanisation or reurbanisation	Urbanisation or reurbanisation (Centripetal migration)	-

The central point of my interest is suburban development (Tammaru 2001), which includes all the processes stated in second column of the table. As you can see, not all the processes of suburban development could be considered as suburbanisation. Different character has tangential migration – mobility of people within suburban zone and migration of population from areas outside metropolitan region. Investigation of source localities of suburban migration was one of differential factors for defining suburbanisation and other processes in peri-urban environment in the studies of Tania Fisher (Ford 1999; Fisher 2003). Fisher recognized four different processes of suburban development: centripetal migration from rural to suburban environment; population retention caused by increased period of residence and reduced out-migration from sub-urban environment; counter-urbanisation and suburbanisation.

Among other differential characteristics Fisher mentioned the degree of eco-nomic and social connectivity with the metropolitan area maintained by migrants, migrants motivations and qualities of destinations chosen (accessibility, amenity value and location or site).

Regarding these added qualitative characteristics of urbanisation processes, we can define suburbanisation as process of population deconcentration from the core to the suburban zone of metropolitan regions. Main motivation for the migration is improving of residential condition of (young) households and at the same time the maintenance of urban lifestyle and strong connection with core city.

Development of Prague and suburbanisation

From the beginning of 1993, Prague (Praha) is capital of the independent Czech Republic. According to the latest population census held in March 2001 Prague has - within administrative boundaries of the city - 1,2 million people. Whole Prague urban region, consisting of Capital city of Prague and two adjacent administrative districts of Prague-East and Prague- West, covers area of 1.666 square km with more than 1,3 million inhabitants. Other major urban centres in Czechia are Brno (380), Ostrava (320) and Pilsen (170 thousand).

Figure 1: Position of Prague urban region in Czechia.

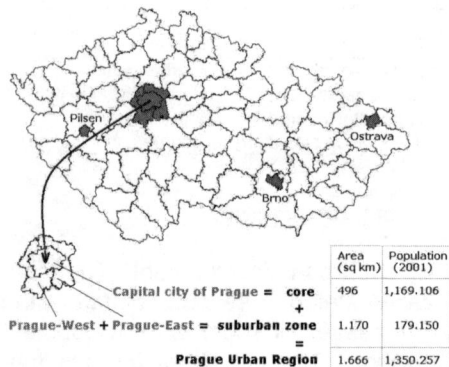

	Area (sq km)	Population (2001)
Capital city of Prague = **core**	496	1,169.106
+		
Prague-West + Prague-East = **suburban zone**	1.170	179.150
=		
Prague Urban Region	1.666	1,350.257

Source: Population census 2001, Czech Statistical Office

Prague grew quickly during the interwar period with annual net migration of 15-19 thousand people. Prague reached 1 million inhabitants in 1939, but during 1940s it lost 50 thousand people and one million regain in the beginning of 1960s. World War II and radical change of political and economic climate after communist coup resulted in state control of population growth of Prague and other big cities. Typical features of 1920s and 1930s - massive concentration of people (urbanisation) from countryside and residential deconcentration (suburbanisation) either in the periphery of Greater Prague or more remote localities alongside rail corridors - were replaced by stagnation of population development.

Although the restriction of natural growth of the capital was reappraised in 1960s and after, the character of development and distribution of new housing was in sharp contrast with urban development in Western countries and also with the past development of Prague. The consequent concentration of state investments to building of large housing estates and very limited individual construction of family houses (mainly in the countryside) led to complete non-existence of suburban development in Prague's surroundings.

Socialism was time of development of large housing estates, which considerably changed previous patterns of suburban development from classical suburbanisation to development of New Towns of panel houses. Al-though the trend of population deconcentration from inner city and de-velopment of suburban zone had the same quantitative characteristics (using plus and minus in population changes of core and periphery), character of residential areas, motivations of migrants and social struc-ture of migration were completely different from western style subur-banisation. The development beyond the city limits was restricted only to quite a few communities, which were established as centres. It has to be allowed to invest money for building infrastructure or housing only to the-se communities. The rest of small communities (noncentres) became de-presssed inner periphery with recreation and agriculture function, with high loses of people, aged and less educated population.

The change of political regime has brought significant changes in economy and society, which started to be gradually observable also in the spatial context. Economic restitutions of formerly private houses and agricultural land situated in urban and suburban areas were important preconditions of new urban development. This led directly to establishing of new functional land use of inner city and to partial changing from residential to commercial uses of buildings, but due to rent regulation also to stabilisation or occasionally trapping of original residents inside re-stituted property. Restitution wasn't in progress in prefabricated housing estates built during socialist era, but instead privatisation became an im-portant stabilisation factor of these areas. Apartments here retain re-latively expensive and that is way they are inaccessible for population with low economic and social status. Restitution of land, on the other hand, was the key accelerator of suburban development in communities surrounding big cities.

Post-socialist suburbanisation
The process of new suburbanisation started in the beginning of 1990s. However, more intensive migration from core to suburban zone was observable from 1995. Forms of suburban development differ significantly from place to place and vary from greater and rather autonomous new settlements to individual projects of separate family houses. New construction is located either on empty lots within existing settlement or as new satellite villages more distant from former settlement. Distinctive aspect of suburban development in Prague urban region is realisation of small projects consisting of 20-50 family houses or quite widespread realisation of individually built houses. These individual projects are realised either on single lot or as a part of larger developed area but using own project and independent of other builders.

Figure 2: Net migration in Prague, suburban zone (districts of Prague-East and Prague-West) and entire Prague metropolitan area (PMR) 1988-2000

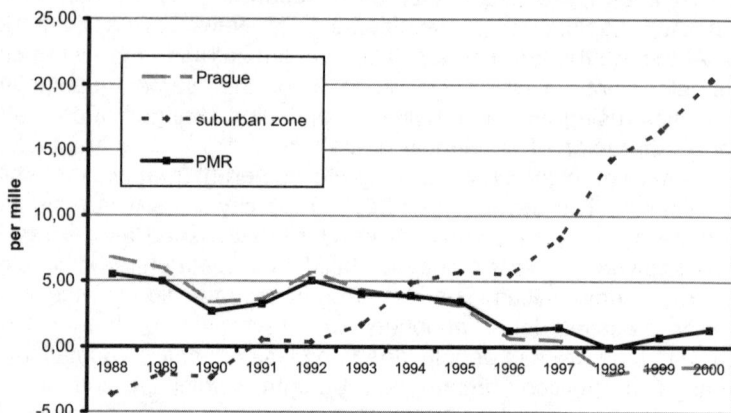

Source: Czech Statistical Office, own calculations

Suburban communities, which were during the communist regime neglected and restricted for investment, have today plans of large residential and commercial development. The extent of proposed development would exceed several times area and number of population of existing community. On the other hand, these large projects of uniform family houses typical for US or Western European suburbanisation are still missing in Prague's suburban development.

It would be hard work to find out within the whole metropolitan area locality without newly constructed family house and in this context some analysts warn against urban sprawl. Indeed many builders don't respect any regulative documents and spatial distribution of new housing therefore depends almost exclusively on activity of new restituents. On the other hand, it must be noted, that small communities have enormous underdeveloped potential for growth. Population of large cities and namely citizens of Prague got quickly reached and are able to spend relatively high amount of money for suburban housing. State support of mortgages and building savings contributes to growing number of people from middle strata, which can afford family house. It has clear impact in spatial spread of communities with net migration growth in suburban zone and in variety of costs and forms of construction in individual localities. In general we can assume that initially were developed houses of higher standard in attractive localities and later also more peripheral communities with cheaper lots and housing. The evidence of communities with migration increase supports this idea. Their number increased from 73 communities in 1991 to 135 in 1999. It is also obvious from table 2 that in 1995 suburban development was concentrated within the administrative boundaries of the city. Six years later the zone with higher rate of migration and total increase were districts Prague-East and Prague-West.

Table 2: Components of population growth in zones of Prague urban region in 1995 and 2001

Year	1995			2001		
Zone	Natural increase	Net migration	Total increase	Natural increase	Net migration	Total increase
	Per 1000 of inhabitants					
Centre (Historic city)	-10,00	-12,98	-22,98	-7,50	-12,65	-20,16
Inner city (Pre-war city)	-6,99	0,68	-6,31	-5,44	-2,72	-8,16
Outer city (Housing estates)	1,57	1,86	3,43	1,46	0,37	1,82
Periphery (Prague´s villages)	-2,88	13,93	11,06	-0,32	13,05	12,74
Prague total	-4,71	0,79	-3,93	-3,35	-4,18	-4,84
Suburban zone (Prague-East and West)	-4,51	5,18	0,68	-2,35	20,41	18,05

Source: Czech Statistical Office, own calculations

The theoretical section of this paper deals with differentiation of processes of suburban development. It is obvious from the investigation of Prague's hinterland that deconcentration moves of population from Prague to the districts of Prague-East and Prague-West cover 61 per cent of in-migration to the suburban zone. Almost one quarter of new-comers originates from communities inside suburban zone (15 per cent) together with other localities within neighbouring districts of Central Bohemia (9 per cent). This short-distance migration (tangential migration) has increasing importance and its internal structure is quite complicated as suburban zone is not homogenous but consisting of small towns, developing and peripheral villages. Only small part of migrants comes from more remote areas of Czechia. The share of international migration is not accurate due to statistical deficiency. High proportions of „foreigners" in suburban zone are Czech re-emigrants, while most of Western Europeans rather concentrate to the inner city. The autonomous locality of Americans in Malá Šárka on the north-western edge of the city is rare exception.

Figure 3: Structure of in-migration to Prague´s suburban zone by source destinations in 1997-1999.

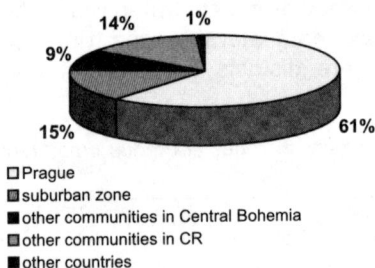

- □ Prague
- ▨ suburban zone
- ■ other communities in Central Bohemia
- ▨ other communities in CR
- ■ other countries

Source: Czech Statistical Office

When we zoom out on the level of Czech administrative districts, we can recognize following general trends (see map 1 and 2). Prague urban region (with absolute dominance of Prague) has positive migration balance with districts contained the largest Czech cities. On the other hand, Prague loses people with own hinterland and also with more remote small towns in neighbouring districts of Central Bohemia and country districts around Brno and Pilsen. We can see similar picture in the case of migration balance of suburban zone. Most important (dark red) source areas of growth of suburban area belong again the largest Czech cities. Is migration out-flowing from Brno or Olomouc to the hinterland of Prague suburbanisation?

Figure 4: Net migration of Prague urban region in 2001.

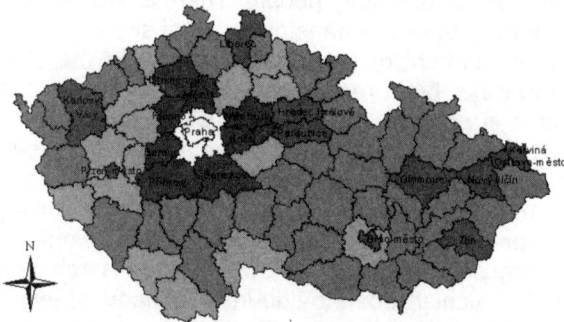

Note: Blue shades are regions with active net migration and red shades with passive balance. The darker districts the more intensive migration flows.

Source: Czech Statistical Office

Figure 5: Net migration of suburban zone in 2001 (see note for figure 4).

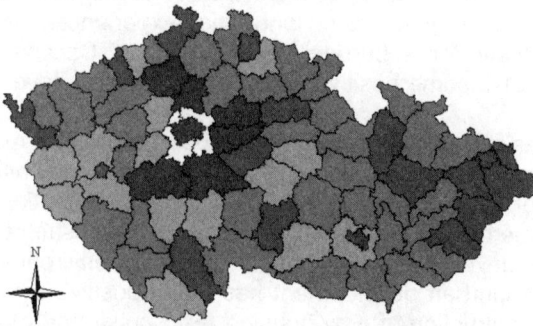

Source: Czech Statistical Office

To identify suburbanisation and other urbanisation processes only on the base of source destination of in-migration is rather insufficient. There are also other very important characteristics of urbanisation processes, which include motivations of migrants and connectivity with the core city (Ford 1999). These characteristics are important for proper differentiation of particular migration flows and urbanisation processes (urbanisation – suburbanisation – counterurbanisation – tangential and centripetal migration etc.). In the case of Czech cities and namely Prague local conditions of urban-to-rural migration play an important role. For instance, among the communities with the fastest migration growth, there are all these with localised rest homes for elderly people. There is also another specific kind of suburban development - transformation of second homes in recreational areas to permanent or seasonal housing. On the other hand, in Prague there has not been recognized outflow of urban poor from the city, trend that is in progress in the South-East Europe. These residential moves have different character and they differ from sub-urbanisation in the right sense of this process. The low degree of con-nectivity of migrants from Brno, Olomouc and other more remote cities is than reason why these processes of suburban development would be considered as different from suburbanisation. However no research deal-ing with diversification of particular urban-to-suburban streams of migra-tion has been done up to date.

Is suburbanisation negative or positive process?
Suburbanisation (and moreover urban sprawl) is traditionally perceived as a negative process. Suburbanisation or suburban development pro-duces functionally homogenous zones. It raises requirements for traffic and technical infrastructure. Suburban buildings occupy formerly agri-cultural land; suburbanites bring alien features to architecture and social environment, and deepen socio-spatial polarisation and segregation. But are these postulates generated from long-time experiences from Western cities appropriate for suburban development in Czechia? I would like to advocate also some positive aspects of suburban develop-ment around Prague.

It was argued that virtually no development had to been allowed in most of communities around Prague during socialist era. Many of communities were in the beginning of 1990s underdeveloped and had big potential for residential (and commercial) growth. Appearance of first suburban pioneers started a new development of social and physical environment and it is obvious that suburban development has many positive conse-quences. Firstly, the construction of new housing (with noise and mood from heavy machines and strange workmen walking through the village) is not perceived as positive feature for local people. But builders often cover part of expenditures for the whole village in case of infrastructure, new lighting or roads. Construction of new buildings brings more oppor-tunities for local firms. Activities in suburban zone pull in more people who use local services. Specific feature of Czech settlement is relatively dense distribution of small towns serving as centres with supply of all elementary goods and services. New suburbanites are not fully depend-ent on commuting to the core city and big amount of travels is realized in short distances. Suburban development therefore supports local firms. Secondly, to the suburban zone migrate rather more affluent people. Their homes are more luxurious, their cars more expensive, but they share common space with residents of former neighbourhood. Although in the first years after they coming the newcomers are rather separated, the co-existence of both social groups becomes tighter. Suburbanites start to participate in local governments, many of them use local firms during construction of family house, and all of them need local services and offices. The most intensive connections are soon done between parents of children and young people generally. Thirdly, suburbanites are more educated people and their social status and life-style is different from former inhabitants. Newcomers bring new activities and there is no doubt that their lifestyle has strong impact on social environment of villagers. They pay more attention for appropriate services and infrastructure and improved facilities serve equally for entire village. New lines of metropolitan buses were set up around Prague, many communities have own newspapers etc.

The special sorts of suburbanites are people, who move towards the cheaper and more remote or/and less accessible localities within metropolitan area. Many of them often don't build new family houses but they purchase and renovate older houses or transform second homes into permanent housing. Typical trend of current suburban development is migration inflow of middle social strata. Many of newcomers are young people in childbearing age, who try to find an affordable housing. For many of them it was really shock therapy, when responsibility for housing was transferred at once from state to individual person. Housing of average standard in suburban zone and daily commuting are most reasonable solutions for numerous young families.

Conclusion

Suburbanisation and suburban development are not new processes in Prague urban region. Intensive suburban growth was traditional form of city enlargement in 19th century and in the era of First Republic. Current residential suburbanisation is relatively moderate process, up to now it has not bring big problems observed in the past development of Western cities. As certain threat we can consider growing number of cars per person, which is evenly consequence of increasing car ownership of firms and individuals within both inner and suburban zones of the city. Suburbanisation could be perceived not only as a negative trend but even as upgrading of social and physical environment of suburban localities, as revival of natural development of Czech cities. There is no doubt, that there exist plenty of threats of suburban development. What is believed to be positive in suburban area would have negative impact in other places of metropolitan area. For example selective migration of people with higher social status out from inner city or housing estates could lead to socio-spatial segregation. Concentration of poor people inside declining areas of the inner city would lead to physical or/and social downgrading of source destinations of suburban migrants. However, experiences from urban development of Western countries tell us that big problems are derived from rapid growth. The post-socialist residential suburbanisation is rather steady rehabilitation of natural urban development.

References:
Champion, A.G. (2001) Urbanization, Suburbanization, Counterurbanization and Reurbanization. In: Paddison, R. (ed) Handbook of Urban Studies. Sage. London. 143-161.
Cheshire, P. (1995) A New Phase of Urban Development in Western Europe? The Evidence for the 1980s. Urban Studies 32(7), 1045-1063.
-, Hay, D. (1989) Urban Problems in Western Europe: An Economic Analysis. Unwin Hyman. London.
Enyedi, G. (1996) Urbanization under Socialism. In: Andrusz, G.; Harloe, M.; Szelenyi, I. (eds) Cities after Socialism: Urban and Regional Change and Conflict in Post-socialist Societies. Blackwell. Oxford. 100-118.
- (1998) Transformation in Central European Postsocialist Cities. In: Enyedi, G. (ed) Social Change and Urban Restructuring in Central Europe. Akadémiai Kiadó. Budapest. 9-34.
Fielding, A. (1982) Counterurbanisation in Western Europe. Progress in Planning 17, 1-52.
Fisher, T. (2003) Differentiation of Growth Processes in the Peri-urban Region: An Australian Case Study. Urban Studies 40(3), 551-565.
Ford, T. (1999) Understanding Population Growth in the Peri-Urban Region. International Journal of Population Geography 5(4), 297-311.
Geyer, H.S. (1996) Expanding the Theoretical Foundation of the Concept of Differential Urbanisation. Tijdschrift voor Economische en Sociale Geografie 87(1), 44-59.
-, Kontuly, T.M. (1993) A Theoretical Foundation for the Concept of Differential Urbanization. International Regional Science Review 17(2), 157-177.
- Kontuly, T.M. (ed) (1996) Differential Urbanization: Integrating Spatial Models. Arnold. London.
-, Kontuly, T.M. (2003) Introduction to special issue: Differential urbanisation. Tijdschrift voor Economische en Sociale Geografie 94(1), 3-10.
Halfacree, K. (2001) Constructing the Object: Taxonomic Practices, Counterurbanisation and Positioning Marginal Rural Settlement. International Journal of Population Geography 7(5), 395-411.
Hall, P.; Hay., D. (1980) Growth Centres in the European Urban System. Heinemann Educational. London.
Halliday, J.; Coombes, M. (1995) In Search of Counterurbanisation: Some Evidence from Devon on the Relationship between Patterns of Migration and Motivation. Journal of Rural Studies 11(4), 433-446.
Kok, H.; Kovács, Z. (1999) The Process of Suburbanisation in the Agglomeration of Budapest.. Netherlands Journal of Housing and the Built Environment 14(2), 119-141.
Kovács, Z. (1999) Cities from State-Socialism to Global Capitalism: an Introduction. GeoJournal 49(1), 1-6.
Lindgren, U. (2003) Who is the Counter-Urban Mover? Evidence from the Swedish Urban System. International Journal of Population Geography 9(5), 399-418.

Mulíček, O. (1999) Prostorové suburbanizační změny v JZ sektoru velkého Brna. Acta Facultatis Studiorum Humanitatis et Naturae Universitatis Prešoviensis XXXII - Folia Geographica 3, 63-66. [Spatial Suburbanisation Changes in South-West Sector of Greater Brno].

Musil, J.; Ryšavý, Z. (1983) Urban and Regional Processes under Capitalism and Socialism: A Case Study from Czechoslovakia. International Journal of Urban and Regional Research 7(4), 495-527.

Ott, T. (2001) From Concentration to De-concentration – Migration Patterns in the Post-socialist City. Cities 18(6), 403-412.

Ouředníček, M. (2003) Suburbanizace Prahy. Sociologický časopis 39(2), 235-253. [Suburbanisation of Prague].

Ptáček, P. (1997) Suburbanizační proces v zázemí Prahy v 1. polovině 90. let. Územní plánování a urbanismus XXIV(1/2), 13-14. [The Process of Suburbanisation in the Hinterland of Prague in First Half of 1990s].

Ruoppila, S./Kahrik, A. (2003) Socio-economic residential differentiation in post-socialist Tallinn. Journal of Housing and Built Environment 18, pp. 49-73.

Sailer-Fliege, U. (1999) Characteristics of Post-socialist Urban Transformation in East Central Europe. GeoJournal 49(1), pp. 7-16.

Sjöberg, Ö. (1999) Shortage, Priority and Urban Growth: Towards a Theory of Urbanisation under Central Planning. Urban Studies 36(13), 2217-2236.

Sýkora, L. (1999) Changes in the Internal Spatial Structure of Post-communist Prague. GeoJournal 49(1), 79-89.

-, ed. (2002) Suburbanizace a její sociální, ekonomické a ekologické důsledky. The Institute for Environmental Policy. Prague. [Suburbanisation and Its Social, Econonomic and Ecological Consequences].

-, Čermák, Z. (1998) City Growth and Migration Patterns in the Context of Communist and Transitory Periods in Prague's Urban Development. Espace, Populations, Societes 3, 405-416.

Szelényi, I. (1996) Cities under Socialism - and After. In: Andrusz, G.; Harloe, M.; Szelényi, I. (eds): Cities after Socialism. Urban and Regional Change and Conflict in Post-Socialist Societies. Blackwell Publishers. Oxford. 286-317.

Tammaru, T. (1999) Differential Urbanisation and Primate City Growth in Soviet and Post-Soviet Estonia. Tijdschrift voor Economische en Sociale Geografie 91(1), 20-30.

-, (2001) Suburban Growth and Suburbanisation under Central Planning: The Case of Soviet Estonia. Urban Studies 38(8), 1341-1357.

TESG (2003) Special Issue: Differential Urbanisation. Tijdschrift voor Economische en Sociale Geografie 94(1).

Timár, J.; Váradi, M.M. (2001) The Uneven Development of Suburbanization during Transition in Hungary. European Urban and Regional Studies 8(4), 349-360.

van den Berg, L.; Drewett, R.; Klaassen, L.H.; Rossi, A.; Vijverberg, C.H.T. (1982) A Study of Growth and Decline. Urban Europe. Vol. 1. Pergamon Press. Oxford.

Weclawowicz, G. (1992) The Socio-spatial Structure of the Socialist Cities in East-central Europe. The Case of Poland, Czechoslovakia and Hungary. In: Lando, F. (ed): Urban and Rural Geography. Papers from 6th Italian-Polish Geographical Seminar, September 15.-23., 1990, University of Venice. 129-140.

-, (1998): Social Polarisation in Postsocialist Cities: Budapest, Prague and Warsaw. In: Enyedi, G. (ed): Social Change and Urban Restructuring in Central Europe. Akadémiai Kiadó. Budapest. 55-66.

Wiegandt, C.C. (2000) Urban Development in Germany – Perspectives for the Future. GeoJournal 50(1), 5-15.

Vendina, O.I. (1997) Transformation processes in Moscow and intra-urban stratification of population. GeoJournal 42(4), 349-363.

Regions in Transition: New Roles in a Global Economy. The Case of Ukraine

Olga Mrinska

Every country in Central and Eastern Europe (CEE) has experienced different levels and types of success over the last fifteen years in their transition to a market economy. This has led to ongoing discussions about the main pre-conditions for success: why does one state quickly attain high international standards, while another is left behind, as the map of Europe is being re-drawn? The answers to this question are complex, and it is widely recognised that apart from sound macro-economic and structural policy and changes towards democracy, a country now needs many other things in order to become competitive in a modern, global economy, including the right mentality and attitude, an open-minded population, and active public participation in this process. The country's historical legacy is another factor that can play a positive or negative role.

If all this is true at the national level, it is even more obvious at the sub-national level. Whilst this may not be an issue in small European transition economies with more homogenous territorial and demographic patterns, such as the Baltic States, Slovenia or Slovakia, in bigger countries with a large population and traditionally diverse territorial regions, development is experienced in different regions 'with different velocities'. This happens not only because of economic and social reforms, but also the impact of social mobilisation, and wider changes that alter a region's overall geo-political or geo-economic position. Ukraine provides a good example of this diversified transition to a free market. Ukraine's pattern of decline followed by strong economic growth encouraged a situation whereby development in different regions progressed along very different paths. Though back in 1989, Ukraine had one of the highest economic potentials in Europe, it has been ranked as one of the least advanced transition economies in CEE over the last decade. However, looking at the dramatic pace of economic development over the past five years, and the many structural changes which have accompanied this development, there are reasons to expect that Ukraine may once again strengthen its position and rebuild this potential.

This paper is aimed at showing the diversity in trends of regional development in Ukraine: why some regions have managed to find a suitable position in both the national and international economy and why others are finding it difficult to preserve or strengthen their competitiveness. Economic success is dependent not only on industrial potential, the size of the labour force or the level/quality of infrastructure in the region: some of the worst performing regions today were formerly among the most industrially powerful territories. Meanwhile, some traditionally peripheral regions with underdeveloped economies and minimal experience in international economic relations are today among the most well-placed regions in the country, and in Eastern Europe more widely. This relative advantage is the result of a change in the type of production (from large-scale production to individually tailored products, from supply-driven to demand-driven output), quality of production, strong human capital, and, most importantly, due to the eastward movement of the European Union (EU)'s borders.

Regional disparities in Ukraine – the economic context

Ukraine's quick economic growth over the last five years has significantly accelerated regional differences. This is due both to external factors, such as the rapid development of a global innovative economy and fluctuations in international markets, and to internal factors such as the considerable gap between different regions' capacity. For example, in 2003, the difference between maximum and minimum levels of FDI attraction to Ukrainian regions was at a factor of 43. A third of Ukrainian regions each attracted less than 1% of national FDI, while one city – Kyiv – managed to attract more than 35%. Regional disparities began to increase noticeably from 1999, when the national economy entered a period of strong growth (the Gross Domestic Product (GDP) - growth rate constituted 9.2% in 2001, 5.2% in 2002, 9.4% in 2003, and 12.5% in the first 8 months of 2004 – State Statistics Committee of Ukraine (SSC)). With sustained rapid economic growth forecast for the next few years, it can be predicted that regional disproportions will continue to deepen and that social stratification will increase.

Graph 1

Dynamics of some macroeconomic indices

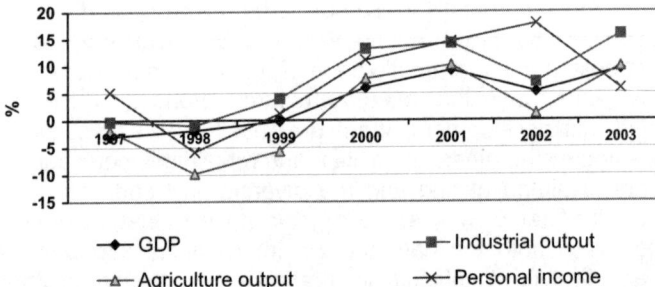

Source: State Statistics Committee, International Centre for Policy Studies ICPS, 2004

Ukraine is a very diversified state in terms of regions' natural resource endowment and economic potential, while human capital is distributed quite evenly. Historical factors have also left a complicated socio-economic patchwork across the country, with different parts of the country demonstrating significant differences in national identity, in their general attitudes and mentality, and not least in their aspirations and preferences in foreign policy. There is a widely recognised approach to regionalisation whereby Ukraine's 25 oblasts are divided into 8 macro-economic regions with significant similarities in economic structure and social portrait (Table 1).

Table 1: Some relative economic indices of Ukrainian regions (in %)

Macroregion / Oblast	Territory 2002	Popula-tion 2003	GVA 2002	Ind. Output 2002	Agr. Output 2002	FDI 2003	Export 2003
Ukraine	**100**	**100**	**100**	**100**	**100**	**100**	**100**
Donetsky	**8,8**	**15,1**	**16,6**	**28,3**	**8,4**	**7,4**	**27,4**
Donetsk	4,4	9,9	12,4	20,6	5,8	6,5	21,5
Lugansk	4,4	5,2	4,2	7,7	2,6	0,9	5,9
Carpathian	**9,3**	**12,8**	**9,0**	**5,3**	**11,4**	**9,0**	**7,2**
Zakarpatska	2,1	2,6	1,6	0,6	2,2	2,7	1,8
Ivano-Frankivsk	2,3	2,9	2,2	1,6	2,6	1,4	3,0
Lviv	3,6	5,4	4,2	2,7	4,6	4,6	2,1
Chernivtsi	1,3	1,9	1,0	0,4	2,0	0,3	0,3
Southern	**18,8**	**15,1**	**12,9**	**7,7**	**15,0**	**11,3**	**9,1**
ARC	4,5	5,0	3,7	1,8	3,1	3,8	1,6
Mykolayv	4,1	2,6	2,3	2,4	3,3	1,1	2,4
Odessa	5,5	5,1	5,3	2,6	5,3	5,4	4,5
Kherson	4,7	2,4	1,6	0,9	3,3	1,0	0,6
Podilsky	**10,1**	**9,0**	**5,8**	**3,7**	**13,0**	**2,1**	**2,4**
Vinnytsa	4,4	3,7	2,6	1,8	5,7	1,0	1,4
Ternopil	2,3	2,4	1,3	0,6	3,0	0,4	0,3
Khmelnitsky	3,4	2,9	1,9	1,3	4,3	0,7	0,7
Polisky	**16,9**	**10,1**	**6,8**	**5,0**	**13,1**	**4,4**	**2,6**
Volynska	3,3	2,2	1,5	0,8	3,0	1,3	0,9
Zhytomyr	5,0	2,9	1,7	1,1	3,3	1,2	0,9
Rivne	3,3	2,4	1,7	1,2	3,0	0,8	0,7
Chernigiv	5,3	2,6	1,9	1,9	3,8	1,1	1,1
Prydniprovsky	**13,9**	**13,7**	**14,7**	**24,7**	**14,1**	**16,5**	**23,5**
Dnipropetrovsk	5,3	7,4	8,8	15,7	6,0	9,0	15,6
Zaporizhzhia	4,5	4,0	4,2	8,1	3,8	6,6	7,5
Kirovograd	4,1	2,3	1,7	0,9	4,3	0,9	0,4
Eastern	**13,9**	**12,1**	**11,7**	**13,1**	**14,4**	**8,7**	**8,3**
Poltava	4,8	3,4	3,8	4,9	5,0	2,6	4,4
Sumy	3,9	2,7	2,1	2,3	3,4	2,1	1,5
Kharkiv	5,2	6,0	5,8	5,9	6,0	4,0	2,4
Central	**8,3**	**12,1**	**22,5**	**10,5**	**10,6**	**40,6**	**15,1**
Kyiv	4,8	9,2	20,6	8,8	6,0	39,1	13,8
Cherkasy	3,5	2,9	1,9	1,7	4,6	1,5	1,3

Source: State Statistics Committee (2003); Monitoring of Socio-Economic Development of Ukrainian Regions, the Ministry of Economy and European Integration (2002), own calculations

The Donetsky and Prydniprovsky regions are traditional industrial centres of Ukraine with a highly developed heavy industrial sector. The share of industrial output in these two regions constitutes 53% of all production, and they now provide more than half of national exports and a third of value added. This could be explained by the disproportionate structure of national exports, with products from the metallurgical and chemical industries accounting for about 45% of overall exports (SSC, 2003). However, the importance of these sectors is declining, because their extensive use of resources, environmentally unfriendly technologies, and products with low value added make them uncompetitive over the long term, and changes in international markets may accelerate this process. Therefore, if radical steps are not made to diversify production structures in these regions, they may suffer severe economic degradation within a few years.

Another peculiar characteristic of Ukraine's traditional industrial centres is that they get only 24% of FDI. This is a consequence of the sector structure of investments, which are mainly directed into sectors such as retail, food industries, light industry, machinery production, power generation, and the service sector – all of which are generally characterised by quick returns on invested capital. Unless new investments and new technologies are introduced into extensively depreciated assets (90% of assets in agriculture and 60% in industry), these traditional industrial regions will face dramatic development problems in a few years' time. It would be fair to note here that significant flows of investments are coming to these regions from Russia, where the type of production and development priorities are similar. Another positive factor that attracts Russian investors to these mostly energy- and material-intensive productions in Ukraine is the low cost of fuel and energy supply.

The Eastern Ukrainian region used to be one of the biggest machine-building centres in the former Soviet Union. In the 1990s, however, the share of machinery in the export structure has reduced drastically, and this fact has had a negative impact on the factories' capacities. The collapse of traditional links with former Soviet republics and acute financial problems resulted in shrinkages in cash flows and high debt levels. The low competitiveness of Ukrainian machinery has led to recession in this traditionally high-priority branch. Between 1991 and 2000, employment in the machinery and equipment sector of Ukraine dropped by 65%. Ukraine lost its traditional markets, and even machinery and equipment exports to Russia constitute only 6% of total exports to this country (SSC).

Over the last 4 years, however, the situation has being improving, and both domestic and foreign capital investment in the machinery sector are increasing considerably. The share of machinery in GDP and exports is rising, not only in the low-tech, but also in the mid- and high-tech segments, meaning a gradual improvement of situation in the *Eastern region* can be predicted.

Ukraine's Central region, which contains the capital city, Kyiv, has the biggest share of FDI – more than 40% of the total amount, despite the fact that its share in Gross Value Added (GVA) and industrial output is equal to 22.5% and 10.5% respectively (See Table 1). This fact greatly supports the idea that the crucial factors in deciding where to invest include the existence of a developed infrastructure, highly qualified human resources, an efficient administrative system, and a 'central location' in economic terms. Kyiv is also the country leader in productivity rates: though it has half the population of the biggest and most industrially powerful oblast (Donetsk), it has a greater share of national GVA and of some other macro indices.

The Podilsky, Polisky and Carpathian regions are traditionally agricultural with a low share of industrial output. After a period of deep crisis, over the last couple of years these regions are finally experiencing dynamic development in sectors such as machinery, light industry and the service sector, especially tourism. These sectors are becoming more important in terms of local economic growth and have in part helped to diminish social tensions by reducing the local unemployment rate. With the exception of Lviv, the oblasts in these regions had an insignificant amount of both national and foreign capital investments in the 1990s. However, EU enlargement gave them a powerful impetus to develop their local economy due to the re-location of European industrial capacities. These are border oblasts, which are experiencing both the positive and the negative effects from the accession of Poland, Hungary and Slovakia to the EU. The European Neighbourhood Policy which was presented by the European Commission (EC) in 2003 promotes the further deepening of integration with Ukraine, particularly in the economic sector and in terms of harmonising policy and social standards.

The Southern region of Ukraine has a mixed structure with a more or less equal share of industry and agriculture. It is specialised in the maritime complex and services, especially maritime transport, which is becoming a more important part of the gross regional product. In total, this region provided 12% of national export of services, which totalled USD 5.2 billion in 2003 (National Bank of Ukraine (NBU)). This is particularly true for the Odessa oblast, where Ukraine's major seaports are located and all main transport lines cross; this forms a good pre-condition for developing an international multi-modal transport node. It is worth stressing that 75% of Ukrainian service exports are in transport services, dominated by pipeline transit services. In combination with the dynamically developing telecommunication sector and high intellectual potential, this creates unique opportunities for the Southern region to become one of the most significant and strategic regions in Europe.

The impact of the demographic situation and social capital on regional differentiation

Since independence, Ukraine has suffered from relatively high levels of depopulation. Its population dropped from 52.24 million in 1992 (the fifth highest in Europe), to 47.42 million by the middle of 2004. In 2003 alone, the Ukrainian population decreased by 380,000 due both to negative natural growth and migrations flows. According to the recently published National Demographic Concept, Ukraine's population is expected to be about 45 Million by 2015 (Graph 2). At the same time, life expectancy will rise from 74 to 76 years for women and from 62 to 67 years for men.

Graph 2: Ukraine's Population

Ukraine's population

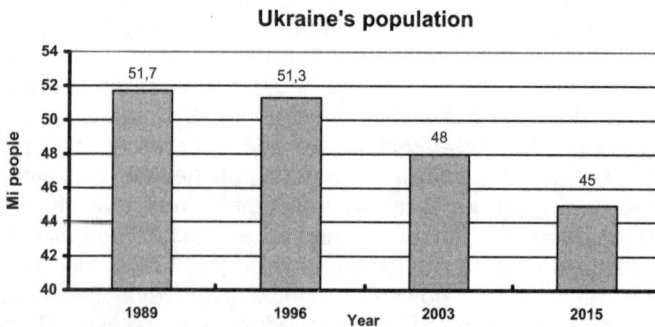

This negative tendency can in part be explained by the fact that in the twentieth century, many millions of Ukrainians lost their lives as a result of two world wars, and famines and repression in the Union of Soviet Socialist Republics (USSR) in the 1930s, 1940s, and 1950s. Ukraine's population had been gradually decreasing since the 1960s, but this process speeded up significantly over the last ten years. The main cause of this process is the decline of the national economy. For two-thirds of the population, the quality of life has deteriorated while poverty has grown, hitting families which used to be relatively well off during the Soviet period. Due to such 'immediate poverty' and negative expectations for the future, many people prefer not to have many children (or not at all) and the fertility rate has dropped to 1.2 (the average in Europe is 1.8). Only in 2003 did the number of births start to grow (by 5%), and experts attribute this phenomenon to the dynamic economic growth of the previous 4 years. Nonetheless, natural growth in 2003 was equal to –7.5 (16 deaths against a birth rate of 8.5 per 1000). This is the worst index among the fifteen former Soviet republics, and one of the worst in Europe.

The high proportion of elderly persons as a percentage of total national population – a trend that is increasing – presents problems over the long term, since it will have a considerable impact on national macro-economic stability. Given that 17.3% of the population are youths, and 23.8% are elderly, there is a heavy burden on the economically active population, which is expected to grow over the next couple of decades. This is further compounded by high emigration flows, since it is generally the most active and talented people who are the first to leave the country.

The Ukrainian Soviet Republic traditionally had a highly qualified labour force and considerable intellectual potential. There are several big educational and Research and Development (R&D) - Centres: Kyiv, Dnipropetrovsk, Kharkiv, Lviv, and Odessa. However, since the collapse of the Soviet economic system and the loss of co-operative links with other former Soviet republics, Ukrainian scientific and educational centres are struggling for their position in the market economy with little success. The amount of time required to turn an invention into a concrete product is usually extremely long and uncompetitive in comparison to other countries. Furthermore, in the qualified specialists market, supply does not meet demand: the number of registered unemployed who are graduates of Ukrainian universities increased 2.6 times between 1995 and 2001. There is also a big gap between the demands of business and the supply from the scientific and educational spheres. In 2002, only 10% of Ukrainian companies implemented innovative activities and products. The share of innovative products and services in the gross national output is equal to 7%, while in developed countries this index constitutes between 70% and 90%. This means that high intellectual potential is not being transformed into economic strength and does not contribute to an increase in productivity in the Ukrainian economy.

The consequences of ten years of economic and social crisis include: a considerable 'brain drain'; the loss of the most qualified and educated people, who would otherwise contribute to the increase of the national productivity; and losses to the Ukrainian economy. According to official statistics there are only 300,000 Ukrainian labour emigrants in different countries. Most of these found jobs in Western and Central Europe, as well as the US, Canada, Israel (mainly Jewish Ukrainians) Australia and Russia. However, this data is very unreliable since in the majority of cases Ukrainians are illegal labour immigrants and are not officially registered with the Ukrainian consulates abroad. According to the Ukrainian Ombudsman there are 2-7 million Ukrainians working illegally, which at worst would mean about 15% of the whole population (!). They mainly migrate from those regions that have the highest unemployment rates (Western Ukraine) where the population is also more proactive. It is said that that there is somebody working abroad in every third family from Western Ukrainian oblasts.

On the one hand, this reduces social tensions in the regions and brings additional sources of income (if we assume that on average, a Ukrainian worker gets 500 USD per month and that the number of illegal workers is directly between 2 and 7 million – 4.5 million – this means that Ukrainians earn about 2.25 billion dollars monthly (!), and that the amount of work remittances sent home is potentially a considerable source of domestic capital).

On the other hand, this 'drain' brings a whole range of social problems, related to broken families, a general deterioration of social and moral standards, and the appearance of so-called 'social orphans' (children whose parents are working abroad and receive no other support but money). This leads to distortions in many children's systems of values and behaviour, and lowers respect and understanding of social rules and norms. This in turn raises levels of criminality among the young, and aggravates drug and alcohol addiction and other health problems.

The weakness of social capital, understood as a complex of social relationships and social networks which play an important role in economic success both at the micro and macro levels, could be characterised as one of the limitations of Ukrainian economy at the moment. The collapse of the Soviet system, whose main characteristic was collectivism, caused a significant decrease in people's level of trust in collective efforts and strengthened tendencies towards individualism. In the majority of cases, social networks do not extend beyond one's family, relatives and circle of friends. Civil society as such is just in the process of formation, and will take many more years to develop fully. Social initiatives are still too weak to play much of a role in increasing the transparency and accountability of power, which would strengthen Ukraine's position as a truly democratic and open state.

Nevertheless, it should be noted that there are significant differences in the parameters of social capital in different parts of the country. The Eastern and Southern regions of Ukraine have a higher percentage of Russians in the population, a surplus of qualified human resources, a high level of urbanisation and an exhausted environment. These regions belonged to the Russian Empire for centuries and thus experienced an immense centralisation of power and an almost complete lack of basic human freedoms. The majority of the local population is not indigenous Ukrainian; it is more passive, less eager to take risks in the private sector, and more used to relying upon the decisions of the central and regional governments. This is a tradition inherited from the centrally-planned Soviet economy. There are no strong traditions of civil society, which has begun to emerge only in the last 5-7 years.

Western Ukraine has a much stronger national identity: it is the cradle of Ukrainian independence, and inherited traditions of civil society and private ownership. For several centuries, this part of Ukraine belonged to the Austro-Hungarian Empire. Although there were problems relating to discrimination against national minorities, the Austro-Hungarian Empire nonetheless provided a basic framework and conditions for the development of community life and civil initiatives. The Western oblasts of Ukraine have a consumer-orientated, medium-developed industrial sector, a large share of employment in agriculture, a developed service sector, and a better ecological situation. The population here is more socially flexible and 'looks west': Western Ukraine has more links with its Central European neighbours and with Western Europe, and is not very dependent on Russian markets.

The implications of transition on the spatial socio-economic development of Ukraine

Most Ukrainian regions and territories experienced a serious shock during the transition to a market economy. This was due to losing a considerable share of their industrial capacities and intellectual potential, a decrease in productivity, social collapse and the 'immediate poverty' caused by radical structural changes in the economy. Due to a serious financial crisis, the Government found itself in a position where there is chronic under-funding in spheres such as science, education, R&D, telecommunications and infrastructure, all of which are fundamental for development in a modern knowledge-based economy. Nor is the private sector yet fully 'fledged' to the extent that it can substantially fund research and innovation itself, meaning that the number of companies which actually produce innovative products and services is marginal (only one tenth).

Structural changes to the national economy are not going as smoothly as expected, and Ukraine is still well behind the majority of Central European states. Though small and medium scale privatisation has been successfully completed, the Government is still struggling to privatise some big strategic companies, and many sectors are over-regulated by the state, unlike in most developed market economies. Especially in such strategically important sectors as machinery, financial and insurance services, the internal market is still quite closed and protectionism still dominates. Some tentative calculations suggest that if the Ukrainian market were to become completely open now, only about 20% of companies would survive, with foreign competitors overcoming the rest. For this reason, state policy is aimed at strengthening 'national producers' so that the market could later be opened to international players without dramatic domestic sector losses. This is quite a lengthy process, however.

By mid-2004, Ukraine managed to attract about 7.3 billion USD FDI, which constitutes approximately 154 USD per capita. This is one of the lowest levels among transition economies – the new EU members from CEE received ten times more investment. Between 1996 and 2002, Ukraine attracted FDI equal to 1.5% of GDP annually, while during the same period, Poland for example attracted 22% of GDP annually (World

Bank (WB)). These low levels of foreign investment are explained not only by the off-putting effects of protracted economic reforms (e.g. tax, land, budget, property, foreign trade, and corporative code), but also by the relative inaction of domestic investors. If domestic investors find the local climate unattractive and over-complicated, foreign investors are likely to find it even harder. According to an analysis by the World Bank, Ukraine has one of the most difficult environments for entrepreneurship in the world: too many procedures are required in order to register and run a business; norms and regulations are over-complicated and change too frequently; the legal situation is unstable and an imperfect judicial system is unable to provide a sufficient framework for settling commercial disputes.

The results of the WB Investment Climate Survey in 2002 show that the biggest problems for businesses in Ukraine are imperfect national policies, unpredictability in interpreting legislation and regulations, corruption, and an underdeveloped financial sector. Inconsistencies in the requirements for domestic and foreign businessmen lead to a multitude of disputes, and the court procedures are so imperfect that settling these disputes turns into a very lengthy and costly endeavour. Taxation is another area that remains quite problematic, and though reforms are in progress, overall, the situation does little to facilitate business. As a result, a considerable share of corporate income is not declared, instead circulating in the shadow economy. Local companies find it much harder than foreign companies to get loans, which are still quite expensive, and relatively uncommon due to a lack of mechanisms for collateral management.

There are differences, however, between the quality of the business environment in different Ukrainian regions, which explains why both domestic and foreign investment is scattered unevenly. There are several methods used for classifying regions according to local conditions. The Regional Investment Rating prepared by the Kyiv-based Institute of Reforms is one of the most comprehensive approaches, since it is based on analysis of five aggregated groups of indices which characterise (1) economic growth, (2) market infrastructure, (3) financial sector, (4) human resources, (5) entrepreneurship and local government. Hence each region gets five 'partial' indices characterising different aspects of the business climate and the general situation. In addition, the Institute of Reforms offers a dynamic index which outlines the quality of changes which occurred over the last year, which is quite important in a period where the national economy is changing rapidly.

The capital city, Kyiv – which is separate from the surrounding Kyiv oblast (this corresponds to the official territorial structure of Ukraine, whereby there are 24 oblasts, 1 Autonomous Republic (Crimea), and 2 cities of state significance (Kyiv and Sevastopol)) – leads, as it has done for the five years of the Rating's history. However, Kyiv is not as overwhelmingly dominant as it was before, and other regions, such as Odessa, Dnipropetrovsk, Kharkiv and Lviv, are gaining considerably from higher investment flows. This can be explained firstly by significant levels of economic growth in these regions and by rising support from local government. The Donetsk oblast, which is still the most powerful region economically, is placed just 7th in terms of investment, and has one of the worst situations regarding human resources (26th in the sub-rating) and in quality of entrepreneurship and local government services (17th). Among the 'losers' in the investment rating are oblasts with weakly developed industrial and service sectors, poor human capital and weak infrastructure, particularly financial infrastructure. They are not able to use their relative advantages (clean natural environment, location, demographic situation) and have failed to attract much domestic or foreign investment.

Judging from how the different Ukrainian regions have reacted to social and economic changes, to movements in the external environment, and to the increasing openness of national markets, it is possible to distinguish three groups of regions that have profited most successfully from their situation and have managed to occupy comparatively advantageous positions in the national and international economy.

The first group comprises the biggest cities in Ukraine – Kyiv, Donetsk, Lviv, Odessa, Kharkiv, and Dnipropetrovsk – which have a modern economic structure, well-developed technical, transport, and social infrastructure, and a network of educational and R&D institutions. Kyiv is a European-class metropolis and serves as a channel of information exchange with other European and world metropolises, while the other cities are of regional significance and have active links with their neighbours (Poland, Russia, other countries in the Black Sea region). These cities have high intellectual potential and a rapidly developing network of financial and business-supporting institutions. Investors both from other Ukrainian regions and from abroad are attracted by their high concentration of economic activity and their developed social infrastructure, the result of sufficient funding through the years of decline. These cities also have a more concentrated population with relatively higher incomes, demands and higher mobility rates, resulting in flourishing consumer markets and service sectors.

The second group is made up of the traditional industrial centres, which provide the greatest share of national GDP, industrial output and export.

These are the Donetsk, Dnipropetrovsk, and Zaporizhzhia oblasts. However, it would be fair to say that their recent economic successes are based mainly on the extensive use of old industrial capacities. The long-term investment deficit hinders the wide-scale modernisation of production and the introduction of modern technologies. Depreciation of capital assets sometimes reaches 75-80%, and without significant injections of capital, in a few years time the majority of big enterprises may have ceased to function. A tendency towards re-industrialisation is prevailing over a more advisable pattern of neo-industrialisation and diversification of industrial output structure. There is also a big gap between the volumes of industrial and consumer outputs, and an under-developed service sector.

Most income in these oblasts is generated by large, formerly state-owned enterprises, which are firmly under the influence of the Government or powerful economic clans, leaving small and medium-sized business far behind. In general, this distorts regional and national competition, and as a consequence decreases the competitiveness of Ukrainian commodities and services. The strength of these regions is in many cases dependent on frequently-used state exemptions, overt or hidden subsidies, and tax holidays for particular branches, enterprises or territories (there are several Special Economic Zones and Territories of Priority Development). This in turn creates rather a negative image of these regions among foreign investors, who prefer to work in a transparent and justly regulated environment, with equal conditions for national and international companies.

The third group of regions consists of the Western border regions of Ukraine – the neighbours of the enlarged EU (Volyn, Lviv, Zakarpatska, Chernivtsy oblasts). During the last 13 years, these regions have greatly intensified their formal and informal economic and social relations with their neighbouring countries in Central Europe. In this way, standards of living have improved (when compared to the national average) and social tensions which resulted from the collapse of the state economy and widespread closures of large enterprises have reduced. Moreover, these oblasts are currently experiencing an economic boom due to the toughening of technical and economic requirements and labour standards in the new EU member states, which has driven up costs. Since 2001, companies have been re-locating from the eastern regions of Poland, Hungary, Slovakia and other countries to Western Ukraine. The *advantages* of this phenomenon are: geographic location, which causes no considerable change to the production/delivery cycle; a well-developed transport infrastructure; a cheap but qualified labour force; and the potential for expansion in the Ukrainian market, which is one of the largest in CEE. Steadily rising personal incomes mean Ukrainians have

increasing purchase power, another reason why Ukraine may be con-
sidered a very dynamic and attractive market. Ukraine may also act as
an entry point towards other markets in the former Soviet Union, in
particular the large Russian market. The *disadvantages* are also quite
serious: the most mobile companies are 'jumping' into Ukraine looking
mainly for a cheaper labour force, but they are not rooting themselves
too deeply into the network of national producers by outsourcing
productive operations. As income levels increase they will leave Ukraine
looking for more profitable sites where they can cut costs, which may
cause knock-on effects in the regions if suitable measures to diversify
risks are not taken in a timely manner.

The spatial characteristics of socio-economic development illustrate the
fact that economic growth is much more dynamic in traditional industrial
regions (in the East) compared with agricultural oblasts and those with
the most dramatic economic decline (in the West and North) (Map 1).

Map 1: GVA per capita in Ukrainian Regions, 2002 (Ukraine=100)

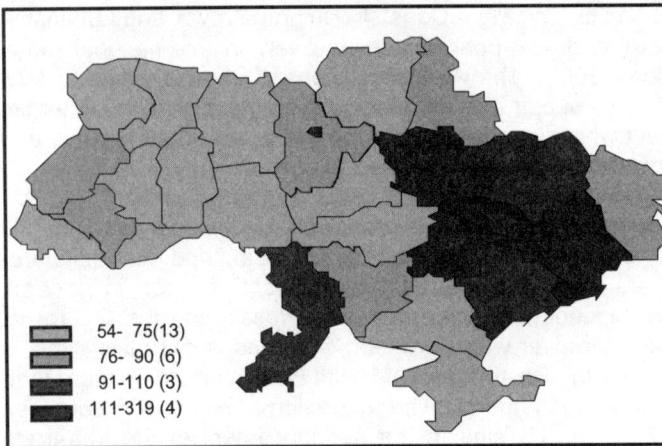

Legend:
- 54- 75(13)
- 76- 90 (6)
- 91-110 (3)
- 111-319 (4)

Source: State Statistics Committee, 2003

At the same time, if we consider the main regional social indices, it
becomes clear that economic success has no real impact on the local
population's social standards and living conditions. Explaining this
phenomenon is quite complicated, but initial analyses have demon-
strated that low productivity rates and the lack of effective and trans-
parent distribution mechanisms have caused a disproportionate spatial
spread-ing of generated income: there is a high concentration of income
among a small number of economic agents, which is not being included
in social expenditure at the national level. Being very resource-intensive,
the Ukrainian economy has not developed mechanisms to redistribute

profits generated from old industries into more modern (more innovative, competitive and profitable) branches. Deep analysis of financial flows is required, as is a special approach to the development of different types of region; this in turn requires the establishment of specific tools and mechanisms to control regional policy at the national level.

In general, Ukraine's spatial socio-economic organisation can be clearly divided into two parts – East and West. Many experts would argue that this approach is too simplistic; nonetheless, it may justifiably be argued that the River Dnieper marks a boundary between two distinct regions as far as many social and economic processes are concerned. Eastern Ukraine is more prosperous in macro-economic terms, securing the major portion of the national income and industrial output. At the same time, it is experiencing social problems that are much more severe than the national average. For example, according to the Regional Human Development Index, which measures social stratification in Ukraine and designates the most poor, socially excluded regions, three of the most powerful oblasts economically – Donetsk, Dnipropetrovsk and Lugansk – occupy 26th, 24th and 27th positions respectively in this national rating (out of 27 regions, 2001). The Western regions of Ukraine, having a less developed industrial sector, are more socially stable and have higher life standards, a fact which is in large part due to the individual mobility and skill flexibility of its inhabitants (Table 2).

The Eastern oblasts have strong, extensively developed ties with the former Soviet republics, in particular with Russia, and are quite dependent on them in their economic development. Though in general, Ukraine is less dependent on the markets of Russia and the CIS for its foreign trade and turnover with European countries is increasing, this is still not the case for the Eastern regions, with Russia providing more than half of both exports and imports[1]. The accession of some CEE countries to the EU in 2004 led Ukraine to the denouncement of the free-trade agreements it had previously had with most of them, which has also had a negative impact on international trade turnover.

---

[1] In a way, the reduction of trade turnover with Russia and other CIS countries is a major reason for the signing of the Single Economic Space (SES) Agreement. It is widely accepted that the standard of Ukrainian commodities are not high enough to allow them to compete on Western European markets now or in the near future. Hence a free-trade agreement with the FSU republics is currently more profitable for the national economy than a similar agreement with the EU. This is a good demonstration of the clash between the geo-political and geo-economic interests of Ukraine.

Table 2: Regional Human Development Index in Ukraine, 1999–2001

Regions/oblasts	Human Development Indices			Rank of the region		
	1999	2000	2001	1999	2000	2001
AR of Crimea	0.521	0.573	0.569	16	2	2
Vinnytsia	0.572	0.561	0.559	3	4	4
Volynska	0.524	0.502	0.507	13	19	17
Dnipropetrovsk	0.501	0.500	0.480	21	20	24
Donetsk	0.449	0.466	0.431	27	26	26
Zhytomyr	0.502	0.500	0.492	20	21	19
Zakarpatska	0.524	0.554	0.547	14	6	7
Zaporizhzhia	0.533	0.514	0.511	11	17	16
Ivano-Frankivsk	0.536	0.527	0.493	10	15	18
Kyiv	0.546	0.530	0.546	8	13	8
Kirovograd	0.492	0.508	0.485	24	18	20
Lugansk	0.452	0.434	0.409	26	27	27
Lviv	0.550	0.536	0.538	7	12	11
Mykolayv	0.481	0.470	0.481	25	25	23
Odesa	0.502	0.518	0.485	19	16	21
Poltava	0.579	0.572	0.564	2	3	3
Rivne	0.541	0.474	0.530	9	24	13
Sumy	0.500	0.491	0.470	22	22	25
Ternopil	0.559	0.541	0.541	5	10	10
Kharkiv	0.514	0.544	0.549	18	9	6
Kherson	0.499	0.484	0.482	23	23	22
Khmelnitsky	0.555	0.547	0.535	6	8	12
Cherkasy	0.570	0.549	0.543	4	7	9
Chernivtsy	0.531	0.538	0.523	12	11	14
Chernigiv	0.519	0.530	0.519	17	14	15
City of Kyiv	0.694	0.705	0.697	1	1	1
City of Sevastopol	0.523	0.557	0.557	15	5	5

Source: "The power of participation". Ukraine Human Development Report 2001, UNDP

Conclusions

At the present time, state practice in Ukraine is not aimed at making radical changing to economic structure. In fact, it merely complicates the traditional economic system by giving the wrong incentives to low-productive and old-fashioned industries with obsolete and environmentally unfriendly technologies. This contrasts with an officially proclaimed policy of moving towards an innovative economy. However, this policy is not yet supported by specific mechanisms and instruments which might help to stimulate the development of innovative, knowledge-intensive industries.

The gap between the potential and the actual state of affairs in the Ukrainian regions is immense. This is due to: the slow progress of legislative and economic reforms; weak links between education, R&D and production; high levels of bureaucracy and rent seeking among government officials; and a public financing deficit, which leads to underfunding of the whole social sector. Only those regions which historically did not have an over-developed social infrastructure or which managed to rationalise it according to real needs are relatively safe from the dangers of considerable social tension and social degradation. Several traditionally well-financed old industrial regions, which for decades benefited from social privileges and their special status in a centrally-planned economy, have a surplus in social infrastructure and no big private sector to which to transfer it. Hence these regions are currently experiencing significant difficulties in trying to sustain this infrastructure, and are slowly losing the assets they had previously accrued in this sector.

For a region of Ukraine to be competitive now, it has to be able to adjust to rapid economic and policy changes, to be able to predict these changes and turn them to its advantage. Regions also benefit if they can influence these changes – both at the local and at the global level. As the global, innovation-driven economy becomes stronger, countries are less and less able to influence and protect the interests of their regions. Multinational companies and supranational organisations have in effect taken part of national sovereignty. For this reason, regions need to become more independent actors in the world arena, and they need to make their voice heard. To do so, they must network and work in association with other regions. Unfortunately, at the current time, Ukrainian regions are still strongly influenced by old habits, and are waiting to be told what to do by the centre, when already they are being expected to act independently. Furthermore, they are still unaware that it will be necessary to co-operate and share both responsibility and profits with other regions. Unless such a philosophy takes root in their identity and in their understanding of the contemporary world, there is little chance that they will benefit from the global economy, but will instead suffer only the negative impacts of further globalisation.

References:
Concept of Demographic Development of Ukraine till 2015 (2004). Ministry of Family, Children and Youth, Kyiv.
Investment Rating of Ukrainian Regions (2004). Institute of Reforms, Kyiv.
Mateju P. (2002) Social Capital: Problems of its conceptualisation and measurement in transforming societies. Paper presented at OECD-ONS Conference on Social Capital Measurement, London.

Monitoring of Socio-economic Development of Ukrainian Regions in 2002 (2003). Ministry of Economy and European Integration of Ukraine, East-West Institute, Kyiv.

OECD (2001) The Well-being of Nations. The role of human and social capital. OECD, Paris.

Mrinska,O. (2002) Specifics of Regional Policy as for old industrial regions in UK (Merseyside) and Ukraine (Lugansk oblast) Contemporary municipal management, №10-12 (8).

Progress in Addressing the Issues of Regional Development and Regional Policy in Ukraine (2001). World Bank Report, Kyiv.

Quarterly Predictions (2004). ICPS, Kyiv.

Romaniuk, S.; Mrinska, O. (2001) Analysis of Regional Discrepancies and Regional Policy in Ukraine. Report prepared for World Bank, Kyiv.

The Power of Participation. Ukraine Human Development Report 2001 (2002). UNDP, Kyiv.

Ukraine in Figures 2003 (2004). State Statistics Committee, Kyiv.

World Development Report 2005 (2004). World Bank, Washington.

Suburbanisation in Sofia: Changing Spatial Structure of a Post-communist City

Yani Valkanov

Introduction

Suburbanisation has been one of the most important processes shaping the spatial structure of cities in the developed, and increasingly in the developing, countries. It has been a subject of considerable debate among academics, planning professionals and the general public in Western Europe and North America. Although attitudes towards sub-urbanisation differ, much is known about its incidence, causes and negative effects on society and nature. Less is known, however, about the similar trend in the post-communist transitional cities of Central and Eastern Europe. After 1989 most countries in the region began massive transformations of their societies towards the Western welfare capitalism. The process of political, economic, social and cultural restructuring has an immense impact on major cities in the region. Although 13 years is a relatively short period of time in the life of cities, some new social and spatial trends are readily observable in Prague, Budapest and other post-communist cities – initial residential and commercial suburbanisation, commercialisation, growing differentiation between different areas (Sýkora, 1999b; Sýkora and Čermák, 1998; Kovács, 1994; Tosics, 2000). Sýkora (2001, 1999a, 1999b) argues that the post-communist development of cities in Central and Eastern Europe should be generalised into a model of transitional post-communist city, which, unlike other models of urban spatial structure, should be dynamic, rather than equilibrium-based. He poses five topics/questions for future research – migration flows into and out of cities (*population growth or decline?*); internal migration patterns (*urbanisation or suburbanisation?, compact city or urban sprawl?*); inner city neighbourhoods (*growth or decline?, gentrification or ghettoisation?*); the future of housing estates (*overall social downgrading or differentiation?, rehabilitation or redevelopment?*); socio-spatial disparity, polarisation and segregation (*increase or decrease?, where are the future ghettos and citadels?*) (Sýkora, 1999a).

This paper investigates the changes in the distribution of population within the territory of the city of Sofia and Sofia Municipality from 1992 to 2001, with the general purpose of drawing a picture of the suburbanisation process and changes in the urban spatial structure in post-communist Sofia. The distribution of population within the metropolitan region is one of the two (the other being the distribution of land use) most important characteristics of urban spatial structure and any significant population redistribution indicates serious spatial restructuring. The main question/hypothesis debated here is that *in the post-communist period after 1989, Sofia (like other cities in Central and Eastern Europe) experienced initial suburbanisation trends and changes in urban spatial structure, caused by the socio-economic transformations and the transition from a 'socialist' to a 'market' city.*

Although the paper directly addresses one of the Sýkora's topics/questions, it throws some insights into the other four. Moreover, it attempts to generalise them into a broader framework. It is argued that the suburbanisation in post-communist transitional cities should be considered in the context of the general transformations of their spatial structures. The paper begins with an analysis of socialist cities' spatial structure. A comparison is made between population density profiles of 'socialist' and 'market' cities, which is used as a basis for generalising the transformation process. Then population data from 1992 and 2001 are used for an analysis of the population redistribution within the territory of Sofia Municipality. Finally, some conclusions are drawn about the nature and causes of suburbanisation in Sofia and other post-communist cities and attempts are made to hypothesise about the future and to formulate some policy guidance.

Socialist City's Spatial Structure

A general model of a socialist city's spatial structure was suggested by French and Hamilton, identifying several concentric zones from the centre to the periphery of a typical socialist city – the historic core; inner commercial, housing and industrial areas from the capitalist period; socialist zone of transition; early socialist housing; integrated socialist residential districts; countryside with satellite towns and villages (Carter, 1995, p.329; Smith, 1994, p.192). Although French and Hamilton's concentric model may resemble Burgess's concentric model, socialist cities had some important features, quite distinctive from their Western counterparts.

Low utilisation and low commercialisation of city centres. Due to the lack of land market and differential land rent, there were no incentives to invest and redevelop city centres and, as a result, little physical and land-use changes were observed there, except for some representative buildings and monuments. Centres preserved, to a considerable extent, their residential functions (Musil, 1993).

Significant proportion of industrial areas in inner cities. Socialist cities preserved their overwhelmingly industrial character, the transition to a service-oriented city progressed slowly (Enyedi, 1997; Pichler-Milanovich, 1994). Industrial land use took up 15 to 30 per cent of the total built-up area of socialist cities, compared to only 5 – 8 per cent on average in West European cities (Bertaud, 2001; p.64). Large part of industrial land was located close to the city centres (Bertaud and Renaud, 1997).

Large high-rise panel housing estates on the periphery. These estates were substantially larger than analogous housing estates in capitalist cities and considerable part of the population lived there. They were relatively heterogeneous in terms of the socio-economic status of residents (Smith, 1994; Musil, 1993).

Sharp contrast between the compact high-density core city and the outer sparsely populated suburban ring. Socialist cities were, in general, more compact and dense as compared with West European and especially with North American cities, with little or no suburbanisation taking place (Tosics, 2000; Pichler-Milanovich, 1994). Small towns and villages in the suburban belt largely preserved their rural character (Enyedi, 1997).

Bertaud (2001, p.67, Fig.4) provided population density profiles of various European cities, measured by concentric circles of 1 kilometre from the centre to the periphery – Figure 1. Most post-communist cities in Central and Eastern Europe have high residential densities in the city centre (where no commercial CBD existed), which fall off in the inner city areas (due to the large proportion of industrial spaces and low-density pre-war housing), then rise up in the ring of socialist housing estates, and drop off rapidly again in the sparsely-populated suburban zone. Of course, there are differences among cities reflecting their different policies, cultures, traditions, pre-socialist patterns, as well as local topographic conditions. Nevertheless, there is a similar '*camel back*' pattern of population density distribution in many cities in Central and Eastern Europe. Two cities that exhibit significant variations from this pattern are Moscow and Budapest. The centre of Moscow, with its high concentration of governmental and cultural institutions, representative buildings, and large squares, has very low population densities. Budapest lacks secondary rise in density, reflecting the Hungarian authorities' more liberal housing policies and less public investments in high rise residential estates (Kessides, 2000, p.11). However, despite these variations, both cities' spatial structures are generally consistent with the '*camel back*' model of population density distribution of socialist cities.

Bertaud and Renaud (1997) attribute the specific features of socialist cities' spatial structure to the absence of land markets, which has impaired the ability to allocate and recycle urban land. In market economies, changing land prices exert powerful pressure to recycle already developed urban land if the type and intensity of the existing land use is less than optimal. Over time this produces a negatively sloped population density function, in general accordance with Alonso's model, as illustrated by density profiles of London and Paris. Density gradient is gradually and smoothly falling from the centre to the periphery, except in the CBD, where the commercial function outbids the residential one. By contrast, in socialist cities, where no land and real estate markets were allowed to exist and all development decisions were taken trough an administrative-command process, once land was allocated, it was almost never recycled. In the absence of price signals, there were no incentives to re-develop already built-up areas. It was administratively easier to meet land demand by developing at the periphery than to redevelop areas with obsolete land uses. A spatial outcome of the failure to recycle urban land, was the existence of industrial belts in the inner areas of most socialist cities. Usually developed before World War II, most of these industrial zones have never been recycled. As cities grew outwards they became under-utilised *'bottlenecks'* with rusting factories and warehouses, old railway infrastructure and enclaves of *'dead land'* within the urban fabric (ibid).

A comparison between population density profiles of 'socialist' and 'market' cities is given in Figure 2. A typical socialist city has a population density curve more or less similar to the thick line. If the same city were in a market economy, its population density curve would probably look more like the thin line. The figure depicts the specific characteristics of socialist cities' spatial structure – lack of commercial CBD; low utilisation of inner city areas; high-density large socialist housing estates on the periphery; and little suburbanisation.

Post-communist Transformations

After 1989 most countries in Central and Eastern Europe began massive transformations of their societies towards democratic political systems and market economies. The main outcomes from the transformation process, which influenced urban development, were re-establishment of land and real estate markets; emergence of a large number of private actors operating in the city; and opening of the urban environment to the international economic forces (Sýkora, 1999b). It is reasonable to expect that the functioning of land and real estate markets would produce changes in the urban spatial structure and population redistribution within the urban territory, which would lead to gradual flattening of the *'camel back'* curve. The arrows in Figure 2 indicate the anticipated trends in population densities in post-communist cities – fall in the CBD and panel housing estates and increase in the inner city and suburban areas.

Although land and real estate markets have been quickly established, they are still underdeveloped in most cities in the region (Kessides, 2000, p.11,12). Due to the fall in real incomes and the lack of well-developed credit system, most households are too financially constrained to actively participate in the market and make the expected adjustments in population densities. Nevertheless, the period after the fall of communism witnessed some visible changes in the spatial structures of cities in Central and Eastern Europe. Sýkora (1999b) summarises the most important trends and processes, readily observable in Prague.

Commercialisation of city centre. Residential function is rapidly declining in the city centre and there is a sharp increase in commercial functions – business offices, retail, hotels, restaurants, and so forth. The most common mechanisms for commercialisation are: change from residential to commercial use within the existing building stock; demolition of existing residential buildings and construction of new commercial building; and intensification through in-fills and additions.

Commercialisation and gentrification in inner city areas. As the supply of sites suitable for commercial development in the city centre rapidly declined, since the mid-1990s large new office and retail projects have decentralised away from the historical core towards inner city locations with good accessibility along major roads and public transport nodes. Older buildings have been redeveloped and transformed into office space and luxury housing for higher income residents, especially foreigners. New residential buildings with condominium apartments are being constructed on vacant plots. However, the process is highly selective, affecting only certain neighbourhoods (especially in the northwestern part of the inner city) with relatively higher quality residential environment and higher socio-economic status.

Suburbanisation in outer zone. Residential suburbanisation takes two forms – individual developments within existing villages, and emergence of new residential districts, spatially attached to existing settlements. However, residential suburbanisation has been slow, limited by the low purchasing power of the population. Nevertheless, the process significantly changed the socio-economic status of the suburban zone, which now has two contrasting population groups – rich and better-educated newcomers, and lower-income, less-educated indigenous inhabitants. Commercial suburbanisation has important consequences on the transformation of the outer area of Prague as well. New shopping centres, hypermarkets, and do-it-yourself stores, as well as warehousing and distribution facilities and increasingly office developments, have mushroomed along major highways and important transport intersections.

In fact, what is going on in Prague is a flattening of the *'camel back'* curve – fall in population densities and commercialisation of the centre; intensification and gentrification of some inner city areas; and suburbanisation of the outer zone. Sýkora does not observe major physical and social changes in the large panel housing estates, however there are some signs of differentiation. Those with relatively higher quality infrastructure, better accessibility by public transport, and more balanced social mix, have maintained their socio-economic status and attracted some investments in new housing construction on vacant plots; retail facilities, etc. Others, with lower quality of living environment and higher concentration of manual workers and less educated residents, have begun to decline.

Similar trends have been observed in other cities in Central and Eastern Europe. Tosics (2001, p.11), for example, documents the dramatic fall (30.1 per cent) in population living in the centre of Budapest (districts I and V) from 1980 to 1998. During the same period the population of the outer districts (IV, XV-XXI) grew by 5.6 per sent, although the total population of the city declined by 9.6 per cent. Before going on to analyse the similar processes in Sofia, brief information about the historical development of the city and its spatial structure will be provided.

Historical Development of Sofia

Situated on the main route from Western Europe to the Middle East, Sofia is one of the oldest cities in Europe. It was founded by the Thracian tribe *Serdes* in the 8th – 7th century BC and later given by the Romans the name *Serdika*. From the 1st to the 8th century, during the Roman and later the Byzantine domination, *Serdika* was a beautiful and prosperous centre of a province with many Christian basilicas, heavily decorated public buildings, and Emperor's residence. In 809 the town was seized by the Bulgarians and, with the name *Sredetz*, soon became one of the main administrative, commercial and cultural centres of the Bulgarian Kingdom. In the late 14th century the town was named Sofia after the church *Sveta Sofia* (St. Sophia). From the 15th to the 18th century Sofia was an important centre in the European territory of the Ottoman Empire. According to Turkish registers of that time, in 1740 Sofia had 8000 houses and 50 000 residents (UNDP, 1997, p.27). In the late 18th - early 19th century the town declined, but Bulgarian Liberation in 1878 started the rapid growth and development of Sofia as the political, economic and cultural centre of the new state.

Table 1:   Population of city of Sofia from 1879 to 1934

Year	1879	1881	1888	1893	1900	1910	1920	1926	1934
Population	11.657	20.856	30.928	46.593	68.789	102.812	154.025	213.002	287.095

Source: NCTDHP (1999).

Table 2:   Population of city of Sofia from 1946 to 2001

Year	1946	1956	1965	1975	1985	1992	2001
Population	366.801	593.113	801.111	967.214	1.120.925	1.114.925	1.094 410

Source: NCTDHP (2000).

When Sofia was declared the capital of Bulgaria in 1879 the town had slightly more than 11 000 residents, 55 years later – in 1934 – the population was approaching 300 000 (Table 1). The years before World War I were a period of planned and organised growth and development. During that period the development of Sofia was confined mainly to the area which is now the centre of the city. In the years between the World Wars the development of Sofia occurred mostly in a chaotic and unplanned manner. Large territories were detached from Bulgaria after World War I and a huge number of refugees flooded the country, many of which settled in the capital. Sofia expanded in all directions, especially along the main radial roads and tramlines, connecting the city with several smaller settlements in the outer zone, which had been developed as suburbs. (NCTDHP, 1999)

The extensive industrialisation and nationalisation of agriculture after the Communist regime took power in 1944 led to massive migration flows from rural areas to large cities, especially to the capital. In the early 1960s the 'mass housing construction' programme was launched. Initially several residential districts with 4-6 storey blocks of flats were built using traditional construction methods. In the late 1960s and especially in the 1970s and 1980s many large high-rise housing estates were built with prefabricated elements (panels) on the periphery of the city. At the same time several large industrial zones were developed among the residential estates, and a giant complex for heavy industries (*Kremikovtzi*) some 10 kilometres northeast of the compact city. In the late 1970s the population of Sofia reached 1 million in the city while another 100 000 people lived in small towns and villages in the outer area within the boundary of Sofia Municipality. In 1985 the city peaked 1 120 000 people and began to decline slightly afterwards – Table 2.

Spatial Structure of Sofia

Sofia is situated in the southern part of a small plain (*Sofiysko Pole*) surrounded by several mountains - *Stara Planina* in the north, and *Lyulin, Vitosha, Plana, Lozen* in the south – Map 1. The southern periphery of the city reaches the foothills of *Vitosha Mountain*, which has a National Park status and has played an important role in the development of the city as a favourite place for sports and entertainment of Sofians. The territory of Sofia Municipality covers an area of 1311 square kilometres in the central *Sofiysko Pole* and parts of the surrounding mountains. It includes the city of Sofia and 37 smaller settlements – 3 towns and 34 villages.

The spatial structure of Sofia is typical of most socialist cities. Four concentric zones can be identified – Map 2.

City centre. This is the area with the highest built-up and population density and includes the main administrative, representative and cultural buildings. As most socialist cities, the city centre of Sofia has preserved, to a considerable extent, its residential function. Since 1989 there has been an increasing tendency for commercialisation of this part of the city.

Inner city. Most parts of the inner city were built up and incorporated into the city in the period between the World Wars. As typical of socialist cities, a large proportion of the built-up area consists of industrial land use, especially in the northern part of the inner city. There is a substantial disparity in the quality of living environment between the northern and southern areas, which dates back to the period between the Wars and was not eliminated during the socialist period. Most of the northern districts in the inner city have derelict infrastructure and housing stock and exhibit bad ecological conditions, owing to the proximity of many industrial zones and the lack of major green areas and parks. There was mass housing construction in some of the inner city neighbourhoods, however most of it was implemented in the early 1960s with traditional construction methods.

Socialist panel housing estates. The overwhelming part of Sofia's panel housing stock is concentrated in four clusters of high-rise housing estates on the periphery of the compact city. Some of the housing estates were developed on the territories of existing settlements, which were absorbed into the urban fabric with the growth of the city and transformed into standard residential estates with 30 000 – 60 000 inhabitants. Others, like the largest and having become emblematic ones – *Lyulin* (115 000 inhabitants) and *Mladost* (100 000 inhabitants), were built on previously completely undeveloped land. The planning concept of the socialist residential estates was based on a spatial hierarchy of *housing groups, micro-rayons, rayons,* and *districts,* based on the catchment areas of the respective services – the kindergarten, the primary school, the polyclinics, and the hospital. The purpose of this spatial hierarchy was to maintain effective public service provision and high-quality living environment in the residential estates. Unfortunately, this concept was only partially implemented. In some of the housing estates, especially those built in the 1980s, lack of funds prevented the completion of many elements of public service provision, inner transport infrastructure, garages, public spaces, playgrounds and gardens. The lack of essential services and employment opportunities led to the deterioration of living environment and the transformation of some estates into *'bedroom towns'.*

Suburban ring. Some of the suburbs, situated in close proximity to the compact city immediately beyond the housing estates, have a status of administrative parts of the City of Sofia. Others are independent settlements within the Sofia Municipality. Most of them have preserved their traditional rural character with low-density single family detached or semidetached housing, but there are pockets of condominiums and blocks of flats. As in the compact city, there is a noticeable difference between the southern and the northern part of the suburban ring. The southern territories, situated at the slopes of *Vitosha*, are significantly more attractive. In recent years, some of the settlements and neighbourhoods in this zone have become favourite places for the new rich. The northern parts of the suburban ring are considerably less attractive, because of their nearness to the more unappealing northern parts of the city and the huge industrial complex of *Kremikovtzi*, stretching over a territory of about 1120 hectares.

Analysis and Interpretation of Population Data
For the analysis of the changes in the distribution of population, the territory of Sofia Municipality is divided into 38 territorial units – the city centre (A1), 7 in the inner city (B1- B7), 12 in the zone of panel housing estates (C1 - C12), and 18 in the suburban ring (D1 - D18) – Map 3. Each unit represents a relatively homogeneous part of the city (in terms of population and built-up densities, type of construction, quality of built environment), easily distinguishable within the urban fabric. Using MapInfo GIS software, the population of each unit in 1992 and 2001 has been calculated from census tracts data – Table 3.

The population of the *city centre* (A1) has decreased by more than 50 000 people, or nearly 30 per cent. This is owing to the processes of commercialisation taking place after 1989. Commercial functions were underdeveloped (both in quantitative and qualitative terms) in the city centre during the socialist period. The introduction of market economy created a strong need for new office space. In the early 1990s the demand was satisfied mainly by transformation of residential properties into offices through minor reconstruction. However, such premises usually lack the necessary facilities and infrastructure for office use. By the late 1990s the construction of new offices in the city centre through demolition of old buildings began.

The population of the *inner city* as a whole has considerably increased – by 10.9 per cent. However, this growth is unevenly distributed over the inner city territory. The population growth of the southern areas (B3 and B4) exceeds 30 per cent, while the population of the western and northern parts of inner city (B5 and B6) has slightly declined. This fact is attributable to the difference in the quality of living environment between the northern and southern parts of the city, discussed earlier. After 1989 this disparity brought about noticeable disproportion in the operation of the emerging real estate market. Because of their pleasant environment and high status, some southern districts (*Lozenetz* – B3; *Ivan Vazov, Beli Brezi* – B4; *Yavorov, Geo Milev* – B2;) have become one of the most attractive in the real estate market and most of the new housing construction is being concentrated there. By contrast, in the northern inner city areas (*Orlandovtzi, Malashevtzi* – B6) there is virtually no new housing construction and housing prices are among the lowest in the city. Unit B7, although situated in a relatively unattractive part of the city (northeast of the centre in the proximity of industrial facilities and railway infrastructure), has experienced considerable population growth – 12.4 per cent. Probably, part of the explanation has something to do with the fact that there is a high concentration of Roma population with traditionally high birth rates (*Hristo Botev, Suhata Reka*). Moreover, some large public investments made in the mid-1990s (reconstruction of the railway station and construction of two transport links with the city centre) considerably enhanced the attractiveness of the area. The availability of vacant land with relatively low prices gave rise to some new housing construction. The population decline in B2, located southeast of the city centre (5.8 per cent) is due to the commercialisation of this part of the city, which has become a secondary business node.

The large *panel housing estates* as a whole exhibit slightly larger population decline (1.6 per cent), than the total population decline (1.3 per cent). In 9 from the total 12 territorial units the population decline varies from 0.1 to 6.9 per cent. Out-migration from the panel housing is, to a certain extent, offset by in-migration in newly built condominiums and individual detached or semidetached houses on vacant plots, among panel blocks. Nevertheless, the intensity of the spatial restructuring process is modest, when compared with inner city areas. There is one notable exception, however. Unit C6, which includes the housing estates *Ovcha Kupel 1* and *Ovcha Kupel 2* in the southwestern part of the city, has experienced population growth of 17.7 per cent. The reason for this serious growth is probably attributable to the fact that these housing estates are situated in the immediate proximity to one of the most attractive suburban areas at the foot of the mountain – *Gorna Banya*. The existence of many vacant plots and the lower land prices (as compared with those in the near suburbs and inner city areas) are conducive to new construction of condominiums and individual detached houses. In all other panel housing estates, including the largest ones – *Lyulin (C8), Mladost (C2), Nadejda (C10)* and *Drujba (C1)*, no intensive spatial processes are observed. As yet, there is no serious social restructuring either. Most of the wealthier population has moved out to the high-status inner city and suburban areas. However, the huge part of the population of the housing estates consists of *'socialist middle class'*, which is too financially weak to take an active part in the real estate market. Most of the transactions involve minor adjustments in social status and/or life cycle – substitution of a larger flat for a smaller one (or vice versa), moving into another housing estate, and so forth.

Much more intensive socio-spatial processes are taking place in the *suburban zone*, which exhibits 12.3 per cent population growth as a whole. All but three territorial units have experienced population increase. The three exceptions in the eastern and northeastern parts of the municipality, which slightly decline, should be explained with their proximity to the airport (D5 and D17) and to the huge heavy-industrial complex of *Kremikovtzi* – a major contaminator in the region (D18). The population growth in the other territorial units in the northern part of the suburban ring varies from 0.9 to 4.8 per cent and increases from east to west with the distance from *Kremikovtzi*. The suburbanisation process in the southern parts of the outer ring is significantly more pronounced both in quantitative terms and in terms of qualitative changes in the socio-spatial structure. Most of the territorial units in that area exhibit population growth of more than 20 per cent, D11 (*Gorna Banya*) recording the highest population growth in the municipality – 36.9 per cent. The traditional rural character of many of the settlements is gradually changing. Large 'castles' of the new rich, with tennis courts and swimming pools, spring up among the old village houses. The process of socio-spatial transformation is most pronounced in D9, which has become emblematic of the new suburban landscape in post-communist Sofia. The high-status neighbourhoods of *Knyajevo*, *Boyana*, *Kinotzentara*, *Dragalevtzi* and *Simeonovo*, as well as several villa zones among them, have practically merged, forming a suburban agglomeration belt at the foot of *Vitosha Mountain*.

Suburbanisation in Sofia and Other Transitional Post-Communist Cities

The spatial restructuring processes, analysed above, correspond with similar trends observed in Prague (Sýkora, 1999b) and other post-communist cities. The transformation process towards market economy results in gradual flattening of the '*camel back*' curve and changes in the urban spatial structure towards that of the 'market city'. The suburbanisation process in Sofia, and in other post-communist transitional cities in Central and Eastern Europe, should be considered in the context of these general transformations. From this point of view, the suburbanisation process in the post-communist cities exhibits certain different characteristics than the similar process in the cities of Western Europe and North America.

First, it is to a large extent a consequence of the transformation process from a 'socialist' to a 'market city'. Socialist cities' distorted spatial structure is inefficient from the perspective of an evolving market economy. The lack of adequate commercial space in the city centre, low utilisation of inner city areas, and the excessive domination of the central city over the metropolitan region are sources of many local and regional imbalances and inefficiencies. Thus, the current changes in Sofia (and in other transitional post-communist cities) could be looked upon as a process of balancing the urban spatial structure and making it more suitable for the requirements of the modern market economy. From this perspective, some suburbanisation might, to a certain extent, produce more efficient balance between the city and its hinterland. Some settlements in the outer zone of Sofia, for example, have attracted better-educated population with higher incomes, thus enhancing their economic viability. The problem is, however, that such settlements are situated almost exclusively in the southern part of the suburban zone, which is a base for another spatial imbalance.

Second, suburbanisation in Sofia (and in most other post-communist cities) is a far less pronounced and universal phenomenon than in the Western cities. In spite of the observed significant transformation trends, the process of spatial restructuring is relatively slow. In fact, the spatial macro-structure of Sofia has not substantially and dramatically changed since 1992. The suburban zone's relative share of the total population of the Municipality has increased by less than 2 per cent – from 14.0 to 15.9 per cent. The share of the large panel housing estates has decreased by only 0.3 per cent, and more than a half of the total municipality population still lives there. Even the city centre, where the physical and functional changes during the post-communist period have been most visible, has decreased its share of the total population by slightly more than 4 per cent.

Third, often the primary motive for moving to suburbs is escaping from the panel apartments, not from the city. After many years of 'collective' living in high-rise panel blocks, now there is an increased demand for more spacious living in individual houses and condominiums. Sometimes this demand could only be satisfied in the suburbs rather than in the city, where it would be prohibitively expensive. Tosics (2000, p.19) argues that in many cases the motives for suburbanisation in Budapest are not the 'push' of the negative conditions in the core city, nor the 'pull' of the positive features of the suburbs, but certain expectations for the quality and size of the dwellings.

Future Directions and Policy Implications

The fact that suburbanisation in Sofia is a relatively limited phenomenon does not mean that it does not have negative effects, nor that it will not intensify in the future. Commercial decentralisation (especially retail) is increasingly promoting car-oriented lifestyles. With the growth in real income this process will tend to gain momentum as well as the negative effects associated with it. Some of these effects are observable in Sofia today. The intensive development on the south periphery of the city has incurred the criticism of many activists and environmentalists for spoiling large amounts of green areas and open spaces with great importance for the city as well as for the natural habitat. So far, suburbanisation in Sofia has no serious negative social consequences. The escape of most affluent people into the suburbs does not pose serious problems as long as the main part of the population lives in the city. However, this may change in the future.

There are several possible factors that might contribute to the future intensification of the suburbanisation trends. With the advancement of the transformation process towards a 'market city', the suburbanisation trends will be increasingly driven by the factors and causes determining suburbanisation in Western cities. With the growth in real income of the middle class, increasingly more people would be willing and able to leave the panel housing estates, in quest of more attractive living environment in the suburbs. This could lead to various social problems and imbalances – socio-spatial polarisation, isolation of disadvantaged groups, downgrading and physical degradation of the panel housing estates and some inner city areas.

The decay of the panel housing estates is the other factor that could accelerate suburbanisation. A significant part of the panel housing, built in the late 1960s and 1970s, is at the end of its lifespan and the first signs of serious structural defects are already observable. The panel housing accounts for 46.4 per cent of the total housing stock in Sofia and considerable part of it will fall into disuse in 20 – 30 years' time (NC TDHP, 2000, p.34). In the lack of reconstruction and renewal, this would result in new housing construction on the urban fringe and in the suburbs.

The third factor has to do with commercial decentralisation. Experience indicates that greenfield developments are preferred by most investors. The existence of large industrial areas in key locations in the inner city is both a liability and an opportunity for the city. It is a liability because the redevelopment of a large industrial area is costly and requires public investments. However, it is also an opportunity because, after conversion, it allows for a response to the future demand for office and retail space in the inner city, and reversal (or at least a slowdown) of the process of commercial decentralisation.

Currently, the city of Sofia is in a process of preparation of its new Master Plan – the first one after the fall of communism – that will shape the future of the city into the 21st century. Suburbanisation and commercial decentralisation are some of the key new processes that have been taken into account, and in fact stimulated in the plan. The allocation of land for future residential developments in the suburban zone and for commercial developments on the urban fringe is expected to enhance the economic viability and competitiveness of the city, by increasing residential choice and making the city more attractive for investments. However, unless significant emphasis is placed on the reconstruction of panel housing estates and the redevelopment of the inner city industrial areas, this could result in rapid increase of suburbanisation trends in the future, and an array of social and environmental costs on the society.

Conclusions

The spatial structure of cities is dynamic and constantly, though relatively slowly, changing over time with developments in society at large. The spatial structure of the cities in Central and Eastern Europe has been deeply influenced by almost half-a-century totalitarian government and command economy, which has resulted in a specific *'camel back'* shape of their population density profiles. The transformation process after 1989 has resulted in several new trends observable in most cities in the region – commercialisation of city centres, gentrification in inner cities, and suburbanisation in outer zones. All these trends indicate serious processes of population redistribution within the urban territory and a general direction towards flattening of the *'camel back'* curve. However, the intensity of these trends considerably varies – the transition towards 'market' city has produced sharp differentiation of urban areas.

Suburbanisation in post-communist cities has some different characteristics and underlying causes from the corresponding process in Western European and North American cities. It is less pronounced and still does not generate serious social problems. In fact, it brings about some economic revitalisation of the outer urban regions, which have long been over-dominated by central cities. The problem with suburbanisation in most cities in Central and Eastern Europe is not the suburbanisation *per se*, but its uneven spatial incidence over the territory of the urban region, which is a source of other spatial imbalances. However, as the transition towards a 'market' city progresses, the suburbanisation trends, and their negative effects on society and nature, are likely to considerably intensify, unless massive public investments are made in the panel housing estates and inner city industrial areas.

Appendix

Figure 1: Population density profiles of selected European cities

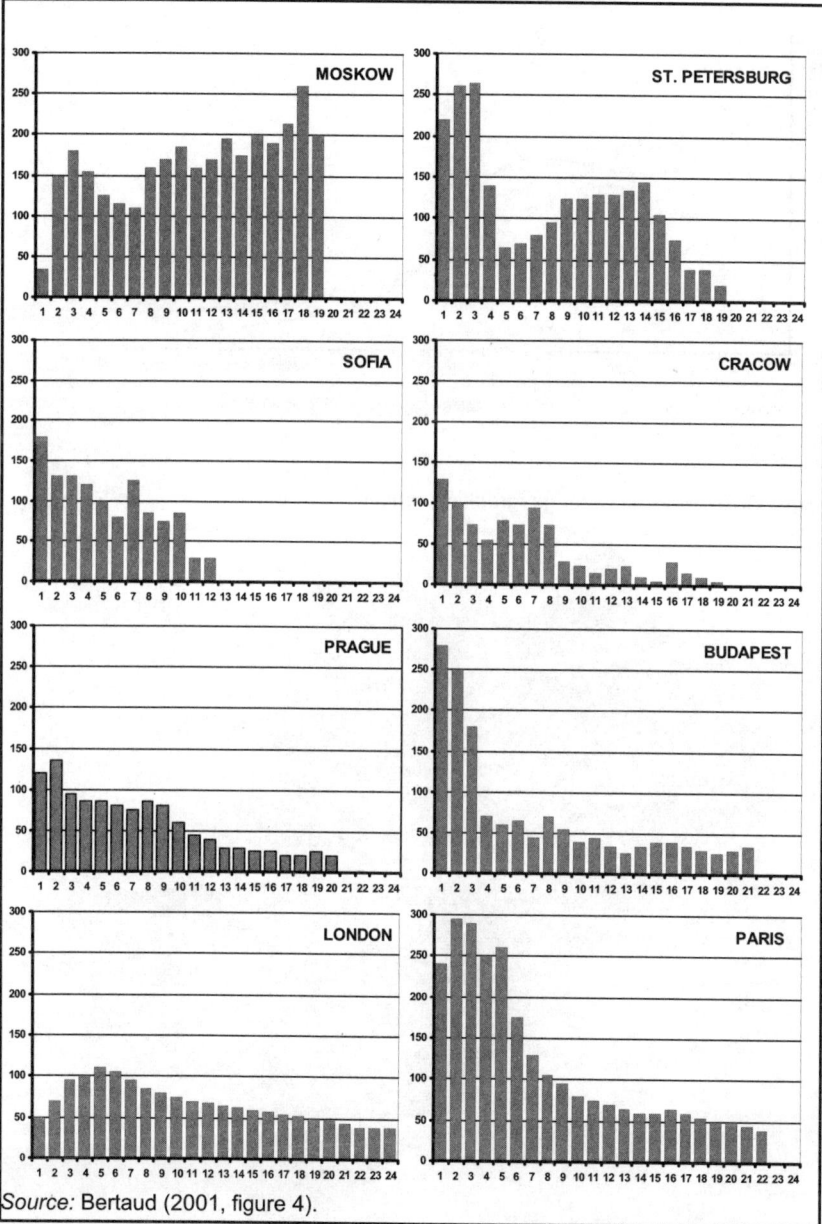

Source: Bertaud (2001, figure 4).

Figure 2: Population density profiles of a 'socialist' and a 'market' city

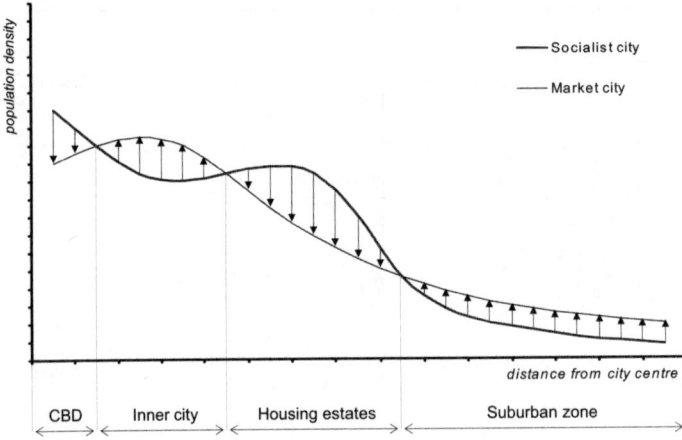

Map1: Sofia within its wider geographical region

Map 2: Sofia Municipality, macro-spatial structure

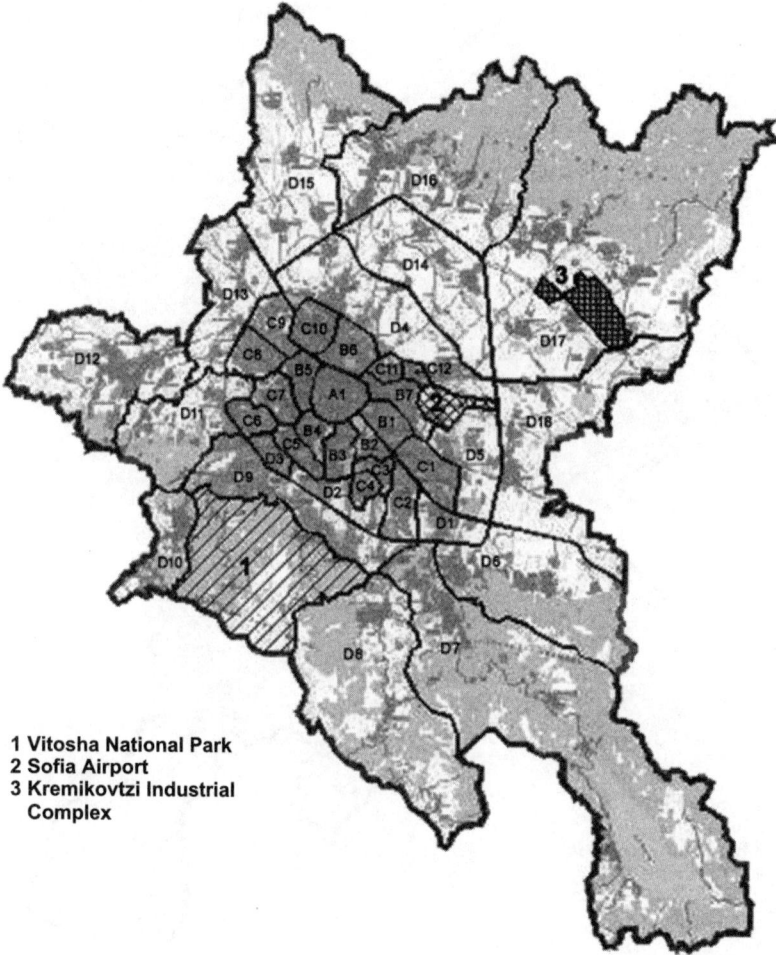

1 Vitosha National Park
2 Sofia Airport
3 Kremikovtzi Industrial
  Complex

Map 3: Sofia Municipality, territorial units for analysis of population changes

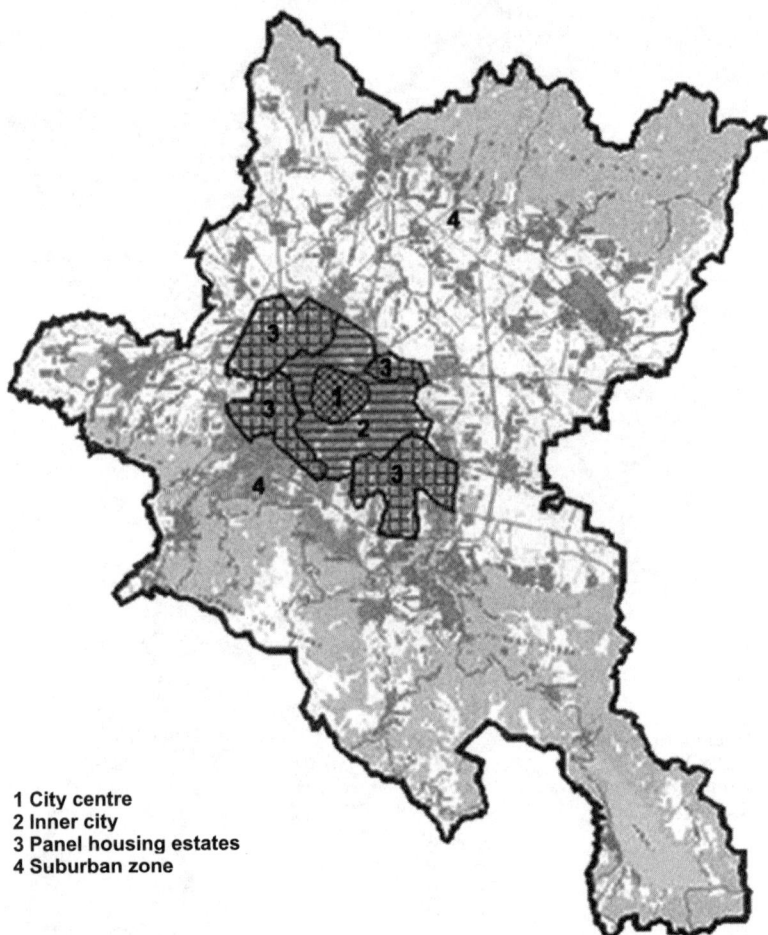

1 City centre
2 Inner city
3 Panel housing estates
4 Suburban zone

Table 3: Population of Sofia Municipality in 1992 and 2001, absolute change and percentage change, relative share of total population

Territorial Units	Population 1992	Population 2001	Absolut change	% change	Relative share 1992	Relative share 2001
A1	177 215	125 717	-51 498	-29.1%		
Total City centre	*177 215*	*125 717*	*-51 498*	*-29.1%*	*14.9%*	*10.7%*
B1	63 378	67 260	+3 882	+6.1%		
B2	24 019	22 636	-1 383	-5.8%		
B3	28 093	37 277	+9 184	+32.7		
B4	41 468	53 897	+12 429	+30.0		
B5	46 118	45 834	-284	-0.6%		
B6	15 012	14 779	-233	-1.6%		
B7	13 523	15 205	+1 682	+12.4		
Total Inner city	*231 611*	*256 888*	*+25 277*	*+10.9*	*19.5%*	*21.9%*
C1	67 481	66 410	-1 071	-1.6%		
C2	93 164	86 721	-6 443	-6.9%		
C3	29 936	29 268	-668	-2.2%		
C4	32685	33056	+371	+1.1%		
C5	36312	37426	+1 114	+3.1%		
C6	24 938	29 355	+4 417	+17.7		
C7	52 639	50 274	-2 365	-4.5%		
C8	107 426	104 775	-2 651	-2.5%		
C9	29 860	28 926	-934	-3.1%		
C10	78 945	77 846	-1 099	-1.4%		
C11	43 409	43 344	-65	-0.1%		
C12	18 197	17 736	-461	-2.5%		
Total Housing Estates	*614 992*	*605 137*	*-9 855*	*-1.6%*	*51.7%*	*51.5%*
D1	5 087	6 222	+1 135	+22.3		
D2	9 165	12 059	+2 894	+31.6		
D3	17 478	21 821	+4 343	+24.8		
D4	13 797	14 192	+395	+2.9%		
D5	4 906	4 883	-23	-0.5%		
D6	7 451	8 057	+606	+8.1%		
D7	4 358	4 848	+490	+11.2		
D8	5 280	5 627	+347	+6.6%		
D9	19 462	24 705	+5 243	+26.9		
D10	4 344	4 848	+504	+11.6		
D11	6 856	9 387	+2 531	+36.9		
D12	8 560	9 900	+1 340	+15.7		
D13	5 892	6 546	+654	+11.1		
D14	6 626	6 851	+225	+3.4%		
D15	6 085	6 377	+292	+4.8%		
D16	15 184	15 327	+143	+0.9%		
D17	7 248	7 203	-45	-0.6%		
D18	18 529	17 836	-693	-3.7%		
Total Suburban	*166 308*	*186 689*	*+20 381*	*+12.3*	*14.0%*	*15.9%*
Total Municipality	1 190	1 174	-15 695	-1.3%	100.0	100.0

193

References

Bertaud, A.; Renaud, B. (1997) "Socialist Cities without Land Markets", Journal of Urban Economics, Vol. 41, No. 1, 137-151.

Bertaud, A. (2001) "Sofia's Development and Spatial Structure", Annex 3 in Sofia City Development Strategy: Assessment Report; The World Bank.

Carter, H. (1995) The Study of Urban Geography, 4-th Edition; London: Arnold.

Enyedi, G. (1997) Integration of the urban system in East Central Europe; Bonn: Bundesforschunganstalt für Landeskunde und Raumordnung.

Kessides, C. (2000) Strategising for the Future in Four ECA Cities: Budapest, St.Petersburg, Sofia and Split; The World Bank.

Kovács, Z. (1994) "A City at the Crossroads: Social and Economic Transformation in Budapest", Urban Studies, Vol. 31, No. 7, 1081-1096.

Musil, J. (1993) "Changing Urban Systems in Post-communist Societies in Central Europe: Analysis and Prediction", Urban Studies, Vol. 30, No. 6, pp. 899-905.

NCTDHP (2000) Regionalen plan za razvitie na oblast Sofia; Sofia: Sofproject Master Plan.

NCTDHP (1999) Administrativno-teritorialno ustroistvo na Stolichnata obshtina i organizatsia na upravlenieto i; Sofia: Sofproject Master Plan.

Pichler-Milanovich, N. (1994) "The Role of Housing Policy in the Transformation Process of Central-East European Cities", Urban Studies, Vol. 31, No. 7, 1097-1115.

Sýkora, L. (2001) "Post-communist City", in XII Konwersatorium Wiedzy o Mieście. Miasto postsocjalistyczne – organizacja rzestrzenl miejskiej i jej przomiany, 41-45; Łódź: University of Łódz and Łódz Science Society.

Sýkora, L. (1999a) The Geography of Post-communist Cities: Research Agenda for 2000+; Conference paper presented in 2nd Slovak-Czech-Polish Geographical Seminar, 1 - 4 September 1999, Bratislava.

Sýkora, L. (1999b) "Changes in the Internal Spatial Structure of Post-communist Prague", GeoJournal, 49 (1), 79-89.

Sýkora, L. and Čermák, Z. (1998) "City Growth and Migration Patterns in the Context of 'Communist' and 'Transitory' Periods in Prague's Urban Development", Espace, Populations, Sociétés, 1998 (3), 405-416.

Smith, D. (1994) Geography and Social Justice; Oxford: Blackwell.

Tosics, I. (2000) Market Forces and Planning Tools Influencing Urban Migration: Residential Mobility in Central and East European Metropoles at the Beginning of the New Millennium; Paper presented in conference "Housing in the 21st Century: Fragmentation and Reorientation", 26 – 30 June 2000, Galve, Sweden.

UNDP (1997) Doklad za Razvitieto na Choveka 1997: Grad Sofia; Sofia: UNDP.

Suburbanization and its consequences in the Budapest Metropolitan Area

Gábor Soós and Györgyi Ignits

Introduction

There is only one metropolitan area in Hungary which compares to the metropolitan areas in Europe as a whole. Budapest, and the suburbs having close ties with the capital, have underwent a deep transformation since the collapse of Communism. Up until the eighties, people living in the suburban area longed to move into the city. Living conditions and, consequently, the prestige of the suburbs were comparatively poor. In the 1990s, Budapest lost 15 percent of its population, while its suburban area grew by 20 percent. Many of the emigrants out of Budapest moved to the new suburban areas, looking for a 'greener' environment. At the same time, the suburbs which had been totally neglected by Communist central planning, quickly improved their infrastructure attracting wealthier people who increasingly sought new lifestyles. As a result, the suburban areas expanded and the settlements developed rapidly. In 1990, the Local Government Act devolved numerous competences to the municipalities as well as providing them with a constitutionally guaranteed autonomy status. At the same time, this act did not establish any institution to govern the metropolitan area and the issue became a bone of contention between the district governments and the city government. In general, the extensive local autonomy of the former came into conflict with the city government's aspirations to coordinate development.

These demographic and administrative changes provide the starting point for this paper. We aim to set out the current challenges faced by the Budapest metropolitan area. The first section describes how the area evolved both before and during the Communist system. The second part presents the main socio-economic characteristics of the area while in the third part, we discuss the main problems of governing an area with strong internal links but lacking any overarching administrative units. The rest of the paper focuses on the micro level dimension. The fourth section compares political patterns within Budapest and the suburban areas, followed by an analysis of some of the main conflicts caused by the rapid suburbanization process of the 1990s. This part of the papers is based on original qualitative research carried out by the authors. In the final section we make some conclusions. As this paper is the first product of a research in progress, these conclusions are only tentative.

1. The Budapest Metropolitan Area Before and Under Communism

Budapest was established in 1872 by the unification of three towns: Pest, Buda, and Óbuda ('Old Buda'). This administrative act resolved most coordination problems until the end of the nineteenth century. By the beginning of the twentieth century, urban development had created a circle of settlements that were closely connected to Budapest. In the first half of the twentieth century, the administrative independence of the suburbs as well as the nature of the conservative-authoritarian regime, which tended to regard Budapest as a potential seat of revolutionary activity, made large-scale administrative reform impossible.

Reforms implemented by the Communist power in 1950 led to the establishment of 'Great Budapest'. These reforms lacked the sophistication of earlier scientific plans, primarily because its main considerations were political. The 23 settlements annexed to Budapest were selected so that the 'correct' mixture of workers, peasants (potential workers) and intellectuals was reached. No feasibility investigation preceded the reforms.

No actual planning for the integration of these newly annexed territories was begun until 1960. The suburbanization process, which occurred within the city borders in the 1950s, was neither spontaneous nor planned. Individual decisions often determined the development of the city. As a corollary of forced industrialization, these tended to occur very quickly. The population of Budapest steadily grew until the 1980s, although between 1956 and 1957 92,000 inhabitants not only left the city, but also the country as a consequence of the revolution that was crushed by Soviet tanks and Hungarian Communists.

With regards to the period before 1989/90, we can confidently state that both qualitatively and functionally, suburban development was substantially different after the change of the regime. During the years of state socialism, the agglomeration processes were determined by the growing needs for labor in Budapest. The capital was the focus of the state-socialist development of industry[1] which generated an enormous demand for labor which was not satisfied by the entry of women into the labor market nor by the migration of workers into the capital. This influx was a major contribution to population growth in the outlying areas and was accompanied by a rapid rise in the volume of suburb-to-city commuting.

Additional reasons for settling outside the city center city included the administrative difficulties involved in settling within the city boundaries and, secondly, an under-financing of urban infrastructure which arose out of the preoccupation with industrial development. This, in turn, led to

---

[1] In the 1950s, 60% of the industrial output in Hungary was concentrated in Budapest. After the 1950s, this ratio began to decrease.

long-term housing shortages in Budapest[2]. As infrastructural development and housing construction could not keep pace with immigration, after 1962, the population inflow was administratively regulated. As a result, a new wave of population growth or, alternatively, population congestion began in the 1960s in the metropolitan area beyond the city. The peak of population growth in the Budapest Metropolitan Area was recorded in the 1960s.

This situation was exacerbated by still current land regulations that protect all agricultural areas. Home construction can only take place in the centers of communities around Budapest. Thus, the labor force catchment area extends along major highway and railway lines as far as 60 to 70 kms from Budapest and, in some cases, even beyond that.

The growth in the suburban population came about through the migration of a population from provincial cities, towns and villages to Budapest[3]. After the 1960s, the expansion of the Budapest labor market began to slow down, as did the growth of the metropolitan area. During the 1970s and 1980s, only those areas where the state carried out home construction projects associated with industrial development (as in Százhalombatta, Szigetszentmiklós, Dunakeszi and Gödöllő) or which possessed scenic beauty and favorable location (Szentendre, Solymár and Pomáz) witnessed any significant population growth.

One of the main indicators of the expansion of the metropolitan area was the growing number of commuters, which resulted in the creation of a relatively urban employment structure in these communities. While at the nationwide level, 20% of active earners commuted to work in 1970 and 25% in 1980, in the Budapest Metropolitan Area, there were some communities (e.g. Gyál, Üröm, Göd, Isaszeg, Halásztelek, Budakeszi) that in 1970 had 80% of workers commuting to work from their place of residence. During this time, a total of 200,000 commuters were recorded in the Budapest Metropolitan Area (Beluszky 1999). At the time of the 1990

---

[2] As a result of this delayed urban development (to use the term employed by Szelényi & Manchin 1972) the number of industrial city workers grew faster than the number of city dwellers. This contributed greatly to a process which saw nearby villages and towns swallowed up by the metropolitan area. As a result, while the level of industrialization was relatively high, large portions of the country's population resided in rural-type settlements and carried on a dual existence. At the time of the change of political regime, 40% of the country's population still resided in villages. Participation in the "second economy" (rural work as a second job) made it possible for village dwellers to accumulate goods and invest in large-scale home construction in villages. At the same time, the infrastructure continued to be underdeveloped, creating a handicap for the local governments of the post-regime-change metropolitan area of Budapest.

[3] As we will mention later, the history of suburbanization of Budapest was a gradual process which at this stage took place largely within city boundaries and only extended beyond them later, in the 1980s and mainly in the 1990s.

census, 61% of active participants in the labor market commuted from suburban communities to the city.

At the same time, infrastructural developments in the outlying areas lagged behind. In this period not only were such developments under-financed, they were also tied to specific industrial investments. The ban on industrial development[4] in large parts of the metropolitan area contributed to the emergence of unfavorable living conditions, since, as we have mentioned, state-financed home construction projects only took place in a very few locations. The Municipal Development Concept of 1971 offered no special provisions for the problems in the Budapest Metropolitan Area. As a result of the great influx of people and attendant increase in demand for infrastructural development, these municipalities were disadvantaged in comparison with other villages.

In summary, with a few fortunate exceptions, the suburban communities in the Budapest Metropolitan Area were dormitory communities in this period. They were residential areas serving the labor market needs of the capital and, as such, they lacked many of the features of suburban life, such as developed infrastructure, suburban landscape, and an urban lifestyle. Quite the contrary, these communities suffered from congestion and under-urbanization.

2. The Transformation in the 1990s
Demographic Changes

After the 1980s, the lopsided functional relationship between the suburban communities and the city began to change, gradually becoming more balanced. During this period, the demand for labor in the capital started to decrease and this continued after 1989. The population total in the Budapest Metropolitan Area showed no significant increase throughout the 1980s and only started to rise in the 1990s. However, the recent population growth is increasingly due to suburbanization. This decade witnessed the transformation of the urban growth pattern into one that resembled most post-industrial societies. The true suburbs of the state socialist era were formed within the city boundaries (Szelényi & Ladányi 1997). In other words, suburbanization in the 1960s and 1970s saw the creation of high-prestige, socially homogeneous communities within Budapest, specifically in some districts of Buda close to the city center. A little later, suburbanization slowly spread to the outlying districts, away from the city center, until it reached low-density housing areas (family homes) on the outskirts. At that point, it moved beyond the city boundaries. Budapest suburbanization was a gradual process and only in its last

---

[4] In 1959, 64 communities in the Budapest Metropolitan Area were included in the ban of industrial development, to protect the labor market of the capital.

phase was there a migration of the middle class away from the city center.

Compared to Western European countries, the suburbanization process in Hungary can generally be described as rather belated and one in which the villages played a great part, thereby narrowing the circle of potential settlers. Generally speaking, economic and residential suburbanization in the 1990s took place at the same time. It was motivated by the mass privatizations of apartment buildings, the winding down of state-financed home construction projects, the appearance of an affluent entrepreneurial class and the availability of cheaper real estate and utility prices in the suburbs. The process was also strongly encouraged by a booming real estate market and local government policy incentives for people moving out into the suburbs. The process was further helped by the high ratio of weekend cottages, one part of which at least lent them readily to suburbanization.

It is, however, important to distinguish between two types of motivations for moving into the suburbs: the middle class was inspired by the suburban landscape and environment while pensioners and low-income families moved there for the area's significantly lower costs of living. The result was that the Budapest Metropolitan Area experienced a spatial segregation of different social classes. In conjunction with the business boom, suburban differences became spectacular. In the mid-1990s, Iván Szelényi and János Ladányi predicted that a significant proportion of the low-income families moving from the capital would be forced to settle in communities farther away from the city. According to the authors, in these areas they will form a new "village underclass" (Szelényi & Ladányi 1997). At the same time, deteriorating inner districts of Budapest will creating a "ghettoization" phenomena whereby a higher concentration of underprivileged, mostly Roma people, will fill the space vacated by the middle class. The authors predicted that this inner district misery will spread. As it turned out, in some case, the development seems to have been effectively countered, for example, by the rehabilitation projects in the 9th district.

If we look at the figures behind these changes, it appears that in the 1980s the population of Budapest was more or less stagnating (the migration balance still being positive) and, after 1993, it began to decline. In the first three years of the 1990s, the migration balance was still positive, but in the following years more people left Budapest than moved into it. The volume of people moving out of Budapest continuously rose. The natural decline of the population accelerated, due to the decreasing number of births and the steady but still high number of deaths. In the last 7 to 8 years, the population decline in Budapest has been significant with an annual rate of decrease of 1%. In 2000, 10 out of every 1,000 Budapest residents moved into the suburbs in Pest county. The volume of steady migration into this area underwent a dramatic increase after 1992. The migration balance of Budapest versus Pest County has been negative since 1988, but after 1994, it became negative in respect of all other parts of the country as well. Budapest residents move most intensely to the suburbs bordering on or near the city boundaries.

In the Metropolitan Area in 1990, despite the natural decline, there was a rising trend in the population. Between 1990 and 2000, the population of the suburbs in the Metropolitan Area grew by over 100,000, a 19.13% increase. At the same time, Budapest experienced a 12.77% decline in the number of residents. By the time of the 2001 census, roughly one-quarter of the country's population (2,434,603 people) lived within the Budapest Metropolitan Area. 72% of this population resided in the city, down from the 78% that was recorded in 1990. It is important to keep in mind that the population growth of the suburbs is solely due to the people settling there as deaths outweigh births and the natural trend is declining. In other words, the general population decline that characterizes the entire country is just as observable in the Budapest suburbs, despite the lower average age there. The most significant population increase took place in Telki, a village on the Buda side, where the population grew from 629 in 1990 to 1892 in 2001. This tripling was the result of a Budapest-rooted population. Already in 1995 three of four inhabitants (73.3%) in Telki were immigrants from Budapest (Daróczi 1999) and in all probability this ratio has since grown.

One important demographic consequence of the migration from Budapest to the suburbs is that the population within the city center is much older than that of the suburbs. 23 percent of the population of Budapest is more than 60 years old, while the equivalent ratio is only 16,9 percent in the suburban area. The national average is 20 percent.

Compared to 1990, the number of residences in the suburbs grew by 23% by 2001, while the growth in Budapest was only 3%. With regards to the intensity of home construction, there is a clear North-vs-South dividing line in the suburbs, with most of the construction work taking place in the areas north of Budapest. Lately, rising land prices has led to a leveling-off of new house building.

Economic and Infrastructural Changes

The fact that suburban communities managed to shake off their status as dormitory communities of Budapest was primarily due to the economic boom. After the change of the political regime, a process of homogenization began between Budapest and the suburban areas, the most important feature of which was the strengthening of the local economies. For a wide array of production facilities, the suburban areas possess a number of attractive qualities, such as space, ample labor supply, relatively developed infrastructure, complex labor market, favorable tax conditions, more affordable real estate, close proximity to Budapest as a market for goods, access to information and so on. This all means that the former division of labor is undergoing significant changes and the spatial system of business relations is also being transformed. One of the most significant changes within the Metropolitan Area is the decreasing centralization of the capital city.

Looking at the number of business enterprises per 1,000 people, at the end of 2001, there were 95 business enterprises recorded in the suburbs. While this maybe lower than the Budapest average of 138, at the same time it is significantly higher than the national average. These figures attest to an economic growth that is more dynamic than the national one. The suburbs saw a 250% increase in the number of business enterprises between 1990 and 1995 and a further 33% expansion between 1996 and 2001. Within this, the number of companies increased by 89%, while the number of single-person businesses (self-employment) saw only a modest increase of 4%. What is also noteworthy is that the growth rate in the villages and towns exceeded that of the cities. During this period in Budapest, growth was less dynamic with an overall increase of 22% while the number of self-employments actually decreased. By the end of 2001, 36% of all domestic business enterprises were registered in the Budapest Metropolitan Area – 79% in Budapest, 21% in the suburbs (Central Statistical Office 2003).

The economic development of the area is even more conspicuous if one looks at the figures for business enterprises incorporating foreign capital investment. For every 10,000 residents, Budapest had 81 such companies and the suburbs 25. As much as 60% of all domestic companies with foreign stakeholders are registered in this area while 68% of all foreign capital was invested here. In the Budapest Metropolitan Area, foreign capital was invested in and around the four edge cities of Gödöllő, Budaörs, Vác and Dunaharaszti.

As regards the number of business enterprises and the rate of unemployment the Southern Gyál area is the most disadvantaged while the number of business enterprises is highest in the areas west of the city (Budaörs and Törökbálint) and in Szentendre, located North of Budapest. In the 1990s, there were emerging differences not only between suburban municipalities but also between the part of Pest County belonging to the Budapest Metropolitan Area and the part which does not. The number of commuters in these suburban communities not only refused to grow since 1990 but, in fact, a slight decline was recorded. According to the 2001 census the proportion of commuters out of the economically active population was 59%. Suburbanization is responsible for the fact that this ratio did not drop by an even greater extent. The smallest decreases were recorded in communities where the ratio was already rather low in 1990 as well as in those outer suburban communities that are farthest from Budapest.

Increasing tax revenues facilitated enormous infrastructure developments in the suburban municipalities. The most dynamic growth was recorded in the case of the natural gas pipeline system. Whereas in 1990, only 36% of all households were connected to the system, by 2001 this figure grew to 86%. Most of the communities undertook the development of sewer systems. The number of communities without a sewer system dropped from 46 in 1990 to 29 in 1997 and to 13 in 2001. During the same period, the proportion of households connected in the central city grew from 80 to 89 percent. In 2001, 49% of all households were connected to a sewer system and whereas the figure may not seem all that impressive, progress is undeniable as in 1990 the corresponding rate was only 20%. In this respect, villages and towns experienced a significantly higher rate of progress than cities. The relative underdevelopment of the suburbs under Communism is indicated by the fact that, already in 1990, 88 percent of households were connected to the main sewage system.

In the years following the change of the political regime, the suburbs became increasingly differentiated both socially and economically. On the one hand, we can draw a dividing line between the inner and outer rings of suburbs. On the other, differences are pronounced between various sectors within the suburban areas. Generally speaking we can posit that various social statistical indicators demonstrate that the conditions in the outer ring are the least favorable, while there is also an East vs West divide. For example, the inner sectors on the Buda side have the highest ratio of people with higher education, per capita personal income tax and number of business enterprises. The southeastern sector of the suburban area displays the most halting process of urbanization, the lowest ratio of business enterprises and a high ratio of commuting blue-collar workers. Residents here are still very much involved in agrarian production, earning the region the description "a working class district in a rural environment." (Beluszky 1999)

3. The Governance Challenge

As in other metropolitan areas, governance in Budapest exhibits a tension between administrative fragmentation on the one hand and socio-economic unity on the other. Successive political regimes have been unable to respond to this challenge, although it probably would be as accurate to say that they have not made much attempt to resolve the situation.

There has never been one administrative unit that covered both Budapest and its suburbs. The administrative system has never considered the specificities of the municipalities around the city, treating them in the same way as the rest of the country. Most suburbs belong to Pest County. Nevertheless, this county has a large, mostly southern part, which does not belong to the suburban area. Moreover, there are several suburbs that belong to other counties.

The 1971 Law on Councils[5] already allowed the establishment of a special administrative unit, the so-called 'city environs' ('városkörnyék'), but for many years this institution was not used. Only in 1984 did city environs replaced the previous, highly centralized district system, providing more opportunities for self-determination to the towns around Budapest.

The 1971 law was followed by Government Decree No. 1005 in 1971, which established the official Budapest Metropolitan Area. This Area incorporated 44 suburban communities, towns and villages within its boundaries. The criteria for inclusion in the Budapest Metropolitan Area depended on the labor force needs of the capital and the existence of easy access from the community to Budapest. In other words, communities with a high volume of commuter traffic to the capital were included in the Budapest Metropolitan Area. In practice, the establishment of this Area had no consequence and the importance of the decree was rather symbolic than practical.

The new general development plan (the so-called 'ÁRT') did have more practical relevance. Not only did it cover Budapest, it included the suburban municipalities in a single document. This was a very significant new development, although the suburbs were still treated from the perspective of the development of Budapest. There were no plans to devolve functions to them, but undoubtedly the outer districts of Budapest did gain a new impetus. The scheme was prepared from 1980, but came into force only in 1989.

The 1990 Local Government Act brought about an enormous change. Freely elected, autonomous local governments replaced the centrally commanded local units. The local government system became one of the main pillars of the new political regime and local governments obtained genuine rights and competences. The Act contains a separate chapter on Budapest, which received a special administrative system of its own. The districts of the capital received broad authorities and complete legal autonomy. This paved the way for the development of the previously subordinate outer districts, resulting in the emergence of several sub-centers within the city. Despite these advance, the law did lead to three, as yet unresolved, problems:

1. The 23 district governments and the capital government are legally equal and, in principle, their competences exist at different levels. However, the law is not entirely clear in this regard which in the be-

---

[5] In this case 'Council' means 'Soviet', i.e. the local unit of the Communist party-state.

ginning led to many conflicts between the two tiers. Practice, precedence and minor legal changes have subsequently improved this situation.

2. The central government and the national parties often stir up strife between the liberal-socialist-led city government and the district governments and between the inner and outer districts. More importantly, the central government often attempts to limit the financial autonomy of the municipalities, creating tension between the wide legal and narrow financial autonomy. The underfunding of compulsory services resulted in some community property being sold off. Thus, municipalities are mortgaging their future.

The municipalities of the suburban areas emerge as the losers in the privatization deals. With respect to infrastructure, the suburban communities were handicapped from the start. As state socialism neglected to bring about fundamental developments in these areas, by now, certain infrastructure developments simply cannot be put off any longer. As the state had no resources for that, it sold the gas and electricity companies (in practice monopolies!) to foreign investors (often state-owned firms like the Gaz de France). Even though some suburban communities share infrastructure systems with the city of Budapest, neither they, nor the district governments of Budapest received a share of the revenues from privatizing these systems and had no say in how privatization was done.

3. The fragmented nature of the Budapest Metropolitan Area is not counter-balanced by any kind of metropolitan institution. Because the governmental structure in the suburban areas is rather fragmented, so far no solutions have been found to problems such as managing and coordinating public services and organizing regional development across municipal boundaries. The capital government is not really interested in a metropolitan government because it would take competences away from Budapest, hamper their ability to divert resources in their direction, and generally weaken their power vis-à-vis the suburbs. On the other hand, the suburbs want to preserve their independence and are still very conscious of the centralization times when they occupied a subordinate position in relation to the center.

The 1990 Act relied upon the voluntary cooperation of the local governments to resolve problems of coordination. While local governments did form some associations, their interests in autonomy mitigated against a voluntary solution. The amendment of the Local Government Act in 1994 did attempt to solve some of the institutional problems. In the debate between the capital government and the districts, by centralizing decision-making within Budapest the law gave priority to the capital, which happened to be of the same political color (liberals and socialists) as the parliamentary majority. Still, the district governments did make skillful use of their few competences in order to effectively blackmail the capital. The dispute remains unsettled.

The redrawing of the boundaries of the Budapest Metropolitan Area had long been on the agenda of urban development professionals but it was not until 1996 that the earlier boundaries were modified. The redrawing incorporated 78 communities into the Budapest Metropolitan Area, and, in 2003, 17 of these communities had city status. The change ultimately became necessary because of the shrinking of the Budapest labor market and the consequent diminishing of commuter traffic. In addition, there was the evolution of a new system of relationships, with higher degrees of cooperation between suburban production units, modernization of the suburban infrastructure, an expanding circle of services available in suburbs and an intensifying process of economic and residential suburbanization. Simultaneously, phenomena such as intensive land-use, blurring of boundaries between communities, the decline of the natural environment and certain segregation patterns have also become apparent in the Budapest Metropolitan Area.

The Development Act in 1996 led to the most promising change in the metropolitan governance of Budapest. The Budapest Suburban Development Council (Budapesti Agglomeráció Fejlesztési Tanács - BAFT) was established in 1997. That was the first institutional framework to include all stakeholders: the central and capital governments, districts, suburban municipalities, and chambers. Despite this, the experiment largely failed. The ministries were over represented, the relationship between Pest County and the BAFT was undefined, and, most importantly, the Council did not receive any serious funding and the body became insignificant. Its most important competence was the right to express opinions on development plans, but this opinion was not compulsory. The Council produced many conceptions, schemes, and recommendations, although on the whole without much effect. In 2000, it was abolished and its functions transferred to the development council of the Central Hungary Region. The region includes Budapest and Pest County, but not the suburbs belonging to other counties. The region is a statistical one, so it has no administration and no elected bodies. The regional development council does distributes real funds, but lacks a strong metropolitan perspective.

As a result of these changes, several main problems persist:

1. There are three systems of mass transportation which overlap each other. A monthly pass for Budapest transportation, for example, is not valid for trains and coaches. Moreover, commuters cannot buy passes covering both Budapest and the suburbs. The parallel infrastructure is costly and this is especially so for people living around the city. The Budapest Transportation Association (BKSZ) has been planning for more than a decade, while the actual government announces a new im-

plementation scheme almost every year. Despite this no steps forward, not even little ones, have been made since the beginning of the 1990s.

2. Municipalities share certain communal services which they cannot operate without a coordinating institution. Communities that sharing infrastructure systems are often at odds over how much each of them should contribute to the development, maintenance and operation of these systems. Moreover, fragmented municipalities have mush less bargaining power against the privatized electricity and gas companies, which cover the territory of Budapest and its environs.

3. As the first part of the paper outlined, many people within Budapest have been migrating to the suburbs where new residential zones have replaced green areas (including many forests). Since 1990, 2000 hectares of green surface have disappeared around Budapest. All municipalities, including Budapest, have an interest in converting agricultural territories into building plots. Collectively, however, all would benefit from regulations that could slow down the loss of the green areas.

4. Suburban people use educational and health institutions of Budapest, but pay taxes in their home municipality. The capital as well as districts often raises this issue, but they cannot force the suburbs to contribute. The usual counter-argument of suburban leaders is that commuters go not only to hospitals and high schools, but also to shops, and they pay business taxes to the municipality of Budapest. A mutually satisfactory solution will not be reached without an institution that covers both Budapest and the suburbs.

In sum, several attempts have been made to resolve the challenge of metropolitan governance, but so far without much success. As a result, the metropolitan problems persist.

4. Political Patterns

As far as electoral patterns are concerned, the true dividing line lies not between the city of Budapest and its suburbs but between the Buda and Pest sides of the Danube.

In the first round of the parliamentary elections, voter turnout in the suburbs generally followed the national pattern. By contrast, in all three election years there was a voter turnout in Budapest that was well above the national and, of course, the suburban average. In 1994, 73.4% of Budapest residents cast their ballots, 6% more than people in the suburbs (67.5%). The difference recorded in the 1998 elections was the same (63.1% and 57.5%) while by 2002, this difference diminished slightly (76.6% and 73.1%). In the suburban area, the Western and Northwestern sectors on the Buda side – where other development indicators are also significant – produced a higher turnout than the rest of the suburbs in all three elections. Likewise, in Budapest, areas west of the Danube (the Buda side) produced higher turnouts.[6] In all three elections, the North Buda area produced the highest and the Inner Pest area the lowest voter turnout in Budapest.

An examination of election results (voting patterns) highlights the regional differences within the Budapest Metropolitan Area.

As for the parliamentary elections in Hungary, the most important temporal change is that by 2002, an essentially bipolar party system had evolved which resulted in a great concentration of votes on the right (Fidesz-Hungarian Civic Association) and the left (Hungarian Socialist Party, the former Communist party). In the suburban communities, Fidesz only gained an average of 7% of votes in 1994, rising to 28% in 1998 and 41% in 2002. While 27% of Budapest voters cast their ballots for Fidesz in 1998, this rate only went up to 31% in 2002, 10% less than the size of the Fidesz vote in the suburbs.

The party on the other end of the spectrum, the left-wing Socialists gained 5-6% more votes in Budapest than in the suburbs in all of the three election years. In the suburbs the Socialists recorded 28%, 28% and 38% of the votes respectively while in Budapest the corresponding figure was 35%, 33% and 43%. At the same time, if we look at the different areas of Budapest separately, it becomes apparent that in the two Buda areas, Fidesz have done much better than its Budapest average. In these areas, the other right-wing party, the Hungarian Democratic Forum (MDF) also did well with respect to other Budapest areas. At the same time, the Socialist Party secured a much lower percentage of the vote in these areas than in other Budapest districts in all elections. The Socialists did best in the Outer Pest region which appears to be the most left-leaning area in all of the Budapest Metropolitan Area. Here, they secured 40% of the vote in 1994, 36% in 1998 and 44% in 2002. As for the suburban areas, the Socialist were mostly supported in those sectors which were adjacent to the Outer Pest region, i.e. the Southern and Southeastern sectors, while Fidesz was dominant in the Northwestern suburban areas, adjacent to the North Buda area of Budapest.

We must point out that Fidesz did not receive the kind of support in the Buda districts as it did in the Buda sectors of the suburban areas. One of the reasons for this is that in the Buda districts of Budapest, the liberals (Alliance of Free Democrats, SZDSZ) and the far-right (Hungarian Life and Justice Party, MIÉP) exhibit similar support patterns, receiving more votes on the Buda than on the Pest side. Both these parties have a stronger voter base in the city than in the suburbs. Not surprisingly, the agrarian party (the now extinct Independent Smallholders Party, FKGP)

---

[6] When examining electoral patters, we divided Budapest up into four areas: 1. North Buda (Districts 1, 2, 12) 2. South Buda (11, 22) 3. Inner Pest (5, 6, 7, 8, 9, 13, 14) and 4. Outer Pest (4, 10, 15, 16, 17, 18, 19, 20, 21 and 23).

did better in those suburbs with strong ties to agriculture, securing twice the number of votes there than in the city. By 2002, FKGP had become utterly insignificant in all areas.

In the Budapest Metropolitan Area then, the principal dividing line for the large political parties is the Danube. West of the river, both in the city and in the suburbs, the conservatives (and liberals) are the better supported side while to the east of the river, in Pest and in the adjacent suburbs, the Socialists are the main political party of choice. The liberals and the far-right, which constitute a special political subculture, do better in Budapest than in the suburbs.

One can find some interesting patterns concerning the local elections. Voter turnout at municipal elections grew between the 1998 and 2002 elections in the suburban communities. While in 1998, an average of 48.4% of eligible voters cast their ballots, in 2002, 52.37% turned up at the voting booths. These rates are somewhat higher than the national average. Voter turnout rates actually decreased in a quarter of the municipalities and increased in three-quarters. In those municipalities where voter turnout increased, the rate of increase was 7% though the base rate (initial condition) was 45%. In 1998 those municipalities that exhibited decreasing tendencies had a voter turnout rate above the national average (56%). Thus, the changes really amount to a leveling of differences. Above-average voter turnout increases were recorded in the Eastern and Southern sectors of the metropolitan area. Cities exhibited a rate increase that was twice that of the villages. In the fast-growing municipalities[7], voter turnout was several percentage points above the suburban average both in 1998 and in 2002 while the growth rate in these suburbs was only average.

We tried to find out whether the political races in the municipal elections had intensified in the suburbs by examining the number of candidates for the representative (council) and the mayoral seats. In 1998 an average of three candidates contended one seat and this remained largely the same in 2002 (2.95 and 3.03). At the same time, in 55% of the communities races did seem to intensify. It is interesting to see which municipalities had the most intense races and, out of these, to see which of them saw the greatest degree of intensification. In both 1998 and 1998, the races were twice as intense in the cities as in the villages. At the same time, the cities exhibited a decreasing number of candidates per seat while by 2002 in the villages there was an average of 0.24 more candidates for each seat, in other words there was one more candidate for every four

---

[7]We looked at 27 suburbs separately – these communities between 1990 and 2001 exhibited a population growth rate higher than the average of 25%. These 27 suburbs were included in our „fast-growing community" category. 89% of the fast-growing communities have a status of municipality and there are only 3 cities among them.

seats. The cities however, did exhibit a decreasing tendency which out-stripped the increase in villages: in 1998 there were 4.5 candidates per seat and in 2002, only 4.1. Two-thirds of the villages can be said to have had a wider election contest in 2002 while this is true for 25% of the cities. Of course, the growing number of candidates might have some-thing to do with the population growth: in fast-growing municipalities, the race intensified by 0.25 candidate, while other suburban communities re-corded no change in intensity. At the same time, the fast-growing com-munities in 2002 were still behind other municipalities with respect to the number of candidates, 2.74 and 3.18 per seat respectively. It would ap-pear that the status and particular features of the municipality has more to do with the changes in the intensity of political races. In the case of vil-lages experiencing an average or slower growth, we witnessed an in-tensifying pattern but cities in the same category recorded a significantly higher rate of intensification. This growth can be observed in both fast-growing cities and fast-growing villages.

The examination of changes in the number of candidates for mayoral seats yields similar results. The average number of candidates grew slightly between 1998 and 2002, but the growth rate is less than im-pressive (0.11). The average number of candidates remained unchanged in the cities but increased in villages, where there were 0.2 more can-didates in 2002 than in 1998 per race on the average. At the same time, the average number of candidates was less in the villages than in cities. In 2002 there were 3.25 candidates in mayoral races in villages while in the cities this figure was 3.94. Though the difference is still striking, it has been diminishing since 1998 when cities had one more candidate per race than the villages. In municipalities with an above-average popu-lation growth rate, there were 0.5 more candidates per seat in 2002 than in 1998, which is a significant growth rate by any calculation. Similarly, slower-growing municipalities exhibited a decreasing intensity in mayoral races. Again, we come up against the question whether this interesting observation could not be explained by the make-up effect, that is, by the fact that the village category always had a higher rate of municipalities with higher population growth rates. It seems however, that this could not be the reason. In both cities and in villages where we found an above-a-verage population growth rate, we also recorded an increase in intensity in elections.

5. Suburbanization and Socio-Political Tensions Within Suburbs

Suburbanization has resulted in a significant reshaping of a good number of municipalities in the Budapest Metropolitan Area. This section ex-amines the changes in the political life of the suburban communities wrought by the rapid and voluminous population influx from Budapest. Our observations are based on three qualitative case studies – Diósd,

Veresegyház, Pomáz – therefore our primary objective is to highlight certain phenomena and effect mechanisms rather than measure their scope and extent.

To summarize our research, we can conclude that the population explosion throughout the 1990s in the suburban communities in the Budapest Metropolitan Area created conflicts. These were not so much between the immigrant and resident populations but between the municipal authorities and certain groups of the population. One problem area common to all the municipalities in our analysis was the struggle to diminish the "infrastructure deficit" that emerged between the growing population and the infrastructure needed to sustain them. As we have indicated earlier in this study, the municipal authorities have had to deal with a "terrible legacy" from the previous regime. This, of course, is true for other parts of the country, but in the communities of the Budapest Metropolitan Area, because of the high growth rate of the population the demands for infrastructure development are more intense and pressing. Needless to say, different authorities have different means at their disposal to manage this process. From this perspective, the starting point i.e. municipal infrastructure, real estate market and general economic conditions, does play especial significance. In the following section, we will highlight the main conflicts and their manifestations in the political life of these communities.

Physical Infrastructure
Infrastructure represents a key problem area. Many areas without the necessary infrastructure become overloaded and the local authorities cannot develop at the same pace that people move in to the area. The situation is exacerbated by construction or additions that take place without permits, as well as by the slow, "informal" transition of resort areas into inadequately regulated residential areas. Diósd and Pomáz are both good examples of this tendency. The municipal government of Diósd re-zoned the extensive resort areas of the municipality into residential areas last year. Because the resort zones were already in a more advanced initial condition in comparison to other, similar areas in the region, lacking only a sewer system but possessing all other forms of infrastructure, the area was already populated mainly by permanent residents. Some still maintained a Budapest apartment, some moved here in the hope of cheaper living costs. As the municipal government could only apply for state development funds for residential areas and because it could not possibly build roads, sewer systems etc. from its own resources, it decided to rezone the area. Simultaneously, the residents themselves placed some pressure on the government. They benefited from the rezoning in various ways, for instance, only property in residential areas can serve as collateral to loans. The rezoning did not be-

nefit the municipal government financially, but it certainly did the property owners of the rezoned area, whose plots went up in price.

Social Infrastructure

The rapid population growth placed a great strain on social infrastructure, such as the congestion of nursery schools and kindergartens. In 1990, in the suburban cities, there were 122 children for 100 nursery school places, in towns and villages the equivalent figure was 130. In the same year, there were 115 children for every 100 kindergarten places. Needless to say, that these problems have intensified with the growing population influx. In Veresegyház, for instance, a new 24-room school was recently completed, but it is already clear that its capacity will be exhausted in the near future and another school will have to be built. Nor is the "doctor density" in health care as it should be -- the physician-per-resident rates in suburban communities lag behind the national average. At the end of 1998, for every 10,000 residents, there were 20 physicians in the suburbs of the Budapest Metropolitan Area, 66 in Budapest while the national average was 36.

Budget Challenges

While tax revenues are rise significantly, in most communities, these resources do not cover the skyrocketing costs of education, infrastructure development and social services. When planning their long-term objectives, municipal governments were depending on revenues from local personal income tax. In the early 1990s, 100% of the personal income tax went to local governments, this first dropped to 50% and currently, only 10% of income tax revenues go to local governments. With the drying up of central, redistributed sources, local governments have had to find alternative means to finance public tasks out of their own sources. However, even communities with strong economic backgrounds have difficulties dealing with their infrastructure deficit. Budget deficits are plugged by rezoning and selling more and more land. This is a vicious circle[8] which reproduces the deficit in infrastructure. Different local governments have varying means to break out from this vicious circle. These are usually determined by their initial conditions and the growth rate of their municipalities. Some local governments scope for action depends on whether they have privately owned lots or revenues from other sources[9].

---

[8]Local residents in Piliscsaba, Telki and Pomáz have already staged demonstrations against rezoning and incorporating new lands into residential areas.

[9]The local government of Pilisjászfalu, for instance, is the only player on its real estate market and the community is not only well-located but it also inherited infrastructure from the previous regime with which it is now able to attract companies to open facilities there. (Váradi 1999) The local leadership envisioned a slow, long-term

The other obvious strategy to raise revenue is to increase the industrial zone, in other words, to attract business into the locality. As we have already seen, there are great differences in this respect between the sectors within the suburban area. The main business incentive tool in the hand of local governments is the granting of municipal tax breaks. At the same time, industrial projects may come up against resistance from residents and often it is difficult to find any solution that is both environmentally and resident friendly. Veresegyház is a good example of this struggle. In the last decade, the population has practically doubled. As the influx is constant so the local government tries to keep up by attracting industry. Recently, a factory manufacturing car batteries tried to move to the municipality but the resistance and protest of the residents thwarted the project.

Difficulties of Land Use Planning
One of the primary preconditions which made large-scale settlement possible was the privatization processes of the 1990s. This saw many old-time residents regain their property which was nationalized under the Communist regime. However, one of the primary features of the land privatization in Hungary was that it created a highly fragmented lot structure. New owners received small and frequently scattered plots. Needless to say, speculators kept a close eye on privatization deals and bought up many of these lots. As a result, the owners of privatized lands exerted pressure on the local government to help them capitalize on their property interests (especially if the land owner also happened to be a local representative) resulting in the rezoning a lot of the land. In many cases, "exerting pressure" smacked of corruption or bribery.
It is however, very difficult to create a comprehensive zoning plan for heavily fragmented areas without injuring the interests of at least some of the owners. As the mayor of Diósd put it,

> "These plots were not originally formed to be residential plots but were divided for agricultural production, narrow strips of land from 6 m to 12-20 m wide. These lots had to be merged but people had a hard time coming to agreements with their neighbors, let alone with anybody else and these difficulties slowed down the process of settlement."

In many cases, when it clashed with the interests of some owners, the construction of a road that was wide enough proved to be a problem. Infra-structure developments also ran into similar difficulties.

---

growth, tightly controlled by the local government, which would see infrastructural development followed by subdivision and sale of lots with the provision to develop.

Wherever municipal governments were less influential players on the real estate market, their scope for action in regulating and controlling settlement also suffered. In Diósd, most of the land is in private hands. The municipal government does not subdivide its own lots, yet the rate of influx is one of the highest in the Budapest Metropolitan Area. At the other extreme, we have the case of Veresegyház, where the municipal government is the only player on the real estate market. During privatization, the municipal government bought from all local residents albeit entering into a debt spiral as a consequence. It used the lots as collateral in order to take out mortgage loans. In turn, they could only pay these loans back by selling off the lots to people moving into the municipality. This amplified the rate of settlement. At the same time, this local government is in the fortunate position of being able to stop subdivision whenever it wants to, yet if it did chose to go down this route it would have to find substitute sources for financing the infrastructure developments demanded by the new settlers. Thus, from the perspective of local government's room to maneuver it is very important what alternative sources of income it possesses.

Social Segregation

The influx of a population into a non-residential or infrastructurally underdeveloped areas often goes hand-in-hand with social segregation. This is what happened in Pomáz: the resort area, though lacking infrastructure, is situated in a pleasant, forest environment and many people moved there in the hope of lower living costs. Today, the municipal government has to tackle the problem of cottages and shacks constructed without permits which gradually become residential dwellings and constitute a drain on social policy funds. Usually, it is lower-income people who move to the underdeveloped areas, but once they are there, the local government must look after them. Further conflicts arise when people of extremely different financial background become neighbors – especially in situations when all neighborhood residents need to come up with their own share to contribute to infrastructure development.

Social Integration of Newcomers

The social integration of newcomers constitutes a difficult task in certain communities and severely taxes the resources of the local government that has to organize community events, cultural programs, support civic activities and set up the institutions necessary to administer these. Social integration proved less difficult in communities where waves of new settlements took place before the change of regime, in other words where some of the newcomers have been residing in the locality for decades and where some of the population was employed in industry, as in Diósd for example. Communities that were dominated by agrarian populations exhibit clashes of very different mentalities. Long-time residents of what became suburbs are usually suspicious and wary of people migrating into the communities especially as the newcomers tend to quickly become the dominant group in local politics.

Conflicts arise not so much between the newcomer and the long-time resident populations but between the municipal authorities and certain segments of the population with diverging interests. For instance, a source of conflict can be where a road is to be built. „If they pave one road, others elsewhere will start complaining and even offer money for the same work in their area but the local government must come up with its own share of the costs," said a Diósd journalist. Another source of civic discontent is the growing volume of traffic – in Pomáz and Diósd, among the locations in our case study – but this kind of conflict is geographically determined. In other words, people living in the same neighborhood will protest regardless of whether they are new or long-time residents. Many of the communities have civic associations that preserve local traditions and respondents in our survey revealed that events and meetings of these are attended by newcomers as well as long-time residents.

Protest Against Municipallty Growth

Ironically, the great influx of population destroys the very value that motivates many to move into the suburbs (peace and quiet). Increased volume of population results in an increased volume of traffic in communities and the mushrooming construction sites can also constitute a source of inconvenience. There are many problems which plague everyday life due to such phenomena as traffic jams, the underdeveloped nature of public transport systems and so on. In many places, commuting has become practically impossible. This is why newcomers, once settled, turn against further settlement and thus become ranged against not only the local government which needs revenues but also against long-time residents who still possess land to sell to newcomers. There is always a great pressure on the local governments to rezone private lands, thereby increasing their value. This pressure is even greater if the lands in question belong to local representatives or officials. In an indirect way, local residents, especially those in the construction business, also benefit from growth. Permitting further growth in these communities has become one of the most important issues that is debated.

The Representation of Newcomers

As for the specifics of political life, our case studies have shown that bodies of representatives did undergo changes under the influence of the newcomer population. On the one hand, political candidates might emerge from the ranks of the newcomers and on the other, newcomers might vote in local elections according to party sympathies, not knowing the candidates personally. In Diósd, the population increase brought party politics into the municipality. Before the 2002 elections, people voted not so much along party lines but along personal preference for the candidate. Long-time community leaders hope that the party sympathies of the newcomers will only last until the first election after which they will get to know the candidates and local conditions better and will cast their vote on the basis of performance rather than party colors.

6. Conclusions

The aim of the paper is to report the socio-economic and political development of the Budapest Metropolitan Area. Its main findings are as follows:

1. The suburbanization process started in the 1960s and gained momentum in the 1990s, when the population of the suburban area grew by 20 percent. Suburban municipalities established new residential areas and significantly decreased the extent of green surfaces around Budapest.

2. The establishment of autonomous and democratic local governments created a favorable environment for the development of the suburbs, something which had been disliked by the Communist planning agencies. The infrastructure has improved and is doing so quickly in the suburban area. Still, the development is not fast enough in many places, finding it difficult to keep pace with the growth of the population. This led to protest against further growth in most suburbs, though in varying intensity.

3. Since the beginning of the 1970s, several attempts have been made to create an institution of metropolitan governance, but these attempts have more or less failed. As a consequence, the problems of mass transportation, land use, shared communal services and educational and health institutions remain unresolved.

4. Concerning political parties, the dividing line is primarily between the Buda side, where the right is more supported, and the Pest side of the metropolitan area, where the socialists (ex-Communists) are stronger. As far as electoral patterns are concerned, the border between Budapest and the suburban area, which is so important administratively, is less important.

5. The integration of newcomers in suburbs is surprisingly smooth. The main conflict is between local government and those who ask for better infrastructure and slower growth.

References

Bartha, G. (1999) Gazdasági folyamatok a budapesti agglomerációban. In: Bartha, G.; Beluszky, P. (szerk.) Társadalmi, gazdasági átalakulás a budapesti agglomerációban. Regionális Kutatási Alapítvány: Budapest.

Beluszky, P. (1999) A budapesti agglomeráció kialakulása. In: Bartha G.; Beluszky P. (szerk.) Társadalmi, gazdasági átalakulás a budapesti agglomerációban. Regionális Kutatási Alapítvány: Budapest.

Central Statistical Office (1991a) Budapest Statisztikai Évkönyve 1990. Budapest: Central Statistical Office.

Central Statistical Office (1991b) Pest megye statisztikai évkönyve 1990. Budapest: Central Statistical Office.

Central Statistical Office (1992) Az 1990.évi népszámlálás: Pest megye adatai. Budapest: Central Statistical Office.

Central Statistical Office (1996) „Mekkora a budapesti agglomeráció?" Közlemények a budapesti agglomerációról 7. kötet. Budapest: Central Statistical Office (KSH).

Central Statistical Office (1998) „A budapesti agglomeráció az ezredfordulón" Közlemények a budapesti agglomerációról 8. kötet. Budapest: Central Statistical Office (KSH).

Central Statistical Office (2000) „A lakosság egészségügyi állapota és egészségügyi ellátása" Közlemények a budapesti agglomerációban 9. kötet. Budapest: Central Statistical Office (KSH).

Central Statistical Office (2002a) A 2001.évi népszámlálás Pest megye 1-2. kötet. Budapest: Central Statistical Office.

Central Statistical Office (2002b) Budapest Statisztikai Évkönyve 2001. Budapest: Central Statistical Office.

Central Statistical Office (2002c) Pest megye statisztikai évkönyve 2001. Budapest: Central Statistical Office.

Central Statistical Office (2002d) Területi statisztikai évkönyv 2001. Budapest: Central Statistical Office.

Central Statistical Office (2003) „Vállalkozások a budapesti agglomerációban" Közlemények a budapesti agglomerációról 10. kötet. Budapest: Central Statistical Office.

Daróczi, E. (1999) Ki a fővárosból: Változás Budapest és az ország vándorforgalmában. In: Bartha G.; Beluszky P. (szerk.) Társadalmi, gazdasági átalakulás a budapesti agglomerációban. Regionális Kutatási Alapítvány: Budapest.

Kocsis, J.B. (2000) A szuburbanizáció jelenségének főbb elméleti megközelítései. Tér és Társadalom No. 2-3.

Kovács, K. (1999) Szuburbanizációs folyamatok a fővárosban és a budapesti agglomerációban. In: Bartha G.; Beluszky, P. (szerk.) Társadalmi, gazdasági átalakulás a budapesti agglomerációban. Regionális Kutatási Alapítvány: Budapest.

Nagy, S.G. (1998) A külföldi működőtőke a budapesti agglomeráció kereskedelmében. In: Budapest: nemzetközi város. MTA: Budapest.

Perger, É. (1999) Közigazgatási dilemmák. In: Bartha, G.; Beluszky, P. (szerk.) Társadalmi, gazdasági átalakulás a budapesti agglomerációban. Regionális Kutatási Alapítvány: Budapest.

Sági, Z. (2000) A külföldi tőke szerepe a budapesti agglomerációs övezet feldolgozó-ipari térszerkezetének kialakulásában. Tér és Társadalom No. 2-3.

Szelényi, I.; Ladányi, J. (1997) Szuburbanizáció és gettósodás. Kritika 1997/7.

Szelényi, I.; Róbert, M. (1972) A késleltetett városfejlődés. Szociológia 1972/1.

Szirmai, V. (1998) A budapesti agglomeráció társadalmi problémái. Társadalmi Szemle 1998.7.

Valuch, T. (2001) Magyarország társadalomtörténete a XX. század 2. felében. Osiris: Budapest.

Váradi, M. (1999) Szuburbanizációs minták és konfliktusok az agglomeráció budai oldalán. In: Bartha, G.; Beluszky, P. (szerk.) Társadalmi, gazdasági átalakulás a budapesti agglomerációban. Regionális Kutatási Alapítvány: Budapest.

Constructing the "city of mine" within the globalised space

Anna Karwinska

1. Introductory remarks.
Spatial dimension of globalisation in a post-socialist city.

The process of globalisation must be the most talked about issue of social life. In the ensuing discussion several aspects of the process and their mutual relationships are tackled, as well as the social determinants which decide about the course of the process and its positive or negative consequences for all walks of life. One of the important elements of the discussion must be, beyond any doubt, the globalisation of space, particularly of the urban space. Cities have always reflected the basic features of a socio-economic system thus becoming, in a certain way, its showcase. The basic characteristics of economy, of a political system, culture, of social order are more or less apparent in the way space is organised and utilised. Globalisation of economy has been bringing ever stronger supranational relationships. That is due to the fact that economic institutions are no longer rooted in a certain country, a definite spot on the map, and their assets and scope of activity often exceed the potential of small countries. A similar process has been taking place in the realm of politics. In line with the emergence of larger and larger international organisations, the course and consequences of political conflicts often spread beyond the borders of a given country. The sphere of culture has been undergoing a similar process which is intensified with the advent of recent mass media coverage. Consequently, in the process of its formation a global society is becoming more and more consolidated. Hence, a significant part of society has been undergoing a transformation in the way of describing its identity, relationships with tradition, needs for modelling their own world. This refers in particular to those categories of people who can be either described as contemporary "nomads" or "metropolitan class" (Jałowiecki, 2000) or a peculiar category of city dwellers labelled by H.Gans as "the cosmopolites" (Gans, 1962).

The consequences of globalisation can be observed in various areas of social life, in making the world a uniform place to live, in making culture a universal and homogeneous product, by allowing mass participation in various realms of culture. A global society has been more and more active in the creation of global social space. That "globalisation" is most apparent in the area of production (a consequence of the globalisation of economy) or the area of exchange. However, even the space of consumption has been assuming a universal character (uniformity of accommodation facilities, the use of green areas, duplication of recreation and entertainment facilities). Even the area of symbols has not been immune to the process despite the fact that, by definition, its functions closely related to the ways of expressing culture of a certain community should be individualistic. As stated above, the realm of culture has been largely influenced by the pressure of globalisation processes and their universal drive.

However, at this point I want to indicate the complexity of changes of the modern world. Globalisation processes have been taking place parallel to strongly emerging processes of strengthening local identity and attempts at displaying separateness and individualist features. Both processes have been interwoven and to some extent may be considered as complementary to one other, thus satisfying various individual and communal needs.

The complementary character of needs has been reflected in the evaluation of the near and remote physical and social space, as well as, in different attitudes to the place of residence (expressed by building one's future around it, or the desire to migrate).

Those issues have become the subject of numerous analyses which have been recently conducted within urban sociology studies, particularly related to the "restitution"[1] of cities after the decline of the socialist system. In place of centrally planned, uniform space[2] catering for the needs of an egalitarian, collective "socialist" society with the uniform culture, class system and ideology[3] the last decade brought new ways of organising and utilising space. What I am referring to is the space conforming to the "McDonald's world" principles so as to suit the needs of consumers influenced by mass pop culture or the "universal" space meeting the wants and demands of "eurospecialists" or "world citizens" being "in transit" or enjoying the ex-pat status.

---

[1] By the „restitution" I mean the processes aiming at returning some important features to the city (both within the social organisation concept as well as an organised space) which vanished in the course of the "socialist transformation". It should be noted that the consequences of global economy and culture have been overlapping the post-socialist *residua*, thus multiplying the problems of transforming the social and spatial structure of cities and balancing their development.

[2] In the course of classes in urban sociology my students were viewing the pictures of housing estates that had been built in various parts of Poland within the same period. It turned out that unless they were given some clear reference (a subtitle or an element of background, e.g. an architectural landmark) there were unable to decide which city the estates were a part of (including the estates of their home town). The "sameness" of estates was thus proved beyond any doubt, which was not necessarily the intention of the architects. In the course of implementation of "A block of flats program" aimed at revitalisation of large housing estates we found that one of the children living in the estate drew a colourful flower next to the entrance so that to facilitate the recognition of her dwelling.

[3] I am referring to the assumed provisos which were not always implemented.

2. Urban environment. Typical versus individual character.

Human habitat may be considered from the global perspective, making reference to human kind "in general". However, this category does not appear very useful in a sociological discourse. Consequently, that habitat is set in time and space and analysed as "somebody's". Hence, we talk about a "Polish" or an "Italian" town or, in a different dimension, about "Provancal" "Upper-Silesian" town, etc, referring to the habitat created by social interaction within a certain whole, a typical habitat which is jointly experienced and which constitutes a common basis for the development of features of a certain community. In turn, the experiences of an individual, his interaction with the social environment create a highly individualistic habitat which is made up from the selected elements of space, tangible and intangible elements of culture, and the framework of social interaction (Rybicki, 1972).

Yet, contemporary cities often assume a character which is not as much regional or national, but "European" or "worldly", devoid of the characteristic features of a certain culture. They are converted into an environment which due to the organisation of space, the type of institutions, patterns of behaviour, type of social intercourse becomes a "universal" setting, catering for the needs of huge entities which Huntington labelled as civilisations or even, at least to a some extent, for the needs of the global society (Huntington, 1997). Such a city becomes a habitat (mostly contemporary) for the modern "cosmopolites", eternal nomads who do not have the time measured in generations, not even years, to adopt to a new location. The lifestyle characteristic of that category of people, who need "instant" institutions, everyday objects and inter-human relationships often result in maintaining very superficial individual relationships and assuming the role of a "user" rather than of an "inhabitant". On the other hand, such lifestyle demands from every habitat the provision of a set of typical features and certain institutions which will allow cashing in a flash a cheque made out by a bank from another part of the world. A fast food outlet has to serve familiar dishes, and the more discerning patrons must be able to find a place providing their favourite, exotic cuisine. Global space moulded by McDonald's culture not only facilitates functioning without the necessity of adopting to or familiarising oneself with the new surroundings. It also satisfies the needs of all those who neither belong to the metropolitan class of people nor are "in transit". This is the need of clout, pride of the attained social status, the feeling that the surroundings are "European", "modern", "good taste", etc. Social and individual expectations of people towards their environment are dependent on the cultural impact, mostly derived from popular culture. Local, folk values are often considered to be too modest, and they are no match for a loud and colourful offer which is often considered to be "high society", "modern", "American", etc. On the other hand, most people feel the need of personal space distinguished by selected, accepted elements facilitating the expression of their individualism. The universal habitat is built by the professionals, yet those who inhabit it, i.e. the "real people" transform it through the on-going interaction from the "potential" (creating opportunities) into the "effective" (satisfying needs) surroundings.

We create, either through an individual or a collective effort, our own small worlds which are, despite the high level of uniformity, different for various social classes of people, for men and women, for various ethnic groups, social strata, and cultural circles (Boehm, 1981). The more diverse social status determining the needs and aspirations of those groups, the more differentiated are their habitats.

3. The relationships between man and space.

The relationships between man and his habitat may be described with the four interwoven processes: learning, valuation, usage, and formation. They are conditioned by the individual and shared values, by their hierarchy, and by the accepted methods of their expression and realisation, by the existing social needs, by the ways of their satisfaction, the scale of unfulfilled or deferred needs, as well as by the common and individual interests.

The process of evaluation of the elements of habitat runs parallel to their creation, recognition, and utilisation (Karwinska, 1998). Various elements of man's habitat, once they have been appropriately organised and provided with the means of their realisation, allow to satisfy both basic and superior needs. The degree and the scope of satisfaction constitute an important basis for evaluation. The elements which are evaluated comprise natural environment, physical space, cultural environment as a whole, and, needless to say, its external aspect, i.e. the landscape. The applied criteria are of different kinds, e.g. those involved in the satisfaction of various individual and communal needs, aesthetic criteria, criteria related to the functioning of certain areas, to the degree of order (spatial, cultural, and social) that has been achieved in the process of creating and modifying the elements of cultural environment. Those processes of relationship between man and space are conditioned by the multidimensional character of man's existence (man as a social, psychic, creating culture, and conducting economic activity being). Hence the multitude of man's needs and aspirations.

The use of space changes depending on the agent. Some areas are "private" (e.g. an apartment), others are shared by a certain community as e.g. the inhabitants of a block of flats, people living in the same precinct, in the same street, people with common interests, at least partially integrated. Finally, there are spaces used by a number of groups such as city centres, a train terminal, an airport, a commercial district. Urban space may be further subdivided into the space used sporadically (a park, a grove, or a sports stadium) and systematically (a road leading to a school, a shop, or a company)

In this way, while satisfying their everyday needs, particular individuals create their own vision of a city, their own version of their habitat. In a big city an individual first becomes familiar with, and then utilises a primary set of elements connected with his everyday life, viz. an apartment, a building and its surroundings, a road to work, a place of work, basic services and their access, finally recreation areas with the roads leading to them. Hence, by choices and rejections, an individual constructs his own system built along the axis organising everyday and leisure time behaviour. Therefore, a city does not appear the same to all its dwellers. The city which an individual knows and "inhabits" is made up from the objective features of the elements contributing to that individual's version of a social and spatial environment. Below I will answer the question how a city is perceived by that individual, and what conditions it offers for living and development.

4. The characteristic features of the individual versions of Krakow.

In my discussion I will use two sources for reference; the results of "My backyard" contest held by the media, and "My Krakow" projects prepared by the students of Cracow University of Economics attending an urban sociology class.

The letters sent by the contemporary and former residents of Krakow told stories about their backyards, about the past, about their childhood, about emotional ties with some places, buildings, trees, and also about people who they shared backyards with. A significant part of those stories was the garden, either real or symbolic. One of the authors wrote this, "When my parents moved in here in the early 1950s, the backyard was a charming, green garden, grown with many fruit trees and shrubs, with a romantic summer-house and not so romantic, furtively bred chicken". Another letter written by a resident of a block of flats describes a "yard" made up of two adjacent balconies packed with flower pots. It is worth noting that the balconies full of flowers or tiny flower beds fenced off from public lawns used to be, and still are, a way of "familiarising" the impersonal space of a high rise development. Other important elements are the borders of the private world (fences), gates, as well as mysterious spots offering space filled by people's imagination. It might be a stained glass window, a shut door, or even a view from the window.

Those real, as well as symbolic yards evoked the feeling of security, homeliness, possessing one's own place on the earth which could be filled with dreams and play. To use the notions that were analysed during two consecutive Seminars on Polish Contemporary Architecture, the backyards belonged both to the "personal", as well as, to the "memory lane" sphere. Creation, cultivation, feeling, and expression of those spheres is related to the satisfaction of psychic and social needs, the need of self-fulfilment of individuals and social groups that are functioning within a city. A city devoid of those social spaces can be merely populated and not lived in. I am referring to an important emotional relationships between man and his turf.

That emotional feeling for the city was recurrent in almost all comments as well as the students' projects describing their individual versions of Krakow. What seems interesting is the fact that such attitude was shared both by the born and raised Krakow residents as well as by the immigrants. The latter treat Krakow not only as a city in which they are living and studying, but also as a place where they make new acquaintances, meet people, start their own life. Another thing Krakow has to offer is a big city atmosphere and a variety of experiences, various social intercourse, a chance to free oneself from a small town atmosphere. Krakow has been perceived as an important centre of culture, a "European" city, a metropolis, and as such it chosen as an attractive place for studying. Adaptation to a new environment and building "one's little world" are not always easy. The feedback from respondents shows that big city qualities can be, at times, a drawback. Feelings of loneliness, being a misfit, extreme pace of life, temporary character of relationships, excessive commercialisation of social life, the "McDonald's world" impact on space are the drawbacks of a big city which is hard to familiarise (domesticate).[4] For the natives of Krakow that city is a little homeland, and their feelings are not merely the consequence of peculiar features of that place, but also the aftermath of family traditions. Students reports are full of the memories of leisurely strolls with the family members, soccer matches watched in the company of fathers and grandfathers. That tradition is still continued for the grown-ups. Those people whose roots in the city reach a few generations back have many special "spots" in the city. Some of them still exist, some have been destroyed by the unavoidable changes in the city structure, some have been made obsolete by the changes in the style of urban life (e.g. corner shops). Those stories may be used to reconstruct a nostalgic map of the city of the childhood days showing the spots where you could buy the best ice cream, the best doughnuts, where you could visit a city park with the swings, the first soccer pitch...

The authors of other reports highlight a peculiar melding of some features of the city perceived as a social environment. The most important issues are stressing the co-existence of the past and the present. For

---

[4] Despite the fact that I have been living in Krakow for over three years I still answer the question "Where are you from?" with a spontaneous "From Polaniec" writes one of the students describing her version of "My Krakow"

many Krakow is a place where you can "stumble on history" with every step you make. In the oldest part of Krakow many houses, squares and streets are connected with major or minor historical events.

Another important feature is the combination of the "local" and "big city" character. A personal version of a city usually comprises many elements which decide about its homeliness, endowing it with the characteristics of a "good place to live". Some descriptions are worth quoting, e.g. " I live in Bajeczna (Fabulous) street, which really deserves its name. In the summer and in the spring it is fabulously green, there are lots of birds and cats living in it, and lilacs bloom by my window" (a narrative by a student from Polaniec). Another confession, "I like best shopping at Ms Irena's who sells great croissants and cottage cheese. There is a pastry shop across the street from her outlet" (a student from Oswiecim).

The areas endowed with big city features, bearing the stigma of globalisation are mostly used for entertainment or doing business. Sometimes they are the places where we work. We value those places for their accessibility, functionality, yet mostly they are not the parts of the city which have earned our special emotional reaction. Frequently they deserve our negative opinion for their lack of character, banality, excessive commercialisation. More refined leisure time activities, aesthetic needs, experiencing art are fulfilled in places with a special ambience, places which are unique or "magical". That style of life calls for bar crawls through the pubs of the Old Town, often intended to change the mood (a different type of music, a different atmosphere), to meet people from different circles of the society. The same variety may be found in numerous shops, in places evoking special " climate"; from the serenity of the narrow streets of the Old Town or the former Jewish town called Kazimierz to the hustle and bustle of the Main Square; from the peaceful green suburbs to the green areas called the Blonia or the parks, to jogging and leisurely walks along the river embankments. That wide selection produces the effect of variety, changeability, richness and intensity of human relationships within the perimeter of the city.

Most students' projects highlight the magical character and uniqueness of Krakow. The words "atmosphere", "ambience", "enchanting", "unusual", "beautiful", "one of the kind" come up in every phrase substantiating the choice of the place to study or the emotional attitude towards the city.

5. The "effective" environment – functional and symbolic sphere.

The effective environment which the students created comprises certain elements common to their group. Those elements are most closely related to the course of their studies as well as various errands and health care. Needless to say, to those elements belong Cracow University of Economics campus and other facilities, students outpatient clinics, and libraries. Common effective environment includes some cultural facilities, cinemas, art galleries, museums, theatres. The above mentioned facilities which are involved in the participation in culture should be supplemented with an element crucial to many students' lives – places of religious worship. The churches were mostly ranked in the projects as "significant" spots (historic landmarks, beautiful, famous). Students seem to have special feelings for two of them: the church of Dominican Friars and St.Anna's Church. It is interesting to note that both churches located in the city centre are frequented by the students living in the dormitories in Nowa Huta, a suburb 10 km away. Strolls along the Old Town streets constitute an important element of experiencing the city due to the silence, calmness, the ambience of a Medieval town.

To some degree, certain elements of the globalised space have been included in the effective environment. Satisfaction of many consumer needs involves the use of various types of institutions belonging to the "globalised" space (e.g. the shops of international networks, large banks, supermarkets and hyper markets. Curiously, almost all comments on shopping in those places were made with the proviso that those facilities were frequented merely for convenience and not real satisfaction). It is very hard for them to qualify as a part of the "one's own individual city" as they are too large and often too tiring.

Meeting places make an important part of the effective environment. Here the dominant role is played by various clubs and pubs, especially those located close to the Main Square and in Kazimierz (considered to be the best and most interesting). The Main Square has been quoted for many reasons; as a place for randez vous, as the most important part of the city that gives it a special charm, as a place with "ambience", finally a backdrop for the city (or rather metropolitan) life. It is also called the heart of the city, one of the prettiest squares in Europe. It is a place with clout (many companies are doing their best to have their offices here), an important point for meetings. Students living in far away suburbs make arrangements to meet in the Main Square, even those who also live at a considerable distance.

Jewish Kazimierz has been posing real competition for the Main Square. That part of the city is much less commercialised, much less crowded. As such, it has much more local character, retaining the ambience of an old Jewish quarter. It is the turf of budding, still not very "professional" artists who give that place the air of spontaneity. [5] What enhances that place with an additional flavour is a unique blending of various social circles

---

[5] It is Kazimierz that will accommodate the second edition of Genius Loci festival. The festival will present unconventional artists who will stage various, at times controversial artistic events, discuss philosophical concepts, hold discussions and comment current situation.

(including colourful at times social misfits), variety of venues ranging from respectable establishments to conspicuous joints, mysticism and vividness of the reproduced Jewish culture (despite the accusations of some students who consider it a fabrication intended to please the tourists). That part of the consumption area, or to be more precise, a Rest and Recreation area belongs, at least in a certain sense, to a common effective habitat. Most students mentioned the Vistula river embankments (the place for walking, roller skating, jogging), Lasek Wolski (hilly, forested area in the suburbs), H.Jordan city park and Krakowski park.

Student Town has a very special role. Many students, not necessarily those who are living on the premises, consider it "their own" area, their turf. It is quite independent from Krakow, it is governed by its own laws, has its own ambience and the pace of life, its areas for entertainment, its "centre" and its own "peripheries", its commercial outlets (shops and services), and also "forbidden" places and "weirdoes" mentioned by the students. This is the place to meet friends, get things done, when necessary to find a place to stay overnight and a helpful hand, and surely to run into some party.

The students carve out from the "potential" urban habitat offered to all its inhabitants their unique, "effective" environment which meets their needs and expectations, and which comprises the elements of both the global and the local culture.

6. Various versions of "Krakow of my own". Social and economic determinants.

In each of my students comments, despite of a certain "uniformity" of students' effective habitat, I found a basically individual image of the city as seen by its dwellers. The differences can be found in various dimensions. The most conspicuous is a Krakauer versus non-Krakauer dimension. People falling into the former category have a much wider spectrum of their own Krakow including places from early childhood, grandparents' and aunts' apartments, favourite places for meeting school friends. The latter mostly cherish the vision of Krakow formed, on the basis of "tales about the city", guidebooks, common stereotypes, myths about the city that emerged during "festive" contacts with the city.

Another dimension worth mentioning is affluence. Among the authors of students' projects there are people who drive cars (both in the city and beyond), who can easily afford visits to restaurants, coffee shops, pubs, and other venues a few times a week, and who shop in the most ex-pensive outlets located in the main streets.

Finally, the most important feature determining the version of "Krakow of my own" are personality traits, different interests and needs. Consequently, students either seek their own "mystery places" or they go with the crowd. They either choose a visit to a movie theatre or Jewish music festival in Kazimierz because of its special ambience, or prefer to stay in the "prestigious" Main Square.

Needless to say, those individual traits bear on the manner of participation in cultural events and decide about the selection of entertainment. Some would prefer the "Aquapark" (the Waterworld) or "Atomic", an entertainment centre at a shopping mall where you can bowl, go to a disco, visit a coffee shop. Others would rather choose small pubs, or gyms, fitness clubs, places which have a special meaning (a street from the childhood days, a students' club where they met a girlfriend, a tenement-house, a spot in the park, etc.).

Other determinants include places, institutions, areas of individual interest, places of residence, financial standing, independence from public transportation system, a circle of acquaintances and friends.

6. "Favourite" versus "excluded" areas.

The area most frequently absent in "Krakow of my own" stories was Nowa Huta (a socialist era precinct built around steel works) viewed through recurrent stereotypes (a dirty, polluted district, a social and spatial margin of the city). The only less critical group of people were students living in the dormitories located in that part of the city. Yet, even that group would rather meet their friends in "Krakow", especially In the Main Square and its surrounding area. Those people would frequent a swimming pool in the centre of Krakow and would prefer roller skating on the Vistula embankment to Nowa Huta.

Another area of Krakow which has traditionally enjoyed the reputation of being "dangerous" is Kazimierz. Despite the fact that, as indicated above, that reputation has been radically changing (to many Kazimierz is an interesting and elite place) some people (particularly visitors) still tend to avoid Kazimierz, especially after dark.

High rise building estates or city suburbs were absent in "Krakow of mine" stories for different reasons. To quote one of the authors, " I have no reason to go there, no friends to meet". Another says, "No reason to go there, nothing that would interest me".

In turn the favourite spots could be divided into various categories. In the first place the greens: the Vistula embankments, the Blonia, Lasek Wolski,(green areas) the Zoo, city parks. Then historical landmarks which have their own ambience and belong to the so called Great Tradition. Another category are pubs and coffee shops. Finally, the "memory lane" spots, the soccer stadium where my grandfather took me to a match, the place of the first date, the route to my date's house, the backyard remembered from the childhood days.

Hence, a place may become someone's favourite for a variety of reasons. However, most often those places have some common features; beauty of the natural surroundings, historical significance, a special spot in memory, connection with the history of the family or my own life, hence the possibility to fulfil superior needs, psychological needs, social needs, self-fulfilment. An effective "students'" habitat has been described by the most important spheres of life of its participants: learning, socialising, participating in cultural events and satisfaction of basic needs. The type of institutions and places included in that category depends on the age profile, financial standing, time management, pace of life (classes, examination sessions, students festivals, days off) as well as on the group of similar needs and expectations related to the life style, recreation, and participation in cultural events. Also, the elements of "production" space (university facilities, libraries), "consumption" space (the campus, pubs), symbolic space (museums, art. galleries, "important" spots, old town streets), commercial space (adjacent shops).

In sum, when trying to reconstruct how the "city of mine" is produced we have to focus on the influence of the place of residence(city centre, students village, the outskirts of the city etc.) territorial origin, affluence, individual interests, and experience.

It might be also interesting to find out what kind of expectations and needs the residents of Krakow have verbalized as "the most important". New needs which come into play vary between people of different ages and different social backgrounds. Many new aspirations and ambitions were revealed in the course of opinion poll (Zybura, Percepcji 2002) testing the needs and expectations of Krakow residents, conducted in keeping with the modernizing of the city. Some needs can be considered postponed, since even though they were realized, they could not be satisfied under the command economy. The issues the residents want settled are the improvement of the quality of goods and services and a wider selection of offered merchandise so that people with certain lifestyle have no problems in following it (e.g. vegetarians, health-food buffs, etc.). Also special needs people (disabled, chronically ill, senior) want to be independent, having access to certain goods and services. Meeting their demand was greatly facilitated with the introduction of private shops, services, private transportation lines, etc. which complemented state-provided products and services. The needs which were voiced in a 2002 survey included construction or remodeling of sports facilities, recreation areas, greens and parks, improvement of neighborhoods, keeping the city clean, upgrading the city Master Plan, increasing the number of cultural facilities providing entertainment, giving the neighborhood a "metropolitan" character. (responses given by the youth). Adults ranked their needs differently: at the top of the list came "improvement of neighborhoods, cleanliness and order", then "increasing the number of retail outlets and services or improving their performance", and finally, in the third spot came "increasing the number of green areas, sports facilities and recreation areas". Within the group of students "cleanliness, law and order" came third after "sports facilities and recreation grounds" and "meeting places, discotheques and metropolitan cultural events". An important need indicated by both groups was also a protection of cultural cityscape to preserve its unique character. As mentioned above, the economic system of the city and its facilities, transformed in the result of privatization, reprivatization and restitution satisfy many of the needs, and create better opportunities for making people's aspirations come true. The most significant gain is the departure from centralized planning of investment projects under which decisions about the type and distribution of retail and service outlets were made at the government level, and which even imposed one scheme for all regions of the country, regardless of cultural differentiation and needs.

One of the most significant higher order needs is the desire to shape one's environment, both creating it directly as well as indirectly, by participating in management at the local level. This might be another meaning of the "city of mine" – the possibility to be a kind of "author" ("co- author") of the city.

References

Boehm, A. (1981) O budowie i synergii wnętrz urbanistycznych, PK, Kraków.
Gans,H. (1962) The Urban Villagers. Free Press, New York.
Huntington (1997) Zderzenie cywilizacji, Muza S.A., Warszawa.
Jałowiecki, B. (2000) Społeczna przestrzeń metropolii, Scholar, Warszawa.
Karwinska (1998) Wartości i potrzeby społeczne a przemiany środowiska miejskiego. Wyd. AE, Kraków.
Rybicki ,P. (1972) Społeczeństwo miejskie, Warszawa.
Zybura, P. (2002) O Percepcji i waloryzacji krajobrazu kulturowego, Master Thesis (mentor:A. Karwinska), Krakow.

Housing Inequality:
Changes of *First-Order* in Sofia, Bulgaria

Elena Vesselinov

The research in this chapter reports the empirical changes in the housing conditions among homeowners in Sofia, Bulgaria during the period of market transition, based on the analytical distinction between a *first-order* urban inequality and a *second-order* urban inequality. The central research question is whether the *first-order* housing inequality has increased during the market transition period as opposed to the socialist period. The changes are studied based on a representative survey data from 2000.

The general expectation has been that the *first-order* inequality, the stratification of housing conditions at individual level, increases during the period of transition to markets. While this expectation is not supported by the data, the findings show a nuanced and complicated setting of social change with three central tendencies. (1) Levels of housing inequality are rather low before 1989 and they continue to be low in 2000. (2) Housing inequality among homeowners, as captured by the size of unit, seems to have declined a little over the market transition decade, an effect that is robust across social categories. (3) The study of the period-based stratification shows that employees in the private sector of Sofia's economy are benefiting the most during the transition. The old nomenclatura and the intellectuals have had a privileged housing position during socialism and they have maintained it during market transition. From a sociological point of view the results show the steadfast reproduction of social advantages even during the most turbulent of times.

The purpose of this chapter is to analyze the changes in the housing conditions among homeowners in Sofia, Bulgaria during the period of market transition. The central research question is whether housing inequality has increased during the market transition period as opposed to the socialist period. This question translates also in specifying two types of social groups in the city: those, who have benefited the most in housing conditions and those, who have lost the most during the period of study.

All aspects of housing are a traditional subject of urban inquiry because housing change is a focal point in many urban transformations. The housing sphere has quickly become central for both national states and local authorities in Eastern Europe because in the new market society it generates substantial revenues. Thus in postsocialist changing Europe housing becomes an intense terrain of private and public interests, economic and political interests and is a subject of conflicting points of view in molding national and local policies.

The new conflicting social reality of postsocialist housing change has been most prominently interpreted by the theory of market transition. The theory has originated with the Nee's (1989) propositions and has been developed further by many scholars including Szelenyi, Stark, Kostello, Rona-Tas, Walder, Bian, Logan, Zhou, and others. The most engaging aspects of the market transition academic debates, which also make the theory particularly relevant to the current study, revolve around issues of stratification and inequality. Those debates lay the theoretical foundations of what I call the *first-order* urban inequality.

Being a student of urban sociology, I propose the analytical distinction between two stratification orders in the city, which captures the differences between social and spatial relationships: the *first-order* urban inequality, namely the stratification of people, individuals and groups; and the *second-order* urban inequality, the stratification of neighborhoods. The two orders of inequality are interrelated and they usually reinforce each other in the city. Although related, the distinctions between the two orders necessitate the investigation of each of them separately. Each order involves disparate types of agents and requires differential attention from policy makers. The *first-order* is more directly related to the institutional organization of the city because the social stratification of individuals and groups rests upon economic and political institutional positions within the city. At the same time, the *second-order* is more directly connected to the environmental and spatial urban outline, as well as to the overall history of the built environment. Understanding the *first-order* housing stratification will serve as a key into the changing spatial *second-order* of the city, which is a subject for another study.

The empirical study of the *first-order* inequality in this chapter is based closely on the established debates of the changing social stratification of postsocialist societies within the theory of market transition. The first step I take in the following pages is to analyze the new housing conditions in Sofia within the context of the changing sources of housing inequality from an institutional perspective (Brinton and Nee, 1998). The discussion shows that the withdrawal of the state from subsidizing housing at all levels should lead to an increase in housing inequality. The next section, Social Stratification during Market Transition, summarizes the market transition debates as they relate to housing inequality. Here as well, the analysis leads to an expectation that the *first-order* housing inequality should increase. The fourth section, Research Design, explains the data and the methods of comparison between the beginning and the end of market transition. If the beginning point of the transition is clear, November 1989, the end point here is taken to be the pronouncement of Bulgaria as a "functioning market economy" by the European Commission in October of 2002 (*Capital*, 2002). Section five of the chapter, Key Differentiation Factors, discusses the findings along the most important differentiating social characteristics: tenure, age, education, and income. The focus of section six is on the three social groups, central to the market transition period, the groups of the nomenclature, the intelligentsia and the employees in the private sector.

Institutional Housing Change in Sofia

During the period of socialism (1944-1989) the state subsidized housing in all of its different aspects from production of building materials, through construction and maintenance of housing, to housing finance. Thus the most dramatic changes in the housing system in the period after 1989 stem from the changing role of the state. The state no longer allocates housing subsidies nor is it responsible for construction and maintenance of housing, which is a typical process for many postsocialist countries (Sailer-Fliege, 1999). In the context of market transition the new sources of housing inequality are ultimately related to the withdrawal of the state from its previous heavy involvement in regulating all aspects of the housing system. The most important new generators of inequality are: the privatization of construction companies, the transfer of responsibility for social housing from the state to the municipalities, the changes in mortgage lending, and the new housing markets.

In this section I show that the new generators of inequality should lead to an increase in differentiation among the homeowners in Sofia at the end of the transition period. Sofiantsi have long established a housing tradition in homeownership, whereby 88.2 percent of housing units were privately owned in 1992 and 93.6 percent in 2001 in the Bulgarian capital city. The already existing high levels of private ownership in Bulgaria after the onset of market reforms facilitated the emergence of dualistic housing model in the country. In the dualistic model (Clapham, 1995; Kemeny, 1993), dominant in the Anglo-Saxon world and most Western European countries, private and public rented housing are distinct and the public sector is prevented from effectively competing with the owner-occupied sector.

The impact of market reforms on the housing system has been especially profound, given the previous large state subsidies. As a direct consequence of implementation of market instruments at the urging of IMF, since 1992 no further direct subsidies for housing have been included in the state budget (Vesselinov, 2000). Two important implications follow from this fact: (1), there are no longer state subsidies for municipal housing construction and (2), the state no longer subsidies all different aspects of housing construction such as building materials, etc. Therefore freeing the prices in Bulgaria in February 1991 resulted in an initial 10- to 15-fold jump in the price levels of building materials, equipment and labor (Clapham et al., 1996; Tsenkova, 1998). A further increase in prices followed a rise in fuel costs and continued to keep pace with high inflation. The liberalization of prices led to steep increase in house prices and was among the strongest factors of differentiation among homeowners, particularly related to the first time owners and those who had plans for upgrading their housing conditions.

The new prices also affected the construction of housing. The construction of housing decreased dramatically over this period of time, in Bulgaria as a whole as well as in most other postsocialist countries (Bodnar, 2001; Sykora, 1999; Tasan, 1999). The privatization of construction companies was the main factor responsible for the sharp decline. Privatization of former state-owned construction companies follows the logic of general rules of privatization in the country (Vesselinov, 2004). Monopolistic enterprises have been broken down into smaller autonomous units operating on market principles. The production of building materials in 1990, for example, was concentrated in 6 firms but in 1991 their number increased to 36 (Hoffman *at al.*, 1992). The decentralization of housing production, as an initial step in privatization, resulted in the subdivision of construction enterprises into 350 economically autonomous units (Clapham *et al.*, 1996).

The privatization of construction companies goes hand in hand with the transfer of housing responsibilities from the state to the local municipalities. Municipalities were responsible for allocation of housing, maintenance, and in many cases production. However, they had to negotiate five-year plans with the 'center' and had to comply to some degree with allocating housing according to need. Since there is no longer central planning, the corresponding responsibility of accommodating poorer families is no longer enforceable either. As Motev argues (Nacionalen Centar po Teritorialno Razvitie i Zhilishtna Politika, 1999), since 5-year plans are no longer enforceable, there are no more direct subsidies in the form of public housing investments, and none of the levels of government has the legal obligation to provide for newly emerging housing needs. Therefore the privatization of housing construction industry, together with the shift of responsibility to the municipal government in Sofia, create new sources of housing inequality by favoring the insiders of the housing industry during socialist times on the one hand, and by limiting the municipal resources for social housing on the other hand.

Housing finance constitutes a central institutional source of housing inequality. In the period before 1989 there was relatively equal access to housing loans, available through the only financial institution – the State Savings Bank (Vesselinov, 2004). In a second phase, a period of price liberalization, the interest rates skyrocketed and became prohibitively high for most housing consumers. In a third phase, after the fiscal crisis of 1996-1997 (Avramov, 2000; Miller, 1999), compensation measures were introduced. In the last phase, the latest policy change corresponds to the transformation of SSB to a commercial bank together with the introduction of mortgage-based securities. In 1999 alone there has been an increase (from 5 to about 10) in the percentage of housing trans- actions where housing credit was used (*Capital*, 2000); still, mortgage lending is far from servicing all social groups. It is quite obvious that the trend in housing finance policy has moved from rather equal access to housing loans to step-wise narrowing of the pool of people able to ac- cess credit.

All factors discussed in this section – the privatization of construction companies, the transfer of responsibility for social housing from the state to the municipalities, the changes in mortgage lending, and the new hou- sing markets – lead to the expectation of an increase in housing dif- ferentiation. Does the new social stratification follow the logic of an in- crease in inequality? In the next section I describe the main arguments related to the postsocialist social stratification as they are laid out by the market transition theory.

Social Stratification during Market Transition

The changing stratification order in postsocialist societies has been the central research project of market transition theory. Two scholars, Victor Nee and Ivan Szelenyi, have had the most influence in shaping the aca- demic debates. Nee attributes the roots of the market transition theory to Polanyi's concept of redistribution and nonmarket trade, whereby the so- cial mechanism of redistribution is the principle of *centrality* or a hier- archically organized system of decision-making. He contends that "in state socialist societies redistribution constitutes the integrative principle of the economy" (Nee, 1989), an argument that is widely accepted by transition scholars.

Nee formulates central theoretical propositions relative to the shift of po- wer and privilege from redistributors to direct producers in the newly for- ming market conditions (Nee, 1989, p. 663). He argues that the direct producers are favored because they are involved in a new set of market relations and their remunerations no longer depend on redistribution of resources but on the market exchange. This idea constitutes Nee's first theoretical thesis, which he terms as the *market power thesis*. Second, he argues, is the *market incentive thesis*, whereby direct producers have far greater incentives within market relations. And the third thesis, *market opportunity thesis*, captures the alternative avenues for socioeconomic mobility: the career prospects are no longer confined within the bu- reaucratic order, but the market conditions structure entrepreneurship as a viable alternative.

Both Szelenyi and Nee accept Polanyi's redistributive principle as central to the former socialist economies. Szelenyi (1983) however, dis- tinguishes the redistributive mechanism under state socialism from that of the welfare state in capitalism. Whereas the redistribution through the welfare state serves to elevate poverty, the redistribution within the socialist state only contributes to the advantages of the key players who are in charge of redistributing goods. Thus redistribution in socialism leads to a greater inequality than expected where the introduction of market mechanisms can only reduce inequality, once the powerless and disadvantaged enter free market transactions. In later publications however, Szelenyi and Kostello (1996) argue that there is in fact a U-curved pattern of inequality during market transitions: in the initial period immediately after the changes inequality declined, but as the reforms widened, inequality began to increase. The inequality in question here is income inequality, and it increases, according to the authors, mostly because a labor market is introduced. With my survey data I can only make comparisons between the period before 1989 and the year 2000, when the survey was conducted. Therefore, I cannot test the U-curved pattern, but I can make conclusions of whether or not inequality has increased.

Very helpful in Szelenyi and Kostello's synthesis of market transition debates are the three types of market penetration: the existence of local markets, socialist mixed economy and capitalist-oriented economy. Capitalist-oriented economies characterize the Eastern European societies after 1989, but not China: in all Eastern European countries privatization of public assets is a major state-governed process; in China the public sector is maintained. According to Szelenyi and Kostello this new phase changes the dynamics of market penetration qualitatively: one, inequality during this period is mostly generated by the market; two, nomenclatura wins, but part of the bureaucratic elite also loses, so the cadre advantages are mixed. Hanley (1995) explains this more specifically when he outlines two new classes: a new corporate bourgeoisie and a new petty bourgeoisie. The first comes mostly from the technocratic fraction of the old nomenclatura; the new petty bourgeoisie is more likely to come from the former middle and lower middle class.

The market transition debates so far have not been conclusive regarding the explanatory power of market transition theory. The empirical evidence are both *pro* and *contra* and suggest a more complex reality. In another influential paper Nee introduced the concept of "partial reform" (1991). Sustained cadre privileges in China he attributes to the partial character of reforms in China during early 1990s. But as the market reforms proceed, those privileges will be wiped out and the inequalities of state socialism will be overcome. Until now however, research continues to show that cadres are the main winners of market transition (Hankass, 1990; Staniszkis, 1991; Rona-Tas, 1994). The conflicting empirical evidence is due on the one hand, to the conceptual formulations of the market transition theory, and on the other, to the research designs, data quailty and variable definitions.

The theoretical conflict lies mostly in the fact that market transition theory emphasizes the emergent markets, which alter the stratification order (Nee, 1989, 1991, 1996). Other scholars point to the influential political power of groups and institutions. These explanations vary with emphasis on the role of local governments (Walder, 1995), the persistence of political power (Bian and Logan, 1996), the translation of political power into economic resources (Rona-Tas, 1994), the liberalization of political markets seen as important as the liberalization of economic markets (Parish and Michelson, 1996), the coevolution of politics and markets (Zhou, 2000), and the interplay between political interests and property (Stark and Bruszt, 1998).

Given the fluctuation of the stratification planes during the period of market transition I introduce the term *interim mode* of stratification. Three important social groups comprise the interim social structure – the old nomenclatura, the private entrepreneurs and the cultural bourgeoisie. The *interim mode* represents the limited social differentiation during market transition based on three central arguments advanced in the literature on market transition. In my study the three groups signify the link between the changing stratification order and housing advantages during market transition.

First, the widely-shared conclusion is that the state nomenclatura has benefited during socialism and continues to benefit now. The former nomenclatura is benefiting economically during the transition period, because it has the opportunity and the access to resources. If that is the case, have the members of the old nomenclatura (before 1989) been able to better their housing conditions during the period of study?

Secondly, Nee's proposition is that the new direct participants on the market benefit in housing. With my survey data I can identify all people employed in the private sector of Sofia's economy. If Nee's proposition is correct, then I expect that most people engaged in the private sector have improved their housing over the last decade.

And the third argument, to which I pay special attention, is the argument advanced by Eyal, Szelenyi and Townsley (1998). In their book the authors qualify the gaining power of the nomenclatura by arguing that in the socialist societies the power was grounded in the possession of political capital rather than economic wealth and in the postsocialist society the intelligentsia has undertaken the building of capitalism in its role as a "cultural bourgeoisie". The cultural bourgeoisie consists of the unlikely symbiosis between former dissident intellectuals and the Communist technico-managerial elite. The authors further point out that these are "two fractions of the intelligentsia". The strongest aspect in defining this group is that they belong to the "educated class," where the common feature seems to be the level of education achieved by the members of this group. In a later paper Szelenyi (2002) also points out the historical aspect in defining the group of the cultural bourgeoisie who, as the members of intelligentsia, have undertaken the project of building capitalism. They are part of a "modernizing elite," however, the logic of the argument, quite contradictory at times, seems to stress the importance of having high levels of education, rather than being a part of the governing elite.

There are counter arguments that point to the fact that intellectuals in Eastern Europe after an initial (about 2-3 years) dedicated engagement with the political and economic changes, later withdrew from positions of political power (Koleva, 1998). In the present work I am not interested in adjudicating between the arguments of what constitutes a governing elite, modernizing elite or intellectual elite. I am mostly interested to discover which urban groups have a housing advantage during market transition. Therefore, I use a broader concept for the "cultural bourgeoisie," stressing the advanced levels of education, namely people who hold Ph.D. and professional degrees (Tilkedzhiev, 1998).

In the next section I describe the research design for my empirical study of the *first-order* inequality, or the postsocialist housing stratification in Sofia, based on survey data.

Research Design
Data
In order to study the changes in housing differentiation I conducted a representative survey in Sofia in 2000. The instrument of the data collection, the survey questionnaire, is based on a questionnaire used by John R. Logan and Yanji Bian in Shanghai and Tianjin, China, in 1993. I modified the questions according to the need to compare two periods of time, before 1989 and after. Then I translated the core questions in Bulgarian, adapted them to the Bulgarian housing and cultural conditions, and introduced new questions related to my own inquiry. A pilot study was conducted before the actual administration of the survey to test the instrument. Unclear and confusing questions were further modified and corrected, based on interviewers' reports.

The sample selection was a two-stage stratified sample, based on electoral districts. In all 24 smaller municipalities in Sofia Greater Region there are 1,586 electoral districts. Based on the proportion of electoral districts in each small municipality 174 districts were selected. Within each district a simple random selection of respondents was applied to a complete sampling frame of all residents 18 years of age and older, based on the information from the EGN administration.[1] The survey was

---

[1] The EGN administration in Bulgaria assigns identification numbers (similar to the Social Security Numbers in the US) to every Bulgaria citizen since birth. It possesses the most updated information about the full count of the population in every city, town

conducted by a certified agency for survey research in Sofia, Bulgaria, the official agency affiliated with the Bulgarian Parliament (NCIOM). The response rate is 97.2 percent,[2] the number of respondents generated was 1,008, the final sample size is 980 people, aged 18 and older. The purpose of the survey was to interview people who are of mature age capable of making independent choices about their housing. The mean age is 48 (18.3 is the standard deviation; median - 46) and 55.8 percent of the respondents are female. According to the last Bulgarian Census, 2001, the female population is 52.6 percent, which is reflected very closely in the survey.

The age structure of my survey data is also representative of Sofia's population as recorded by the 2001 census. In the census the proportion of the age groups used in the survey is as follows: (1) ages 20-34 comprise 31.3 percent of the population of 20 years of age and older; (2) ages 35-44 comprise 16.5 percent; (3) ages 45-54 comprise 19.4 percent; (4) ages 55-64 comprise 13.4 percent; and (5) people 65 and older comprise 19.4 percent. The age structure of my survey data is as follows: (1) ages 18-34 comprise 30.0 percent of the survey respondents 18 years of age and older; (2) ages 35-44 comprise 18.2 percent; (3) ages 45-54 comprise 14.9 percent; (4) ages 55-64 comprise 12.9 percent; and (5) people 65 and older comprise 24.0 percent. The only noticeable difference is between the proportions of people age 65 and older who are slightly overrepresented in the survey data. The magnitude of the difference, however, cannot jeopardize in any way the generalizations made from the sample to the general population.

The correspondence between the level of education of the general population in Sofia and the educational levels in the survey is also very high. The 2001 census yields the following proportions: (1) people with less than a high school education amount to 13 percent of those 20 years and older; (2) people with a high school diploma are 52.9 percent; (3) people with Associate Degrees are 6.8 percent; and (4) people with Bachelor's degrees and higher are 27.3 percent. My survey respondents have the following proportionate group participation: (1) people with less than a high school education amount to 11.9 percent of those 18 years and older; (2) people with a high school diploma are 49.2 percent; (3) people with Associate Degrees are 6.0 percent; and (4) people with Bachelor's degrees and higher are 32.5 percent. Thus, there are no discrepancies between the sample and the general population which would require adjustment of the survey results.

---

or village in Bulgaria. The National Statistical Institute uses that information in its sampling frames for survey analysis.

[2] This response rate is standard for Bulgaria.

Variables

I use three dependent variables as aspects of housing inequality: an Index of Housing Quality (IHQ), square meters of the housing unit, and number of rooms. The IHQ is made of four dichotomous variables, which record the presence (or absence) of heating, wooden stove, bath, and telephone. Basic conditions such as running water and electricity were excluded because they are universally available in both times. After initial consideration having a cable connection was excluded also because it was thought that it artificially increased the differentiation among home-owners. It is important to note that IHQ is a measure of the interior quality of housing as opposed to exterior, such as type of building and structure, year built and others. The later characteristics are much more commonly used in housing sociology, whereas the interior characteristics are somewhat understudied. All three variables are measured for the period before 1989 and for the period after that.

The survey was conducted only at one point in time (June, 2000) but I included several retrospective questions about housing conditions and work history. I asked my respondents to tell me about the conditions they live in now and to tell me about the conditions they lived in before 1989. The question about housing conditions in the current residence im-mediately precedes the question about the housing conditions in the re-sidence before 1989. The wording of both questions is unambiguous and it records the presence or absence of ten aspects of housing quality, the size of unit and the number of rooms. Even though the retrospective questions maybe problematic, because they relate to people's memory, in my case the questions concern very basic and objective housing con-ditions. In addition, people in Sofia tend to live a long time in one apart-ment, which further limits the chances of inaccurate recollections.

The best aspect of using all three housing variables is that the change in housing does not necessarily mean a change of residence. It maybe a change of residence, but it also means a change in living conditions, an improvement or a deterioration of housing conditions. Maybe somebody built an extra floor to his or her house (would reflect in the number of rooms), or had a telephone installed. This way the change in housing captures the "in-place" housing adjustments. Mandic (2001) points out that the *in situ* changes are much more important where residential mobility is generally lower (the case in most postsocialist countries). Ba-sed on a survey data for Slovenia she shows that 26 percent of the inter-viewees engaged in in-place modifications at their last place of residence in 1994. Therefore the variation of housing changes is increased and the more subtle changes in that variation are included in the analysis of inequality.

Methods

The methods of study here are those of descriptive analysis. I use the measures of variation – variance, standard deviation, range, interquartile range, deciles – to assess the differences between the variables in the two periods of the study. I apply several statistical tests to assess whether or not the differences between groups are statistically significant: one-way analysis of variance (ANOVA), t-test, Wilcoxon Signed Rank Test, and Mann-Whitney Test. In addition, I also calculate Gini coefficients for size of unit. The Gini coefficient is based on the Lorenz curve, a cumulative frequency curve that compares the distribution of a specific variable with the uniform distribution that represents equality. This distribution is represented by a diagonal line, and the greater the deviation of the Lorenz curve from this line, the greater the inequality (Stiglitz, 1993). When applying this index to size of unit, the cumulative proportion of the population is generally shown on the X-axis, and the cumulative proportion of size of unit on the Y-axis. The greater the distance from the diagonal line, the greater the inequality. The Gini coefficient ranges from 0 to 1, 0 representing perfect equality and 1 representing perfect inequality.

In the following two sections I report the results from the analysis of the key differentiating social characteristics – tenure, age, education and income – and of the most important social groups, which constitute the temporary, transition-specific *interim mode* of stratification.

Key Differentiating Factors: Tenure, Age, Education, and Income

As demonstrated in Table 1, the average Sofia resident experienced improvement in the three dimensions of housing: housing quality, number of rooms and size of unit[3].

---

[3] All comparisons in my survey data, unless otherwise noted, are based on categorization of groups as recorded in 2000: I have selected the owners in 2000 and looked at their living conditions in 2000 and before 1989; I have selected the age groups based on the respondents' age in 2000 and looked at the conditions at present and before, *etc.*

Table 1: Descriptive Statistics By Tenure in 2000

Housing Characteristics	All N=870		Owners N=818		Renters N=52	
	Mean	Std. Deviation	Mean	Std. Deviation	Mean	Std. Deviation
IHQ, 2000	2.96	0.89	3.01	0.88	2.25	0.76
IHQ, before 1989	2.47	1.14	2.49	1.13	2.21	1.18
IHQ-change	0.49	1.02	0.52	1.00	0.04	1.22
Number of rooms, 2000	2.77	1.10	2.83	1.08	1.85	0.92
Number of rooms, before 1989	2.71	1.12	2.72	1.13	2.54	0.83
Number of rooms, change	0.06	0.84	0.11	0.79	-0.69	1.20
Size of unit, 2000	75.83	26.37	77.55	25.19	48.90	29.82
Size of unit, before 1989	72.79	25.72	73.04	25.87	68.75	23.00
Change in size of unit	3.05	21.53	4.50	19.14	-19.85	38.22

The average housing quality, measured by the Index of Housing Quality (IHQ), increased from 2.47 to 2.96, the average number of rooms increased from 2.71 to 2.77, and the average size of unit increased from 72.79 to 75.83. The period effects for IHQ and number of rooms are significant, measured by the Wilcoxon Signed Rank Test (Table 2)[4].

Table 2: Period Comparisons

GROUPS	IHQ		Number of rooms		Size of unit	
	Before 1989	2000	Before 1989	2000	Before 1989	2000
Direct Producer	2.60**	3.11**	2.75**	2.94**	72.37**	79.83**
Nomenclature	2.57**	3.18**	2.74	2.87	77.00	82.92
Intelligentsia	2.75**	3.27**	2.75	2.86	76.77	80.49
All owners	2.49**	3.01**	2.71**	2.77**	72.79**	75.83**

Note: For IHQ and Number of Rooms I use Wilcoxon Signed Rank Test, for Size of unit - t-test.
** $p<.01$
* $p<.05$

The comparison of the IHQ as recorded in 2000 with the IHQ before 1989 in the values for range, standard deviation and variance reveals that the variability among Sofiantsi decreased during the last decade. The decrease in variation is very small and it is due to the fact that people have overall improved their housing quality. Therefore there is

---

[4] The test was used because it requires a less stringent assumption about the variable distribution: the assumption is not that of normality but of a symmetric distribution (Sheskin, 1997).

less variation around the mean of IHQ in 2000 than there is around the mean in IHQ before 1989.

The look at the size of unit before 1989 and now also shows that the average size increased over the studied period of time. The survey data in this respect confirms the findings based on Census data for Sofia, Table 3. The analysis of variance reveals that the difference in size is also statistically significant. The standard deviation and the variance show that there is a slightly higher variation among the residents at the present moment than a decade ago. The group responsible for this small increase is the group of renters, featured on Table 1. Renters, unlike owners, seem to be disadvantaged during this time period, since the average unit size decreased from 68.75 sq. m. to 48.90 sq. m. The look at the standard deviations shows that there is a much wider variation experienced by renters in 2000 than before 1989. The same direction of change is recorded by the average number of rooms in 2000 and before 1989: 1.85 and 2.54 respectively.

Table 3: Housing Characteristics, Census 1992 and Census 2001

Housing characteristics	Bulgaria		Sofia	
	1992	2001	1992	2001
Population	8,487,317	7,932,984	1,190,126	1,173,988
Number of Buildings	2,007,707	2,123,271	86,794	96,744
Newly built (percent)	13.0	5.4	15.7	10.3
Total Number of Housing Units	3,395,633	3,686,269	473,996	515,958
Units by Number of Rooms (percent)				
One-room	11.8	11.7	19.4	17.7
Two-room	29.8	33.2	39.7	40.6
Three-room	31.0	31.9	32.7	32.1
Four-room	16.5	15.0	6.2	7.1
Five-room	4.2	4.9	1.0	1.5
Six and more	6.7	3.3	1.5	1.1
Tenure				
Private (percent)	93.2	97.0	88.2	93.6
Population and Housing Ratios				
N units per 1000 people	400	466	398	442
Average people per unit	2.5	2.1	2.5	2.3
Usable unit area (square meters)				
Total	215,745,106	233,943,830	29,407,283	33,541,630
Living area	140,538,169	150,530,803	17,825,977	20,453,361
Additional area	46,780,558	50,816,615	7,607,256	8,590,621
Kitchen area	28,426,379	32,596,412	3,974,050	4,497,648
Usable area per person	25.4	29.6	24.7	28.76
Additional area per person	16.6	19.05	15.0	17.53
Kitchen area per person	5.5	6.43	6.4	7.36
Average usable area per unit	63.5	63.5	62.0	65.01

Tenure

Compared to renters owners seem to benefit to a greater extent during the transition period in all three dimensions of housing: they have improved their quality more, live in larger residences as recorded by the average number of rooms and by the average size of unit. This finding is not unusual, because owners are far more interested in making im-provements to their property in general than renters. Certainly, both groups try to reach the optimum conditions between costs and benefits, but owners plan for a longer term when they buy a residence, while ren-ters are more likely to look for accommodation of their immediate needs. Renting is a temporary condition in Sofia and people who rent are mostly concerned with affordability than with the residence's other characteristics. The private rents in Sofia have increased sharply during the transition period, which is one explanation for the decrease in average size of unit and the average number of rooms. Another explanation is that the group of renters is not only very small but also is a very unstable category: about half of the respondents in this group are between the ages of 18-30 in 2000, and about a half lived in their parents' owned homes before 1989. This group is also characterized by lower levels of education – 88.5 percent have a high school diploma, while only 11.5 percent have a Bachelor's or higher degree. (Among all survey respondents 32.5 percent have a Bachelor's or higher degree.) In addition, 33 percent are students in 2000, which explains the fact that they live in smaller residences and in those of less quality. This also explains the fact that this group has a relatively lower educational attainment on average.

The calculation of the Gini coefficients for size of unit in 2000 and before 1989 confirms the differences between owners and renters, but we have to be very careful in how much weight we give to this story, given the unstable nature of the renters' category. Table 4 shows that the magnitude of the Gini coefficient for all homeowners in Sofia is almost the same in 2000 as it is before 1989. There is one rather unexpected finding, which shows that the inequality at least in one aspect of housing – size of unit – among Sofia residents has not changed during the last decade. When we look at owners and renters separately however, we notice that inequality in size among renters has increased, while the inequality in size among owners has declined. The latter can be explained by the fact that in the new social conditions the majority of Sofiantsi cannot afford to own a very large place: either because of the utility costs or because of the house prices. Most of the housing demand has been for two-room apartments, which means an increase in number of mid-size apartments. This is recorded by the Census data in Table 3, where we can see a small increase of the proportion of two-room apartments: from 39.7 percent in 1992 to 40.6 percent in 2001.

Table 4: Gini Coefficients

GROUPS	N	Size of unit	
		Before 1989	2000
Among Owners:			
Direct Producer	157	0.153	0.133
Not Direct Producer	661	0.180	0.164
Nomenclature	152	0.165	0.139
Not Nomenclature	666	0.176	0.161
Intelligentsia	133	0.152	0.137
Not Intelligentsia	685	0.178	0.161
Renters	52	0.190	0.338
Owners	818	0.175	0.158
First Quartile	188	0.171	0.150
Second Quartile	195	0.183	0.158
Third Quartile	189	0.160	0.142
Fourth Quartile	178	0.169	0.150
Age 65 and Older	196	0.174	0.159
Age 18-64	621	0.174	0.156
All Sofia Residents	870	0.175	0.172

Age

A second differentiating factor related to unequal housing conditions is age. I have divided my respondents into 5 age groups: 18-34, 35-44, 45-54, 55-64, and above 65. None of the age groups seems to have suffered a decline in their housing conditions, considering all three aspects of housing change. The first age group, 18-34, was chosen because of the period effects, namely those are the people most of whom (82 percent) lived with their parents before 1989. In 2000 66.4 percent of this group still lives in housing owned by their parents. The three cohort groups, ages 35 to 44, 45 to 54 and 55 to 64, experienced improvements to different extent in the three aspects of housing conditions. Housing quality (IHQ) improved most for the age cohorts 45 to 54, and 55 to 64, mean change 0.63. Since these groups are less likely to move than younger cohorts, they probably targeted their resources in improving the quality of houses they already live in. The age cohort, 45-54, seems to have benefited the most from the transition in the other two aspects of housing quality: in number of rooms and in size of unit. The age cohort ages 35 to 44 has the highest averages in IHQ and size of unit, for both periods, before 1989 and 2000. This is an interesting finding and it attests to the fact that this has probably been the most dynamic age group during the period of transition – from people who have come of active working age during this period to people who were well e-stablished in their careers, this cohort consists of people willing and able to take advantage of the new opportunities. Almost half of the people in this group (46.4 percent) have attained a Bachelor's or a higher degree, about a third (32 percent) have household incomes of 600 leva in a time when the average monthly household income for Sofia was 294 leva (National Statistical Institute, 2003), and 81.4 percent live in housing owned either by themselves or by their spouse.

Education
Education is a central human capital characteristic which structures differences among groups. In a society which is undergoing such fundamental changes as the Bulgarian society, affecting in profound ways the class stratification, education attains particular significance as a status symbol. Unlike other social characteristics, education bridges the two periods as an important status symbol and as such is a consistent measure of differentiation. As Weber points out, in times of large societal transformations, when the class structure is in flux, status groups come to signify the major divisions in society.

To ensure a more detailed approach, I have divided the homeowners in my sample into five educational categories: the first category consists of people with less than high school education; the second group includes people who have graduated from technical high schools in Sofia, which means that they have acquired very particular skills, with a wide range: electro-technicians, plumbers, people trained to work in ship-making and repairs, people trained in culinary arts, technicians to work in chemical industries, etc. The third educational category is the people who graduated from liberal arts high schools, the fourth category comprises of people who finished specialized high schools (*e.g.* language and math high schools), and people who have obtained an associate degree. I have combined these two categories, because specialized schools have demanding curricula, whereby the level of education corresponds to that of associate degree. And the last category consists of people with Bachelor's or higher degrees.

People with less than a high school education have the lowest levels of housing quality, number of rooms and size in both periods of time. In 2000 these groups had an average IHQ of 2.42, whereas the group of respondents with college degree or higher had an IHQ of 3.24 on average. The size of unit differences are even bigger: 66.3 sq. m. as opposed to 81.0 sq. m. on average respectively (in 2000). The most problematic aspect of this level of inequality is that two thirds of the group of people with less than high school (71 percent) consists of people ages 60 and above. Even though there was some improvement in housing conditions over time (IHQ change was 0.62 on average, and the size of unit increased with 3.0 sq. m. on average), this is one group, which will not be able to do much for their housing in the future.

Naturally, the differences are greatest between people with less than high school and people who have achieved higher education. People graduating from different types of high schools do not seem to differ very much, although the liberal arts graduates have a bit higher average IHQ in both periods, whereas people graduating from technical high schools have improved their unit sizes and number of rooms on average. What is interesting about the most educated people is that the variances on most characteristics are smaller than the variances for the other three educational groups. This means that people with higher education are most alike with less differentiation among them, especially given the higher number of observations in this group.

Income

It seems that in the group of homeowners the biggest differences surface when we look at the housing characteristics (measured by the number of rooms and the size of unit; in INQ the biggest differences are in education) for each quartile based on owners' income distribution (Table 5). The differences in housing between the first quartile and the last quartile are widest; given all other possible divisions I have investigated. People in the first quartile of the income distribution have an average IHQ score of 2.78 for 2000, while people in the fourth quartile have an average IHQ score of 3.32. Both groups also differ importantly in number of rooms and size of unit, shown on Table 6. In addition, it seems that the fourth income quartile has benefited the most between 1989 and 2000, even though this group had a high standard of housing before 1989 as well as in 2000; for them the number of rooms increased by 0.22 on average and the size of housing increased by 6.51 sq. m. on average. People who fall within the first income quartile have a lower starting position before 1989 *and* they have experienced a small decline in average number of rooms and the smallest increase in size of unit too, respectively −0.01, and 1.55.

Table 5: Descriptive Statistics for Owners, Quartiles of the Income Distribution*

Housing Characteristics	First Quartile N=188		Second Quartile N=195		Third Quartile N=189		Fourth Quartile N=178	
	Mean	Std. Deviation	Mean	Std. Deviation	Mean	Std. Deviation	Mean	Std. Deviation
IHQ, 2000	2.78	0.89	2.85	0.92	3.07	0.85	3.32	0.69
IHQ, before 1989	2.23	1.19	2.33	1.14	2.59	1.05	2.82	1.00
IHQ-change	0.55	1.00	0.52	1.05	0.49	0.89	0.50	0.99
Number of rooms, 2000	2.39	0.87	2.85	1.13	2.79	0.87	3.24	1.26
Number of rooms, before 1989	2.40	0.93	2.81	1.30	2.64	0.94	3.02	1.28
Number of rooms, change	-0.01	0.62	0.04	0.83	0.15	0.85	0.22	0.83
Size of unit, 2000	66.36	17.84	77.06	25.87	78.88	20.16	85.98	30.78
Size of unit, before 1989	64.81	20.14	73.98	27.70	73.76	21.19	79.87	31.71
Change in size of unit	1.55	14.20	3.08	17.63	5.12	19.47	6.11	20.40

* The total number of observations is different because of the listwise deletion.

Interestingly enough, people in the fourth quartile of the income distribution in 2000 live in the best housing conditions not only in 2000 but also before 1989. This finding shows that there is a consistency of the housing advantages: urbanites in the highest quartile of the income distribution do not seem to be a new group formed during the market transition period; on average, those people obviously managed to maintain *and* improve the most their housing conditions.

In the period 1989-1996 the differentiation of households by income is steadily increasing, shown by the Gini coefficient for each year: 1989 – 21.7%, 1990 – 22.8%, 1991 – 23.5%, 1992 – 33.1%, 1993 – 33.7%, 1994 – 36.6%, 1995 – 37.8%, 1996 – 39.0%. The gap between the richest 20% and the poorest 20% is increasing also and in 1996 the ratio is 5.8, higher than in many West European countries (Vesselinov, 2000). As shown above the differences in housing conditions between the first and fourth quartiles of the income distribution are the strongest I have found. Given the fact that the differentiation in income is increasing it will certainly lead to further differentiation in housing conditions as well.

The *interim mode* of stratification

If during socialism there was one stable stratification plane stemming from the Communist Party power-hold on society, during market transition this plane is in flux. The new stratification plane has been under formation for more than a decade now, and Tilkedziev (1998) argues that in fact there is no longer one social hierarchy but a range of multiple hierarchies. As a summary of these multiple hierarchies I introduce the term *interim mode* of stratification, which is specific to the period of market transition. As mentioned earlier, the *interim mode* consists of three social groups: direct producers, nomenclature, and cultural bourgeoisie.

The "Direct Producers"

Following Nee's proposition (Nee, 1989) I have defined the private sector employees, or using Nee's terminology the "direct producers," as people who identified their jobs as private sector jobs. More specifically, the selection of the respondents was based on the following question: "Question 51: Please read through the categories on Scheme 1 and choose the category, which best reflects your duties on your job now". The respondents I have selected as "direct producers" chose the following categories: private businessmen and trader (who works alone; who has one employee; who has 2-9 employees; who has 50 or more employees; who works in a family business) and employees in the private sector, who are not engaged in physical labor (job requirements involve routine office work; job requirements involve a minimum of decision-making; job requirements involve substantial level of decision-making; manager in charge of making decisions, *e.g.* department supervisor, university professor, school principal, etc.)

Direct producers seem to have somewhat of a market transition advantage compared with the rest of Sofiantsi. The advantage is mostly in the average number of rooms and size of unit in 2000. The statistical test of difference of means in Table 6 confirms this finding[5].

Table 6: Group comparisons, Means Significance Tests

CHARACTERISTICS	Direct Producer		Nomenclature		Intelligentsia	
	Yes	No	Yes	No	Yes	No
IHQ, 2000	3.11	2.98	3.18**	2.97**	3.27**	2.95**
IHQ, before 1989	2.60	2.46	2.57	2.47	2.75**	2.44**
IHQ-change	0.51	0.52	0.61	0.50	0.52	0.52
Number of rooms, 2000	2.94*	2.80*	2.87	2.82	2.86	2.82
Number of rooms, before 1989	2.75	2.71	2.74	2.72	2.75	2.71
Number of rooms, change	0.19	0.09	0.13	0.10	0.11	0.11
Size of unit, 2000	79.83*	77.00*	82.92**	76.32**	80.49*	76.97*
Size of unit, before 1989	72.38	73.20	77.00**	72.14**	76.77**	72.32**
Change in size of unit	7.45	3.80	5.92	4.18	3.72	4.66

Note: For IHQ and Number of rooms I use Mann-Whitney Test, for Size of unit - ANOVA.

** p<.01

* p<.05

---

[5] I have chosen Mann-Whitney U test because it does not require that the variables are normally distributed. It assumes that the population variances in both groups are the same. This assumption cannot be tested, but the variances of the two groups in my sample are very close. I have also performed ANOVA, which is a more conservative test of significance and the results are the same.

The largest difference seems to be related to the size of unit: the average direct producers' housing unit increased by 7.34 sq. m., while the average size for the rest of urban residents increased by 3.80 sq. m. The Wilcoxon Sign Test (confirmed by a paired-samples t-test) shows that the direct producers are the only group which has consistently improved its housing for all three characteristics over the market transition decade (Table 2).

What conclusion can we draw about the housing benefits of direct producers during market transition? It seems that this group has benefited consistently over the transition period, especially given the fact that they were not better off than the rest of homeowners before 1989. This finding supports Nee's proposition that the transition would bring benefits to those employed in the private sector.

The "Old Nomenclature"

The old nomenclatura is operationalized as the "politico-military, industrial and intellectual elite" (Harloe, 1996). In my survey data the old nomenclatura is selected in connection to two dimensions: 1. Position of authority (how many people the respondent supervises) and 2. Area of expertise (politics, industry, finance, culture and entertainment, military, religion).

As members of this group I have selected the respondents following in four categories: 1. A respondent, whose parent was a government employee with authority to make decisions, when the respondent was 16 years old. The question in the survey, which corresponds to this selection is: "Question 68: What type of job did your parent have when you were 16 years old? Please answer about the parent, who had a better paying job." I have also selected the respondents between the ages of 27 and 72, because these ages bracket the period from 1944 to 1989. 2. A respondent, whose parent was employed in the military, supervising at least 10 people, when she/he was 16 years old. 3. A respondent, who was a government employee with authority to make decisions before 1989. I selected the respondents over the age of 41, because these respondents were over the age of 30 before 1989. This is a more conservative approach in defining the nomenclatura in order to ensure that people were at higher ranked positions. 4. A respondent, older than 41, who was employed in the military, supervising at least 10 people, before 1989. The addition of the aspect of authority is again to ensure the clarity in defining this category as the political and military elite.

This group seems to fare a bit better than the group of direct producers in housing quality and size of unit. However there are no striking advantages for nomenclatura in either aspect of housing inequality in 2000 and before 1989. Interestingly enough, still, is the fact that the differences between its mean size and the rest of the population mean size are statistically significant (Table 6), both before and after the societal changes. The differences in IHQ for 2000 are also significant. The period effects for IHQ are significant as well (Table 2). It seems, as expected, that the nomenclatura have had continuous housing advantages before and during the period of market transition. The Gini coefficients are in alignment with the results for the direct producers and owners as a whole: the inequality has declined a little and the coefficients are somewhat smaller compared to the rest of Sofia residents.

The "Cultural Bourgeoisie"

The last group under consideration is the cultural bourgeoisie, or the group of intellectuals. As group members I selected the respondents who fell into two categories: 1. Respondents, who answered the question about their type of work now as being professionals (doctor, lawyer, artists, etc.), people engaged in the public or private sector in charge of making decisions as section managers, school principals, directors, professors, etc.. 2. Respondents, who themselves have a B.A. or a higher degree *and* whose parent has a B.A. or a higher degree. This is one way to correct for the fact that I cannot identify people with M.A. or Ph.D. degrees. Children tend to achieve at least the level of education as their parents, and many times they would surpass the level of their parents' education.

Like the other two groups, the intelligentsia also seems to have some advantages compared with the rest of Sofia residents. While direct producers on average have advantage in IHQ and room size, intellectuals like nomenclatura have a significant advantage in both IHQ and size, on average. In addition, compared to nomenclatura, the intelligentsia has an IHQ advantage before 1989 as well. Also, the intellectuals like the nomenclatura seem to have significantly improved only their IHQ during the last decade. The indicators of inequality, the Gini coefficients, show nothing surprising or very different from the stories above: inequality is less within the group than between the group and the rest of urbanites. As with the other two groups, this is not unusual, since each of these groups has been selected based on a couple of criteria. One expectation based on the literature review was that the housing conditions of intellectuals might differ depending upon position of authority. The tests show that being in a position of authority does not introduce additional differentiation among intellectuals. In fact, average room number and size of unit are higher for intellectuals not involved with supervising others. One explanation of this effect is that after 1989 many intellectuals work for non-governmental organizations, and while they do not supervise others they still receive higher salaries. Also, college professors may not have answered affirmatively the question "At your present job do you supervise people or not?" Overall, it seems that being an intellectual during the transition to markets on average does render some advantage in betterment of the housing conditions; but intellectuals, like the old no-menclature, seem to have maintained their privileged socialist housing position during the transition to markets.

Conclusion

In this chapter I studied the differences in homeownership conditions during the period of market transition. What conclusion can I draw about housing inequality during the period of market transition: has housing inequality increased? First, I would like to point out that there has not been a dramatic change in the urbanites' housing conditions. On the one hand, all three characteristics show an overall improvement in housing conditions for homeowners. On the other hand, Gini coefficients show rather low levels of inequality, also identical levels for 2000 and for the period before 1989. The same magnitude of the coefficients, however, cannot be interpreted as if there was no change at all. For one, the groups of owners and renters have quite different standing on aspects of housing change. In the very simplistic analytical duality of winners and losers it appears that at this first instance the owners are on the winning side of housing change, while renters are on the losing side; renters are on the losing side temporarily, since half of them are younger than 30 years old, which means that there is a strong possibility for them to improve their housing conditions with age.

Still, has housing inequality increased? The short answer is "No". On a-verage homeowners have benefited from the overall betterment of housing conditions in the Bulgarian capital, but that does not necessarily mean that all homeowners improved their living conditions equally. As can be expected people at the lower end of the income distribution not only have overall lower scores on the housing indicators, but they have experienced the least improvement. The second most disadvantaged group is the group of people with less than a high school diploma. This is the most problematic group because two-thirds of this group consists of people ages 60 and above with little chance to improve their housing in the future. And the group of renters is also among the disadvantaged groups, however, this is a group in transition and with chances to improve their status in the future.

The story that emerges here reveals three central tendencies: first and foremost, levels of housing inequality are rather low before 1989 and they continue to be low in 2000. One issue needs to be kept in mind: there is some ambiguity introduced by the way questions about conditions before 1989 were asked. Nevertheless, the census data for Sofia (Table 3) confirms the survey differences in size of unit. Therefore, this gives me enough confidence to take the results from the survey as representative both for the beginning and the end of the market transition period.

Secondly, housing inequality among homeowners, as captured by the size of unit, seems to have declined a little over the market transition decade, an effect that is again robust across all categories. This is an interesting finding and a contradictory one to my central research expectations. I interpret the results as supporting an argument of uniformity in housing conditions (Vesselinov, 2004). Uniformity in living conditions was inherited from the socialist period. Given the low rates of residential mobility in most former socialist countries in Europe (Ruopilla, 2002) and the conservative nature of the built environment of which housing is a part, it is not completely surprising to discover that there is a very little change in housing conditions. The slight decrease in inequality most likely is a function of two events: (i) the popularity and the increase of small (most often two-room) apartments; and (ii) the difficulty to reach and interview the newly rich. Still, as observed above, there are no unusually wide distinctions among homeowners along the most significant social axes of age, education, income, and occupation. Exceptions are two groups: people in the first quartile of the income distribution (as compared to the fourth quartile) and people with an education level of less than high school diploma (as compared with the people with Bachelor's degree or higher).

The study of the *interim mode* of stratification shows that employees in the private sector of Sofia's economy on average are benefiting the most from the transition. The old nomenclatura and the intellectuals have had a privileged housing position during socialism on average and they seem to have maintained it during market transition. In contrast to the three disadvantaged groups discussed above, the *interim mode* is indeed the mode of housing advantages. The three groups to some extent overlap: they consist of people with command over different types of societal resources, educational, political, economic or all three. The command over those resources makes the groups part of the social elite understood in a broad sense. From a sociological point of you, the results from my analysis show the consistent reproduction of social advantages even during the most turbulent of times.

Here lays one explanation of the discrepancy between my expectations and the findings in this research: the *first-order* housing inequality does not seem to have increased because those who were privileged in terms of housing conditions before the changes remain in a privileged position in 2000 as well. A second explanation has to do with the strength of the welfare state during socialism and the slow erosion of it during the period of market transition. The redistributive power of the state could not be extinguished overnight in all aspects of social life: unemployment benefits, health benefits, education, housing subsidies, etc. Which means that all of those safety nets combined did not allow the individual level of housing inequality to increase dramatically. We should not forget also that there was a socialist government elected in Bulgaria between 1994 and 1997, which slowed down the process of privatization and structural reforms, attempting to prevent the increase in unemployment. A transition period does mean a transition period, where the general direction of economic development has changed radically, but the implementation has gone through various gradual and often contradictory steps (for more details see Vesselinov, 2004).

More analyses are needed to further disentangle the advantages and disadvantages for each group. The market transition literature suggests, for example, that only certain segments of the old nomenclature gain during market transition. Which are these segments in Sofia? Still, at this stage, it is important that the conclusions based on the empirical analysis of data are considered in the larger context of change during market transition. As Briggs (2003) observes, "the embeddedness of households, neighborhoods and cities in larger regional and global networks requires a modicum of peripheral vision," it requires an understanding that there are indirect place effects which cannot be controlled for in statistical analysis. In section two, Institutional Housing Change in Sofia, I discuss several aspects of the housing system, which seem to be the new generators of inequality: the lack of state subsidies for housing, the privatization of construction companies, the transfer of responsibility for social housing from the state to the municipalities without a corresponding transfer of funds, the changes in mortgage lending, and the new housing markets. All of these new sources of housing inequality limit the wide access to housing, which existed during socialism, and particularly to homeownership, thus ultimately setting the stage for new differentiation among homeowners. The larger context of continuous political agenda in emphasizing economic growth and the further measures of economic liberalization work in the same direction. Even though the *first-order* housing inequality does not seem to have increased in Sofia during the market transition, this finding unfortunately cannot be extrapolated as a future trend. The urban scholars, the urban leaders, and housing policy makers should consider the multitude of empirical, contextual and regional aspects in setting up the new paths for housing transformations.

References:

Avramov, R. (2000) "The Role of a Currency Board in Financial Crises: The Case of Bulgaria." Discussion Papers. Bulgarian National Bank. http://www.bnb.org/

Bian, Y.; Logan, J. (1996) Market Transition and the Persistence of Power: The Changing Stratification System in Urban China. American Sociological Review 61, 739-58.

Bodnar, J. (2001) Fin de Millenaire Budapest: Metamorphoses of Urban Life. University of Minnesota Press.

Borocz, J.; Rona-Tas, A. (1995) Small Leap Forward: Emergence of New Economic Elites. Theory and Society. 24(5), 751-81.

Briggs, X. (2003) "Re-shaping the Geography of Opportunity: Place Effects in Global Perspective," Housing Studies, 18 (6), 915-936.

Brinton, M.; Nee, V. (1998) The New Institutionalism in Sociology. Russell Sage Foundation. New York.

Capital. (2000) "Zhilishtnite Stroiteli Shte Poluchat Tri Stotinki na Spestovno Chislo." Capital, June 30, 2000. http://www.capital.bg/

Capital. (2002) "Bruksel Ne Dade na Balgaria Kart Blansh za Chlenstvo." Capital, October, 2002. http://www.capital.bg/

Clapham, D.; Hegedus, J.; Kintrea, M.; Tosics, I. (eds.) (1996) Housing Privatization in Eastern Europe. Greenwood Press.

Clapham, D. (1995) Privatization and the East European Housing Model. Urban Studies, Vol. 32, No. 4, 679-694.

Eyal, G.; Szelenyi, I.; Townsley, E. (1998) Making Capitalism Without Capitalists. Verso.

Gerber, T.; Houst, M. (1998) More Shock than Therapy: Market Transition, Employment, and Income in Russia, 1991-1995. American Journal of Sociology, 104, 1-50.

Guthrie, D. (1997) Between Markets and Politics: Organizational Response to Reforms in China. American Journal of Sociology, 102, 1258-304.

Hanley, E. (1998) Capitalism from Below: The Emergence of a Propertied Middle Class in Post-Communist Eastern Europe. Dissertation Abstracts International, UMI, Ann Arbor, MI. Order No. DA9807612.

Hankass, E. (1990) East European Alternatives. Oxford: Clarendon Press.

Harloe, M. (1995) The People's Home?: Social Rented Housing in Europe & America. Blackwell Publishers.

Hoffman, M.; Koleva, M.; Ravicz, M.; Mikelson, M. (1992) The Bulgarian housing sector: An assessment. Bulgaria Paper No. 1C. Washington, DC: The Urban Institute.

Kemeny, J. (1995) From Public Housing to the Social Market: Rental Policy Strategies in Comparative Perspective. Routledge.

Mandic, S. (2001) "Residential Mobility vs. 'In-place' Adjustments in Slovenia: Viewpoint from a Society 'in Transition'". Housing Studies, v. 16, No. 1, 53-73.

Miller, J. (1999) "The Currency Board in Bulgaria: The First Two Years." Discussion Papers. Bulgarian National Bank. http://www.bnb.org/

Nacionalen Centar po Teritorialno Razvitie i Zhilishtna Politika – Konsultansko-Ekperimentalen Sektor. 15.04.1999. Predvarotelni Prouchvania na OGP – Sofia, Razdel "Obitavane i Zhilishten Fond", Etap "Analiz i Diagnoza". Rabotna Grupa s Arh. Stojcho Motev.

Nacionalen Statisticheski Institute. 1994. Zhilishten Fond. Sofia, 1994.

National Statistical Institute. 2003. Housing Fund. Sofia, 2003.

Nee, V. (1989) The Theory of Market Transition: From Redistribution to Markets in State Socialism. American Sociological Review 101, 908-49.

Nee, V. (1991) Social Inequalities in Reforming State Socialism: Between Redistribution and Markets in China. American-Sociological-Review. V. 56, No. 3, June, 267-282

Nee, V. (1996) The Emergence of a Market Society: Changing Mechanisms of Stratification in China. American-Journal-of-Sociology. V. 101, No. 4, Jan, 908-949.

Oi, J. (1992) Fiscal Reform and the Economic Foundation of Local State Corporatism in China. World Politics 45, 99-126.

Parish, W. and Michelson, (1996) Politics and Markets: Dual Transformations. American Journal of Sociology. V. 101, No. 4, Jan, 1042-1059.

Peng, Y. (1992) Wage differentiation in Rural and Urban Industrial China. American Sociological Review, 57,198-213.

Ravicz, R. M. (1992) The Bulgarian Banking System and the Housing Finance Market. The Urban Institute, Bulgaria Paper, U.I. Project 6127-95, April.

Rona-Tas, A. (1994) The First Shall Be Last? Entrepreneurship and Communist Cadres in the Transition from Socialism. American Journal of Sociology. 100 (1), July, 40-69.

Ruoppila, S. (2002) Residential Differentiation in Socialist Cities: A Comparative Study on Budapest, Prague, Tallinn and Warsaw. Paper presented at the XV Congress of Sociology, Brisbane, Australia, July 7-13, 2002.

Sailer-Fliege, U. (1999) "Characteristics of post-socialist urban transformation in East Central Europe," GeoJournal 49, 7-16.

Stark, D. (1996) Recombinant Property in East European Capitalism. American Journal of Sociology 101, 993-1027.

Stark, D.; Bruszt, L. (1998) Post-socialist Pathways. Transforming Politics and Property in East Central Europe. Cambridge University Press.

Stiglitz, J. (1993) Economics. MIT Press.

Sykora, L. (1999) "Changes in the Internal Spatial Structure of Post-Communist Prague," GeoJournal 49, 79–89.

Szelenyi, I. 1983 Urban social inequalities under state socialism. Oxford University Press, London.

Szelenyi, I. (1988) Socialist Entrepreneurs: Embourgeoisement in Rural Hungary. Madison, University of Wisconsin Press.

Szelenyi I.; Kostello,E. (1996) "The market transition debate: toward a synthesis?" American Journal of Sociology v.101, 1082-1096.

Szelenyi, I. (2002) An Outline of the Social History of Socialism or an Auto-Critique of an Auto-Critique. Research in Social Stratification and Mobility. 2002, 19, 41-67.

Tasan, T. (1999) Warsaw under transformation: new tendencies in the housing market. GeoJournal 49, 91–103.

Tilkedziev, N.; Koleva, S.; Zlatkov, C.; Kelian, M.; Kostova, D. (ed.) (1998) Social Stratification and Inequality. Sofia, 1998.

Vesselinov, E. (2004) "The Continuing Wind of Change in the Balkans: Sources of Housing Inequality in Bulgaria" Urban Studies Volume 41, Number 13, 2601-19.

Vesselinov, E.; Logan, J.R. "Mixed Success: Economic Stability and Urban Inequality in the New Sofia". In: Hamilton, F. E. I.; Dimitrovska-Andrews, K.; Pichler-Milanovich, N. (eds.) Transformation of Cities in Central and Eastern Europe: Towards Globalization. UNU/IAS Press. Forthcoming.

Vesselinov, E. (2000) "Housing Inequality in Sofia, Bulgaria." Paper presented at the European Network for Housing Research Conference Housing in the 21st Century: Fragmentation and Reorientation, 26-30 June, Gavle, Sweden.

Walder, A. (1995) Career Mobility and Communist Political Order. American Sociological Review 60, 309-28.

Xie, Y.; Hannum, E. (1996) Regional Variation in Earning Inequality in Reform-Era China: 1949-1994. American Journal of Sociology, 101, 950-92.

Zhou, X.; Moen, P.; Tuma, N. (1998) Educational Stratification in Urban China: 1949-1994. Sociology of Education 71, 199-222.

Zhou, X. (2000) Economic Transformation and Income Inequality in Urban China: Evidence from a Panel Study. American Journal of Sociology. V. 105,No. 4, January, 1135-74.

Tirana Urban Challenges

Enkeleida Tahiraj, Elidor Mehilli, Luan Deda

Long talks took place between the authors of this paper, as to which aspect of particular importance in contemporary Tirana our contribution would focus. The reason for joining forces in this paper is to offer more than one dimensional perspective of what Tirana is today seen from the eyes of three interdisciplinary scholars. This paper will not just emphasise data and statistics[1] nor rely heavily on theorising. Instead the three contributions as a critically-reflective approach highlight three different perspectives that most affected our cross-cutting observation also as residents of Tirana. Metropolis or megalopolis, cities as space of modernity, the 'new' urban city is thought to be used, yet, not understood mainly because the combination of the past [as old] and present [new] is producing a new type of so-called 'post-socialist' city whose trajectory of urbanism will very much produce a local outcome, unlike perhaps western models, and whose typology is still to be studied, understood and internationally compared. The paper does not aim a single conclusion. Instead it serves as a genuine attempt to highlight issues that deserve further scholarly attention.

Tirana -The capital dream of unconventional other cities?!

Enkeleida Tahiraj

This section will analyse two levels of Tirana urban transformations. First, the impacts of the transformations on the people, by challenging the fears of ruralisation and the death of the old city. Secondly, a critical view of the authorities-led transformations. Other city[2], post-socialist city, transitional city of extremes, modern and cosmopolitan, fancy colored buildings city– these are all terms that are commonly used to describe Tirana. Among the category of post-socialist cities these cities aim to distinguish between past and present, old and new (Sykora, 2001). Although these cities are changing based on capitalist principles, their spatial pattern is not yet capitalist [new], nor communist [old]. Tirana offers an example of a city in transition, thought to be changing on those

---

[1] For brief statistical data on Tirana, see note 1.
[2] On a previous publication of mine on urban space on Tirana and London, the editors found that Tirana does not belong to any of the well-know western typologies of cities, therefore they created a new group called 'other cities' where Tirana was put along other what I would prefer to call un-conventional cities.

principles, yet, what city type will emerge from this 'in-between process of transformation' is still to be seen.

The political system change, post 1991, was associated by economic downturn and enormous social problems. A governmental decree issuing freedom of movement was what today is thought by general opinion[3] to be the first mistake in the governmental handling of urban crisis in Albania, mainly in Tirana as the receiver of the highest number of the internal migratory movements. From 250,000 inhabitants in 1989, in just 15 years Tirana counted over a million people extending the borders of the greater city beyond existing infrastructure. It is estimated that by 2015 Tirana will be numbering 1,5 million people. The population growth of Tirana is one of the highest in the world, 5-7% per year (Aliaj et.al 2003), 2% as a result of natural growth and 3-5% from mechanical growth as a result of internal migration.

Photo 1: Tirana block of flats painted

Photo © E.Tahiraj

The rapid flux of people toward the capital could be interpreted as related to at least two factors. First, finally people could settle anywhere in the

---

[3] I tend to disagree with the 'naming and shaming' of this decree. It only opened up the already 'slow and hidden' process of in-country mobility, which as other studies show (Sjoberg, 1992; Alimehmeti 1986) was happening before the system change. Therefore, it only legitimised a phenomena which would have forced the government to pass the decree because of the mass movement pressures. That would have been the case of a 'decree because of a need' not as a future vision forsight.

country if they wanted to as opposed to the previous system where movement was regulated by the state - and in this case of intra-city move Tirana was a target as just another city. Secondly, they had the right and the choice to decide to live where they thought their life would be better – in this case only the capital was perceived to be able to offer that. Tirana is the case where both rural-urban and intra-urban move combine. As section three will show below, the infrastructure to welcome the flow that Vehbiu calls 'epic deplacements' was non-existent mainly in the peri-urban areas, and major governmental attention was needed. While the inner city was originally designed to accommodate only a small fragment of it's current population.

The 'capital dream' however, is not a recent phenomenon. Sjoberg (1992) argues that even during communism there was the tendency to settle in Tirane and since movements were strictly centrally regulated, the flow was slower. People approached the capital via the suburbs such as Vora and Kamez which make today the extended borders of greater Tirana.

Tirana's 'satellite-view-from above[4]' in simplistic terms would very much look like a unity of extending rings, with a degree of fluidity between each other. Chicago school of thought can serve as an explanatory model to understand some of Tirana transformations. The city is composed by the central business district (CBD) which is also the smaller central / centrifugal ring. This is the centre of culture (The Culture Palace, Opera House), the headquarters of the international organisations (sometimes even of those organisations whose work would be strictly rural) main Governmental ministries etc. Here, residential areas are also existing, and people living there are thought to be well off. It represents the area with the highest density, doubling during the day due to business commuters. The intra-city trend is observed also within the zones as an intra-ring fluidity with tendency towards the CBD[5]. The wider the rings (two and three) the less well off people are thought to be and the same applies to businesses. In between the borders of the city and the greater city are settled businesses that have extended. The less well off or comparatively poorer people, settled in the peri-urban areas in the total absence of infra-structure.

---

[4] If seen from above, the urban expantion of Tirana, starting from the centre would much look like floating rings with a high percentage of fluidity among the rings.
[5] Ring fluidity in Tirana seems to have been overcome by the extend the external borders have changed introducing the concept of greater Tirana.

Photo © E.Tahiraj

Faced with the highest levels of unemployment and total lack of go-vernmental ability to deal with 'change' people started to aim for self-so-lutions. In the space of a few years all green parks in Tirana became the grounds of metal kiosks. The only river-like space was invisible to the public, leading so to a decade of constant uglisation of the city, con-tributing this way to making Tirana today the noisest and most polluted city in Europe. Getting used to the 'bad' is worse than the bad itself ma-king Tirana a frustrated city.

The city as melting-pot of mini-cultures and professions was much dif-ferent to what it was before, and the newcomers to the eyes of old Tirana people were substantially different. They were the first to get named and shamed for destroying the 'good old city'. Derogatives such as *malok* - for northern people, or even more *chechen* were common bullying at-tacks of everyday conversations almost at the level of english gentle-men's conversation about the bad english weather. In a previous re-search of mine, one of the respondends identified *chechens* as the *ma-loks* that destroyed his city. To sceptics they were negatively different, they had taken the city's breath by settling down and building kiosks any-where they could as they had done in the villages they were coming from. They [the new comers] showed no respect for the city and had fi-nally and un-reversably ruralised the city. This mentality dominated, des-pite studies showing that it was not true that the new comers had van-dalised the city. Along the river Lana only 15.3% were illegal con-structions by north-east migrants, the rest were mainly from 'old' residents of Tirana (42%) and migrants from the south (38%)(CO-Plan, 2001). Media reports[6] indirectly yet constantly were feeding information on how Tirana used to be nicer, and anciently recognised by the travel writers. These regular daily historical reports aimed at educating Tirana people about its historical heritage, yet indirectly they generated the need of authentic Tiranas.[7]

Photo © E.Tahiraj

These un-grounded panic fears often expressed as ruralophobia or new-comers-phobia, fears of the death of the city (see note 3), or 'pacific in-vasion'(Vehbiu) surfaced perhaps forcefully the need of many Tiranas to distinguish their identity of having for generations belonged to the capital with all it embodies. 'You walked down the street, and didn't recognise anybody, anymore. The effect of this overdose of new faces was night-marish, especially when you became aware that you weren't recognised either'(Vehbiu). Automatically there were distinctions between 'we –the tiranas' and 'them – the outsiders', despite quite often among the 'we' there were even people who had settled in Tirana not more than a

---

[6] For an example of daily historical reporting on getting to know the city see Note 2.
[7] Tiranas – the term is equivalent to people who are from Tirana for many ge-nerations, as Londoners – for London residents. The only difference being that the former does distinguish between being a resident of Tirana and yet originally from another town, then automatically one is considered 'i ardhur' [new comer]. It is not clear how many years are considered to be the criteria for 'being recognised / up-graded as a Tiranas' to the mentality of people from the capital.

decade before 'outsiders' appeared. Unsure about what and how long does it take for a person to consider 'himself/herself' tiranas anyone post 1990 comprised the outsiders.

The second line which looks at the time period from 2000 is closely related policies attributed (rightly or wrongly) to what the international media called 'The regeneration pop star major' (BBC; Guardian, 2003). In most European cities, not only socialist ones, the nation-state has played an essential role in the hierarchical, bureaucratic form of regulation of the cities. The power shift from national to local authorities encountered today, makes the role of the governance actors essential in understanding the city as interactive arena. Le Gales (2001) referring to Weber early work, and later to Bagnasco and Negri (1994) emphasises the importance of the city as a group equipped with an apparatus and a leader that regulates the economy, an issue that has been acute in American cities in early twentieth century. In an attempt to revive the city, with the power shift to local authority, the new Major, Edi Rama, an artist by profession approached the city plan by what has been previously experimented in European cities, the cultural approach.

Photo © E.Tahiraj

Culture and art has been widely called upon to rescue European cities. It has become a key element in the city' image and representation (Le Gales, 2001). The symbolic dimension of this approach as an economic tool is the work to make cities attractive to tourists, consumers and business firms (Judd and Fainstein 1999 in Le Gales 2001), that in the long term will improve the living standards in the city. With this belief, Tirana main street residences of the CBD were painted in vivid colours.[8] It has been argued (Bianchini and Perkinson, 1993, ibid.,) that in European cities cultural policies also serve to recreate a sense of belonging, to assert an identity and to bring life back to public spaces. A typical application was the project 'Return to Identity' which aimed the renewal of cultural heritage of the facades of main Ministries within the CBD as they were when originally built by the Italian architects.[9]

Neither residents of Tirana nor visitors could miss this visual reform. Furthermore, it was sight-enjoyable, and, slowly building a nice feeling that different from few years ago, 'this city now can be done'. Policies extended into demolishing illegal buildings and regreening public spaces that, were overtaken by kiosks initially at the Rinia park (CBD) and along river Lana.

Although changes were welcomed, a survey carried out by NACSS[10] in 2002 shows that, out of 1500 Tirana residents interviewed, 54% were not happy with the living environment, considering it dirty/very dirty, while 72% of the respondents were not happy with the number of the green areas and parks close to where they live. For others, changes were felt only at the 'noisy budget of the municipality'.[11] There are yet no data to prove that the cultural approach did have an economic tangible output or vice-versa if there was any, was it only due to that approach, and whether it did improve the standard of life in the capital. There are more green areas in Tirana CBD now, and buildings are colourful there, yet, the 400 business activities destroyed as illegal along the river Lana must have generated at least the triple of that number of unemployed people, more panicking families were added to the economic aid and unemployment benefit lists.

---

[8] 'These are the things we are fighting for' is what reads one of the painted residential buildings in the main road close to Zogu i zi.

[9] Similar approaches where culture serves as a political, social, economic tool to get a particular outcome are known in France during the 1980s. Most typical approach as the one applied by the Major of Tirana, was tried by the new Italian Majors in 1980s.

[10] NACSS – National Albanian Centre for Social Studies, is an non-for-profit organisation working on general social services issues. This survey was requested by the Municipality of Tirana.

[11] This is what one of the respondents of a previous research of mine said: 'Changes in Tirana are mainly felt in the noisy budget of municipality rather than in direct impacts to citizens'

Photo © E.Tahiraj

Once the eye is pleased with the colourful facades, residents of inner
Tirana continue their ever-since cohabitation with kilograms of dust in the

summer and mud in the winter[12]. Furthermore, residents of Blloku continue to experience the added value – the unbearable noise of their own existence. First, because the ground floors of all buildings, which by the way seem to be increasingly frictioning and flirting with each other, are the host of coffee shops[13] and bars, with not much difference, they are places were loud music throughout the day is a MUST[14]. By personal experience, one would feel powerless, even more laughed at if dares to ask for the music to be lower to enable a civil conversation – meaning to enjoy a morning coffee without needing to shout. Secondly, because of the timely 24-hours demolition & construction industry[15] the level of noise during the night is reaching resident's ears, mixed on the way with night club's bumping music. And, again here the resident feels powerless. To add to the uncomfortable living of what in the first part of my paper was considered the favourite area of the well off, lately a new policy was introduced by the municipality to ease the life of people in that zone. A car-free zone for evening hours, has not only not helped the residents, but, on the contrary has rendered the lives of many even more difficult. All it helped was to increase the flux of teen-agers frequenting the bar-and-night club- life in that area. Based on the above observations, it would not be a surprise if in less than a decade because of these policies or due to lack of resident-friendly ones the process of gentrification will happen.

Tirana as a city and the capital, is a typical example of dynamic, fast, intense and unregulated transformation and urbanisation, typically classified as a post-socialist city. I argue that the city is not dissapearing, not being ruralised (as often feared). Tirana today represents a city that is dynamically being transformed, and so are its values. Quite often actors of transformations conflict with each other for agreable outcomes. A city

---

[12] Ardian Vehbiu in his critical essays of Tirana describes the city as 'smoking in the winter and dusting in the summer'.

[13] Coffee shops were thought to be so numerous, as the most expressed form of small business, as illustrated by the humorous saying: 'Half of Albanians serve coffee and the other half drinks coffee'. This saying perhaps had basis, especially at a time of high unemployment, immediately post 1991.

[14] The first case of resident action against the violation the right to reside in a non-noisy area, was done only a few days ago when a resident of Blloku sued the owners of the pub underneath his flat for damaging his hearing ability due to very high level of music sound that the resident had to put up everynight.

[15] Askold Krushelncy in 'The independent' quoted in Gazeta Shqiptare, October 26, 2004 called Albania: The country where streets have no names', an issue that came to surface when the EU asked for the Cencus data. As a matter of fact quite often addresses contain explanations such as 'The green building, opposite the former statue of De Rada, next to ex-Aulona Bar, close to Fefad bank, the entrance from the construction side, sixth floor extention [shtesa e pallatit]'.

is not a first come first served place of identity and people will move in and out. Instead it can be seen as a mosaic of social worlds and depending on the subject of study different pictures could be obtained, yet the citizen stands at the heart of its understanding. Whether surface beautification approach of attractive city will solve or just temporarily hide the real social problems is still to be researched. I tend to be a critical optimist.

Abolishing the Private / Claiming the Public

Elidor Mehilli

A commonly used slogan in Albania throughout the socialist experiment was "Let us change the reality of our villages by getting rid of our old habits." By "old habits"—notably, the Albanian term *mbeturinat* also refers to physical waste—one generally meant religious attachments, superstitions, individualism, and, inevitably, private property. The regime was, in fact, actively invested in the transformation of rural communities, and it wanted to achieve its collectivization goal through the extension of industries and the massive mobilization of "volunteers" who offered to work and live in these emerging communities. The guiding maxims of the time were "Let us love and learn the profession of the farmer," and "Let us transform our hills and mountains into fertile fields!" The desire to move towards cities was in turn deemed "a petty bourgeois attitude" but the government prided itself in the systematic planning of new towns and the expansion of residential areas in the capital, Tirana.[16]

The criteria that were established for the recognition of existing communities as cities included a requirement that over 85% of adult residents be employed by the state, that the inhabited area has more than 2000 residents, the density of the inhabited area within the yellow line be over 80 residents/ha, and, finally, that there is some consideration for the built tradition and the perspective of the residential area.[17] Forty-one new

---

[16]The English language literature that deals with issues of urban planning in Albania is fairly modest. For a general overview see Derek Hall's "New Towns in Europe's Rural Corner," Town and Country Planning 55, (1986):354-356, and his "Albania," in Planning in Eastern Europe, A. H. Dawson, ed., 35-67. New York: St. Martin's Press, 1987. On questions of urban development and rural transformations see Örjan Sjöberg. Rural change and development in Albania. Coulder, Colo.: Westview, 1992.

[17] Arkivi Shteteror (Central State Archive), Ministria e Ndertimit, Drejtoria e Ndertimeve Qytetare Fondi 499, Dosja 205, 20.2.1974. Recently opened archives in Tirana offer documents that better inform us on the processes of urban planning in socialist Albania. Particularly helpful are the sections under Ministria e Ndertimit and

towns and urban settlements were established in post-war Albania until 1989.[18] At the end of World War II, Albania had only had 26 towns for a total urban population of 238,000.[19]

Such tension between the urban and the rural constituted an important frontier in the Party's socialist struggle. It often marked the split between the public and private realms and the official rhetoric and the clandestine acts of resistance in the periphery. The repression of rural behavior, similarly to acts of prominent demarcations like the writing of party slogans on mountains and hills, was necessary for the exercise of control, which was to be pervasive in order to successfully manage the project of modernization. It initially sanctioned and then completely denied possibilities for privacy. Slogans and political portraits were abundant in cities too, where public space was transformed into a location of propaganda; a theatre of political performances and pompous manifestations of resolve; a blank page (as a consequence of the erasure of religion and old markets from the urban fabric of Albanian towns) for the writing of the official history and the production of the image of the new socialist city. The reason why post-socialist urban transition in Albania is so interesting and challenging has much to do with the legacy of extremism inherent in Albania's dictatorship. The regulation of space and its infusion with ideological meaning during that regime are crucial aspects of that history, I would argue, if we want to understand the Albania of today.

Thus, post-socialist urban developments largely reflect previous socialist policies and restrictions. Albania's rigid political system firmly rejected the concept of private ownership until the very last days of its existence.[20] It consistently maintained an image of resolve and self-

---

Keshilli i Ministrave. Arkivi Qendror Teknik (Central Technical Archive) in Tirana has master plans, projects and orginal documents.

[18] See Dean Rugg, "Communist Legacies in the Albanian Landscape," Geographical Review, Vol. 84 (1994), pp. 59-73. Works relevant to the subject, written in Albanian, include Koco Miho's Trajta te profilit urbanistik te qytetit te Tiranes. Tirane: 8 Nentori, 1987 and Petraq Kolevica's personal account as an architect working under the regime, Arkitektura dhe Diktatura, Tirane: Marin Barleti, 1997.

[19] Faja, Enver. "Urbanistika e qyteteve te reja te ndertuara pas clirimit dhe blloku i banimit," (Disertation), Katedra e Arkitektures Tirane, 1984, 5.

[20] On economic issues in Albania at this time and, particularly, the issue of self-reliance see Berit Becker, "Self-Reliance under Socialism. The Case of Albania," Journal of Peace Research, Vol. 19, No.4, (1982) 355-367. See also Michael Kaser, "Economic Continuities in Albania's Turbulent History," Europe-Asia Studies, Vol. 53, No.4, 2001, 627-637.

sufficiency.[21] Since public space—which included not only squares and workplaces but also smaller neighborhoods and venues for gathering and celebrations—was tightly connected to the official propaganda that it accommodated, the collapse of the public went also hand in hand with the collapse of the regime. Some public spaces were aggressively confronted because they had been so closely associated with the ideological apparatus they served and others because of the dramatic demographic shifts which increased the demand for housing in urban areas.

Post-socialist Tirana thus, initially suffered the denigration of public spaces and the monuments that marked them as symbols of an oppressive regime, and, eventually, the consequences of their unruly appropriation precisely because they had been symbols of that particular system. What had been, until the early 1990s, unattainable for ordinary individuals was now a valid option within the emerging framework of a capitalist society. I look at two kinds of urban appropriation distinguishing between commercial and residential needs although these were not always so clearly distinct on the ground. The example of *the Block*, for instance,—a formerly forbidden urban section of Tirana reserved for the ruling class and the highest members of the *nomenklatura* and now the most exclusive setting for both businesses and high-end residences—is a case in point.

The appropriation of public space for profit initially took the form of a widespread emergence of small merchants and their kiosks—small prefabricated containers used by petty businesses for the sale of newspapers, tobacco and alcohol—which, in turn, signaled a prevalent urge to claim more space and reinvent oneself within the emerging logic of individual economic initiative. Like the dissemination of propaganda under communism or the collective paranoia that resulted in the construction of hundreds of thousands of concrete bunkers across the Albanian landscape that would protect Albania from a foreign invasion, kiosks, too, became a collective endeavor in what was perceived as the spirit of a free market economy. Their establishment was, of course, unlegislated, and in certain areas of the city they developed into massive belts of mixed businesses, entertainment venues, casinos, illegal enterprises, and so on. Increased frustration with their public presence as well as the urban degradation that they promoted placed them on the agenda of politicians.

---

[21] Many of these issues, and more, were discussed in official publications such as Akademia e Shkencave e RPSSH, Konferenca kombetare per problemet e ndertimit socialist, Tirane: Shtypshkronja e Re, 1980. This is a comprehensive review of talks held at the national conference on problems related to socialist building in November 1979. Enver Hoxha was quoted more than 100 times and every other quotation came either from Marx, Lenin or Stalin.

Throughout the last few years, they have been mostly demolished in campaigns that have sparked controversy.

The second example involves the unlegislated appropriation of public space for residential purposes which has been an on-going process and effectively reflects the restrictions that housing policies had placed during socialism as well as the complete failure of post-socialist attempts to tackle the issue. Following the collapse of the regime, residents themselves instantly demanded more living space for their families and engaged in individual interventions in the architecture of their apartment blocks. From simple closures of balconies, to internal modifications of the standard living units and entirely new and illegal partial constructions or whole buildings attached to formerly existing blocks, these interventions have profoundly altered the urban fabric of Tirana and its image of itself. This may seem superfluous, at first, but the extent to which such interventions have happened in Tirana is unparalleled and paralyzing for many residential communities. It has introduced issues of living quality, air quality, absence of adequate light and basic sanitary and emergency concerns. Recently, there have been attempts to start demolishing some of these developments, particularly those which serve purely commercial purposes or are utilized as storage spaces or garages. Attempts are also being made to come up with a legal framework for legalizing "informal" residential interventions and constructions.

The two examples of public appropriation are related. Both have their roots in the legacy of a previous system. Both also mark Albania as a very different case from her neighbours where similar developments have not happened at this scale. Those who have been eager to advocate free market reforms and extensive privatization would still recognize positive elements within the developing urban fabric of the capital: numerous business centers, bourgeoning residential construction enterprises, increasingly tourist-friendly services, and so on. What makes Tirana a particularly vulnerable case, however, might be precisely what accounts for its charm, namely, the profound mixture of private and public spaces; the diversity of both luxurious developments and slums; high-end retail stores flanking petty illegal traders; exclusive private clubs where the visitor is often approached by seven-year-olds selling cigarettes. At first glance, it seems that Tirana's diversity is a sign of its transition as well as the infusion of western concepts and capital into Europe's poorest and previously most isolated country. What this mixture produces, however, is increasingly isolated routes of communication. Tirana manifests signs of passing from "a past dictatorship of ideas to a future dictatorship of markets," as Albanian writer Ardian Vehbiu has aptly noted, where individuals operate within strictly isolated realms avoiding external contact with those who do not belong there. The privatization of formerly state-sponsored services such as health care, entertainment, and leisure has contributed to the emergence of these segregated realms.

Under socialism, architects and planners followed strict official guidelines to "to build quickly, cheap and do it well." With the advent of the market economy and the emergence of land prices, their preoccupations with well-functioning residential areas have also changed. Besides the gross speculations with public space, the vast appropriation and the un-legislated interventions in buildings for commercial purposes, Tirana has seen the emergence of tall apartment buildings with offer the highest revenue for developers by minimizing living space as much as possible. The irony is that these families, who moved to cities after years of frus-tration under socialism, will soon find themselves living in apartments comparable to Soviet-type housing. The new apartment blocks are often situated within existing complexes, without any consideration to the urban context and leaving no open spaces for recreational purposes, green parks, or even emergency routes, since space is now an ex-pensive item. The desire to live as close as possible to the centre of Tirana has produced apartment buildings in the most unlikely locations throughout the city, disturbingly unconnected and dramatically altering the image of the capital. Those who cannot afford to do otherwise, live in overcrowded areas where services have significantly deteriorated. In a recent ORT/USAID survey, a majority of the respondents claimed that the largest effect of the demographic shift in post-socialist Albania was "the decline of urban culture." Three in four respondents thought illegal construction and kiosks had greatly damaged the environment.[22] What we notice in the case of Albania's urban development following the col-lapse of the socialist regime is that each group, from the single individual or family to the small entrepreneur or the larger business has used the resources available to them (and, often, appropriated them illegally) to integrate themselves into the new economic order. During this process the legacy of the past, such as allocation practices, have significantly shaped the process.

The social status in the previous system has had much to do with this process since many who could not move to urban areas in the previous system have now been able to do so, and those who instantly converted their social capital into tangible resources and wealth have managed to segregate themselves within the new system. Development in Albania

---

[22] See ORT/USAID Programi i Rrjeti i Demokracise ne Shqiperi, "Udha e Shqiperise drejt Demokracise," Mars, 1999, 249.

might well lead to a mixed result where illegal enterprises and smaller merchants, segregated private areas and the legacy of socialist housing together with newer trends all coexist in hybrid form.

The two edges for the legalization of informal settlements in Greater Tirana – a political, social and economic dilemma.

Luan Deda

The post-communist urban development story of Tirana starts in early 1990 when the social and political movement against the dictatorship resulted in a change of regime to pluralism and market economy. This section aims to provide briefly some information on the main steps the urban development have gone through in Tirana during the transition period and also focus on the legalization option for informal settlements, which is increasingly receiving more political importance but unfortunately with poor prospect for benefits from the residents.

The first outcome in terms of urban development from the political changes was the free movement of population within the country as well as abroad. The internal migration was not only an expression of elongated denied aspirations to move from rural to urban areas but also a way to escape from places no longer serviced with basic needs of health, education, infrastructure and governance[23].

Therefore, Tirana almost doubled its population during the period from 1989 to 2001, particularly in the peri-urban areas (see Table 1). Studies regarding urban land management during the mid 1990s have reported dramatic figures of population growth, up to 7% a year (PADCO, 1996) which has slowed down since than. Similarly, despite the fact that official administrative boundaries of the city have not changed, the urban area has almost "de facto" doubled, for the same period[24] (see map1). In this process of expansion, the city has integrated many other, recent and existing, urban areas surrounding it, and is now referred to as the Greater Tirana.

---

[23] With the political changes all specialists forcefully employed in remote areas left towards major urban centers leaving behind schools without teachers, health centers without doctors and governance without specialists.

[24] The recent Strategic Development Plan for Greater Tirana proposes the new borders of the factual urban area (Greater Tirana), which includes the Municipality of Tirana, and other surrounding (existing before 1990 or developed during transition) urban areas. It is important to mention though that officially, a considerable part of the newly urbanised area within GT is still considered as rural. Consequently, the statistical information from official sources refers separately to Tirana Municipality and other areas

Table 1: Population of Greater Tirana, 1989 and 2001

Area	1989	2001	Change 1989-2001	Annual Avg % Change 1989-2001
Municipality of Tirana	253,000	343,078	90,078	2.57%
Other Greater Tirana	82,000	148,015	66,015	5.04%
Total Greater Tirana	341,503	491,093	149,590	3.07%

Source: PADCO 2002. Strategic Plan for Greater Tirana

Map 1: Expansion of Tirana in the period 1990 to 2001

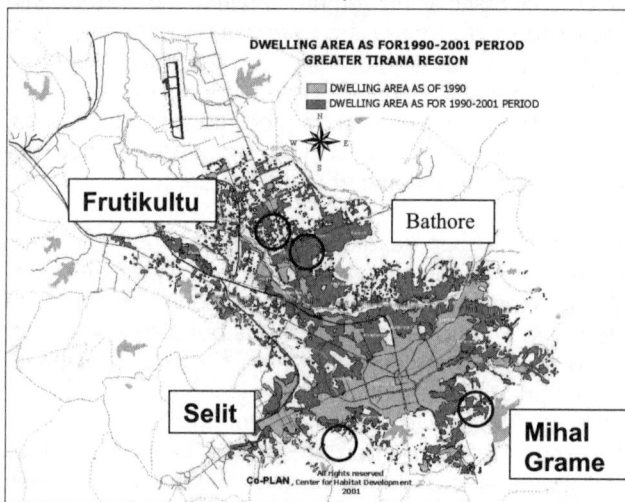

Source: Co-Plan & IHS, 2002.

Such rapid growth of population in circumstances of inexistent state structures was only made possible by the other phenomenon of public and private land occupation process. Almost the entire new development took place in surrounding agriculture land, which was either publicly or privately owned as agriculture land, informally converted to urban land[25]. In addition, the new housing stock is almost entirely not conforming the existing planning regulation, therefore illegal. Apart from the conformity with building regulation, the professional elite claims that these new developments are of poor construction standard and do not consider the urban space development standards. And yet if we consider the figure from the 2001 census that the number of constructions in Tirana has doubled

---

[25] Similar process occurred in the city center where people started to construct in any available public land either with or without building permissions, which however is not the focus of this article.

in the period after 1990s we can guess that approximately 80% of such constructions are informal and/or poor construction standard.

As a result of this process first the land restitution to former owners became even more difficult in the new urban reality while the chances to legalize the new urban dwellings become unacceptable.

The phenomenon to take actions against the "new form" of urbanization started from the government in 1995. The prime minister himself engaged police forces to evict the new comers and force them to return to their places of origin. The attempt failed to achieve its objectives due to resistance of residents.

The picture from a local newspaper illustrates the anger of new settlers against the government actions for eviction. This outcome served as an important lesson for the political and professional lobby to consider other alternatives for solving this problem.

In response to such situation, with the support of the World Bank, the government of Albania committed to start a program of rehabilitation for the informal settlements with final objective for legalization. This program used the experience from other countries with similar problems such as Rio De Janeiro in Brazil to embody a new approach on the legalization process. Therefore it involved communities in the decision making process and tried to integrate the selected pilot areas in the formal urban structure before coming to the formal act of legalization. Although the program was not entirely completed as initially designed it laid out the basic benchmarks for a normal legalization process. However, it is only the recent years that have brought the legalization discussion in the top political agenda. As shortly as was described, the history of urban development in Tirana during transition is in broad terms similar to many other urban processes of developing countries either in political or economic transition or in the structural adjustment process. There are similar outcomes from similar situations where public administration is both incapable and inexperienced to respond to growing demand for housing due to rapid and uncontrolled movement of population. At the same time there is lack of political will to focus on urban development agenda, insufficient capacity on the professional institutions and lack of proper legal system which add to the very complicated situation of urban development.

It is therefore difficult to draw sufficient conclusions out of complicated circumstances but taking advantage to other experiences there is a great deal of "room for maneuver" to take positive actions. To my point of view, the solution for normalizing the urban reality in Tirana but also Albania wide cannot be found if we do not meet the basic criteria of a just process. First it needs to be socially just and secondly economically just. In few words this would mean that first the whole society accepts and agrees that the informal settlers have illegally got what they legally deserve and secondly it is not fair to expect them to be charged the entire cost.

So far the contingent of informal settlers are only consider as significant potential for votes by politicians while as speculators from the rest of society. There is in general a discriminatory approach in any process that considers the needs of people living in informal settlements and there is little done by public administration to change this mentality at first place among their administration and then to the public.

Furthermore, the discussion becomes even more difficult when considering who is paying the bill. The later approach of Albanian Government in preparing the law for legalization is "who damages pay" as they require the settlers to pay the market value for the land and unfair compensation for former owners as they want to compensate the agriculture land value when the land was occupied adding inflation for that period. This is a typical result of a political process of harvesting votes out of immature decisions which will not only have no impact in solving the problem but will aggravate the social tensions as it has happen in other countries practicing the same approach.

It is unrealistic to think that the resident payment for land legalization alone will pay the bill for compensating the former owners and financing the legalization process. The reason being is that first the cost of legalization is much higher than the formal act of legalization as it includes the cost for provision of infrastructure and other public services as a precondition for integration with the "formal city". Secondly, people are already overstretched financially in these areas with house construction and investment for basic services and they are not willing and actually cannot afford to pay the price of the market value for the land. Thirdly, informal settlers themselves have developed the land with their investment and therefore it would be economically unfair to charge them the development fee during the development period.

For these reasons, the only realistic option for a fair legalization process socially and economically just is if we are able to come up with a plan of action with legal back up for the transformation of informal slums to an integrated part of the entire city by:

Changing our attitude starting from the public administration and professionals of urban development to the wide public in respect to informal urban settlers. The mater of the fact is that the cause for the urban chaos of today is not the people involved with it but the chain of social, political and economic developments during communism and later on the transition period. Therefore, everyone deserves a chance to build a decent life including those living in informal settlements.

Starting the legalization process by an overall property registration including land ownership or land possession in informal areas. It is of vital importance to know who is where and where is what. This process if accompanied by legal acts for recognizing land transactions of informal ownership will open up the land market and therefore the economic development as it revitalize the so called by De Soto "dead capital" which is the basis of income generation. Therefore, the formal act of land and house ownership should be the final step of an entire process of transforming the peripheral slums to habitable areas with basic infrastructure and public services. Such transformation can only be made if there are incentives for people to do so and if there are incentives for private developers to operate in such areas.

Opening public space for future infrastructure and preserving other public space for future schools, hospitals and other public services buildings.

Investing in basic infrastructure from a joint financing scheme of government, residents and donor agencies initially.

Provide favorable conditions for private developers to invest legally in these areas for housing or services industry. These investments will be done according to planning standards and could be as prerequisite and/ or incentive for the land occupiers to legalize.

Complete the legalization process gradually in different parts of the city where communities area ready for such process.

The above steps are conclusions from working with people in such areas who would rather prefer to have a decent amount of water, electricity, education and health care instead of an ownership piece of paper. These conclusions also derive from the lessons of other similar processes around the world and therefore are not new and not part of human imagination. There is no point for Albanian government to waste more time and energy as well as taxpayers resources for practicing something that have proven not to work. We know very well today that we shouldn't have sent the police to evict the residents of Bathore settlement in 1995 and therefore we should understand that we cannot afford to make the same mistake today that can be judged the same in the future.

Notes:

Note 1- Tirana city covers 41.8 km^2 which represents 3.4% of Tirana district (2001 Cencus), in 2001 it had 341,453 inhabitants, 11.1% of the country's population and 26,4% of the population living in urban areas, and has only 6.9% of total buildings available for housing. The housing ownership is extremely high by European standards as 87.9% of houses are owned (bought and paid then and there, no mortgage). Building pre 1945 are greater than the national average 13%, while those post 1996 are double the national average 30%. Almost 51% of the buildings were constructed between 1991 and 2001. Tirana's population is older than that of the country as a direct impact of high emigration, and the elderly represent 9.1% of Tirana's population. The elderly live mostly in the centre than in suburbs. Density-wise Tirana is like any other European city with 8,161 inhabitants per km^2, but the average density of Tirana city is 80 times greater than that of the country. Tirana is the only city in Albania that has expanded between 1989 and 2001. The total population of the country has decreased by 113,142 but the population of Tirana has increased by 43.4%. Tirana city has doubled it's population as a result of internal migration and natural increase. The number of the households in Tirana is 12,3% of the total of the country, the number of the unoccupied dwellings is 12.6%. The post-graduate educational level of inhabitants in Tirana city is 3.2 times higher than the national average but this is explained as all university and post-university educated tend to remain in Tirane as it offers more employment opportunities, although ironically the employment level of Tirana is the same as the national average, 34.9% of the entire population.

Note 2- Nothing has remained from the old heart of the capital. Noises, small shops set by each other are now an old shadow. The old Tirana Bazar exists now only in photos of that time. In 1959, that was destroyed so that the culture palace could be built whose first ever brick was placed by Hrushov. The Bazar was a source of employment not only for Tirana people but also for the new comers at the beginning of XX century, mainly internal migrants who had no other means of living, and roads were decided by the nature of the services, like butchers, coffee makers etc. At the beginning of the XX century Tirana had 12 thousand inhabitants, while the old Bazar contained 700 shops, and the most famous elite gathering coffee place was called Kursal. It was built in 1920 and named coffee shop of the intellectuals but was demolished by the end of 70-ies (an example of daily reporting in newspapers to Tirana's history)

Note 3 - Tirana has turned into an ugly, disgusting, dirty, crazy, noisy full of newcomers (te ardhur) city. It aches to see it like this... Where are all the Tirana people gone? This is not my city anymore, all public spaces are overtaken by ugly illegal coffee making and kebap smelling kiosks, the river is lost and buildings are appearing every day like mushrooms, everywhere. I do not understand this mentality, 'if it's not private, take it...the state will regret having forgotten about this city, about the capital, but it will be too late. This city is gone! No-one knows what on earth is happening here...(Tirana authentic resident, 1999)

References:
Aliaj, B.; Lulo, K.; Myftiu, G. (2003) Tirana – The Challenge of Urban Development. Cetis. Tirane.
Are, S. (October 22, 2003) Regeneration Man. Guardian Unlimited www.guardian.co.uk/elsewhere/journalist/story/0,7792,1068527,00.html accessed on October 25th, 2003
Co-Plan (2001) 'Social economic questionaire along Lana river area'. Co-Plan. Tirane.
Co-PLAN (1999). 'Social Economic Survey for Urban Bathore'. Study for the appraisal of the project "Roads to Stronger Civil Society" in Bathore area. Tirana, April 1999.
Co-PLAN (2000) 'Household Survey for Mihal Grameno, Selita, Bathore, and Frutikultura'. Study for the Social Assessment of the Urban Land Management Project of the Ministry of Public Works and Tourism. September 2000.
Co-PLAN (2002) 'City Made by People II'. New roles of Community in new urban reality. Tirana 2002.
Co-PLAN & IHS (2002) 'Strategic Urban Development Plan for Kamza Municipality'. Report for the program of Strengthening Local Authority and Community-based Initiatives in Tirana. Prepared Co-PLAN, Centre for habitat Development Tirana and IHS (Institute of Housing and Urban Development Studies Rotterdam), April 2002.
De Soto (2000) The Mystery of Capital. Why Capitalism triumphs in the West and fails everywhere else. Basic Books, NW, 2000.
Fiori, J; Riley, E; Ramirez, R (2000) 'Urban Poverty Alleviation through Environmental Upgrading in Rio De Janeiro': Favela Bairro Program. Development Planning Unit Research Report, March 2000.
Gordon D; Townsend, P (Eds) (2000) Breadline Europe: the measurement of poverty : The Policy Press, 2000 Bristol, UK.
INSTAT & World Bank, (2003). 'Albania: Poverty During Growth'. A document prepared by the World Bank and the Institute of Statistics (INSTAT) as input to the 2003 Albanian Poverty Assessment and the National Strategy for Socio-Economic Development. Draft.
INSTAT (2002) The population of Albania in 2001 – Main Results of the Population and Housing Cencus. Repoba.Tirane.
INSTAT (2002) The Statistical Year Book 1991-1999. Instat. Tirane.

INSTAT (2001) Population of Albania in 2001. Main Results from the registration of Population and Housing. Institute of Statistics, Albania.

Kilbridge, M.D.; O'Block, R.P.; Teplitz, P.V. (1970) Urban Annalysis. Harvard University. Boston.

Le Gales P. (2001) 'Social and Political Actors Within European Cities and the Making of Urban Modes of Governance' (Lecture given at EUREX 2001).

NACSS (2002) 'Evaluation of Tirana Municipality work according to people's opinions'. Tirane.

PADCO (2002) 'Strategic Plan for Greater Tirana. Volume 1: Main Report (Draft)'. Urban Land Management Project. PADCO, Inc. Value Add Management Services, Mix Tecnic. February 2002.

PADCO (1996). 'Tirana Structure Plan'. Report for the Urban Land Management Program of the Ministry of Construction and Transport. Tirana 1996.

Sjoberg, O. (1992) 'Urbanisation and the Zero Growth Hypothesis: Diverted Migration in Albania' in Geografiska Annaler, Series B, Human Geography, Vol.74, No.1 (1992), 3-19

Sykora, L. (2001) 'Post-communist city' http://www.natur.cuni.cz.~sykora/text/postcomm.htm accessed July 2004.

Timms, D.W.G. (1975) The Urban Mosaic – Towards a Theory of Residential Differentiation. Cambridge University Press. Cambridge.

Tsenkova, S. (2004) 'Urban Sustainability in CEE' paper presented at ENHR 2004 conference, Cambridge, UK.

Vehbiu, A. (2003) Kulla e Sahatit.K&B. Tirane.

Vehbiu A. other selected undated online essays.

Changing of the Slovene Urban System: Specific Socio-Spatial Trends and Antiurban Public Values / Attitudes

Marjan Hočevar, Matjaž Uršič, Drago Kos, Franc Trček

In the paper we give an overview[1] of the specifics of the Slovene urbanization process, in comparison with the experiences of the other republics of former Yugoslavia, other socialist urbanization in central and eastern Europe and in Europe in general. Through a social analysis we attempt to make a cause-effect connection between Slovene socio-spatial dynamics in the longer period and the value orientation of the spatial practices of the population.

In Slovenia in all of its "history of modernization" none of the more pronounced classical functional and cultural characteristics of urban centralism developed. The national capital Ljubljana is the main administrative, political, economic and cultural center of the country, but with rather weak expressed properties of the materialization of urban culture and urbanism as a way of life. During the Austro-Hungarian period, when Slovenia was a distinctly agricultural land, the town centers and their development dynamics were governed by the German population, and in the western part also the Italian. During this period, Ljubljana had a transit character, lying between Vienna and Trieste.[2] Due to its transit economy and peripheral political role under the wing of the Austro-Hungarian Empire, Slovenia lagged behind in the forming of conditions which would enable faster industrial growth and more pronounced urbanization. These circumstances had a major influence on the socio-spatial organization and the spatial structure of the Slovene territory up to the Second World War.

---

[1] We should emphasize that in this paper we cannot embrace all of the complexity of the development of the urbanization of Slovenia, but are giving an simplified overview and some analysis of various urbanization specifics. Slovene sociology has an otherwise strong tradition of socio-spatial research, the foundations of which were laid by Zdravko Mlinar. With his colleagues he performed empirical research of the urbanization of several Slovene towns (see Mlinar 1972, 1988, 1990; Mlinar, Teune 1972, Kos et al. (2002), Hočevar, M. (2002)). He himself published more than five hundred scientific treatises on the socio-spatial aspects of Slovene development. Urban sociology research in Slovenia is concentrated at the Center for Spatial Sociology at the Faculty of Social Sciences of the University of Ljubljana.

[2] For a comparison and an understanding of the present roles of (and relations between) Ljubljana and Trieste, it is exceptionally important to know that half of the population of Trieste is the result of exogenic (fluctuating) immigration, while Ljubljana is characterized by constant growth of the urban population from the nearby vicinity.

Socialist modernization after the Second World War brought relatively rapid industrialization, but with few of the characteristic classic consequences of urbanization. The Slovene urban system never achieved a level of high urbanization; in fact, a short period of growth of the concentration of people and capital in urbanized areas was followed by a slowing of the growth of the urban population. This is a case of the specifics of a lack of alignment between a relatively high level of economic development and a low level of urbanization. That is to say, Slovenia was the most developed of the Yugoslav republics and the most economically developed area in socialist central and eastern Europe. The standard of living during this period was the highest among all of the Yugoslav republics and also among all of the socialist countries of Europe.

The current Slovene spatial system is characterized by pronounced under-urbanization, which can be at least partly explained through the phenomenon of the "urban gap". In Slovenia today, 63% of housing is in free-standing buildings. Around 1.3 million people live in them, of whom around 200 000 in towns and 550 000 in their vicinities, while as late as 1960 the proportion of such housing was only 27%. These circumstances strongly influence the spatial practice and socio-spatial value orientations of the population, which are expressly antiurban. The values of the population are expressly antiurban, oriented towards living in isolated or very small settlements in free-standing family houses. Public opinion research shows that this antiurban value orientation is growing in Slovenia, influenced by increased physical and telecommunications access.[3]

An Overview of the developmental dynamics and specifics of Slovene Urbanization

While industrialization was crucial to the intensive urbanization in other European countries and the USA at the end of the 19th century, in Slovenia, at that time a part of the Austro-Hungarian Empire, it proceeded much less intensively. The slow growth of industry was also reflected in the slow growth of the urban population. The level of urbanization in Slovenia in 1869 was only 13.6 percent, in 1880 about 15 percent, in 1890 about 15.6 percent and at the turn of the century in 1900 only 17.5 percent (Klemenčič, 2001: 10).

The slow growth of the urban population was also influenced by the poor "ur-ban foundation" (small number of towns[4] and low level of urbanization

---

[3] On sociological analyses of growing IT in Slovenia after 90's see Trček (2003).
[4] Only 31 towns were recognized by the authorities during the period between the wars (Lah, 1999: 14).

before the beginning of industrialization), which obstructed better harmonization of the processes of industrialization with those of urbanization, as was characteristic of other economically developed countries in Europe. The smaller number of towns and small urban population also meant a lower critical mass of entrepreneurs, tradesmen and other economic sectors which could cooperate in the accumulation of capital and the preparations for industrial urbanization. Even during the first wave of industrialism after the First World War, major growth of the urban population never occurred in Slovenia due to delays in the preparation of the conditions for industrialization.[5]

Novak (1991) explains that Slovenia in the period up to the Second World War formed its own important industrial capacities, but only as one of the typical early latecomers to industrialization. Owing to its peripheral role within the Habsburg Empire, Slovenia was late in forming the conditions which would have allowed faster economic growth and urbanization. The process of the gradual forming of the conditions for the first wave of industrialization, which occurred during the period between the two world wars, began relatively late with the land reforms of 1848, when Slovene farmers gained the right to hold title to their own land. The acquiring of the partial self-sufficiency of the inhabitants and the acquisition of the land enabled the independent provision of the basic living conditions. This was also supposed to gradually make possible the concentration of capital and investment in various branches of industry. However, the processes of formation of the preconditions for industrialization were not arrived at through the accumulation of Slovene capital, but through the investment of foreign capital, which was invested only in particularly profitable branches. This led to the development of individual areas, or so-called "enclave industrialization" (Novak, 1991: 132), while Slovenia as a whole lagged behind.

The slow development of the national economy had a significant effect on the processes of industrialization and the spatial development of Slovenia. The low level of urbanization and the relatively slow development of industry in comparison with other European countries partially affected the need to form specific development policies in the period after the Second World War. Normative socialist policies were intended to stimulate the development of industry and accelerate the spatial development of the country.

---

[5] The level of the urban population in 1931 was 22.7 percent.

Socialist countries partially succeeded in stimulating the growth of the urban population through the application of specific spatial policies, but in the majority of cases it never reached the level of western countries. This is also shown in a comparison of the differences between the levels of urbanization among various socialist countries and countries with market economies, where a noticeable gap in urbanization appeared between the western capitalist societies and the post-socialist societies (Graph 1).

Graph 1: Comparison of the levels of the urban population in various western European countries and in eastern European countries (data from 1990-2000)

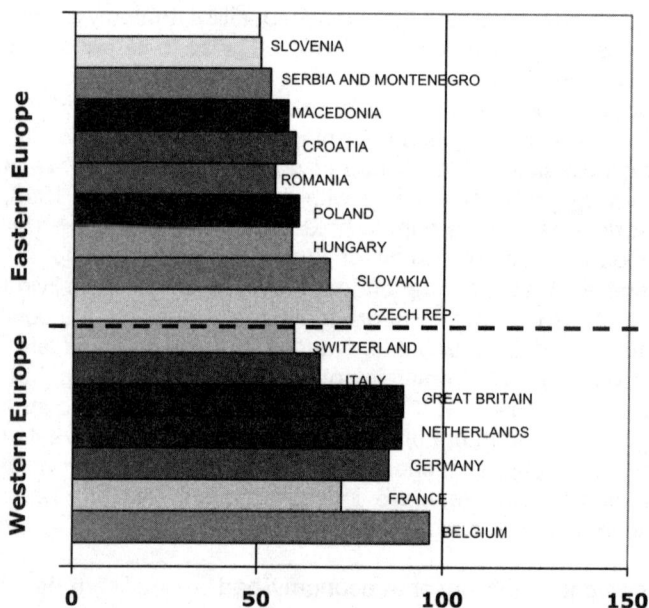

Sources: United Centre for Human Settlements (1996) An urbanising world, Oxford, Oxford University Press, Paccione, M. (2001) Urban Geography, London, Routledge, Vladimir, K. (2001) "Processes of Deagrarization and Urbanization of Slovene Rural Areas". In: Klemečič, M. (ed.) Rural Areas at the Millennium Shift: Challenges and Problems, pp. 7-17.

Undoubtedly, the spatial policies in the socialist countries, including Slovenia, affected the development of the towns differently than the spatial policies in capitalist countries. The scope of the influence of socialist policies differed from country to country. However, all countries which had socialist spatial policies share essentially the following elements: accelerated "deagrarization and industrialization, forced urbanization, partial or substantial nationalization of resources and consequently the freezing of the real estate market, i.e. insufficient attention being paid to the economics of spatial development (Szelenyi, 1996)[6].

In Slovenia in the period after the Second World War but especially from the beginning of 70's a relatively specific relation between industrialization and urbanization developed. A policy of polycentric spatial development with dispersed industry was designed, into which the settlement system was incorporated. Deagrarization and the flow of urbanization were strong, but did not form any expressly metropolitan area. While a trend of intensive metropolization occurred in modern western and certain socialist countries in the period after the Second World War, characterized by strong concentration of the population and economic activities in a few central urban areas and the rapid expansion of cities, this trend was much less intensive in Slovenia. In Slovenia, especially during the initial period of socialism, there was a tendency and normative planning orientation towards harmonized urban and rural development. Despite the initial process of socialist modernization with large-scale long-term spatial plans, the construction of large urban projects, apartment block neighborhoods etc., the Slovene urban system never achieved the high level of urbanization characteristic of developed western countries. The period of short-term growth of the concentration of people and capital in urbanized areas up to the end of the seventies of the previous century was followed by a decrease in the growth of the population in the cities, especially in central and adjoining districts. The transfer of industry and service activities outside the city areas began at the end of the eighties, and intensive suburbanization of trade[7] began at the beginning of the nineties.

Urbanization in Slovenia during the Socialist Era
Slovenia entered the socialist era as the most well-developed Yugoslav republic. During the postwar period Slovenia advanced the fastest of all the republics of the former Yugoslavia and further improved its prewar developmental advantages. The situation with respect to urbanization

---

[6] There are even cases of socialist cities (Budapest) where the town authorities became aware of the deficiencies in urban planning with a limited real estate market. In attempting to simulate market mechanisms – by setting up false, imaginary real estate markets – they tried to form a mechanism which could measure the value of the land in the city. However, since the land in the city center remained monopolized, the processes of the self-regulation of the value of city land could not be established to the extent necessary to influence urban planning. (Szelenyi, 1996: 301)
[7] On the suburbanisation of trade in transition period in Slovenia see Uršič (2003).

was completely different, as Slovenia was caught up with or even overtaken by economically less well-developed republics (Graph 5) and other socialist countries. Whereas in other socialist countries fast-growing industry and economic development was accompanied by major growth of urban populations, Slovenia experienced only moderately fast growth.

Graph 2: Growth of urban population in percent – comparison of Slovenia with other Yugoslav republics 1953-1991

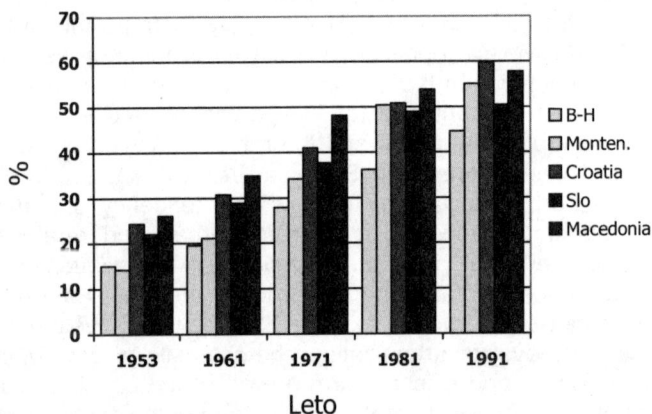

Sources: Statistički godišnjak 1979, 1989, Vladimir, K. (2001) "Processes of Deagrarization and urbanization of Slovene Rural Areas". V: Klemečič, M. (ed.) Rural Areas at the Millennium Shift: Challenges and Problems, pp. 7-17.

In contrast to other socialist countries (Hungary, Czechoslovakia) and various Yugoslav republics (Croatia, Serbia and Montenegro), Slovenia had no metropolized area before the Second World War,[8] where there would be a larger concentration of people, institutions and businesses. Its urban system was therefore characterized by a low percentage of urban population – under-urbanization[9] (Szelenyi, 1971) and an "urban

---

[8] The majority of former socialist countries have at least one large city or metro-polized area which exceeds the average concentration of the population with respect to individual areas of the country (e.g. Budapest, Prague, Belgrade, Warsaw etc.)

[9] Ivan Szelenyi (1971, 1996) explains that industrialization in countries such as Hungary, the former Czechoslovakia, Yugoslavia and Poland was achieved with a "lower level of growth of the urban population" (1996: 287) and a "lower spatial concentration of the population than in the market conditions of capitalist societies at the same level of economic development" (ibid.). Szelenyi's thesis of the "under-

gap". The urban gap is characterized by a gulf between the speed of economic development and the slower growth of the urban population, which was larger in Slovenia than in any other Yugoslav republic or other eastern socialist country, for instance Hungary or the former Czechoslovakia (Kos, 2002).

The structure of the working population in Slovenia in the period 1910-1989 indicates that Slovenia achieved a higher level of employment in industry and lowered the numbers of agricultural employees sooner than other Yugoslav republics, and at the same time increased its percentage of employees in the tertiary sector more quickly[10] (Vrišer, 1978, Statistički godišnjak 1989). Despite the faster modernization of the Slovene economic system in comparison to the Yugoslav system, there was no pronounced increase in the urban population in Slovenia during the period when this may have been necessary in order to avoid later negative influences on sustained spatial development. The policy of polycentric development (e.g. remotely located branch manufacturing plants) fit very well with the dispersed settlement of Slovenia and the increased employment in the tertiary sector, which did not require such spatial concentration of the workforce as heavy industry. The result of these processes is a relatively low level of metropolization in Slovenia. Despite having the highest level of economic development in the former Yugoslavia, Slovenia had one of the lowest percentages of concentration of the urban population.

Therefore, major changes in the employment structure of the population occurred in Slovenia after the Second World War,[11] but this did not lead (partially also because of unrealized metropolization) to the extensive urbanizing which denotes the spreading of the social and behavioral characteristics of urban life to the population. A significant part of the population who did not move to the cities was made up of so-called "half-farmers" and "half-tradesmen", who spent part of their work time in industrial plants, and part on the farm or in a trade. This dual role was reflected in the high share of the informal economy (Kos, 1993), which raised the living standards of these people but at the same time slowed migration into the cities.

---

urbanization" (ibid.) of the socialist societies of eastern Europe in the period of intensive socialist industrialization is one of the key concepts in clarifying the specifics of the urban development of post-socialist countries.

[10] In 1989 the difference between Slovenia and the other Yugoslav republics according to individual economic sectors was between 5 and 10 percent.

[11] The processes of deagrarization and later also the transfer of a large part of the population from the secondary to the tertiary employment sector.

Some public values and attitudes findings toward "Urbanism as a way of Life" in Slovenia

Both the causes and effects of these structural movements in Slovenia, where metropolized areas did not develop, are also socio-cultural. In Slovene towns, even in the national capital of Ljubljana, in all of the "history of modernization" none of the more pronounced classical characteristics of the urban population developed, especially urban cultures and urbanism as a way of life. Emigration from the countryside and migration into the towns is almost completely an instrumentally social phenomenon in Slovenia, but is not also a reflexively cultural one. Urban socialization and the acculturation of migrants into the cities has been relatively low throughout the entire period from after the Second World War to the present.

The process of permanent "defective urbanization" was never seen politically as a problem, but as proof of the humane living conditions. Urbanism as residential and cultural practice was therefore not a social value, and the syntagm "urban culture" was rarely used. If we take the stance of the city administrators and professional pundits of the time with a grain of cynicism, we could say that what was especially important were the "real", human, content-related problems of the humanization of the towns. The social discourse of the tradition of "local communities" predominated, and the culturological discourse of urbanism was marginalized. The ecological and economic aspects of the population's tendency towards extremely dispersed settlement (especially the expensive, state-financed utilities and road infrastructure) were utterly neglected. From the socio-economic viewpoint this consequently led to a low level of residential mobility (migration) and a markedly high level of owned residences, which is among the highest in the world.[12] This increasingly and unavoidably leads to sometimes unpredictable, disharmonious and conflicted situations between the interests of the state, which tends towards a controllable socio-spatial order, and private interests, in which particular subjective criteria for the evaluation of socio-spatial qualities predominate (Hočevar, 2000).

We put forward as a causative factor the findings of various Slovene sociologists, that there are clear historical reasons for the strong antiurban values and attitudes, both in the official political ideology and among the population (Rotar, 1985; Gantar, Kos, 1993; Hočevar, 2002). The ideologies of "Blut und Boden" were crystallized in the Slovene territory

---

[12] In Slovenia approximately 82 percent of housing is privately owned, the rest is rented or state-owned (SURS, 2002).

in the relation to common enemies, especially Germans and Italians[13] and their national or imperial cultures. In exchange for a weak national ideology, a homey and idyllic rural ideology of cultural closed-mindedness and autarchy was established, which was strongly emphasized by every political and cultural elite up to the beginning of the twentieth century. Slovene bourgeois intelligence was markedly weak. The population of the towns and the owners of capital were in the majority either German or Italian. Slovene towns were small. Except for Trieste, today an Italian city, and Ljubljana, which was a main provincial town in the Austro-Hungarian Empire, there were no larger towns where a bourgeois class developed to any significance. The deeply-rooted ideology of blut und boden was maintained in the period of industrialization within the framework of the Yugoslav Federation and continues to represent a significant part of the national culture today.

The latest results of a public-opinion poll entitled *Socio-Spatial Values* from 2004 also indicate the value-laden, antiurban orientation of the population towards dispersed settlement and with it the rejection of urbanism as a way of life.[14] The residential wishes of the population with regard to location and type of residence correspond relatively highly with their expectations.

The most general finding is that the residential preferences of Slovene citizens are markedly antiurban even today. In the questionnaire we posed several questions from which, through correlation of the responses, we can determine with a fair amount of reliability the key qualities of the residential, locational and areal preferences.

---

[13] After the Second World War, all the way to the forming of the national state in 1991, a similar resistance appeared in the form of a rejection of so-called Yugoslavianism. The homogenizing ideology of Yugoslavianism in the former federation was pronounced, although the relatively strong formal autonomy of the republics after 1974 also allowed the formation of national consciousness.

[14] The basic objective of the public opinion poll was to obtain a response to this question or to gain an insight into the trends, i.e. a demographically, socially and geographically (territorially) differentiated socio-spatial overview of the values, and partially a perceptual overview of the population of the Republic of Slovenia at a certain point in time, i.e. between March and May 2004. The sample was representative, N = 1140.

Graph 3: Residential preferences of respondents to values poll (in percent)

Question: We are going to list different areas, would you please choose the one area in which you would most want to live if you had the chance?

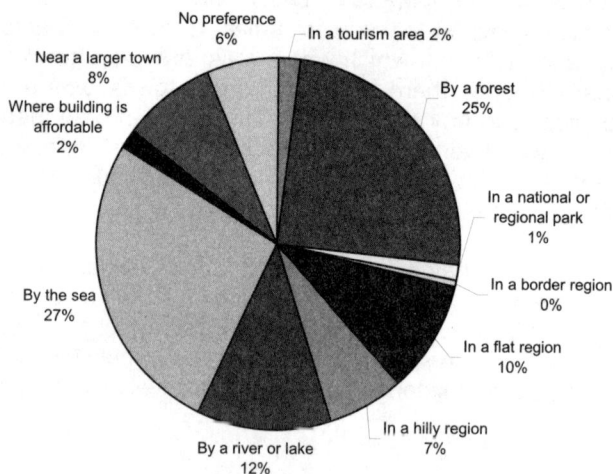

No preference 6%

In a tourism area 2%

Near a larger town 8%

Where building is affordable 2%

By a forest 25%

In a national or regional park 1%

In a border region 0%

By the sea 27%

In a flat region 10%

By a river or lake 12%

In a hilly region 7%

Source: Hočevar, M. et al. (2004). Socio-Spatial Values (3rd phase and final report). Ljubljana, Faculty of Social Sciences, Center for Spatial Sociology.

In terms of regions (Graph 3): 27% of respondents would prefer to live by the sea if they had the possibility, i.e. if they could choose. A quarter of respondents would choose to live by a forest, and 12% of respondents by a river or a lake. Only 8% of respondents would choose to live near a city, which corresponds to the rejection of urbanism as a way of life among Slovene citizens. Differential analysis shows slight variations between age groups, where a preference for living near a city is present among those under 30, but the preference for living by the sea is also higher for this age group.

Graph 4: Residential preferences of respondents to values poll (in percent)

Question: **Where would you most like to live?**

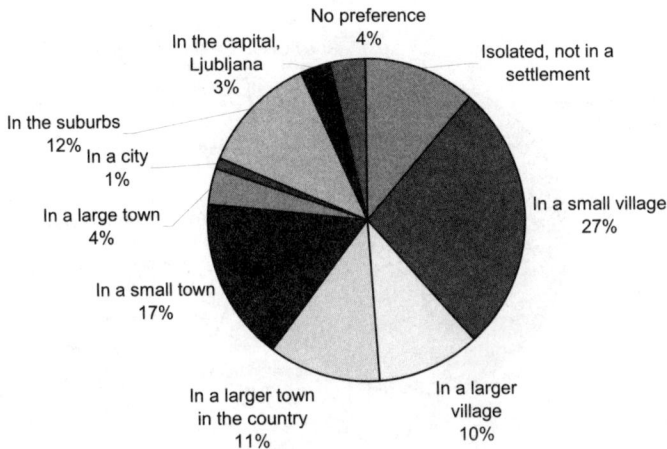

Source: Hočevar, M. et al. (2004). Socio-Spatial Values (3rd phase and final report). Ljubljana, Faculty of Social Sciences, Center for Spatial Sociology.

In terms of settlement type (Graph 4): more than half of respondents would rather live in small or large villages or in the countryside. Over 50% of the people actually live in their preferred settlement type. 5% of respondents would like to live in a city or large town. Just over a quarter of respondents would prefer to live in a small town (between 3000 and 10 000 inhabitants). Despite the fact that large towns and cities in Slovenia include those with over 100 000 inhabitants, and that there are only two, Ljubljana and Maribor, the people would not live there if they didn't have to or if they had a choice. An interesting fact in connection with this is that in a recent international study of the quality of life, the World-Wide Quality of Life Survey,[15] the city of Ljubljana was ranked very high, not just in Europe but in world terms. In the region of former socialist countries in central and eastern Europe it was ranked in first place, ahead of Bratislava, Slovakia.

---

[15] Mercer Human Resource Consulting 2005 (http://www.mercerhr.com/).

Graph 5: Residential preferences of respondents to values poll (housing type, in percent)

Question: We are going to list some types of housing. What kind of housing would you choose if you could?

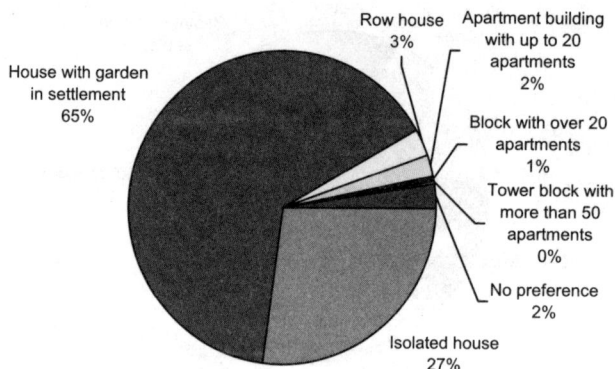

Source: Hočevar, M. et al. (2004). Socio-Spatial Values (3rd phase and final report). Ljubljana, Faculty of Social Sciences, Center for Spatial Sociology.

In terms of housing type (Graph 5): the highest share – 65% of respondents – would like to live in a house with a garden in a settlement. 27% of respondents would choose to live in an isolated house outside of a settlement. Multi-apartment and block lifestyles would be chosen by a total of 6% of respondents, while 2% have no preference in terms of housing type. The conformance of the results is also indicated by the response of 64% of respondents, that if they decided to obtain new housing, they would decide to build (37%) or purchase (27%) a house, and only 19% would purchase a new or old apartment.

The results indicate a clear connection between two residential characteristics among the inhabitants of Slovenia: individualism and anti-urbanism, which in the broader context could be sociologically explained as an ambivalent combination of postmodern and pre-modern value-based social orientations. Nearly three quarters of respondents do not intend to improve their housing standard – either because they are satisfied with it (57%) or they are unable to do so (15%). Some 70% of respondents believe that the size of their present residence is suitable, 17% think it is a little too small, and 7% that it is much too small. The data indicate that the social component here is not at all prevalent. We can indirectly conclude that on average there is relatively high satisfaction with people's present housing conditions and a correspondingly low level of housing differentiation. Such a conclusion is also supported by the data that nearly 70% of respondents will remain where they are presently living until the end of their lives. A further 20% of respondents will probably live where they are currently residing for at least five to ten years. The analysis indicates a markedly low level of expectation of mobility, which however is not connected to social issues. The phenomenon can be partly explained by the ageing of the population, which is more inclined towards sedentariness, and partly by the pronounced Slovene characteristic of being connected to one's primary place of residence (so-called "permanent anchorage").

5 Urbanization in the Post Socialist Period
Despite the relatively low rate of growth of the urban population, during the socialist era Slovenia managed to maintain a relatively high level of economic development, but after the changing of the political system and the transition to a market economy the first negative consequences began to appear, which were the result of the specific type of spatial development. These are mainly processes of dispersed suburbanization and the transfer of economic activities outside of large town centers. With the rapid construction of new infrastructure networks (motorways, telecommunications etc.) the Slovene authorities are attempting to compensate for deficiencies which are the results of the negative effects of the particularities of the spatial development.

The modernization of the infrastructure systems in Slovenia has led to major discrepancies between aspirations towards the fast economic development of the country and the practical consequences of their actual implementation. The accelerated construction of the motorway infrastructure, which in addition to reducing the traveling time between Slovene towns also accelerates the process of dispersed suburbanization, provides a suitable illustration of these discrepancies (Graph 6).

Graph 6: Slovenia – changes in the no. of inhabitants (by municipality) 1991-2002

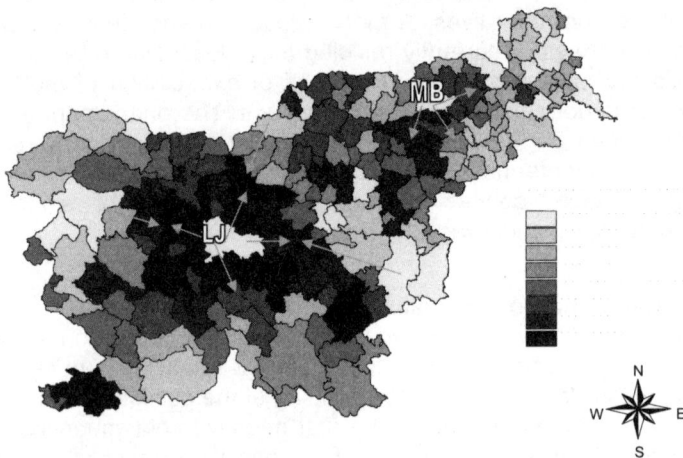

Source: (2004). Census 1991-2002 (dynamic data tables).
At: http://www.stat.si/pxweb/Database/Popis2002/Popis2002.asp (19/5/2004)

Despite the fact that the development of metropolized areas did not occur, trends of suburbanization were strongly present after the Second World War, which is one of the key particularities of the spatial development of Slovenia which we do not observe elsewhere. Unlike other socialist countries, the trend of postwar suburbanization in Slovenia occurred without the presence of strongly metropolized areas. This was due to many reasons, the most prominent of which were the political and ideological conceptual bases and the antiurban values and attitudes. In the period after the fall of Yugoslavia and the introduction of a market economy after 1991, the trend of suburbanization became even more pronounced (Graph 6).[16]

---

[16] The graph shows changes in the number of inhabitants in the 2002 Census compared with the 1991 Census (the arrows indicate the approximate movements of inhabitants over a period of 10 years). The color contrasts in the graph show that in the period from 1991-2002 the number of inhabitants in the vicinity of the larger towns increased (especially Ljubljana and Maribor, marked in the figure with the abbreviations LJ and MB), while the number of inhabitants in the central parts of the larger towns decreased.

An analysis of the census data leads to the conclusion that in the last fifteen years the construction of new housing in Slovenia has become even more dispersed, and empty (abandoned) residences have been poorly utilized in the settlement system. Allowing this trend of dispersed housing construction to continue in suburban areas in Slovenia could have major consequences for the natural environment, the mobility of the workforce and consequently the socio-economic development of the entire country. Correspondingly with the construction of new housing in free-standing houses on the outskirts of large towns, the number of abandoned residences in hard to get to or remote areas of Slovenia is increasing. In 2000, of construction in non-urban areas[17] approximately 93% of housing was in free-standing houses and about 7% of housing was in apartment buildings (2002 Census). One third less housing was built in urban areas than was built in non-urban areas – of which approximately 40% was built in free-standing houses and approximately 60% in apartment buildings. On the basis of an analysis of this data we can reasonably assume that a thoughtless utilization of space is occurring in Slovenia, which is having the effect of creating extremely expensive municipal infrastructures.

The process of the ageing of the population in Slovene towns is also worrisome, especially in the centers of towns, which is similar to the trend throughout Europe, and could lead to major influences on the socio-economic and spatial development of Slovenia in the future. Despite the fact that the birth rate in Slovenia is falling (inverted age pyramid), the number of preschool children in 2002 in non-urban settlements increased in comparison with urban settlements, while the situation was still the opposite in 1991 (Graph 7). The migration of young families to suburban areas can be explained as a change in lifestyle due to economizing of costs in the main urban areas (especially in Ljubljana, coastal and alpine towns) and due to the already discussed antiurban value determination of the Slovene population. The prices and rents for housing in the main urban areas are still exceptionally high,[18] and therefore young families are trying to reduce costs through migration to

---

[17] In the 2002 Census, urban settlements were defined on the basis of four criteria: a) settlements with over three thousand inhabitants; b) settlements with two to three thousand inhabitants and a jobs surplus; c) settlements which are municipal seats and have at least 1,400 inhabitants and a jobs surplus; d) settlements on the outskirts of towns with a lower number of inhabitants, but which are gradually developing into a spatial and functional whole with the town. All other settlements are defined as non-urban settlements (2002 Census, at http://www.stat.si/popis2002/si/teritorij.html (22/5/2004)).

[18] The reasons for maintaining or even raising housing prices are especially: undifferentiated real estate market, very few newly built apartments, delayed denationalization procedures, deficient real estate legislation etc. (Cirman, 2004)

cheaper areas and at the same time (via the new motorways) remain close to their jobs, the majority of which are located in the main urban areas.

Graph 7: Preschool children aged 1-6 by settlement type, 1991 and 2002 census

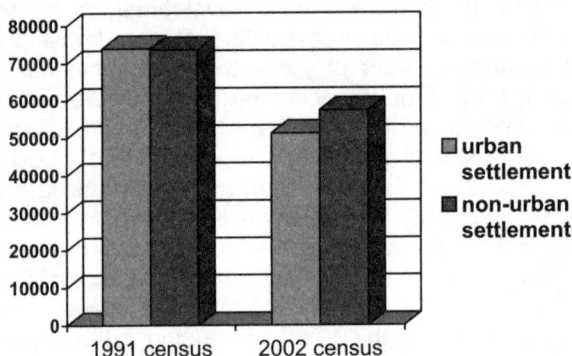

Source: (2004). 2002 Census (2002 Census of Population, Households and Residences). At: http://www.stat.si/popis2002/si/default.htm (18/5/2004)

While the majority of urban regions in developed western capitalist countries went through the first three phases of the urbanization cycle[19] (urbanization, suburbanization and deurbanization) during the periods of industrialization and after the Second World War, and are slowly entering or seeking mechanisms for entry into the fourth phase (reurbanization), Slo-venia is currently at the beginning of the third phase (deurbanization). Before independence, the larger Slovene urban areas, especially Ljubljana, reached only the period of urbanization and "pseudo-suburbanization".[20] After the change of the political system and the transition to a market economy the processes of dispersed suburbanization became significantly more pronounced. Population growth in the larger towns stagnated or even began to decrease (e.g. in Ljubljana), owing to

---

[19] The four phases of urbanization have been written about in various ways by numerous authors, such as H. Geyer, T. Kontuly (1993), A. Champion (1997, 2000), Klaassen (1981), Van den Berg (1982), J. Mercer (1999) etc.

[20] Actually we cannot speak of classical suburbanization, since what happened was not spontaneous suburbanization as was characteristic of western cities in capitalist countries (with the "spillover" or expansion of the city into the hinterland due to excessive concentration and overloading of central areas), but non-spontaneous suburbanization, which was the consequence of partially obstructed development of metropolized areas after the Second World War.

which we can speak of a phase of deurbanization. The process of deurbanization in Slovenia, due to the traditional large dispersion of settlements, which is continuing to increase, because of the lack of large towns and the relatively low population density in the larger Slovene towns, could strongly increase the pressures on the natural environment and lower the current quality of residential life.

Conclusion

The maintaining of a "ruralist" settlement structure (without large cities) had both positive and negative effects on the Slovene settlement system. In the period before the Second World War, the dispersed settlement system made a major contribution to the maintaining of the Slovene cultural identity and even to the strengthening of the national identity. For various reasons, external (foreign) economic subjects had a major impact only in the larger towns, while the majority of the dispersed settlement system remained beyond their influence. The dispersed settlement system, which was also maintained and strengthened during the socialist era, contributed to the diminishing of social differences between the inhabitants, but it hindered the rise of a strong urban middle class. That is to say, the construction of a large number of free-standing houses in the Slovene countryside and on the outskirts of towns helped to raise the residential standard, increase the relatively low amount of housing and lower the costs of the construction of new housing in urban areas. Polycentric development which was either explicitly supported or at least not opposed by the socialist authorities,[21] was in conformance with the Slovene settlement system and the prevailing values of the inhabitants of Slovenia with respect to spatial development, which contributed to rapid economic development.

The individual characteristics of the dispersed settlement system could benefit the further socio-economic development of Slovenia. The maintaining of a dispersed settlement pattern could with well-developed transport and telecommunications infrastructures also lead to the maintenance of a high standard of living among the populace. A high level of infrastructure fluidity could at the same time enable fast access to natural areas as well as urban services. The dispersed settlement pattern could

---

[21] The authorities to some extent allowed illegal construction with the intention of blurring the lines between social differences which appeared due to the lack of housing in the towns. When making up for the lack of housing, people usually helped themselves in the form of private "informal construction" (Kos, 1993). Private construction of individual houses was cheaper and more easily accessible than building apartments in the towns because of the difficult access to large parcels of land in urban areas (nationalization), the possibility of providing their own labor, materials and in the majority of cases also their own land.

also serve as a good basis for further polycentric development, assuming decentralization and the redistribution of functions throughout the entire urban system.

The dispersed settlement pattern in Slovenia, which the populace also holds as preferential, is of course also attended by a number of harmful effects such as large pressures on the natural environment, high costs of expansion of infrastructure networks (increasing the length of utilities installations, roads etc.), the deterioration of public transport and increasing dependence on cars, the loss of regional identity, the preservation of strong antiurban values and attitudes etc. In Slovenia in the period after independence, spatial development was carried out on the basis of "spontaneous and uncontrolled situations", i.e. temporary zoning plans and without detailed spatial development strategies The consequence of this is the poor harmonization of different levels of sub-national spatial organization between the towns, the suburbs and the countryside, in spite of the fact that all of these areas are gradually becoming a part of a unified urban system in Slovenia. Poor cooperation be-tween individual areas leads to increased unproductive and destructive competition within the national urban system, which in turn leads to irrational utilization of natural resources and human potentials.

Continuing with dispersed suburbanization and the expansion of urban areas will lead to increasingly bitter conflicts due to unsettled administrative and political relations between the towns and the countryside. Disharmonies between individual urban areas, which in the urban system are growing into each other on the functional level, could be solved through formal legal arrangement of a unified urban area which extends over a large part of Slovenia. The expansion of spatial planning would perhaps lead to the harmonization of relations between the processes of suburbanization and the development of infrastructure systems, and to the limiting of the effects of explicitly antiurban values and local specificities, which to a large extent hinder the spatial development of Slovenia. The spatial development strategy of Slovenia, in a period of dramatic changes in the speed of connections via modern local and global infrastructure networks (Castells, Borja, 1996, Hočevar, 2000), precisely because of the small size and high value of the limited space, will have to be based on holistic development of all areas and the prevention of sharp divisions between urban and non-urban areas.

We can conclude that the dispersed settlement pattern in Slovenia is attended by various advantages and disadvantages, which have to be combined and aligned with the demands for harmonized socio-economic dynamics. In order to ensure the optimal spatial development of Slovenia it is therefore reasonable to make a compromise between: 1) demands which arise due to economic reasons, 2) demands for the modernization or acquiring of suitable infrastructures which would maintain or even improve the quality of life and 3) the values orientations of the population towards dispersed settlement. From the point of view of long-term socioeconomic development, the integration of spatial planning is therefore a reasonable solution. The optimal approach would seem to be the application of uniform spatial planning criteria and mechanisms so that the entire territory of Slovenia would be treated as a single spatial unit. Thus we are increasingly approaching the idea of a "city-state", which would join the urban, countryside and natural areas in a differentiated but at the same time integrated spatial system.

7 References:

(1996) An Urbanising World. Oxford, United Centre for Human Settlements, Oxford University Press.

(2004) Popis 1991-2002 (dinamične podatkovne tabele).
On: http://www.stat.si/pxweb/Database/Popis2002/Popis2002.asp (19.5.2004)

(2004) Popis 2002 (Popis prebivalstva, gospodinjstev in stanovanj 2002).
On: http://www.stat.si/popis2002/si/default.htm (18/5/2004)

(1979, 1989. Statistički godišnjak Jugoslavije. Beograd, Savezni zavod za statistiku.

(2004) SURS (Statistični urad Republike Slovenije). On: http://www.stat.si/ (17.7.2004)

(2005) Mercer Human Resource Consulting On: http://www.mercerhr.com/ (10.3.2005).

Berg, L. v. d. (1982) Urban Europe - A Study of Growth and Decline. Oxford; New York, European Coordination Centre for Research and Documentation in Social Sciences, Pergamon Press.

Castells, M. (1996). The rise of the network society. Cambridge, MA, Blackwell Publishers.

Champion, A. (1997) Urbanization, Suburbanisation, Counterurbanisation and Reurbanisation. In: Handbook of Urban Studies. R. Paddison in W. Lever (eds.). Beverly Hills, California, Sage.

Cirman, A. (2004): Housing finance in Slovenia : the key role of the National Housing Fund. Housing finance international, Dec. 2004, vol. 19, no. 2, 11-16.

Gantar, P.; Kos D, (1993) "Če bo vodnjak, bo tudi bomba! - O segmentih ruralne ideologije v Ljubljani." Vesela znanost - O hišah, o mestih, o podeželjih (št. 3/4), 97-122.

Geyer, H. S.; Kontuly T. (1993) "A Theoretical Foundation for the Concept of Differential Urbanization." International Regional Science Review, let. 2, 157-177.

Hočevar, M. (2000) New Urban Trends: Locales in the Cities – Networks Between Cities. Znanstvena knjižnica, FDV, Ljubljana (extended summary in English).

Hočevar, M. (2002) Urban Locales and Global Networks: The Case of Coastal City of Koper. In: Hočevar; Trček (eds.). Glocal Localities. Salzburg, Euro Cult, 99-115.

Hočevar, M. et al. (2004) Vrednote prostora in okolja (3. fazno in končno poročilo). Ljubljana, Fakulteta za družbene vede, Center za prostorsko sociologijo.

Klaassen, L. H.; Molle, W.T.M. et al. (1981) The Dynamics of urban development: proceedings of an international conference held on the occasion of the 50th anniversary of the Netherlands Economic Institute in Rotterdam, September 4, 1979. New York, St. Martin's Press.

Klemenčič, V. (2001) Process of Deagrarization and Urbanization of Slovene Rural Areas. In: Klemenčič, M. (ed.) Rural Areas at the Millenium Shift - Challenges and Problems. Ljubljana, Department of Geography, Faculty of Arts, University of Ljubljana, 7-17.

Kos, D. (1993) Racionalnost neformalnih prostorov. Ljubljana, Fakulteta za družbene vede.

Kos, D.; Marušič, I.; Polič, M.; Zupančič-Strojan, T. (2002) Culture, quality of life and Globalization. 17th Conference of the International Association for People-Environment studies. In Coruna: Asociación Galega de Estudios e Investigación Psicosocial, cop. 2002, 794-795.

Mercer, J. (1999) North American Cities - The Micro Geography. In: North America - A Geographical Mosaic. F. Boal in S. Royle (eds.). London, Arnold, 191-206.

Mlinar, Z. (1972) Integration of Rural Areas into Broader Socio-Economic System, TheYugoslav Village, Zagreb, Department of Rural Sociology.

Mlinar, Z. (1988) Phenomenology of the Local Response to the Economic Crisis, Revija za sociologiju, n. 4.

Mlinar, Z. (1990) Territorial Identities: Between Individualization and Globalization in A. Kuklinski (eds.).

Mlinar, Z.; Teune, H. (1972) The Wealth of Cities and Social Values, Bologna, La Ricerca Sociale 1.

Pacione, M. (2001) Urban Geography - A Global Perspective. New York, London, Routledge.

Pešec-Novak, M. (1991) Zamudniški vzorci industrializacije. Ljubljana, Znanstveno in publicistično središče.

Rotar, B. (1985) Risarji:učenjaki - Ideologije v urbanizmu in arhitekturi. Ljubljana, Delavska enotnost.

Szelenyi, I. (1996) Cities Under Socialism - and After. In: Cities after socialism: Urban and regional change and conflict in post-socialist societies. G. Andrusz, M. Harloe in I. Szelenyi (eds.). Oxford, Cambridge, Blackwell, 286-317.

TRČEK, F (2003) Info-technologies and new ways of organising of regional work environment, case of Koper, Slovenia. V: LSE [London School of Economics and Political Science]. EPIC [European Political-economy Infrastructure Consortium]. London: EPIC, 2003.
On: http://www.lse.ac.uk/collections/EPIC/documents/ICTrcek.pdf (7.2.2005).

Uršič, M. (2003) Urban Spaces of Consumption. Ljubljana, Fakulteta za družbene vede (summary in English).

Vrišer, I. (1978) Regionalno planiranje. Ljubljana, Mladinska knjiga.

The European City in Transition

Edited by Dieter Hassenpflug und Frank Eckardt

www.peterlang.de

Peter Lang · Europäischer Verlag der Wissenschaften

György Széll / Carl-Heinrich Bösling /
Johannes Hartkemeyer (eds.)

Labour, Globalisation &
The New Economy

Frankfurt am Main, Berlin, Bern, Bruxelles, New York, Oxford, Wien, 2005.
559 pp., num. fig. and tab.
Work – Technology – Organization – Society.
Edited by Wiking Ehlert, György Széll and Heinz Sünker. Vol. 30
ISBN 3-631-50865-4 / US-ISBN 0-8204-6434-1 · pb. € 79.–*

The dominant form of globalisation, i.e. financial globalisation, is the biggest
challenge for employees and their representations of interest. If it remains
largely unregulated, not only the natural resources will be destroyed, but also
social sustainability will be prevented. The negative effects of this development
are first of all to be felt on the local and regional level. It is here, therefore,
where counter initiatives and strategies have to start. The quality of life and
working-life has not necessarily increased through globalisation and the New
Economy, though the possibilities of improved communication via email and
Internet were positively acknowledged. The biggest challenge is the increasing
inequality on a global scale, which is produced so far by the New Economy.
As education contributes to enlarge this gap, it has to be adapted to the new
social needs to overcome this polarisation. The ongoing development must be
reversed: Real needs demand more spending for public than for private
consumption. Intermediate organisations can play a positive role in this process.

Contents: New forms of economic activities · The role of institutions in the
process of local and regional development · Transnational social regulation ·
Qualification and regional development

Frankfurt am Main · Berlin · Bern · Bruxelles · New York · Oxford · Wien
Distribution: Verlag Peter Lang AG
Moosstr. 1, CH-2542 Pieterlen
Telefax 00 41 (0) 32 / 376 17 27

*The €-price includes German tax rate
Prices are subject to change without notice
Homepage http://www.peterlang.de